CHOP SUEY AND SUSHI FROM SEA TO SHINING SEA

FOOD AND FOODWAYS

SERIES EDITORS:
JENNIFER JENSEN WALLACH
AND MICHAEL WISE

OTHER TITLES IN THIS SERIES

Mexican-Origin Foods, Foodways, and Social Movements: Decolonial Perspectives

The Taste of Art: Food, Cooking, and Counterculture in Contemporary Practices

Devouring Cultures: Perspectives on Food, Power, and Identity from the Zombie Apocalypse to Downton Abbey

Latin@s' Presence in the Food Industry: Changing How We Think about Food

Dethroning the Deceitful Pork Chop: Rethinking African American Foodways from Slavery to Obama

American Appetites: A Documentary Reader

Chop Suey and Sushi from Sea to Shining Sea

CHINESE AND JAPANESE RESTAURANTS IN THE UNITED STATES

EDITED BY BRUCE MAKOTO ARNOLD,
TANFER EMIN TUNÇ, AND
RAYMOND DOUGLAS CHONG

The University of Arkansas Press
Fayetteville
2018

Manufactured in the United States of America

ISBN: 978-1-68226-060-9
e-ISBN: 978-1-61075-636-5

22 21 20 19 18 5 4 3 2 1

Library of Congress Cataloging-in-Publication Data

Names: Arnold, Bruce Makoto, editor. | Tunç, Tanfer Emin, editor. | Chong, Raymond Douglas, editor.
Title: Chop suey and sushi from sea to shining sea : Chinese and Japanese restaurants in the United States / edited by Bruce Makoto Arnold, Tanfer Emin Tunç, and Raymond Douglas Chong.
Description: Fayetteville : The University of Arkansas Press, 2018. | Series: Food and foodways series | Includes bibliographical references and index.
Identifiers: LCCN 2017042834 (print) | LCCN 2017044141 (ebook) | ISBN 9781610756365 (electronic) | ISBN 9781682260609 (pbk. : alk. paper) | ISBN 9781610756365 (Ebook)
Subjects: LCSH: Chinese restaurants--United States--History. | Japanese restaurants--United States--History. | Cooking, Chinese--History. |Cooking, Japanese--History.
Classification: LCC TX945.4 (ebook) | LCC TX945.4 .C47 2018 (print) | DDC 641.5951--dc23

♾ The paper used in this publication meets the minimum requirements of the American National Standard for Permanence of Paper for Printed Library Materials Z39.48-1984.

CONTENTS

FOREWORD

HARLEY J. SPILLER

Chop Suey and Sushi from Sea to Shining Sea: Chinese and Japanese Restaurants in the United States brings readers in and out of the kitchens of Chinese and Japanese restaurants. It portrays these inner sanctums, particularly the swinging doors that lead to and from dining rooms, as nuclei of transnational culture, interpersonal relations, and cuisine. The authors of these essays, insiders and outsiders alike, reveal histories that have spent decades under lock-and-key, drawing conclusions by comparing and contrasting primary historical documents, raw data, and art. The feelings and experiences of Asian restaurateurs in the United States are examined in these explorations of sensitive cultural matters. Careful readers will find that the deeper we delve into these cultures, the harder it is to exit unchanged.

In the past four decades, the United States has seen an explosion in food consciousness. In 1980, there were few cuisine-centric broadcasts, celebrity chefs, or food-studies programs. Collections of menus, cookbooks, and family histories were being assembled, but none had been digitized or made available online to the international public. Today, anyone anywhere can compare and contrast Asian restaurant menus via the impressive online collections at the New York, San Francisco, and Los Angeles Public Libraries, and at Cornell University, the University of Michigan, the University of Nevada, Las Vegas, and at least one public collection focused exclusively on Chinese restaurants, the Harley J. Spiller Chinese Restaurant Archives at the University of Toronto, Scarborough (UTSC).

In 2015, UTSC acquired the archives I spent thirty-four years assembling, and simultaneously launched *Culinaria Research Centre*, a multidisciplinary initiative blending research, community engagement, and student/faculty initiative. *Culinaria* explores new insights into the place of food in cultural identity and expression;

the relationship between food, diaspora, and interethnic/intercultural contact; commodity production and labor; and the links between food systems and family, gender, and health. Scholars in anthropology, cultural studies, East Asian studies, English, geography, history, human geography, library studies, museum studies, and other fields have begun to handle this archive of over 10,000 international Chinese restaurant menus and related artifacts dating back to the 1870s. The prospects for the advancement of understanding, particularly via advanced computer analysis and interdisciplinary pursuit, are bright.

Recently, exquisite culinary histories, such as Andrew Coe's *Chop Suey: A Cultural History of Chinese Food in the United States* (Oxford University Press, 2009) and Anne Mendelson's *Chow Chop Suey: Food and the Chinese American Journey* (Columbia University Press, 2016), have begun to revise long-held beliefs and set records straight. Moreover, legal scholar Gabriel J. Chin's work on the racist efforts to suppress Chinese restaurants through discriminatory law enforcement and biased laws, such as prohibitions on white women working in or even entering them, is also a welcome addition to this growing body of research.

Culture can also be explained by artists like Arthur Dong, who in 1989 with his film *Forbidden City, U.S.A.*, exposed the lives of Asian entertainers who worked in Chinese American restaurants and nightclubs between the 1930s and 1970s. Other eye-opening art has been created by Indigo Som, whose long-running *Chinese Restaurant Project* is a multifaceted "investigation of the place of Chinese restaurants and Chinese food in the American imagination," and conceptual artist Javier Téllez, who explored how the material culture of Chinese cuisine changes when placed in a museum with his video titled after a 1960s board game, *You Don't Have to Be Chinese to Play Chop Suey*. In 2016–2017, the Museum of Chinese in America (MOCA) advanced public understanding of China's regional cuisines with *Sour, Sweet, Bitter, Spicy: Stories of Chinese Food and Identity in America*, an exhibit featuring oral histories and treasured heirlooms of professional chefs and amateur cooks. MOCA deployed a commissioned suite of complex and richly-glazed ceramic artwork to depict archetypal Chinese foodstuffs in their environmental, architectural, and societal milieus.

Beyond the Americanized versions of Chinese, Japanese, and Taiwanese fare discussed in the essays ahead, there are Asian cuisines from Afghanistan, Armenia, Azerbaijan, Bahrain, Bangladesh, Bhutan, Brunei, Cambodia, Cyprus, Georgia, India, Indonesia, Iran, Iraq, Israel, Jordan, Kazakhstan, Kuwait, Kyrgyzstan, Laos, Lebanon, Malaysia, Maldives, Mongolia, Myanmar, Nepal, North Korea, Oman, Pakistan, Palestine, Philippines, Qatar, Russia, Saudi Arabia, Singapore, South Korea, Sri Lanka, Syria, Taiwan, Tajikistan, Thailand, Tibet, Timor-Leste, Turkey, Turkmenistan, United Arab Emirates, Uzbekistan, Vietnam, and Yemen to delve into, not to mention Batak, Hakka, Newari, Okinawa, Yunnan, and untold numbers of other regional cuisines.

I had the opportunity to learn about one of these cuisines from scratch when, in 2014, New York City received its first Himalayan snooker hall, Weekender. This street-level space boasts five pool tables and a small kitchen offering twenty-five traditional dishes from the Kingdom of Bhutan (plus Chinese chow mein, Indian-Chinese chili chicken, and Tibetan *shaptak*). The social lubricant of Weekender's homespun fare, by masterful chef Norbu Gyeltshen, is vital to the venture's success. Gyeltshen prepares Bhutan's national dish, *ema datse*, with white American cheese and a tangle of fiery fresh green hot peppers, and sends out other aromatic Bhutanese standbys like *momo* (dumplings); *jasha maroo* (a hearty broth of minced chicken, bones and all, spiced with fresh chili peppers and *thingay*, Bhutanese numbing peppercorn); *norsha kam pak* (air dried beef with vegetables); and *kangchung* (stewed pig feet with chili, ginger, and garlic), all with a choice of Bhutanese red rice or *tingmo* (steamed wheat buns).

Located on a quiet side street in a Queens neighborhood once called Woodside Heights, Weekender provides a taste of the Himalayan beyond billiards, beef, and butter tea. Bhutanese, and others, are drawn to this relaxed community hub to play snooker, eat, drink, celebrate, commiserate, and every so often join forces to rent an industrial container to ship goods to family and friends back in Bhutan. For these and other reasons, the tiny kitchen functions as the hub of a transnational site that boosts Bhutan's Gross National Happiness index.

The analysis of diasporic Asian foodways is freighted with seriousness and leavened with deliciousness. As concepts like authenticity fall to today's steely-eyed revisionists, it is vital to remember that people from any culture can enjoy the taste, smell, texture, sight, and sound of cooking and eating in another. A popular advertising campaign once featured diverse spokespeople proclaiming "You don't have to be Jewish to love Levy's Jewish Rye Bread," begging the question, "do you have to be Asian to prepare Asian food?" I offer for discussion my original duck liver recipe, published in Jacqueline Newman's Chinese food magazine *Flavor and Fortune* (Fall 2004, vol. 11, no. 3). It can be challenging to find the duck liver and yellow chive, but the rest is easy.

Does it smell good? How does it taste? Is it authentic? Is it Chinese? Chinese American? How can we learn from such questions when the same person in different settings at different times might draw different conclusions? I once asked a former salesman/Buddhist monk why vegetarians eat mock tripe. He replied by saying there are different levels of Buddhism, and went on to describe hermits who eat but one bowl of sesame seeds per day. Surprisingly, some live into their 120s. He said the sesame seed was an ideal and nutritious food, and compared its perfect golden roundness to that of the sun.

Converts can be more intent than those born to a culture. For better or worse, I, a Buffalo-born-and-bred New Yorker with Ashkenazi, Ukrainian, Polish, and Viennese roots, exhibit what E. L. Doctorow describes in his novel *World's Fair* as "the fervent pride of the assimilationist." I have long been infatuated with Asian food; so if it is true you are what you eat, I am Asian. Ha, fat chance! But who does have the final say on who is in and who is out? Delineating culture is never simple.

PREFACE

RAYMOND DOUGLAS CHONG

Chop Suey and Sushi from Sea to Shining Sea: Chinese and Japanese Restaurants in the United States is our eclectic collection of evocative and provocative essays about the diversity of Chinese and Japanese cuisines in the restaurants of America.

With the California Gold Rush of 1848–1849 came Chinese pioneers who brought their Cantonese cuisine which was transfigured into the beloved chop suey. Since then, various types of Asian cuisines have evolved in the American culinary landscape with each new wave of immigrants from Asia. They bring their zesty dishes, assorted cooking techniques, ingredients, and seasonings, adapting and adding to the patina of American cuisine. Now, Americans can savor and devour tasty meals with Asian accents in downtowns, shopping centers, and just about everywhere in between.

Our essayists bring to the table their rich narratives and perspectives concerning the diverse Chinese and Japanese cuisines that can be found at restaurants across America. They describe the textures and contexts of these Asian foods in the U.S. culinary world, discuss the intrepid histories of Chinese and Japanese restaurants, explore culinary ephemera, examine the interactions between specific restaurants and their customers, provide analyses of ethnically hybridized establishments, and illustrate how America is a true feast of Asian cuisines.

We hope you enjoy reading this culinary journey as much as we enjoyed assembling it.

We would like to thank the authors for their contributions, the anonymous peer reviewers for their input and suggestions, and the University of Arkansas Press, especially Jennifer Jensen Wallach, Michael Wise, David Scott Cunningham, and Deena R. Owens, for their support.

CHOP SUEY AND SUSHI FROM SEA TO SHINING SEA

INTRODUCTION

Chinese and Japanese Restaurants in the United States

BRUCE MAKOTO ARNOLD
AND TANFER EMIN TUNÇ

The history of restaurants in the United States is as rich and varied as the ethnicities that populate the nation. Beginning in the late nineteenth century, restaurants began to transform from an institution only for the rich or for special occasions into institutions embodying the working- and middle-class aspirations of consumer choice and variety. When combined with America's growing multiculturalism in the mid-twentieth century, these consumerist aspirations gave rise to a sense of cosmopolitanism that translated into the widespread and continued growth of restaurants serving every imaginable cuisine.[1] Restaurants have been woven into the very fabric of American culture: there are almost one million restaurants in the United States—approximately one restaurant for every 320 people residing in the country—and almost 60 percent of Americans dine at a restaurant at least once a week. Over thirteen million people are employed by the restaurant industry, and almost half of all Americans will have worked in a restaurant in their lifetimes.[2]

Restaurants are an inseparable part of American history and culture and impact the lives of each and every person residing in the nation. The story of Chinese- and Japanese-cuisine restaurants in the United States is complicated and, as this volume will illustrate, is connected not only to the development of public eateries in general, but also to immigration history, the evolution of Asian ethnicities in America, culinary history, the blurring between public and private space, the commercialization of food, and the link between food and identity.

Initially, Asian immigrant, and especially Chinese, employment was circumscribed by American society due to racial prejudice. Individuals of Asian descent were only permitted to work in the service sector, mainly in restaurants and laundries, so out of necessity, they pursued these occupations. Over time, they created a niche for themselves in the provision of such services, and even after employment restrictions were lifted, they continued to work in these areas, passing businesses along from generation to generation and welcoming new immigrants into the fold. Although Asian restaurants in the United States have a racially troubled origin, for many, these restaurants have become a pathway to the "American dream"—a conduit to prosperity and success fueled by consumer demand.

While there are no definitive statistics, the number of Chinese restaurants in the United States alone total over 40,000, with another estimated 10,000 Japanese restaurants.[3] Asian-cuisine restaurants, as a group, are more popular than McDonald's, Burger King, Wendy's, Domino's, and Pizza Hut combined.[4] Even relatively isolated Springfield, Missouri, which straddles the Midwest, Southeast, and Southwest, has over 100 Asian-cuisine restaurants in a city of only 160,000 inhabitants. Springfield's racial makeup is over 88 percent white, and just under 2 percent Asian. It hosts fourteen McDonald's, eight Wendy's, and four Burger King locations; yet, it has a particular fondness for Asian cuisine.[5] The question becomes, why? Clearly, Asian cuisine has made an indelible culinary imprint on the United States, with Chinese- and Japanese-cuisine restaurants playing a significant role in American culinary culture and foodways. This reinforces the need for rigorous study of this subject.

Chop Suey and Sushi from Sea to Shining Sea

As Alice McLean has expressed, "Asian American restaurants range from high-end Chinese banquet halls and Japanese restaurants serving 16-course meals to food trucks and fast-food chains."[6] Add to these other eateries such as bakeries, noodle houses, sake bars, and bubble-tea cafés, and the number of American Chinese and Japanese culinary spaces suddenly expands. Yet, restaurants have been disproportionately understudied and relatively few books, academic or otherwise, have delved into the specifics of these establishments in the United States. The books that are dedicated to Chinese and Japanese cuisine in America overwhelmingly focus on general histories, practices, or literary expressions, at best reserving only a portion of their overall discussion for restaurants.[7] *Chop Suey and Sushi from Sea to Shining Sea: Chinese and Japanese Restaurants in the United States* addresses this gap by providing an examination of the development and current status of Chinese- and Japanese-cuisine restaurants in the United States. The focus of our edited volume—Chinese and Japanese restaurants in the continental United States, from the Atlantic to the Pacific—is reflected in its title. Although a few of our essays refer to Asian cuisine in Hawaii, as editors, we made a conscious choice to exclude Hawaii from this volume since, given its location and immigrant and colonial connections to Asia, it has a complicated ethnic restaurant history and culinary narrative, and deserves consideration in a separate volume.[8] We also feel that American Asian restaurants that extend beyond Chinese/Taiwanese, Japanese, and Pan-Asian cuisines to those of different regions (Southeast Asia, Korea, and the Indian subcontinent, for example) are outside the scope of our work because, like Hawaii, they are far more complicated for many of the same reasons and warrant individual attention.

While chop suey served as the foundation of Chinese cuisine in the United States, our examination will go beyond such basic formulations, offering chapters on the histories of specific restaurants; culinary ephemera such as menus and cookbooks; interactions between specific restaurants and their customers; analyses of ethnically hybridized establishments; and essays on the ways in which Chinese- and Japanese-cuisine restaurants have impacted culture through film and other media outlets. In short, we are interested in the (re)presentation of a variety of voices that both deconstruct, and more accurately reconstruct, "chop suey cuisines," or American Chinese-restaurant narratives of the United States. On the other hand, while sushi is not as widely consumed as ramen or tempura are in Japan, and is usually an expensive dish reserved for special occasions, for many Americans, it is synonymous with Japanese cuisine. In fact, when asked to name a Japanese dish, we would argue that sushi would be the first to come to mind for most Americans, even though many are still unwilling to try it. Hence, sushi has become part of the American perception of Japanese cuisine and deserves consideration alongside the iconic "Chinese" dish chop suey. While a number of our essays address sushi, there is still a great deal of work that can be done on this and other Japanese cuisines in the United States.

As conveyed by the endnotes in this edited collection, a wide range of articles on American Chinese- and Japanese-cuisine restaurants has already been written. However, there currently exists no single multidisciplinary volume of essays dedicated exclusively to this subject. For example, while the edited collection *Eating Asian America: A Food Studies Reader* covers Chinese and Japanese cuisine in America, it does not specialize in restaurants.[9] Written by one of our contributors, John Jung's *Sweet and Sour: Life in Chinese Family Restaurants* focuses on restaurants, but concentrates its efforts on Chinese family establishments.[10] Likewise, Jennifer 8. Lee's, *The Fortune Cookie Chronicles: Adventures in the World of Chinese Food* is dedicated to Chinese restaurants in the United States, but is a personal narrative written by a journalist.[11] Other recent works also offer generalized histories of Chinese food in the United States; however, they, too, focus on one ethnicity or on the subject from a single vantage point.[12] While such works trace the progression of Chinese food from "suspect" to America's favorite take-out cuisine and explore Chinese restaurant culture in the United States, they tend to overemphasize the development of the industry, especially around chop suey, without necessarily engaging with the restaurant business as practiced "on the ground."[13] Moreover, most do not extend into the late twentieth century or transnationally, which our volume does.[14] Specifically, we engage in the postmodern discourse of the global consumption of food, and restaurant food in particular, as a commodified cultural activity that transcends ethnic, regional, and national borders.

The remaining notable publications on Chinese and Japanese cuisine restaurants in the United States are either not specifically dedicated to this subject,[15] or are designed solely for non-academic audiences.[16] There also exist edited collections with essays on Asian American restaurants in fiction and film, but these volumes generally focus on Asian American literature and culture, and not on the actual dynamics of Chinese and Japanese eateries. Other recent publications investigate the personal and political inner workings behind some of America's most iconic Asian-cuisine restaurants, but also are geared towards non-academic audiences.[17]

The goal of *Chop Suey and Sushi from Sea to Shining Sea* is to fill some of the gaps in the literature by revealing and contextualizing the hidden, local histories of Chinese- and Japanese-cuisine restaurants in the United States through a diverse, multidisciplinary blend of academic writing, personal accounts, and methodological approaches, ranging from history, to sociology, anthropology, ethnography, economics, phenomenology, journalism, food studies, and film and literary criticism. We feel that utilizing insights from a variety of disciplines not only complements the existing scholarship and exposes the work that still needs to be done in this field, but also underscores the unique and innovative approaches that can be taken in this area of American food studies. Our volume is a mélange of different genres of writing: we envisioned each essay as a surprise meal, and feel that the variation in style and discipline is a strength of this collection. Such original, engaging, previously unpublished, overlooked (hi)stories, neglected personal accounts, and insiders' testimonies will, we hope, provide readers with the kind of access to Chinese and Japanese restaurants in the United States rarely seen in most published works on this subject. They recount how the taste and presentation of Chinese and Japanese dishes have been (re)created and (re)invented in sweat and hardship over generations of Chinese immigrants who had no choice but to become restaurant owners, chefs, and laborers in the small towns and large cities of America. In our opinion, these vivid, emotional, and detailed portrayals are just as significant as those produced by professional ethnographers and anthropologists, because they reveal the survival strategies deployed in Asian restaurant kitchens over the past 150 years and their impact on the culture, politics, and foodways of the United States. Some of the authors of these chapters are family members of restaurant owners and/or chefs, writing with a passion that can only come from personal investment in these issues, while others are academic writers who have painstakingly mined decades of archival data to reconstruct the past. Moreover, several authors offer a fresh look at the amazing continuity and domination of the "evil Chinaman" stereotype in the "foreign" world of American Chinatown restaurants.

Thus, we feel, this collection illustrates the richness of individuals working in the field, from different racial, ethnic, national, and educational backgrounds, including professional historians, sociologists, ethnographers, and chefs, as well as those who have followed these pursuits as second careers and as a means of providing narrative frameworks for their experiences. There are many stories to be told, and this collection of essays provides a sampling of the various possibilities, while underscoring areas for future research.

(Trans)National Chinese and Japanese Restaurants

Another goal of *Chop Suey and Sushi from Sea to Shining Sea* is to dissect how the development of Chinese- and Japanese-cuisine restaurants manifested itself in different parts of the country and beyond. This ties national geography to transnational geography, while simultaneously interrogating the larger cultural meaning of Asian foodways in America, particularly in terms of their contributions to the construction of (ethnic) identities. As conveyed in Chee-Beng Tan's *Chinese Food and Foodways in Southeast Asia and Beyond*, Asian food in general, but Chinese food in particular, is clearly not geographically fixed, but travels with the Chinese diaspora as individuals migrate across the globe, interacting with local foodways (referred to as glocalization), and leaving a pathway of "de/re-territorialized," hybrid, and fusion cuisines in its wake.[18] Interestingly, these foods are also now re-migrating "back" to their supposed countries of origin, creating a bidirectional, interactive crisscrossing of cuisines.

Over the past couple of decades, American-style Chinese and Japanese food has become a transnational phenomenon, ironically infiltrating the Asian market (its "origin") and catering mostly to foreign ex-pats and locals interested in trying American interpretations of Asian food. As the essays in this volume by Annessa Babic and Tony Liu convey, one such example of the globalization of American Chinese food is the Scottsdale, Arizona–based chain P.F. Chang's which, as of this writing, has restaurants in Argentina, Bahrain,

Brazil, Canada, Chile, Columbia, Costa Rica, Dominican Republic, Germany, Guatemala, Egypt, Jordan, Kuwait, Lebanon, Mexico, Panama, Puerto Rico, Qatar, Saudi Arabia, South Korea, Turkey, the United Arab Emirates, and the United Kingdom.[19] The California-based Asian-cuisine chain Panda Express, mostly found in airports and mall food courts in the United States, has also gone global, with branches in Mexico and Canada, U.S. territories such as Puerto Rico and Guam, as well as Dubai and South Korea.[20]

Another indicator of the transnationalization of American Chinese and Japanese cuisine is the TV reality show *Restaurant Redemption*, which began its run in 2013 on cable channels such as the Food Network, the Cooking Channel, and the Asian Food Channel, reaching audiences in North America, the United Kingdom, and other parts of Europe, as well as the Middle East and Asia (Hong Kong, Singapore, Malaysia, and Indonesia). Hosted by BBC celebrity chef Ching-He Huang, a British citizen of Taiwanese birth and heritage known in the Anglophone cooking world as Ching, the series promises to change "the face of Asian food in America one menu at a time." Ching travels across the United States, helping struggling Asian-cuisine restaurants "update and revitalize their dishes and make over their run-of-the-mill establishments."[21] In other words, to make them more "authentically Asian," which is ironic in an industry that profits from inauthenticity. Despite Ching's efforts to raise standards in these restaurants, many of which are small, family-owned take-out establishments, owners are generally reluctant to explore new approaches, particularly when it comes to changing the menu. Mainly, they fear that making any alterations to "time-tested" recipes (basically what every other Asian-cuisine restaurant in the neighborhood is serving) will drive away the customer base they are struggling to retain.

Restaurant Redemption immediately received criticism from viewers who claimed it reified stereotypes about American Asian restaurants (e.g., that they are unclean) and their owners (e.g., that they cannot speak English, are always bickering, and are more interested in turning a profit than customer satisfaction). Moreover, the show often dramatized the "failing restaurant/failing immigrant/failing family" angle for ratings, depicting arguments between family members and between employers and employees that sometimes occupied more air time than the process of reviving the restaurants themselves. Furthermore, they—the restaurants, owners, and staff members—always awaited "redemption" by Ching, the "infallible expert" who doubled as a therapist.[22] The owners of the Austin, Texas, Satay and Fresh Meadows restaurants, and New York's Kim Yum restaurant have maintained that, in fact, *Restaurant Redemption* "blindsided" them, never expressing its true intentions, and imposing itself on their establishments, which were actually doing quite well before they were featured, reinforcing the notion that "reality shows are not reality" and are exaggerated for drama and profit.[23] In Satay's case, the drama existed between the owner and the host, Ching. Moreover, after the crew departed, owners generally maintained the cosmetic changes made to the restaurants (and paid for by the show), but often removed Ching's menu changes, reverting to the "old school" American Chinese and Japanese restaurant food formula which, because of its deep-rooted history, has become an unshakable and, for many, a comforting American tradition.[24]

In short, *Restaurant Redemption* not only underscored the factors that make Asian-cuisine restaurants in the United States distinctly American, but also conveyed how and why these restaurants are such an intricate and indelible part of the American fabric. Clearly, Chinese and Japanese restaurants have come a long way since the pre–World War II era when, for the most part, they were looked at with suspicion, and often aversion, in the United States. Nevertheless, as this "reality" show reveals, Chinese- and Japanese-cuisine restaurant owners still struggle, especially to remain solvent, in the United States, where they are immensely popular—an irony that will be explored in *Chop Suey and Sushi from Sea to Shining Sea.*

This Collection

The essays in this volume are designed to add to our understanding of what has become an institution in the United States: Chinese- and Japanese-cuisine restaurants. How did individual restaurants begin in the United States? How did they fail or thrive? Who was working behind the scenes? How does the presence of Chinese- and Japanese-cuisine restaurants within the American landscape impact its culture?

And how do these restaurants factor into the daily lives of their customers, owners, and workers? These are just some of the questions addressed by this collection. The answers to these types of questions, and those we have not even considered, are complicated, varied, and exciting. They demonstrate the rigor, creativity, and inquisitiveness in this area of inquiry and reaffirm our opinion that we are only scratching the surface with this edited volume.

Given Chinese cuisine's importance in the United States, it is not surprising that over half of this volume's chapters help illuminate its history, giving us a deeper understanding of the intricacies of the dishes served by these restaurants, the restaurateurs who ran them, and their clientele. The first three chapters present studies of the larger milieu surrounding Chinese restaurants in the United States, in order to illustrate the historical complexities of the eateries so many view as part of the quotidian American landscape. Tanfer Emin Tunç's essay examines the sociopolitical messages conveyed by Chinese restaurant menus between the 1940s and the 1970s. Using menus as primary sources, Tunç analyzes the shifts in how Americans viewed China, and the Chinese, during these decades of upheaval, and explores how Chinese American restaurateurs often felt the need to portray themselves, and their establishments, as "safe" by deploying orientalist tropes. Annessa Ann Babic theorizes about the development of America's Chinese chain restaurants and how they changed perceptions of Chinese cuisine. She illustrates that now, not only is Chinese food "Asian," but thanks to its distribution through chain restaurants, it has also become "American." Tony Liu's chapter rounds out this section by discussing General Tso's chicken and Panda Express, two exemplars of the political landscape surrounding the identity politics connecting the United States, Taiwan, and mainland China.

Several chapters narrate the histories of specific Chinese restaurants. Susan Boslego Carter details the rise of Chinese restaurants in Oshkosh, Wisconsin, in the early 1900s. Many of the Chinese eateries established during that time period were located within the confines of a Chinatown, which provided them with a built-in clientele that was not hindered by racism. Oshkosh, a large town in the middle of Wisconsin, did not have a Chinatown, so Charley Toy, its first Chinese restaurateur, used his intelligence, charisma, and business sense to attract non-Asian customers. Clarence Chan's and Ting Man Tsao's study follows the life of master chef Kai Tai Chan, whose efforts included transforming Chinese cuisine from take-out food into a respected art form in 1990s New York. Staying within the same geography, Chunghao Kuo's essay follows the creation and evolution of Taiwanese restaurants in Flushing, New York, from the 1970s to today. Although Chinese in ancestry, Taiwanese restaurateurs faced resistance from mainland Chinese restaurateurs and patrons who began flooding the area in the 1990s. Raymond Douglas Chong parses through the history of chop suey, a dish that is Chinese in spirit, but American in development. His examination traces the development of the iconic dish back to the Guangdong province and then to its heyday as an American culinary phenomenon in the first half of the twentieth century, while interweaving his own family history in the restaurant business. John Jung looks at the "sour side" of Chinese restaurants across the nation over the course of the twentieth century. Jung's essay illustrates that strained finances, a wary public, mercurial government regulations, and other hurdles always makes opening new Chinese-cuisine restaurants in the United States anything but a guaranteed success. As Jung argues, in order to survive, owners have always had to adjust through accommodation and adaptation.

Frank Jacobs and Bruce Arnold provide us with insight into the evolution of Japanese cuisine in the United States. Jacobs's study looks at the public's perceptions of Japanese food in the United States between 1853 and 1918. He carefully plots changing American opinions concerning Japanese food and restaurants through newspapers from the era, revealing that there were often differing opinions about food from Japan and the Japanese-themed restaurants that served it. Arnold's chapter delves into the history of Japanese restaurants in Tucson, Arizona, and finds that, unlike Chinese food, the desert town had little taste or appetite for food from the Land of the Rising Sun. Restaurateurs faced the difficult task of running restaurants while educating their clientele about their exotic menus, and few early examples were successful. Changes to the American cultural landscape in the late 1980s brought about a new appreciation for Japanese food. However, as the cuisine expanded, its newfound popularity resulted in negative consequences for members of the Japanese American community who had built their ethnic lives around Japanese restaurants.

Several authors shed light on small slices of the history of Chinese- and Japanese-cuisine restaurants in the United States. Shoon Lio and Megan Bott examine the ways in which modern-day hipsters and culinary innovators have reinvented and reinterpreted classic Chinese and Japanese cuisine, first as fusion and then as Pan-Asian cuisine, redefining, through tropes such as cosmopolitanism and authenticity, how Americans conceptualize and relate to Asian food and the spaces that serve it. On the other hand, Andrée Lafontaine looks at 1930s Hollywood representations of chop suey and the restaurants that served it. Using a mixture of techniques developed within film studies and food studies, and borrowing phenomenology from the philosopher's toolbox, Lafontaine analyzes the iconic dish and its influence in film beyond that of a mere trope.

In a turn towards the theoretical and abstract, our last two authors attempt to understand how Chinese restaurants are represented and understood by the American public through cultural products such as fiction and science fiction films. Carmen Birkle illustrates that Chinese food, as understood by the majority of Americans (Chinese Americans, included) is not as precise as we think. In her analysis, she exposes the spaces where Chinese food is produced and consumed, and how it affects, and is affected by, the ethnic identities of those who produce and consume it, who may or may not be Chinese. Rounding out our collection is Ingrid Castro's chapter, which looks at the ways in which Chinese and Japanese food, chefs, and restaurants are represented in science-fiction films. The genre, Castro argues, has a long history of viewing Asian restaurants in orientalist terms, often presenting Asians in a negative light. As Castro concludes, while Chinese and Japanese cuisine restaurants have become an inextricable part of the American fabric, they still struggle with many of the same racial, social, cultural, and economic issues that their originators grappled with over 150 years ago.

CHAPTER 1

Dining at the "Oriental Garden"

The Cultural Politics of American Chinese Restaurant Menus, 1940s–1970s

TANFER EMIN TUNÇ

The 1940s to the 1970s is a significant timeframe within the history of Asian/American foreign relations because it represents a period of intense interaction between "East" and "West," specifically through World War II (Japan), the Korean War, the Vietnam War, the Cold War, increasing fears about Red China and communism in general, and eventually the détente that came with the Nixon administration in the 1970s. Many of the fears that accompanied these political events circulated widely in the United States, and often made appearances in American mainstream popular culture through music, cinema, magazines, comics, book covers, posters, and other forms of ephemera such as restaurant menus. Ethnic restaurants, in particular, were caught in the crossfire of what was occurring globally, and during this period, some customers refused to patronize Asian eateries, whose allegiance and Americanness were suddenly under question.

As suggested by their menus, many Chinese restaurants attempted to allay such fears, which translated into a loss of business, by positioning themselves as safe and harmless dining experiences that in no way were connected to what was happening politically. This strategy often employed self- or auto-orientalization, which, through the use of specific imagery and language, played into pre-existing American stereotypes about the exoticism of the Orient. Some menus, like those found at the Ah Fong Chinese Restaurant chain in Beverly Hills, Westwood, Encino, Anaheim, and Hollywood as late as the mid-1970s, used overtly racist, self-deprecating techniques, including "humbly suggesting" certain meals and serving drinks such as "Coolie Cup," "Vicious Virgin," and "Moment in Peking," as a means to attract white clientele by implying that Chinese women were sexually accessible and Chinese men were at the bottom of the social hierarchy (i.e., they "knew their place") and therefore were not a threat to the nation.[1] Moreover, the management welcomed "guest inspections of Ah Fong's kitchens," to assuage concerns about cleanliness and disease—fears harkening back to the racist yellow peril scare of the nineteenth century. Accommodating as ever, the management also happily offered special assistance during the selection of meals, conveying its desire to serve white customers: "Just beckon your Host to your side. He will be happy to help you order a delightful Cantonese meal that will long be a pleasurable remembrance."[2]

This essay will analyze the social, political, and cultural messages conveyed by such American Chinese restaurant menus between the 1940s and the 1970s.[3] Placing these ephemeral material objects into their proper historical context enables a reading of the menus as objects of knowledge which participated in the framing of a digestible China that managed social, political, and cultural turbulence. Such a reading not only illustrates how menus, as primary sources, reproduce, reflect, and mitigate the climate of their era, but it also provides enormous insight into the position of the Chinese in America during this tumultuous time. One aspect of these menus that emerges is their explicit use of what Frank Chin and Sau-ling Wong have termed "food prostitution" or "food pornography," respectively. As Chin elucidated in his play *The Year of the Dragon* (published in 1981; first staged in 1974), this involves emphasizing the "'exotic' aspects of one's ethnic foodways" in order to benefit, financially and sometimes socially, from, in this case, American interest in Chinese cuisine.[4] Although Chin is highly critical of this approach, others have positioned food prostitution as a subversive survival strategy that deploys expectations concerning minority exoticism in order to exploit the majority. However, this subversion, as Wong delineates, is just as destructive because it also relies on exploitation. For Wong, food pornography is particularly insidious because it involves "reifying perceived cultural differences and exaggerating one's otherness in order to gain a foothold in a white-dominated social system."[5] Even though, superficially, "food pornography appears to be a promotion, rather than a vitiation or devaluation, of one's ethnic identity,"[6] as Wong conveys, it is ultimately a form of self- prostitution which commodifies and capitalizes on food, rather than sex, and is perpetrated by cultural "insiders" for consumption by "outsiders."

As this essay will illustrate, Chinese Americans have not only been on the receiving end of cultural appropriation, but also on the giving end. In other words, they, too, have been "active participants in processes of cultural consumption" and not simply "passive subjects who are merely acted upon and from whom 'culture' is unidirectionally appropriated."[7] Such active processes have culminated in the consumption of alterity through food pornography and food prostitution, which in the context of American Chinese restaurant menus have taken the form of "entertaining antics," pidgin English, the emphasis on orientalness through Asian imagery or cultural caricatures—like the horrific buck-toothed coolie, dragon lady, and China doll—and symbolism (e.g., "Asian font" and characters).[8] While all of these elements have undeniably been used to pander to white consumers with the ultimate goal of social acceptance, they have also contributed to the essentialized and exoticized equation of the Chinese with food, which is the only point of contact many non-Asian Americans have with racialized subjects.[9] This has complicated the racial and cultural position of the Chinese in America, attenuating the acquisition of legal rights, cultural recognition, and socioeconomic equality.

The 1940s and 50s: Americanization and Self-Orientalization in the (Post) World War II Era

The history of American Chinese restaurants is just as racially and politically fraught as the history of the Chinese in America, mostly due to the fact that the restaurant industry was one of the only sectors into which, up until World War II, those of Asian heritage were allowed to enter.[10] For most of this period, Chinese Americans survived in the restaurant business not by cooking their own cuisine, but by serving traditional American meat and potato fare. This was because of the widespread, racialized contention that "Chinese food incorporated all sorts of disgusting things."[11] The Chinese "reportedly ate everything from dogs to rats, cats, and living shrimp, still jumping in the bowl," as well as rotten eggs and snakes.[12] Clientele were warned, especially by newspapers, to be sure of what they were consuming and to be certain that eateries met health standards. By the 1920s, however, tensions between Chinese restaurateurs and non-Asian patrons began to ease with sanitary improvements and the invention of chop suey and chow mein, two stir-fried "concoctions typically involving bean sprouts, celery, onions, water chestnuts, green peppers, soy sauce, and small pieces of either chopped pork or chicken," which were created specifically for such customers.[13] Although these dishes were in no way examples of "authentic" Chinese meals, they spawned a craze that opened the door to the acceptance of Chinese cuisine, serving as conduits between white clientele and Asian restaurant chefs and owners that helped Chinese cuisine spread from Chinatowns in large West Coast urban centers to other parts of the country.

The 1920s chop suey and chow mein crazes and the opening of Chinese cuisine to non-Asians allowed Chinese immigrants to improve their public image, especially in terms of sanitation, and to minimize concerns about what they were serving. The influx of customers also prompted them to improvise dishes using local ingredients, which satisfied the culinary requirements of both Asian migrants and the non-Asian population.[14] For example, restaurants used "American vegetables," such as "carrots, snow peas, green peppers, broccoli, and mushrooms," because vegetables found in China, like "fresh bamboo shoots, hotbed chives, garlic bolt, and wax gourd" were, at the time, difficult to obtain and looked upon with suspicion by non-Asian customers.[15] This process of "re-creation, invention, and representation" rendered Chinese cuisine flexible and adaptable, two qualities that have allowed it not simply to endure through decades of culinary fads, but also to become part of American cuisine despite factors such as racial prejudice and cultural politics.[16] This process, as Haiming Liu notes, involved both "dynamic interaction" between Chinese food and American customers, as well as "an interesting process of cultural negotiation. While the Chinese restaurant business helped shape the American diet, Chinese food was at the same time being shaped, transformed, and altered by American popular taste."[17]

The desire to serve non-Asian customers something familiar-yet-exotic resulted in the creation of Americanized Chinese dishes like chop suey, chow mein, egg foo young, egg rolls, crab Rangoon, shrimp toast, Mongolian beef, sweet-and-sour selections, duck sauce, and the ubiquitous fortune cookie, which were specifically crafted to fit U.S. culinary and cultural expectations. While "the ingredients and preparation methods retain[ed] some loose affinity with other Chinese dishes," for example using julienned ingredients as well as "similar-yet-toned-down spices and sauces," such Americanized dishes demonstrate how successfully American Chinese restaurants were able to adapt and acculturate into the more dominant culture.[18] As Vincent Cheng notes, "much of American Chinese cuisine is quintessentially American." In fact, many Americans do not realize just how American the Chinese food served in the United States actually is: "they still perceive it as 'foreign' in spite of its immense popularity in the U.S.," and despite the reality that it was "made in the U.S.A."[19] Some early menus, such as that found at Sacramento's Oriental Grill in 1916, even had to remind their American customers that Chinese dishes were "foreign" by emphasizing that they were "served without bread and butter."[20]

This Americanization, or some would say prostitution, of Chinese food for the non-Asian masses was also accompanied by essentialist processes which reduced Chinese Americans to racist assumptions concerning the "foreign," "exotic" food they ate. The 1920s orientalist fascination with chop suey, chow mein, and chinoiserie reinforced such assumptions for most of the twentieth century, giving rise to, and subsequently reinforcing, the pornographic props of Chinese cuisine restaurants in the United States. Many restaurants urged using chopsticks for Chinese food, while others deployed costumes, performances, and stage settings to assert their Chineseness.[21] Interwar-era restaurants, such as Boston's Cathay House[22] and Bob Lee's Lantern House,[23] deployed orientalist paintings and paper sculptures of pagodas and dragons, Chinese calligraphy, "gaudy lanterns, colorful wall decorations, and bright red" and gold "facades to match non-Chinese

Americans' stereotypical image of the 'Orient.'"[24] Some restaurants, especially those in California Chinatowns, were even built in the shape of pagodas and externally electrified with neon lighting. This commodified construction of the Orient through physical, visual, and linguistic props not only guaranteed the popularity of Chinese cuisine, but also laid the foundation for the self-orientalism that would persist throughout the twentieth century.[25]

According to Yan and Santos, self-orientalism is a reconfiguration and extension of Edward Said's conceptualization of Orientalism.[26] Self-orientalization "proposes that orientalism is not simply the autonomous creation of the West, but rather that the Orient itself participates in its construction, reinforcement and circulation."[27] It is a result of the Asian's "internalization of the orientalist images that have been developed by Western colonial authority," in this case the United States, which has been asserting itself socially, economically, and politically in Asia and the Pacific Rim since the Open Door Policy of the late nineteenth century.[28] The Asian, as Hirose and Pih note, "then adopts and self-inscribes the images," a process which can involve the adoption of orientalist props such as clothing, font, symbols, and other aesthetic expressions, as well as "linguistic orientalism."[29] While Rey Chow suggests that such self-orientalism needs to be rethought as an empowering "voicing back"—"an elusive process of self-realization, a process that can be vital even when it is, as is often the case, demeaning"—because it disrupts hegemonic discourse by deploying the same orientalist strategies, there is an inherent danger in self-orientalism mostly because it has not had the intended subversive effect.[30] By positioning themselves, through self-orientalization, as perpetually foreign and outside of mainstream (white, Anglo-Saxon Protestant) American society, such minorities have voluntarily given a green light to their subjugation.[31]

As suggested by these restaurant menus, Chinese Americans often engaged in alienating and marginalizing processes in their struggle to gain social acceptance, with the orientalism of white Americans defining, and co-conspiring with, the self-orientalism of Chinese restaurateurs. This process was undergirded by a dynamic that Sau-ling Wong has described as "the ethnic's appeal for acceptance by the mainstream customer, who has the power to decide what is agreeably authentic and what is unthinkably outlandish," usually involving "ethnics in the food trade" being "forced to play up stereotypes of their own group."[32] Between the 1940s and the 1970s, the Chinese in America became "recognized in dominant discourses insofar as [they] resembled the stereotype of [their] ethnicity, safely promoted through 'food, festivals and fun.'"[33] To a certain extent, social and economic success became linked to their ability to perform an exaggerated Chineseness as envisioned by non-Asian Americans, and the naming and décor of Chinese restaurants such as Jade Lion, Lotus Flower, Sichuan Gardens, and Pearl River was part of the strategy designed to generate an exotic hyperreality.[34] The menus of this period, which evoke a fantastic and exaggerated simulation of the "real" China through their ubiquitous use of the colors red and gold, and their depiction of dragons, lanterns, Chinese calligraphy, bucolic "Asian" landscapes, and a wide arrange of "Asian-inspired" characters, reflect this illusionary landscape. New York's Chins restaurant, for example, featured a Chinese child in what seems to be a Tai Chi pose on the front of its 1944 menu,[35] while Chicago's Hoe Sai Gai's 1949 menu displayed a very prominent Buddha figure.[36] Forbidden City's 1943 menu displayed a China doll, transposed over an image of a phoenix, and accompanied by Asian-style font;[37] Boston's Joy Yong Co. Chinese and American Restaurant included a stylized pagoda on its 1945 menu;[38] and the menu at Las Vegas's Chop Sticks Chinese Restaurant and Cocktail Lounge featured almost all of these elements: a red and gold cover, embossed with Chinese symbols, a dragon, and a phoenix.[39] The 1940s menu of the Lotus, located in Washington, D.C., was a masterpiece of chinoiserie, depicting, in vibrant pastel colors, an elegant "Chinese" woman with long braids, perched upon a blooming lotus flower.[40]

Because in American society "food and foodways are often used to build and blur boundaries between categories of people,"[41] Chinese restaurant menus, not so surprisingly, became (self)orientalist stages which built and blurred racial, cultural, and political boundaries, ironically for the purpose of social inclusion. This strategy was even used by Chinese restaurant owners in heavily Asian locales, such as California and Hawaii, the latter of which was a territory, and not yet a state, in the 1940s. P.Y. Chong's restaurant in Waikiki, for example, was advertised as the "largest and most beautiful Chinese restaurant in the whole world." As David Wu elucidates, Chong "reinforced a long-lasting stereotyped image about 'Chinamen' and 'Chinese culture' through his self-advertising in pidgin English—'me P.Y. Chong Namba ["number"] One China Cook.'"[42] Chong's World War II–era menu was replete with such linguistic examples: "Sometams fliends make appointmans. When come, place full no room. Vely sorry. You please wait little while."[43] This language was often accompanied by images of the famous personality in the stereotyped Chinaman cap and Manchu jacket.[44] Dishes were also numbered on menus during this time, as they still are, and customers were encouraged to order by number, which further accentuated owners' supposed poor command of English.

Chong's World War II–era menu also included direct political references to the war. Under the flags of the United States, the United Kingdom, the Soviet Union, and the Republic of China, Chong comments, "Me P.Y. Chong say 'These 4 stlong peoples must stick together for keep peace in world always!'"[45] While depicting himself as a "harmless Chinaman" might have been a protective strategy for Chong in Hawaii in the aftermath of Pearl Harbor—a way to distinguish one Asian group from another and to resist conflation into one indiscernible group by explicitly conveying "we are allies" and implicitly reminding "we are not Japanese"—his menu clearly reinforced and perpetuated damaging stereotypes. Likewise, despite initially serving exclusively Chinese cuisine, the California-based Don the Beachcomber restaurant, which later became a chain at the height on the tiki fad of the 1950s and 60s, employed images from the South Pacific in an effort to distance itself from the Japanese. Its menu, which was copyrighted in 1941 and reprinted in various forms throughout the 1950s and 1960s, depicted imperialist maps that foreshadowed the island-hopping technique that would be used by the U.S. military to reach Japan during World War II, and was decorated with nude hula girls and natives.[46] However, such characterizations, many of which attempted to counteract fears of Chinese immigrants as inassimilable yellow perils by comforting American society with entertaining buffoonery and gratuitous sex, lingered well into the twentieth century, complicating the racial position of Asians in the United States. Instead of deconstructing racist Asian stereotypes, restaurateurs selected those that complemented their goals, ultimately positioning Chinese Americans as inferior to native-born, middle-class, white Americans who were "tasteful, cultivated, clean [and] educated."[47] Early on, Chinese restaurateurs appreciated the profit in this and did little to challenge racial and ethnic hierarchies. Rather, they, sometimes even pornographically, "repackaged cultural differences as an economic asset" that could be prostituted, marketed, and consumed.[48] In fact, some restaurants, like the Led Looster Lestaulant and Allan Lum's New Grand East Café in Los Angeles, were so blatant in their use of this approach that they even used pidgin English in their names[49] and Chinaman photographs on their menus,[50] consistently emphasizing orientalist elements both inside and outside their establishments.

Despite the anti-Asian racism of this period, Chinese restaurants boomed during and immediately after World War II, a phenomenon that was undoubtedly catalyzed by the deployment of such orientalist strategies. As J.A.G. Roberts maintains, "the recognition that the United States and China were allies," at least until 1949, "brought about a substantial, if not a complete, revision of American attitudes towards China and Chinese food."[51] In fact, during the hearings to repeal the Chinese Exclusion Act of 1882, a Missouri congressman even commented that "all at once we discovered the saintly qualities of the Chinese people. If it had not been for December 7 [1941, the attack on Pearl Harbor], I do not know if we would have ever found out how good they were."[52] Moreover, Chinese cuisine was promoted as complementary to the eating habits of wartime Americans and was "especially adapted to the meat rationing situation during the war," a "Chinese dish require[d] only about one quarter the amount of meat which a normal American dish may require,"[53] which undoubtedly did not escape the notice of Americans. Chinese restaurants, such as Toon Tien in the Bronx, also attempted to increase their appeal during this period by presenting themselves as ideal locations not just for meals, but also for American pastimes such as bridge parties, as is clearly stated and illustrated on the back cover of Toon Tien's 1948 menu.[54]

Clearly, eating Chinese food became politicized during the World War II era and was closely tied to Chinese-American relations, a phenomenon that would resurface during the Nixon administration in the 1970s. "In San Francisco, Chinese Americans held 'rice bowl' parties to raise funds to support China's war against Japan. These parties were attended by white Americans" who "regarded the Chinese community and by extension the eating of Chinese food more favourably than hitherto." As a result, "between 1941 and 1943 San Francisco Chinatown restaurants experienced a 300 percent increase in business."[55] The Peking Restaurant in Washington, D.C.'s Chinatown became a favorite with politicians, and was renowned for its "Peking Style Native Foods," especially its moo shu pork and the house specialty, Peking duck. Meanwhile, San Francisco's Kan's restaurant "sought to revive the tradition of the high-end banquet restaurants that had flourished in San Francisco in the nineteenth century," and "culinary tourists streamed to Chinatown for dinner at Kan's or upscale competitors like the Empress of China and the Imperial Palace."[56] Once considered "diseased immigrant slums," Chinatowns gradually became locales to stage Chinese identity. For white Americans, they also became exotic and adventurous geographies where they could absorb allegedly "authentic culture" while expressing their solidarity with non-Japanese groups. The Forbidden Palace, which in an elaborate orientalist menu from 1946 claimed to serve "Chinese food at its best," even made a point to mention that it was located in Los Angeles's "New Chinatown,"[57] as did the Golden Pagoda's 1943 menu which, complete with rickshaw, China doll, and pagoda on its front cover, also reinforced destructive stereotypes.[58] Chicago's Golden Pheasant likewise blended orientalist imagery, a heavily American menu of steaks, chops, and potatoes (for those individuals who were still not comfortable eating Americanized Chinese cuisine in 1946), and the accommodating promise to "cheerfully" prepare any dish to be taken home with the hope that it would, through reasonable prices, attractive (clean) environment, and "homelike atmosphere" "establish a continuous clientele of discriminating patrons."[59] Thus, Chinatowns provided non-Asians with a safe buffer zone, a place where they were "reminded of the distinction between the exoticness of the Oriental other and the neutral and unmarked quality of themselves. When their bodies [were] juxtaposed with racialized bodies, the racially authenticated, cultural differences [were] accentuated," as was the line between Asian and Caucasian.[60]

As Harley Spiller notes, "Chinatown's restaurants catered largely to Occidental tastes," which is why starting "in the late 1930s they began adding live entertainment to their bills of fare."[61] During the 1940s, Chinese cabarets—which were almost always showcased in Chinese restaurants or Chinese-owned/themed bars—became popular since they pornographically deployed familiar stereotypes, like the hypersexual and seductive dragon lady and the cuckolded Chinaman, and self-deprecating humor which Americans found both non-threatening and entertaining. New York's China Doll restaurant, and San Francisco's Fong Wan's Club Shanghai and the Lion's Den, were restaurant-nightclubs that flourished in the 1940s, with the latter promising patrons "America's Only Under-Ground Chinese Nite Club Featuring an All-Chinese Floor Show."[62] At the Lion's Den, Americans could imperialistically conquer and consume exotic Chinese women and culture as they consumed a mix of Chinese American dishes, "including ten different sandwiches, Chicken à la King, steaks, chops, pies, cakes, and ice creams," and "authentic-sounding soups such as Yee Chee (shark's fin), Yeen Wo (bird's nest), Bow Yee (abalone), Gai Choy (mustard green), and Cho Goo Gung (grass mushroom)."[63] Printed in English with Chinese transliterations, the menu also featured "a salad of tomatoes, egg, pineapple, cottage cheese, anchovy, peppers, and celery called 'Shanghai Gesture,'" perhaps "named after the [film] that evokes the sizzling tone of 1930s Shanghai."[64] Clearly, such orientalist associations were intentional, as suggested by the menu's "pencil sketch of a wintry village scene with brick bridges arcing over a river and houses," recalling the "famous bridge over Xi Hu (West Lake), one of China's most fabled natural settings in [the] Zhe Jiang province near Shanghai."[65]

The menu, like those of most Chinese restaurant-nightclubs of the period, also offered a wide range of alcoholic beverages. In fact, at the Lion's Den there was "more booze on the menu than any other item, including long lists of scotch, rye, bourbon, Irish whisky, and rum," as well as sexist and racist Asian-inspired cocktails, which were commonplace at upscale Chinese establishments during this period.[66] Much like the bartenders at the Lion's Den, those at the Sky Room "mixed house cocktails for forty-five cents—Dragon's Neck, Dragon's Tail, Dragon's Eye, and Dragon's Tooth, as well as one called Angel's

Tits, made from white crème de cacao, cherry liqueur, and cream in chilled layers," topped with a maraschino cherry.[67]

The "changing American foreign policy goals in Asia," "the developing alliance with China's Nationalist Party—the [anti-Communist] Kuomintang (KMT)," and the "ideological shifts that accelerated with the anti-Japanese partnership of World War II and extended through the Cold War era" catalyzed the transition of the Chinese from the unassimilable aliens of the Exclusion Era (1882–1943) to a model minority of the second half of the twentieth century.[68] Nevertheless, the popularity of Chinese food waned slightly during the early 1950s after the communist takeover of China and its support of North Korea during the Korean War. Eating Chinese food suddenly became politically dangerous, "a potential signifier of one's Communist leanings."[69] However, this was only a temporary predicament. As Shehong Chen notes, "as a result of its Cold War foreign policy, the United States refused to recognize the People's Republic of China. With direct access to mainland China cut off, many Americans found an outlet" for their "curiosity about Chinese culture in the Chinese American restaurant."[70] The culinary demands of "soldiers who were stationed in the Far East and had tasted the 'real thing'" augmented the "natural outgrowth of an already growing desire to learn more about the food," which helped recuperate the slumping Chinese restaurant industry.[71] Some restaurants, like Sacramento's Coral Reef, even worked with these soldiers to capture the aesthetic of the Orient. As conveyed on the back page of a menu from the 1950s, "the Coral Reef's interior is the product of several years of collecting." "We did the décor ourselves with the help of a group of G.I.s."[72]

According to Andrew Coe, "around the early 1940s, the menus in Chinese restaurants stopped evolving. Their food stagnated into bland and unexciting dishes," and "they were losing ground to the competition. The magic and excitement were gone from Chinese food."[73] Resourceful and savvy entrepreneurs like Calvin Lee, owner of the famous Lee's Restaurant in New York's Chinatown and author of *Chinese Cooking for American Kitchens,* were able to use the growing postwar interest in Chinese food to change what was on the menus of Chinese restaurants, maintaining that they were actually educating Americans about their culture even while their culture was being altered, exploited, and perhaps even prostituted. After the war, menus evolved from those of the chop suey era—when usually chop suey, chow mein, fried rice, and egg foo young were the only items available—to include an increasing variety of Chinese American dishes, such as moo goo gai pan (chicken with mushrooms), barbecue spare ribs, lobster Cantonese, shrimp with lobster sauce, sweet and sour pork, and wonton soup.[74] During the 1950s, Chinese restaurants also helped save themselves from being another cultural casualty of the Cold War by following families to the suburbs, where they found competitors such as diners, pizzerias, and hamburger joints.[75] They adapted by capitalizing "on one of their longtime strengths: the ability to sell large portions of inexpensive food. The centerpiece of their menus was the 'family dinner,' a multicourse meal of Cantonese American favorites for one low price." "Some restaurants divided the choices into columns; hence the 'one from column A and one from column B' that many associate with eateries from this era."[76] In the late 1950s, restaurateurs in large urban centers like San Francisco and New York began to renovate their establishments, hiring architects and interior designers to tear down orientalist elements and create eateries that were sleek and modern. The classic Chinese restaurants of the old chop suey days were streamlined to resemble 1950s diner-style eateries with "booths along the wall, tables in the center, lanterns hanging from the ceiling, a few cheap Chinese prints on the walls, a counter for the cash register, and a display of cigars and cigarettes by the entrance."[77]

Catering to the growing middle class, which had an eye for the exotic and a proclivity for Asian food, Polynesian and Hawaiian-themed restaurants serving Cantonese cuisine also became popular during this period. Coinciding with Hawaiian statehood in 1959, establishments such as Edwin Tan's Chinese Gardens in San Bernardino,[78] and a number "in suburban New Jersey, where the commercial strips were dotted with colorful eateries like the Orient Luau," began featuring Hawaiian buffets and feasts.[79] Most of these restaurants shared the same culinary palate—anything that featured pineapple or maraschino cherries suddenly became Polynesian or Hawaiian—and aesthetic, conflating a variety of Asian and South Pacific cuisines and cultures into menus decorated with hula girls and kitschy tiki artifacts.[80] In

Burbank, California, the China Trader served a number of Hawaiian drinks and dishes, and its 1950s menus deployed sketches of relaxed and sexually accessible Hawaiian girls to sell cocktails, exploiting another culture in much the same way Chinese culture was being prostituted.[81] Hollywood's Mouling Restaurant featured a photograph of a "real" Asian woman on the cover of its menu, proprietor Loretta Mouling Hung,[82] who "cordially invited" customers "to patronize her Chinese-American cuisine," adding a personal touch to the exotic gustatory experience that most non-Asian clients expected from this type of establishment.[83]

The 1960s and 70s: The Expansion and Evolution of the Chinese Restaurant Menu

By the early 1960s, Chinese food had not only become a part of the American diet, but, as the popularity of Calvin Lee's cookbook indicated, Americans were also beginning to cook basic dishes in their own homes, or in cooking classes, which further reinforced interest in Chinese restaurants.[84] "Going for Chinese" had become fashionable, especially for young Americans living in urban and suburban locations, as suggested by the menu cover of Boston's Yee Hong Guey Restaurant, which depicts what looks like assimilated, suburban, Chinese American teens, dressed in the latest fashion, using chopsticks.[85] Many Chinese restaurants even tailored their menus to suit the local suburban ethnic population.[86] "Reaching out to the Jewish community were kosher Chinese restaurants in New York's suburbs with names such as *Glatt Wok*" in Monsey, "*Wok Tov*" in Cedarhurst, and "*Shang-chai*," which served dishes like Matzoh Foo.[87] Many Jewish eateries also described fried wontons as "kreplach (Yiddish for small, meat-filled dumplings)" in order to make the exotic familiar.[88] The *House of Lee* in Oakland, California, which catered to the Italian community, included "fried ravioli" (wontons) on their menu, and *Brillante* in Paterson, New Jersey, featured General Tso's Pollo, which was designed to appeal to its Mexican clientele.[89] As Vincent Cheng has observed, "for many newly arrived immigrants during and after the Second World War, eating at Chinese restaurants was a way of forging a new American identity and was an initiation into American culture," and these "ethnic" ethnic restaurants functioned as interfaces between numerous cultures.[90]

The Immigration and Nationality Act of 1965 encouraged new groups of Chinese settlers from different parts of China to immigrate to the United States, and with them came an assortment of regional cuisines. As Lin and Lin indicate, "between 1965 and 1984, an estimated 419,373 Chinese entered the United States—almost as many as the 426,000 Chinese who had come here between 1849 and 1930."[91] Many of these immigrants took advantage of the liberalization in policies and "opened restaurants serving Shanghai and Sichuan specialties, like the Four Season Maiden Lane in New York," primarily aimed at Chinese immigrants.[92] This led to a shift away from the Cantonese-style food found in Chinese restaurants and towards a diversification of dishes, a new emphasis on "authenticity," and the removal of many American or Americanized dishes from menus. While chop suey and chow mein never completely disappeared, and can still be found on many take-out menus in the United States, they began to take backseats to new dishes, many of which, as Haiming Liu notes, "closely followed the culinary trends of Asia."[93]

During the 1960s and 70s, there was an explosion in specialty restaurants and dishes, like New York's Shun Lee Dynasty, which was one of the first Sichuan restaurants, offering "chicken in hoisin sauce, shrimp in 'Szechuan sauce,' and the like—the hotter the better."[94] San Francisco's restaurant, the Mandarin, also introduced customers to new dishes, including cuisine from "northern China, Peking, Hunan and Szechwan: real Chinese food, with a conspicuous absence of chop suey and egg foo young." "The Mandarin was a success, introducing dishes like tea-smoked duck, pot stickers, and sizzling rice soup."[95] Other popular non-Cantonese restaurants were New York's Mandarin House, which specialized in Shanghai cuisine and unusual dishes such as beggar's chicken, sesame-sprinkled flatbread, and mu xu rou (moo shu pork).[96] New York's Harbin Inn listed its specialties (Peking, Shanghai, and Cantonese cooking) on the front of its 1970 menu, below a picture of a red pagoda and above the note that takeout was also available, presumably so customers could enjoy a "taste of China" at home.[97]

The politics of Chinese cuisine intensified during the 1960s and 1970s, in tandem with the intensification of the Cold War. According to Jennifer 8. Lee, "the Cuban Missile Crisis was resolved in a Chinese restaurant called Yenching Palace in Washington, D.C.," which is now a Walgreen's.[98] Thus, some restaurants literally became cultural and political meeting grounds as they had been during World War II. In fact, in the 1960s, Kuo Wah Café, located in San Francisco's Chinatown, even printed that it was the place "where dignitaries and celebrities meet" on the front cover of its menu.[99] While the Vietnam War caused a slight retraction among patrons in the same way that the Korean War did—some Americans curtailed their consumption of Asian cuisine, but most did not due to the fact that Chinese food was now considered part of American cuisine—in general the 1970s is considered by food historians to be a boom time in Asian cuisine, mostly because of President Richard Nixon's visit to China in 1972, which thawed Sino-American relations and ushered in the era of détente. This visit spurred great interest in Chinese cookbooks, upscale Asian restaurants, "Far Eastern" banquets, and "genuine" Chinese food, especially Peking duck, which Nixon reportedly consumed with delight. As the *New York Times* reported, "Some images were simply beyond words or still photographs, including the sight of Mr. and Mrs. Nixon carefully wielding chopsticks."[100]

American interest in banquet dishes such as Peking duck and shark fin soup, as well as chopsticks, immediately began to increase and "in New York, Chicago, and Washington, D.C., restaurant owners anxious to cash in on the trend quickly whipped up special nine-course menus that supposedly replicated Nixon's meal with Zhou Enlai."[101] In 1975, Los Angeles's Four Rivers Restaurant joined forces with La Société Bacchus et Epicurus to serve a Lucullan banquet that included champagne and an elaborate feast of shrimp, pork, duck, beef, chicken, and fish.[102] Gung Hay restaurant in Gardena, California, whose 1977 menu was decorated with a Chinese warrior, emperor, and sage, offered a range of banquets heavy in meat, poultry, and seafood that varied in price and selection.[103] As Susan Sih, co-owner of Chicago's Dragon Inn remarked at the time, "When we opened…I couldn't give away a Peking Duck. And then President Nixon went to China" and ate one. "He's been the greatest salesman for Peking Duck," which continues to be a favorite dish in the United States.[104]

The menus of the 1960s and 1970s also changed to reflect this growing interest in new dishes, "authentic" cuisine, and the connection between Chinese food and Chinese history. During this period, "menus began to mention the historical, cultural, and geographical aspects of the country," and "emphasized where the ethnic dishes had come from,"[105] often stressing the "genuine," or "gourmet," nature of their food right on the menu. These menus thus function as examples of 1960s/70s culinary "*autoethnography*—texts that undertake to correct, through self-representation, the portrayals others have made."[106] However, in this case, many of the so-called "others" were in fact Chinese Americans themselves. Nevertheless, this paradigm shift, which emerged in tandem with the relaxing of American Cold War strategy—in particular with Nixon's détente policy and his historic visit to China—made an indelible impression on Chinese restaurant menus. Los Angeles's Golden Dragon Café devoted the entire first page of a 1960s menu to a fable-like introduction which intertwined old Chinese aphorisms with a lesson in Chinese culture.[107] In its 1965 menu, New York's Mandarin House provided patrons with a map that explicitly illustrated the regions of China from which its dishes hailed.[108] Chicago's Jade Palace transposed Ming trees, a Chinese peasant, and Chinese characters upon a bamboo screen to produce a sleek and modern menu, devoting its back cover to the story of Kuan Yin, the Chinese goddess of mercy.[109] Likewise, in their 1973 menu, Los Angeles's Jade West combined the aesthetics of the Forbidden City and the Great Wall to produce a tribute to the "city of Cathay" on its back cover, which was specifically commissioned by the restaurant and created by an artist from Taipei.[110] Biographical details about the restaurant owner or the history of the restaurant itself were also incorporated into menus, which in upscale restaurants were becoming encyclopedic in length and breadth. Don the Beachcomber, for example, laid out its entire history and contributions to Cantonese cuisine and American cocktail culture in a menu from 1965.[111]

Chinese restaurant menus also began to include information about cooking techniques, "such as stir fry, and the exotic ingredients, such as pea pods, black or dried mushrooms, bamboo shoots, water chestnuts, bean sprouts, dried shrimp, cellophane noodles, 5-spice powder, [and] oyster sauce, they used."[112] Other restaurants tried to inculcate Americans on Chinese dining etiquette: "For example, at the bottom of a menu, diners were instructed to: Please give your entire order at the same time because in the real Chinese style we served everything together. NO ORDER EXCHANGE AFTER IT IS PREPARED."[113] However, even authenticity had its limits—anything that might have been considered too "authentic" or unusual for the American palate was usually kept off the menu, as was the case at Chin's Village in Wellesley, Massachusetts. The restaurant, which physically resembled an Americanized Chinese village,[114] asked patrons to "please request for special Chinese dishes not listed."[115] New York's Harbin Inn included dishes written solely in Chinese on its menu, presumably because English translations might have driven away non-Asian customers.[116]

The 1970s brought with it the proliferation of Chinese take-out establishments, which enabled Americans to consume even more Chinese food—at lunch, after work, on weekends—without having to gather the entire family for a special outing. The decade also marked the further standardization of Chinese menus, not only in sit-down restaurants, a process that had been underway since the 1950s, but also in take-out kitchens. By fixing names and titles, Chinese restaurant menus "both addressed the fantasy and further created the expectation of identity and uniformity" putting "into place a kind of Chineseness that persists through the dissemination of the menu. The standardization of Chinese dishes produced a soothing sameness in the representation of Chineseness on the menu."[117] By the 1970s, almost all American Chinese takeout menus had the same conformist "roster of dishes like Kung Pao chicken, hot and sour soup, egg rolls, beef with broccoli, and General Tso's chicken," as well as, perhaps, some specialty dishes.[118] However, spicy, sweet, and crispy food, mostly in Mandarin, Hunan, and Cantonese styles, in large quantities, and at low prices, became the expectation of most American customers. Moreover, rather than grouping dishes "American style" into appetizers, main courses, and desserts, as was previously the case, by the 1970s almost all menus grouped dishes "Chinese style" "according to their major ingredients: vegetables, beef, chicken, fish, chow mein, rice, and seafood." Nevertheless, the American tradition of "starting with appetizers or soups; proceeding with options such as seafood, beef, or poultry with rice, noodles, and vegetables; and finally, finishing with a dessert" has persisted.[119]

Food is a vehicle through which ethnicity can be constructed and reproduced, with menus in particular serving as locations for the negotiation and realization of often politicized ethnic identities. While, between the 1940s and 1970s, the Chinese "morphed from the yellow peril to model American citizens…race and ethnicity remained essential components of Chinese American experiences," especially within the restaurant industry.[120] Menus reflect not only changes in the status of the Chinese in America, and how cultural politics impacted these changes, but they also elucidate how many Chinese entrepreneurs deployed strategies such as self-orientalization through food pornography or food prostitution to attract and retain non-Asian customers. While many restaurateurs undoubtedly perceived such survival strategies as necessary evils, they ultimately contributed to the denigration of Asian peoples and attenuated the struggle towards social equality. As Samantha Barbas rightly observes, eating "foreign food" is a "form of cultural and culinary imperialism in which colonizers confirm their dominance over a culture by appropriating" its cuisine. "Chinese Americans as restaurant servers or cooks posed little threat to most Americans—although they could not accept the presence of Chinese Americans in mainstream social settings or businesses, they had little trouble envisioning them in subservient roles."[121]

Some Chinese entrepreneurs were, to a certain extent, complicit in their own oppression, contributing to what Sau-ling Wong has called "the limited vision" for Asian subjects.[122] However, despite the disturbing nature of this self-orientalization, perhaps many had no choice; dismantling such hierarchies is extremely difficult, especially for historically disempowered groups, due to the strong social, political, and economic ties that exist between race, ethnicity, and food in the United States. Further complicating this is the reality that racial meanings, racialization, and race-based discourses have permeated all aspects of American society. The American restaurant business itself operates on a series of racial and ethnic stereotypes—of Mexicans, Italians, Australians, and Asians, among others. As the inheritors of such a system, "Asian restaurant owners make their living on the knife-edge between novelty and familiarity, risk and comfort. Their battle with reluctant palates is not unlike the collective struggle that Asian Americans have to undertake in order to maintain a viable identity."[123] This "knife-edge" includes not only "harmonization and compromise between seemingly contradictory requirements: being authentic and being Americanized, maintaining tradition while consciously modifying it,"[124] but also carving out a niche within the often rigid boundaries imposed by (white) American society.

CHAPTER 2

Importing and Exporting the Ethnic

Thoughts on American Chinese Cuisine, Globalization, and the Dinner Plate

ANNESSA ANN BABIC

Takeaway, or takeout as Americans dub it, serves as a national standby. Americans have crafted fast food into a national product, and they have packaged, frozen, rehydrated, and exported this quick and ready-made creation. Yet, the lure of these high-fat, excessively salt-laden foods goes beyond the popular American drive-through and freezer section at the local grocery. American fast food has woven its way into the global food market, and standby chains like Burger King, McDonald's, and Kentucky Fried Chicken abound in numerous tourist locales. They can also be found in emerging tourist centers like Ecuador; there is a KFC in Quito.[1] In short, the quick, greasy, eat-on-the-go food common to Americans is now familiar around the globe.

The rise of American fast food is not a shocking surprise. Ease, comfort, and even idealist notions of modernity play at the fast food table. Standardized chain food allows American tourists to capture a "taste of home" in the Philippines, or elsewhere, while a local can also "taste America." Fast fare also serves as a cultural ambassador, permitting consumers to travel vicariously from the dining table while never leaving home. Ironically, Chinese food has emerged as a "familiar yet exotic" all-American meal. However, the complexities on the plate extend far beyond the choice of brown or white rice. As journalist Jennifer 8. Lee has remarked, "Our benchmark for Americanness is apple pie. But ask yourself: How often do you eat apple pie? How often do you eat Chinese?"[2] Such questions capture the essence of this discussion at its core. Its availability, pervasiveness, accessibility, and class-crossing undercurrents not only reflect the mobile and fast-paced life of Americans, but also inadvertently bring a sense of community, as pretty standard Chinese takeout fare can be procured from coast to coast. The pluralism of American society intersects with the classic melting-pot analogy to bring a continuous fusion of tastes, cultures, and expectations onto the dinner plate.[3]

In the United States, Chinese takeout restaurants account for more than 43,000 food venues, with 84 percent of Americans reporting they eat ethnic food at least once a month (dining out or takeaway).[4] Since the birth of P.F. Chang's, Panda Express, and Manchu Wok, the nature of American Chinese fast food has changed. Previously, Americans found Chinese restaurants lurking around corners in suburban strip malls, in the middle of historically white, small Midwestern towns, and in an array of urban locations. However, Chinese food has a long history in the American diet. The first Chinese immigrants settled in San Francisco in 1847, mainly to build the transcontinental railroad, and the rapid influx shortly thereafter established their presence in the social landscape. Californians, in particular, saw their foods influenced by this ethnic group. As Chinese communities grew and Americans relied upon them for labor and food services, their cuisine became more diverse. Traditional Chinese food used all of the animal, and Americans were shocked to discover what gave their noodles and rice such rich and distinctive flavor. These restaurants, especially those outside the largest and most vibrant urban Chinatowns—San Francisco, Seattle, Tacoma, New York, Chicago, Philadelphia, Honolulu, Boston, Los Angeles, and Washington, D.C.—altered their menus to create a palatable selection for locals. They also self-described as Chinese American, versus labeling themselves Chinese as did restaurants in Chinatowns. Gradually, the American landscape became dotted with chop suey houses, with dishes rich in cornstarch, thick batters, and sweetened sauces that differed greatly from traditional Chinese cuisine. Wonton soup, egg rolls, barbecued spareribs, sweet-and-sour pork, and beef with lobster sauce were specifically created for, and targeted to, American consumers.[5]

The rise of chain restaurants post–World War II created a conformist culinary culture. Just as Disney World rose to fame in the postwar era, providing ready-made and guaranteed fun-filled family vacations, as this essay will argue, American Chinese chain restaurants gave patrons a safe ethnic experience. They could consume Chinese cuisine without the fear of not liking it. Most importantly, national chains made it "user approved." Moreover, packaging the chain and shipping it abroad enabled non-Americans to interact and engage with American products, voyeuristically consuming modernity and so-called Americanism in much the same way Americans imaginatively travel with their own Chinese dinners. The packaging of Chinese food by (trans)national American chains became a form of modern cultural imperialism, a geopolitical consumer-based force that Americans did not invent, but made their own.[6]

Americanizing Chinese Cuisine

Foodways authors, like Andrew Coe, serve up the gastronomic reader a light and entertaining overview of Chinese food, and examine how the cuisine is largely a commercial and cultural hybrid. Hidden within the cuisine's history are moments of political comedy, such as when national security advisor Henry Kissinger, on a state diplomatic mission to China in 1971, failed spectacularly at using chopsticks. However, such moments also reveal the politics of food, and Chinese food in particular, both within the United States and beyond its borders. As Coe conveys,

> The status of Chinese food in the American culinary scene has always been linked, albeit often loosely, to the state of international relations between the two countries. In 1989, the brutal squashing of the Tiananmen Square protest shattered the illusion of China evolving into an American style democracy. Cultural exchanges ground to a halt; tourist cancelled their China trips; and the US government instituted economic sanctions against the communist government. At the same time, the American culinary world's attention was directed elsewhere, particularly

toward the Japanese and New American restaurants that dominated the white-tablecloth end of the market.[7]

Yet, despite such politicized moments, a worldwide, politically resistant acceptance of ethnic foods has become a part of global cultural dynamics. In the United States, Chinese eateries began to boom in 1848 in Sacramento Valley, California, as the quest for gold drove scores of settlers there. By 1851, more than 25,000 Chinese had moved to California, not entirely in search of gold but in the quest for a stable and prosperous life. San Francisco's Chinatown, with its inexpensive restaurants aimed at miners, served as a strong cultural and economic current that encouraged the formation of other Chinatowns. However, even with their positive social contributions, the Chinese still remained stereotyped as dirty, shifty, rat-eating undesirables.[8] Nevertheless, by World War II, Chinese cuisine had triumphed over such discourse, prompting the *St. Louis Dispatch* in 1940 to call it "among the best in the world."[9]

Yong Chen provides another provocative look at this story by intertwining memories of China and his own immigrant encounters with America and its eateries. He remarks that by 1980, Chinese food served as the nation's most popular ethnic cuisine, and traces the roots of contemporary American Chinese restaurant chains to the social and economic networks established by Chinese immigrants working in the restaurant business. As the Chinese carved out lives, communities, and homes on the American landscape, they came to represent "America's first truly national network of public dining, Chinese restaurants played a vital role in expanding the meaning of abundance and democracy," and the connection between nation-building, imperialism, and food.[10]

The spread of Chinese food was inseparably connected to the geographic and socioeconomic expansion of the United States. This connection is best captured by the notion of "empire food," which was created in the process of empire building for the pleasures of its citizens. Consumption was indeed a significant goal and consequence of empire building, and recognizing Chinese food as empire food helps us appreciate its basic characteristics: ubiquitous but cheap.[11]

Perhaps the true litmus test for Chinese food as a marker of American cultural imperialism is a comparison to McDonald's. McDonald's has long stood as an icon of cheap (and unhealthy) fast food and the problems of the American service industry. However, Chinese restaurants fail this litmus test, mainly because there are far more complicated social, cultural, ethnic, racial, and geopolitical forces at play with this particular cuisine.[12]

Chinese restaurants, as journalist Jennifer 8. Lee remarks, are comparable to apple pie. There are twice as many Chinese restaurants as there are McDonald's locations, and the sheer abundance of them suggests the importance they hold on the American culinary landscape. Her story, encompassing forty-two states and three years of ethnographic research, reveals that the driving force and longevity behind this ethnic cuisine lies in its chefs, particularly its cooks' abilities to integrate local ingredients into dishes, making them feel exotic yet familiar, all at once.[13]

Chinese food, unlike McDonald's and other ethnic foods, has endeared itself to Americans at home and abroad like no other cuisine. A cheap, urban dinner for metropolitan dwellers and a staple of the suburbs, Chinese cuisine has transcended class, race, and culture. It is particularly popular among American Jews, who often celebrate Christmas Day with Chinese and a movie. Even though the Chinese diet is rather free and flexible, and the Jewish diet is bound with restrictions like eschewing pork and shellfish and not mixing meat and dairy, the affinity between these two ethnic groups speaks to the transnationality and adaptivity of Chinese food, which is precisely what has made it a global favorite. Perhaps the shared experiences of the two cultures might have also contributed to this bond. The Jews largely fled Europe because of religious and ethnic persecution, and the Chinese became the target of American racism beginning in 1882 with the first Chinese Exclusion Act.[14] On the surface, this shared history of racism could be one reason for Jewish sympathy. But, with respect to the stomach, any person who has ever had the faintest ache of hunger can attest that emotion is only half of the equation. Taste and accessibility really make the case for culinary desire.

Even though pork and shellfish are used in Chinese dishes, Jewish consumers, especially those who do not follow kosher dietary rules, flock to the satisfying cuisine. Within the Jewish community, it has come to be known as "safe treyf," a mixture of the safe and forbidden, because ingredients like pork are cut up so finely that customers can "safely" overlook their inclusion.[15] Dining on Chinese food has also served a communal purpose as it has become a de facto Jewish tradition on Christmas and a go-to "all-American" family meal. Yet, the beauty of American cuisine is that its constant (re)cycling allows it to fuse elements that are seemingly unconnected. Moreover, interaction with food on a personal, familial, and national level reinforces connections between memory and identity. Chinese food has certainly filled this function in the United States.

The chain restaurant, another American creation, was probably destined for marriage with Chinese food, a national favorite.[16] The first chains—brimming with "American fare" such as ribs, chops, and steak and potatoes—were designed to feed travelers efficiently, while keeping trains on schedule. They were based on an intricate system of organization, but not the fast food and ready-to-eat items of the modern era. Rather, these chains represented the standardization of home food cooked for the masses. However, these restaurants, with their finely-tuned assembly-line kitchens whose style was reminiscent of Taylorism in factories, laid the groundwork of today's fast-food-chain culture.

In the 1980s, only 10 percent of American restaurants were ethnic. By 1997, this number had risen to 33 percent. These ethnic kitchens brought in an annual revenue of $29.5 billion, and by 2005 the income from ethnic restaurants reached $48.75 billion. Throughout, Chinese restaurants have long remained the core of American ethnic eateries. With more than 43,000 Chinese restaurants in the United States alone, it is no surprise that they serve as an international envoy of the American culinary experience. To put the 43,000 in perspective, this staggering number exceeds McDonald's, Wendy's, and Burger King restaurants combined. Moreover, the Chinese eatery typically remains family owned.[17] Ironically, through an ethnic endeavor, the Chinese have achieved the American dream. The tragedy here is that even though Chinese American families have become economically successful, many have still not obtained middle-class status, remaining the "foreigner within." Studies consistently show that Chinese restaurants actually bring in low profits because consumers expect good food at cheap prices. Thus, even the busiest Chinese restaurant in the neighborhood might only see revenues that barely keep the owners afloat.[18]

According to the 2010 census, individuals identifying as Chinese only accounted for 1 percent of the United States population. Yet, the Chinese have blended foods that have become a permanent part of most American diets. Chinese food, which itself is an adaptation, has been further adapted according to regional tastes, with examples including honey pecan shrimp in Louisiana and Szechuan alligator found in Florida and Louisiana. Though, most interestingly, cashew chicken, a long-standing staple of Chinese menus, is not a Chinese dish at all. Cashew chicken is actually a mainstream, middle-class American dish that was rendered Chinese with the addition of exotic nuts: it consists of a gravy type sauce, chopped vegetables, and fried chicken. Likewise, General Tso's chicken is a hybrid Chinese/Taiwanese/American creation. However, the American version with sugar, vinegar, and sriracha or red pepper sauce, occupies a stronger place in U.S. and international markets.[19]

Globalizing American Chinese Food

Consistently, Chinese food remains cheap, but labor-intensive. The small pieces of meat, chopped vegetables, and sautéed dishes require the chef to remain constantly vigilant and engaged. Chinese food remains relatively cheap in the United States because Chinese labor is equated with cheap products in general, with many consumers refusing to pay more than other types of fast food. Not surprisingly, the expansion of Chinese markets globally parallels the growth of American Chinese food chains, such as P.F. Chang's and Panda Express, in Asia, which essentially sell Americanized Chinese food back to Asian consumers as "American food." This dizzying transnational recycling of fast food was catalyzed by changes in eating habits in the 1990s, which is when American taste buds expanded in a new world of trade and connectivity. This largely occurred due to the free, open, and expanded global trade and economic boom that came after the Persian Gulf War. Exotic ingredients like tarragon and raspberry vinaigrette first appeared on grocery store shelves in the 1990s, and in 1993, the first chocolate yogurt tantalized American, and later global, taste buds. The same year, we saw the term "gastroporn" enter the vernacular. A rise in packaged goods and processed foods also fueled our gastro revolution, resulting in the perfect recipe for the expansion of American tastes.[20]

In many ways, one can look at American Chinese food, and our obsession with it, as a case study of American idiosyncrasies. We live in an age when being considered a foodie, or a self-proclaimed one, is considered a cultural medal of honor—when fusing cuisines (a popular Gen-X fad that now seems passé) and reading food magazines are considered everyday activities. Withstanding it all, Chinese food has woven its way into the American market, mixing seamlessly with hamburgers and fried chicken to become, for many, quick comfort food. The geopolitics of the 1990s, the rise of exotic ingredients (everything from mushroom variations to lemongrass), and cheap travel created a unique context, opening the door to other American adaptations (exploitations) of Asian culture, such as kimono dresses, chopstick hair accessories, and Chinese symbol tattoos, all of which, much like Chinese food itself, can be seen as creative examples of ethnic adaptation.[21] However, the reality is that just as Chinese food was appropriated and altered to suit the American palate, the Chinese language has also been hijacked, manipulated, and often outright fictionalized in the name of body art.[22] Yet, these appropriations are largely in the eye of the beholder. For most Americans, partaking in these trends is nothing more than a form of consumerism, filling a cultural or spiritual void, or hunger, in much the same way food does.

By the time Panda Express entered the market in the 1980s, it did not need to mask its fast-food appeal. That cute panda, the glowing red lights, the distinctive take-out box (which has even been used as inspiration for women's handbags over the years), and the comforting guarantee of predictability, even banality, in flavor, told us that we did not have to be brave. Drive-thrus even allowed us to remain in our climate-controlled cars with heated seats, air conditioners, sunroofs, and posh interiors. Safe treyf came in little boxes, wrapped up safe, and the chances of it being inedible, or something we would not recognize, were slim. When exported out, American products convey this mixed bag of feelings, beliefs, and ideas. On the flip side, the foreign becomes the local when we add a dash of alligator, a side of pecan, or simply create a new cuisine staple, like cashew chicken.

CHAPTER 3

General Tso's Chicken, Panda Express, and the Identity Politics of Chinese Food and Restaurants in America

TONY TAI-TING LIU

Accompanying China's rise is an ever-growing interest in the culture, history, and language of the Chinese civilization. In an attempt to balance negative connotations associated with the term *rise*—China is a growing major power that is increasingly discontent with the current world order and seeks change—elites in Beijing jumped on the train of *zhongguore* or "China fever" and sought to correct the nation's image through expressions of soft power. Through the establishment of Confucius Institutes, or Chinese learning centers, around the world, China has successfully exported its language and culture abroad, a phenomenon that prompted Joshua Kurlantzick to coin the term "charm offensive."[1] What often goes unnoticed, however, is the role food plays in China's charm offensive. The identity politics of Chinese cuisine has brewed quietly alongside U.S.-China-Taiwan relations, and is visible through Chinese-cuisine restaurants in America. With this in mind, this essay looks into the development of the popular dish "General Tso's chicken" (*zuozongji*, or *zuozongtangji*) and the restaurant chain "Panda Express" in America, while considering the identity question of "being Chinese" that is entailed by the two case studies.

History aside, politics matters. With the balance of power increasingly tipping in favor of China in recent years, it is becoming clear that competition across the Taiwan Strait is spilling over from politics and economics into the realm of culture.[2] Cuisine defines a large part of Chinese culture, and food plays a significant role in defining Chinese identity. Unrivaled in the preparation of a dish, the Chinese look to the phrase *sexiangweijuquan*, or the complete package of appearance, smell, and taste, as the standard for delivering food onto the kitchen table. As China continues to grow, seeking to gain the favor of the international community through soft power, cuisine becomes an ever more important element. As cultural competition intensifies between China and Taiwan, cuisine may increase as a possible source of friction between Beijing and Taipei.

While food and foodways do not necessarily have to be politicized, as cultural representations and objects, possibilities abound in terms of their ability to create political tension. The 43,000-plus Chinese restaurants in America would certainly be a focal point of this tension, with two nations ostensibly claiming Chinese cuisine, and the identity politics of food potentially becoming a concern for Chinese restaurants in America.[3] With the aim of addressing this dilemma, this chapter moves forward in four parts. Part One discusses the complicated identity politics hidden in Chinese food in America; Parts Two and Three examine the cases of General Tso's chicken and Panda Express, respectively, and elaborate on the challenges of defining a specific identity; and Part Four concludes with some reflections on Chinese identity and its implications for defining Chinese American cuisine in the future.

The Identity Politics of Chinese Food and Restaurants in America

A sense of Taiwan as a separate political entity, with a unique cultural identity, has come into being in Taiwan, particularly among the younger new generation of Taiwanese who were born and raised on the island and feel little historical connection with the "fatherland." Accompanying this development is a renewed examination of the cultural and social roots of Taiwan and what "being Taiwanese" means vis-à-vis "being Chinese." So far, the movement has had limited success, and has been overshadowed by China's continued integration into the global economy. Taiwan, for its part, has invested considerable effort in promoting its separate status and identity, establishing cultural centers and organizing events in the United States. Nonetheless, the continued absence of a distinct cultural object or tradition that represents "Taiwan" remains the Achilles' heel of its efforts and aspirations.

Taiwan's identity challenge is most vividly played out in Chinese restaurants in North America. While Taiwan can make claims to culinary sovereignty within its territorial boundaries with ease and reasonable success, the same cannot be said for similar attempts elsewhere. Such issues come to a head in multicultural societies such as the United States and Canada, where the Chinese diaspora represents different regional origins and cultures. Food has become one of the only umbilical cords that connect the various Chinese communities abroad. An issue that Taiwan confronts in such a setting is how to identify itself separately from China, when "being Chinese" is already ethnically and culturally hybrid. For example, Malaysian-Chinese, Thai-Chinese and Vietnamese-Chinese (or the other way around) are all identities that do not seem to be in conflict with the Chinese culture. Correspondingly, in terms of Asian restaurants, so called "fusion" or "creative" establishments that amalgamate and serve a combination, or combined style, of cuisines have become fairly common in North America. If so, why should things be any different in the case of Taiwan? Does it need a distinct cuisine abroad?

Taiwan's identity challenge seems to be even more problematic when considered in an Asian American context. Since *Asian American* is itself a term that stands for a fused or combined identity—similar to the various combinations of Chinese identities noted above—Taiwanese immigrants abroad, like the Taiwanese in Taiwan, may need to wrestle with the concept of a divided Chinese identity. If China and Taiwan are separate categories, "being Asian American" should be further divided into Chinese American and Taiwanese American, and the Taiwanese diaspora should be offered a range of identities to adopt. The most parochial pries away at the notion of Asian American, while the most inclusive challenges the notion of a singular Chinese national identity.

Identifying General Tso's Chicken: Chinese, Taiwanese, or Chinese American?

Among Chinese dishes associated with chicken—with the exceptions of Kung Pao chicken and sweet-and-sour chicken—perhaps the most renowned dish known in America is General Tso's chicken, a dish named after the famous Qing dynasty Chinese general, Tso Tsung-tang. Kung Pao and General Tso share a large crossover in ingredients: chicken, soy sauce, and hot chili peppers. However, Kung Pao chicken is a spicier Sichuan dish, while General Tso's chicken is a sweeter Hunan dish that is closer to Sesame chicken in the United States. Yet, in an interview conducted by *China Forum* (*shiji dajiangtang*), a popular program produced by Phoenix Television that engages scholarly subjects, Renmin University Professor Yang Dongliang claimed that, in fact, Kung Pao chicken and General Tso's chicken are the same dish. On the other hand, in *The Chinese Kitchen*, chef Eileen Yin-Fei Lo claims that General Tso's chicken is a distinctly different dish that comes from a simple Hunan chicken recipe of humble origin. According to Lo, the dish did not receive its name from the great Qing general, but from a phonetic reference to the ancestral meeting hall or *zongtang* commonly found in traditional Chinese homes. Hence, in Cantonese, the dish is also sometimes referred to as *chung tong gai*.[4]

In 2002, Michael Browning, feature writer of the *Palm Beach Post*, traced the origin of General Tso's chicken to immigrant chef T. T. Wang. In his research, Browning notes an interview with Michael Tong, owner of New York's Shun Lee Palace. Tong claims that in 1972, he and Wang partnered to open the first Hunanese restaurant in the United States. In Tong's words, "the four dishes we offered, you will see on the menu of practically every Hunanese restaurant in America today . . . they all copied from us," and one of these dishes was General Tso's chicken.[5] In a recent report, Kimberly Kohatsu echoes Browning's narrative of Wang's role in introducing the dish, but adds that David Keh, an immigrant chef like Wang, also opened a Hunan restaurant in New York, featuring General Tso's chicken on its menu, around the same time.[6] Yet outside America, both Wang and Keh cannot claim to be the creator of the dish. As Eric Hochman conveys, General Tso's chicken may have originated from a Chef Peng instead.[7]

In 1952, when the relationship between China and Taiwan was particularly tense and hostile, chairman of the U.S. Joint Chiefs of Staff and commander of the Pacific Fleet Admiral Arthur Radford made a formal visit to the island and stayed in the country for four days. Admiral Liang Zhao-xu, Chief Commander of the R.O.C. Navy, hosted Radford with great hospitality and invited his American counterpart to a three-day long banquet prepared by Chef Peng Chang-kuei. In Peng's words, "even though both Radford and Liang seemed quite satisfied by the food for the first two days, I decided it's time for some change on the third day."[8] Forgoing braising and steaming, Peng decided to cut the chicken into big chunks, deep fry the pieces, and finally stir fry the pieces with a mixture of soy bean sauce, vinegar, and red chili pepper. The result was General Tso's chicken.

After enjoying the dish, an intrigued Radford asked Peng what the dish is called. With sudden whim, Peng named the dish "General Tso's chicken" after the great commander of a Hunan army that pacified the Taiping Revolution and unrest on China's border. Peng later explained that as a Hunan chef of Hunan cuisine, the use of "General Tso" seemed appropriate. Peng Chang-kuei later immigrated to the United States and brought General Tso's chicken to America in the 1970s. In 1973, Peng opened his first restaurant, Peng's Restaurant, on New York's Forty-Fourth Street, where he served the dish.

Before the arrival of Peng and others like Wang and Keh in the 1970s, Hunan cuisine was largely unknown in the United States. General Tso's chicken was the dish that helped promote Hunan Chinese cuisine in America. General Tso's chicken was also popularized by then secretary of state Henry Kissinger. After trying the dish at a dinner banquet at Peng's Restaurant, Kissinger became hooked on the unique Hunan flavor. Kissinger's appetite for Chinese cuisine, and General Tso's chicken in particular, was featured in the *New York Times* and *Washington Post*, which catapulted Peng Chang-kuei and Hunan cuisine to fame in the United States. As Peng recollects, "Kissinger visited us every time he was in New York and we became good friends . . . it was he who brought Hunanese food to public notice."[9] In his office in Taipei, Peng still displays a photograph with Kissinger, toasting wineglasses at the restaurant.[10]

After enjoying success in the United States, Peng decided to sell his business in 1981 and return to Taiwan upon the request of former customers who "missed his cooking."[11] In October 1983, he opened the first Pengyuan Restaurant on Linsen Road in Taipei. Since then, Pengyuan has increased to nine branches in northern Taiwan and has become famous for its fine dining and Hunan-style cuisine. In fact, the story of General Tso's chicken and chef Peng Chang-kuei served as part of the inspiration for the documentary film *The Search for General Tso*, released in 2014.[12] The film premiered in Taiwan at the grand opening of a new Pengyuan Restaurant in Taipei, and has developed a cult following on Netflix.

The story of General Tso's chicken speaks to the inherent problem of identity, since China and Taiwan parted ways in 1949. In light of the competition over Chinese identity, how should one refer to a dish such as General Tso's chicken? Is the dish Chinese or Taiwanese? The apparent answer may depend on one's political stance and which of the narratives above one believes to be true. However, attributing General Tso's chicken to a single identity can barely do justice to its rich journey from Taiwan/China to America to Taiwan again, and its evolution according to local tastes. In this respect, the divide between China and Taiwan is superficial, as neither label is sufficient in describing the identity of General Tso's chicken, and perhaps only both labels can describe the Chinese identity of the dish. On the other hand, the fact that General Tso's chicken rose to fame in the United States suggests that any definition of its identity is incomplete without including America. Clearly, important American figures play significant roles in the narrative. General Tso's chicken originated from a banquet prepared for Radford and became popular in the United States because of Kissinger. One is thus left to ponder the issue of what defines General Tso's chicken as "Chinese American." This issue is also at the core of the Panda Express story.

Identifying Panda Express: Chinese, Taiwanese, or Chinese American?

A similar dilemma also exists with the story of Panda Express. With over 1,700 locations across the United States and its territories

(Puerto Rico and Guam), and international branches in Mexico, Canada, South Korea, and Dubai, Panda Express is arguably the largest North American "fast casual" Chinese restaurant chain, maintaining an uncontested lead over Manchu Wok, a Canadian chain, which operates approximately 200 locations in the United States and Canada. Panda Express opened its first restaurant in 1983 in a mall food court on the outskirts of Los Angeles. Cherng Chur-ng, also known as Andrew Cherng, established Panda Express when the developers of the Galleria shopping center approached him and asked him to bring the taste of China to the new complex. Cherng and his wife Peggy soon expanded to more than half a dozen restaurants in the city by 1985.[13] In 1993, the Panda Express reached a franchise milestone by opening its one-hundredth store.[14] In an interview, Cherng has stated that "at the current rate of expansion, if we can reach a growth rate of twenty percent per year, by 2020, there will be more than 10,000 Panda Express restaurants around the world."[15]

Despite entrepreneurial success, Cherng came from a humble background. In 1948, he was born to chef Ming-Tsai Cherng in Yangzou, China. In his early years, Chef Cherng prepared meals for Chiang Kai-shek.[16] In 1953, when Cherng was five years old, his family moved to Taiwan, where he stayed until the age of fifteen. In 1963, the family moved again, this time to Yokohama, Japan.[17] Cherng later pursued an education in the United States, majoring in math. In 1973, the Cherng family moved to Pasadena, California, and opened the Panda Inn, the family restaurant that became the origin of Panda Express, named after the famous giant pandas—Xingxing and Lingling—given by the Chinese government to the Nixon administration as a sign of good will between the two countries.[18]

Panda Express raises many interesting issues concerning identity. While the restaurant was first established in the United States, the restaurant clearly has roots in Taiwan and China. In the case of General Tso's chicken, one can argue that part of its identity lies with its inventor, Peng Chang-kuei. In this sense, Panda Express's identity lies with Andrew Cherng, not in an original dish on its menu that claims a specific cultural identity. Thus Panda Express can be called a Chinese American restaurant—an establishment that is not only

Chinese but American as well. However, one should consider what characteristics contribute to the "Americanness" of the chain.

What defines Panda Express could be the Chinese-style cuisine it offers. Nevertheless, perhaps more important than "being Chinese" is the question of what makes the restaurant American. A possible answer may be the flavor of the dishes offered, which relates to the way the food is prepared. Unlike the various ways the Chinese prepare food, Panda Express emphasizes one methodology—the quick and cheap deep-fry—as evident from General Tso's chicken and similar dishes. Parallels can thus be drawn to other American fast-food chains, such as McDonald's and Kentucky Fried Chicken, which also prepare food in boiling oil. In addition, the substitution of a soft drink or juice for Chinese tea—a staple in Chinese restaurants—at Panda Express cannot be overlooked. In short, one way of defining Chinese American cuisine is the combination of deep-fried food(s) and soft drinks/juices on the menu.

Another way of thinking about Panda Express's identity is to examine its dining setting and style. Panda Expresses are mostly situated in shopping malls, and chopsticks, knives, forks, and "chorks"—a cross between chopsticks and a fork—complete this hybrid Chinese American identity. According to Panda Express spokesperson Jeremy Gordon, "We introduced the world to the Chork, an American Chinese original. The chopstick-fork-hybrid symbolize[s] 'a bridge between two cultures, an admission that chopstick mastery is for some, but rice should be for everyone.'"[19] Moreover, the substitution of the plate for the standard Chinese bowl complements this hybrid identity. In a sense, the restaurant chain may in fact be more American than Chinese: convenient packets of soy sauce and sweet-and-sour sauce (and not self-serve bottles) add to the American feel of the chain. Thus another way of identifying Chinese American is to consider the objects that contribute to the cultural definition of a particular culinary space.

Chinese Food, Restaurants, and Identity in America: Much Ado about Nothing?

This chapter is a short foray into the identity of Chinese food and restaurants in the United States. Clearly, politics is never far from the dinner table. At a time when political competition continues to rage between China and Taiwan and has spilled over to the realm of culture, food may become even more contested in the near future, especially since the Chinese are extremely proud of their foodways.

As this discussion suggests, General Tso's chicken and Panda Express offer alternative ways of defining (culinary) identity: through the origins of a dish and/or its creator, or through a restaurant and/or its founder. The latter approach further complicates identity by bringing in the variable of space. If the location of the restaurant in discussion—in this case, Panda Express—is part of the identity of the food it serves, then it cannot be neglected or underestimated in the overall equation. Moreover, do other elements of space, such as symbols like a panda, dragon, or phoenix, define "being Chinese"? Do the presence of chopsticks, bowls, and tea cups matter as well? Clearly, they do. Chinese restaurants are not only defined by the food they serve, but also by the setting and symbols that reinforce their identity. This is certainly the case in China, Taiwan, and in the United States.

When Chinese cuisine is politicized, mirroring political tensions between China and Taiwan, one is confronted with the interesting problem of what to make of these two distinct cuisines, both of which may or may not be Chinese, depending on one's ideological inclinations. Yet, as this chapter demonstrates, hybrid identities can peacefully coexist alongside other, monolithic identities. Even though General Tso's chicken and Panda Express both achieved success in the United States, they are both infused with elements of Chinese and Taiwanese identity. Ironically, a third identity—"being American"—has underscored, and to a certain extent has helped resolve, this dilemma.

CHAPTER 4

How Chop Suey Came to Oshkosh, Wisconsin

SUSAN BOSLEGO CARTER

The lengthy menu at the Oshkosh China King offers chop suey, chow mein, lo mein, and moo shu—six types each. There are soups—chicken rice or noodle, egg drop, hot and sour, roast pork and wonton, bean curd and vegetable, and the "house special." Moo goo gai pan, roast pork with broccoli, Hunan beef with black bean sauce, shrimp with garlic sauce, along with an assortment of other dishes, are available for takeout by the pint or quart. At the nearby Jade Dragon, proprietors Yan and Steve serve Wisconsin rolls, jalapeno pork, and sweet corn with pine nuts, their own original twists on traditional favorites. Chinese is not the only ethnic cuisine available in Oshkosh. The Royal Kitchen, a tiny place in a strip mall just behind the Landmark Shopping Center, serves Japanese and Thai. For Italian, there is Primo, Benvenuto's, and Christiano's Pizza; for Mexican, there is Durango's and La Cabana; and for Greek, Nikos Gyros. Mandy Potts, an Oshkosh food blogger, even writes of a community chili cook-off.[1]

Like Americans everywhere, Oshkosh residents choose from a vast smorgasbord of restaurant offerings inspired by culinary traditions from around the world. Although almost 90 percent of residents of this central-Wisconsin community are non-Hispanic whites, ethnic food—food identified with an ethnic group other than one's own—assumes a place of prominence.[2]

Oshkosh was not like this in 1900. Then, the town's cuisine adhered far more closely to the culinary heritage of its citizenry. That cuisine is on display in an 1891 cookbook compiled and sold by the Ladies of the Charity Circle to raise money for their good works. Contributors were "experienced housekeepers," almost all native-born women married to eminent men. Not everyone in the community would have cooked all the recipes, but rich and poor alike would have been familiar with many of them. Some replicated the foods of the European countries from which their ancestors came—beefsteak kidney and Yorkshire puddings from England, Indian mutton curry and West India pickle by way of Britain, doughnuts and other rich pastries from Germany, Norwegian pudding, and Swedish coffee brewed with egg shells. Other recipes were American innovations—Boston sherbet, Nahant buns, Connecticut sausage (rich in sage), Delmonico's oyster stew, Philadelphia scrapple, and johnnycakes.

Oshkosh cooks also adapted techniques learned from their mothers to local Wisconsin ingredients—whitefish, Mackinaw trout, cheese and milk, crabapples, and peaches. They found ways to use the many new ingredients imported into Oshkosh from elsewhere. They cooked oysters shipped in from Baltimore and pineapples shipped whole and canned from Florida and Hawaii. They used currants, ginger, cloves, candied lemon peel, Tabasco sauce, and rice to add variety unavailable before Oshkosh became connected to the national railroad grid. Oshkosh cooks were attentive to the salads and salad dressings so popular at the time, and also to the picnic sandwiches—just becoming popular—made of chopped cold ham, sardines, and cucumber pickles with mustard, vinegar, and catsup. The only ethnic food was French, and dishes included fish a là crème, veal fricassee, and French tomato soup. "Hints to Housekeepers" advised adding vinegar to the fish poaching liquid to firm the flesh. "French cooks always do this."[3]

Oshkosh restaurant food reflected this same innovative adaptation of European cooking styles. In months with an *R* in their names, Pelton's Blue Pine brought in fresh oysters packed in enormous, ice-filled barrels shipped directly from Baltimore in refrigerated rail cars. Pelton's oysters were fresh enough to eat raw on the half-shell, or in a cocktail glass topped with a sauce of horseradish, tomato catsup, vinegar, lemon juice, and tabasco. They were also good in oyster patties, made by frying the oysters in butter with a little onion and hot pepper, stirring in a roux-thickened liquor, and serving on pastry shells. Pelton's made its own pastry shells fresh each day and bragged that its recipe was the "best in the world."[4]

The Golden Eagle commanded a handsome, high-ceilinged building in the downtown. It was the place to go for steaks and chops to order, home-style baking, and ice cream. At Christmas it added Continental specialties, such as consommé and duck with jelly, to its festive roast turkey with cranberry sauce and prime-rib roast with gravy. Apple pie with cheddar cheese, a Wisconsin favorite, was a featured dessert. The Chicago Bakery offered cream puffs, Ferris wheels, peanut cookies, Tennessee squares, and other sweet treats. For a quick lunch or supper, Pueppke's Imperial served ham sandwiches, pork and beans, coffee, tea, milk, and pie—each at five cents a serving.[5]

However, sample rooms were the most popular eating places of all. "Sample room" originally described a space, often in a hotel, where traveling salesmen displayed their products and took their orders. In the Midwest, where beer-loving Germans sometimes clashed with their neighbors over community alcohol policy, the term was a euphemism for saloon. Oshkosh had 137 sample rooms—one on practically every corner.[6] Gottleib Pueppke's Sample Room was located on the ground floor of a solid corner building at the intersection of Main and Otter. A heavy wooden bar ran the length of one wall. Behind it sat barrels of Oshkosh Select, the local brew, and bottles of spirits, wine, and more beer. An enormous mirror reflected humidors filled with cigars and a giant cash register. Oversized beer mugs sat below the bar, cuspidors appeared around the room's perimeter, and a potbelly stove sat at the back. As the bar filled, drinkers clinked glasses and offered one another cheery toasts of "Prost!" Tall windows afforded passersby a glimpse of the gaiety within.[7]

Residents agreed that Oshkosh was a "restaurant city." There were so many restaurants, in fact, that a portion of Main Street was known as "restaurant row." Still, times were changing. Some longed for "a fine café" serving refreshments "a little out of the ordinary," adorned with "attractive 'frills'" at "not too great an expense," "an eating place where I would care to take my wife."[8] These wishes were granted when Oshkosh merchant and laundryman Moy Toy Ni, aka Charley (also Charlie) Toy (1860–1955) opened a Chinese restaurant. "Would it not be a decided novelty to enter one of these places?" the *Oshkosh Daily Northwestern* asked rhetorically before going on to describe what patrons expected to find inside. "The air would be filled with the scent of incense, mixed with the appetizing odor of chop suey, bird's nest soup, rice and many other mysterious dishes prepared and served by the expert cooks of the almond eyed race." Adding to the excitement of the food and drink, the décor of a Chinese restaurant would dazzle: fiery dragons, celestial colors, Chinese lanterns dangling from brassy chains, and tables set with odd imported plates, cups, and bowls.[9]

Toy bought out the Delmonico's on restaurant row, hired an expert cook with San Francisco experience, and opened the Hong Kong Low. At first "Fried Chicken, Turkey, Roast Beef, Chicken Mushroom Soup" headed the bill of fare, but within a month Toy shifted emphasis to his "special Chinese dishes." A special feast he cooked for his Euro-American friends featured bird's nest soup, lobster salad, egg subgum, chicken chop suey, lychee, and gamgot. So successful was Toy's venture that when fire destroyed most of his equipment only a few months later, Toy sold the remains "cheap, for cash or auction," relocated to Milwaukee, and built a new Chinese restaurant on a grand scale.

The Shanghai was a sumptuous Chinese fine-dining establishment quite unlike anything that city had ever seen. It was housed in a specially-built six-story structure whose exterior was clad in green stone and topped by a red gabled roof with a sweeping curvature that rose at the corners. Stone dragons and Chinese characters festooned the edges.[10] Its interior was decorated with expensive tables of ebony inlaid with marble and mother-of-pearl, large, painted porcelain vases, beautifully-woven rugs, and other costly objects. The building and the restaurant quickly gained a reputation as one of the unique sights of Milwaukee. Among the delicacies he offered were kai, young bird's nest soup, steamed duck, whole subgum fish, ting lan chicken, long ha deon lobster, turkey, Chinese style, and squab fried in peanut oil. "All the bones had been carefully removed from the fish, fowl, and birds, after which they were put back into their original shape, making a perfect deception," gushed the *Oshkosh Daily Northwestern*, which continued to follow Toy's career even after he had left town.[11]

Once the Shanghai was running smoothly, Toy partnered with an associate to launch a more modest Chinese restaurant in Oshkosh.[12]

Toy was not the only Chinese restaurateur in Wisconsin. Wah Mee and perhaps several others had opened restaurants in Milwaukee in the late 1890s. Another opened one in Calumet (population 4,668)

FIGURE 4.1. Moy Toy Ni, aka Charley Toy (1861–1955). National Archives, Chinese Exclusion Case file No. 2070 (Seattle). Photo attached to a document dated October 5, 1894.

on Michigan's Upper Peninsula in 1897. A "Chinese restaurant helps to add variety to the life of the copper miners," reported Milwaukee's *Weekly Wisconsin*. Yet another delighted the residents of Rhinelander, Wisconsin (population 4,998): "An oriental café, where chop suey and other toothsome dainties . . . will be served, will be quite a new addition to Rhinelander's list of business places and will no doubt meet with popular favor."[13] Oshkosh laundryman Moy Hee moved to St. Paul to open an elaborate Chinese restaurant in the downtown area. Moreover, H.O. You began serving chop suey at his New York Lunch Counter in Stevens Point, Wisconsin (population 9,524).[14]

It was a remarkable development. Before the Second World War, with the exception of Old El Paso's canned enchilada sauce and Chef

Boyardee's spaghetti and meatballs, ethnic food was available only in ethnic enclaves. Yet by 1910, with a Chinese population of only a little more than two hundred and no established Chinatowns, Chinese restaurants operated by Chinese Americans could be found in cities and towns throughout Wisconsin.[15]

How did the Chinese achieve such widespread coverage and popularity in the era of Chinese Exclusion? Using the three-part food choice lens proposed by Warren Belasco, this essay explores how consumers' changing identities, chop suey's unparalleled convenience, and the challenges to responsible eating posed by racist images of the Chinese in popular culture affected demand for Chinese restaurant services.[16] Chop suey appealed to the consumer identity of an emerging middle class whose cosmopolitan, omnivorous tastes embraced the foods of many different groups, the Chinese included. Chop suey was convenient and Chinese restaurateurs supplied it to far-flung cities and towns at a modest price. Low prices were attractive to the middle class unable to afford the French restaurants patronized by the elite, but they were also attractive to working men who liked to drink, gamble, and engage in other minor vices. Appealing to middle-class consumers' sense of responsibility was the most difficult hurdle Chinese restaurateurs faced. Harsh racist stereotypes portraying them as alien and unassimilable, seductively childlike yet threateningly sexual, made them vulnerable to arbitrary and seemingly random attacks from both individuals and the state.[17] To achieve success, Chinese restaurateurs like Charley Toy needed to distance themselves from these ugly stereotypes and signal their exceptionalism.

Chop Suey and American Identity

Excluded from the highbrow cultural institutions of the Gilded Age elite, the growing middle class of the late nineteenth century embraced a cosmopolitan, omnivorous appreciation of the art, architecture, home furnishings, dress, and cuisine of many different cultures. They built bungalows in the Japanese spirit, dressed in Spanish gowns, sipped Indian tea, slept in Philippine lingerie, and shopped in Little Italy. In fictive travel clubs, they climbed the Pyramids and navigated the Rhine. They visited big-city ethnic enclaves and dined in ethnic restaurants, insisting that the foods of Germany, Italy, Spain, Japan, and even that of China were every bit as good as French cuisine.

Though racist imagery described Chinese food with "ineffable disgust," the middle class embraced it. Big-city journalists wrote rhapsodically of the "most delicious tea. . . . No milk or sugar is used with it," and of the rice, "such rice! Each grain is thoroughly cooked yet separate." Even beyond tea and rice "their macaroni, or 'meu,' as it is called, is fully equal to Neapolitan spagatti [*sic*]. They excel the French cooks in making chicken bouillon." In the late 1890s, New Yorkers began considering it fashionable to order chop suey for supper. News of the fad went viral and in what Andrew Coe called "one of the greatest cultural shifts in American culinary history," New Yorkers began "flocking to Mott Street to eat Chinese food." In 1900, the *New York Times* declared the city "'chop suey' mad." The rising middle class inspired the character of Carol Kennicott, Sinclair Lewis's fictional heroine, for whom "cosmopolitan" meant sitting at a "teak and marble table eating Eggs Fooyung" and listening to a "brassy automatic piano."[18] This middle-class cosmopolitanism was everywhere, even in the prosperous community of Oshkosh.

Situated at the confluence of the Upper Fox River and Lake Winnebago, on the eastern edge of Wisconsin's vast pine forests, logging and lumbering dominated "Sawdust City's" mid-nineteenth-century economy. By 1900, the economy had matured and diversified, and the plethora of small businesses meant a vibrant middle class. Proprietors and managers accounted for almost 11 percent of the male workforce, eleven times the level for the non-agricultural workforce of the nation as a whole.[19] Boosters boasted of the city's middle-class character, noting the "utter absence of tenement houses" and a pervasive "bonhomie."[20] Oshkosh supported twenty-five churches and seventy-four societies and organizations, ranging in type from ethnic groups such as the Turners, a German American gymnastics club, and the Ancient Order of Hibernians, an Irish Catholic fraternal order; to labor organizations such as the Knights of Labor (Oshkosh was home to four separate chapters); to benevolent societies such as the Modern Woodman of America; to political organizations like the Young Women's Christian Temperance Union. The Arion Band, and the Canoe and Scat Clubs (Scat was a German card game) promoted relaxation and fun.

The city's Grand Opera House displayed a lavish, modern Victorian design and could comfortably accommodate more than a thousand people. Its opening in 1883 provided a stage for the popular plays of London and New York. Many of the plays were Asian themed, starring white actors in "yellow face," who were made to look Chinese or Japanese. A professional touring company brought *The Mikado* to Oshkosh in 1885, just months after the opera's American debut. Not long afterwards, a local theater group mounted its own production. The opera remained popular among the city's energetic amateur thespians. An 1892 photograph shows Miss Bessie Lou Daggett, an accomplished Oshkosh soprano, along with two other young women seemingly dressed for the roles of Yum-Yum, Pitti-Sing, and Peep-Bo. They appear in heavy makeup, arrayed in silk kimonos and carrying matching oil-paper fans. Their long hair is tied back, piled on the tops of their heads, and adorned with delicate kanzashi.[21] Charles Holt's immensely popular play, *A Trip to Chinatown*, arrived in 1897.[22]

While *The Mikado* and *A Trip to Chinatown* romanticized Asian culture, *A Chinese Honeymoon*, performed in Oshkosh in 1902, focused the spotlight on less savory issues. It claimed to present for the first time "a correct view of a Typical Chinese restaurant . . . its beauty accentuated by the brilliant evening costumes of a party of society leaders who are out 'slumming after the theatre.' . . . The gorgeous hangings with gold embroidered dragons and strange birds, the rich Oriental colorings and the half concealed alcoves for the use of the opium smokers, are accurate representations and furnish a superb setting for some very good acting." Critics blasted it as "plotless and formless . . . neither drama, comedy nor operetta" but conceded that "the Chinese gowns constitute a perfect orgy of splendid coloring."[23] Audiences loved it.

Oshkosh Daily Northwestern editor Colonel John Hicks (1847–1917) fed the city's cosmopolitan appetite. As a charter member of the Associated Press, he had access not only to up-to-date national and international news, but also to a stream of popular human-interest stories, fiction, poems, sports, fashion, and housekeeping articles. Read by people from different classes and backgrounds, these stories reflected the increasingly diverse society America was fast becoming. Many of the stories featured ethnic, specifically Asian, food. One story centered on a former Beloit College student who was opening a Japanese restaurant in nearby Janesville with furniture imported direct from Japan.[24] Others told of strange vegetables that were being grown on a Chinese farm in Queens, New York. *Ong qua* was a "squash with odd convolutions and of weird, grayish green coloring. There is a bloom on it like the bloom of a peach." *Bok toi* had a center "like the heart of the cauliflower," stalks resembling celery, and a top broadened out "in to a very fair imitation of a cabbage leaf."[25] In 1894, Hicks published an extended discussion of other "unusual foods" on offer at San Francisco's Midwinter Exposition: "In the Indian village an old squaw will bake you a tortilla on a sheet of hot iron over a brushwood fire. Japanese girls will serve you with rice and tea in their typical village, and in the mining camp there are plenty of beans to be had and many things to drink. Nearly everyone goes to the Ceylon booth . . . for a cup of tea or coffee and a sight of the quaint little Ceylonese men who serve it."[26]

Oshkosh residents did more than just read about new foods. When they had the opportunity, they tried them themselves. To celebrate his friends' engagement, James Jenkins enlisted the services of Charley Toy. At Jenkins's behest, Toy prepared a "delightful combination of sumptuous Chinese viands" and costumed Jenkins in "the rich silken draperies of a real Chinese mandarin." He assisted him in sending out invitations "arranged in the form of the Chinese characters." Toy must have aided the recipients of those invitations as well because some acceptances were returned in Chinese. The next day the entire town read all about it in the *Daily Northwestern*.[27]

Chop Suey and the Immigrant Narrative

Despite the growing interest in ethnic cuisine, only the Chinese took their food outside their enclaves. In matters of convenience, early-twentieth-century Chinese restaurateurs were nonpareil. Barred by racist prejudice from better-paid employment and united by exceptionally strong and supportive immigrant networks, the Chinese opened their exotic, inexpensive restaurants wherever they sensed a market. Like the Euro-Americans—the Germans and Scandinavians who comprised the majority of foreign-born Wisconsinites at the turn of the twentieth century—Chinese Americans came from rural backgrounds and formed networks based on family and community. Overwhelmingly, Chinese immigrants to Wisconsin came from a single region, Guangzhou (Canton) in the Pearl River Delta of southern China, and formed networks that were large, national, and transnational.[28] These expansive Chinese networks aided immigrants with loans, transportation, housing, employment, cultural goods, and religious and legal services. Above all, they provided a forum for exchanging information.

Because they were excluded from other occupations, the first Wisconsin Chinese worked as laundrymen; because laundrymen needed to be located near their customers, they dispersed geographically. The sixteen Chinese persons present in Wisconsin in 1880 were spread across eight different counties. Milwaukee had the largest number. The official figure is three, but newspaper accounts suggest there may have been more. By 1900, only twenty-two of Wisconsin's 212 Chinese lived in Milwaukee. The rest were widely scattered across the remainder of the state, so much so that forty-seven out of seventy Wisconsin counties had at least one Chinese laundryman. Outside Milwaukee, the largest groups were in the prosperous Lake Superior ports of Ashland and Duluth and in the booming lumber towns of Oshkosh, Eau Claire, and Appleton. No single county was home to more than twenty-three Chinese individuals. For the most part, these were young men who performed laundry services for the single young white men employed in the physically strenuous logging and water transportation industries.[29]

Because Chinese women were largely barred from entry by the 1882 Exclusion Act, most Chinese Americans were men who lived their lives as "bachelors." Unencumbered by family, they lived frugally and responded quickly to changing economic opportunities.

Physically dispersed though they were, the Chinese stayed connected. On weekends and holidays, those living in more distant places traveled to larger Chinese communities to replenish their supplies of rice, dried vegetables, sauces, and other ethnic foods as well as the tickets, detergent, bleach, and starch they used in their laundries. On Chinese New Year, they celebrated with parades, social visits, feasts, firecrackers, and letters and telegrams to far-flung relatives and friends.

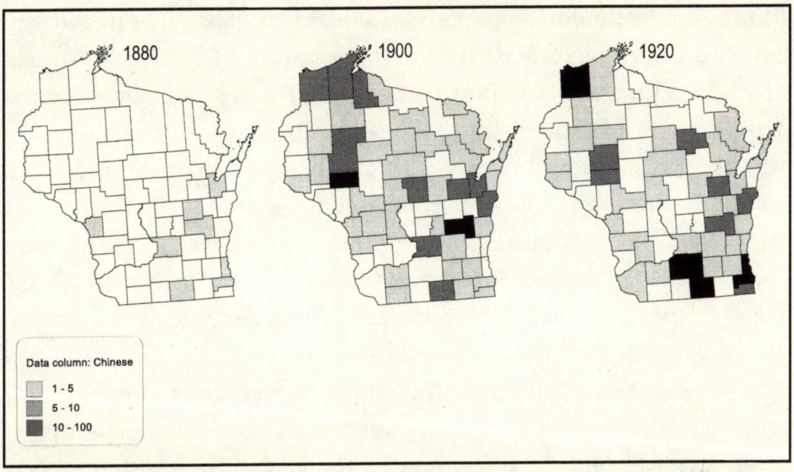

FIGURE 4.2. Chinese by County in Wisconsin, 1880 through 1920. Sources: Chinese by county: 1860 through 1890: Michael R. Haines and Inter-University Consortium for Political and Social Research. Historical, Demographic, Economic, and Social Data: The United States, 1790–2002 [Computer file]. ICPSR02896-v3. Ann Arbor, MI: Inter-university Consortium for Political and Social Research [distributor], 2010–05–21. doi:10.3886/ICPSR02896.v3. 1900 through 1950: Hand-transcribed from published census reports. County boundary shape files from: Steven Ruggles, J. Trent Alexander, Katie Genadek, Ronald Goeken, Matthew B. Schroeder, and Matthew Sobek. Integrated Public Use Microdata Series: Version 5.0 [Machine-readable database]. Minneapolis: University of Minnesota, 2010.

In 1903, about thirty Chinese from cities throughout Wisconsin came to Oshkosh. Charley Toy reconfigured his import store to host a sumptuous dinner featuring Chinese dishes made with expensive foods rarely seen outside of China. He entertained with phonograph music, the playlist including recordings fresh from the leading theaters of China. He arranged live performances on Chinese violins, mandolins, drums, and cymbals. The following year, the Appleton Chinese community hosted a state-wide New Year's celebration.[30]

The Chinese Masonic Society, a nationwide fraternal organization that adopted the symbolism and ceremony of the Freemasons and whose membership topped 20,000, further reinforced ties among the Chinese across the United States and beyond. Gong Hoar, the U.S. Grand Master Mason, regularly toured across the country, presiding at initiation ceremonies and networking with his colleagues.

In 1898, he traveled to Appleton, Wisconsin, to elevate Toy's kinsman, Sam Wah Kee, to regional master. In 1900, it was Toy and his cousin Moy Hee's turn to host. Two years later, Moy Hee was awarded the order's highest honor.[31] This Masonic network provided the Chinese with detailed, up-to-date news regarding business, political, and social conditions across the country and around the world.

At their family, business, community, and fraternal gatherings, the Chinese exchanged news and information not only from China, but also about political and economic developments in the United States, especially within the laundry and restaurant industries. They compared notes on pricing, suppliers, customers' tastes, and employee relations. They gave and received advice on how to take over existing businesses and start new ones. They kept abreast of the rapidly changing legal and political environments in which they operated. They learned of America's latest food fads. They learned to cook their dishes the way other Americans liked them; they found partners and investors; they complained about the rowdies and thugs who assaulted and robbed them, who smashed up their restaurants, and who kept the paying customers away.[32]

These discussions gave rise to a business formula that Chinese entrepreneurs believed would increase their chance of success in the United States: choose a prosperous community with a growing middle class. Befriend the editor of the local newspaper and influential lawyers, businessmen, and politicians. Create an upscale, exotic environment, but keep prices low and keep American-restaurant items on the menu. Appeal to theatergoers, young women, and others in the vanguard of changing cultural norms and gender roles, but not enough to provoke the ire of conservative and reactionary forces. As they soon realized, the last element was the trickiest to negotiate.

Chinese restaurateurs labored under pervasive popular stereotypes portraying them as unassimilable aliens, inveterate gamblers, opium fiends, and sexual predators. These stereotypes made them vulnerable to arbitrary and possibly deadly harassment and arrest, and the Milwaukee Race Riot of 1889 illustrates this danger. In 1889, Milwaukee police arrested two laundrymen, Hah Ding and Sam Yip Ya, and charged them with sexually assaulting young white women. The *Milwaukee Sentinel* labeled Ding and Ya "Chinese Daemons" and reported the story under the headline, "Children Enticed into

Laundry Dens and then Ruined." The next morning, the paper detailed allegations of an elaborate, multi-state alliance in which Milwaukee Chinese allegedly abducted white girls and sold them as brides to their Chicago brethren. Altogether, the paper reported, twenty-two children had made confessions "of such a horrifying nature as to be almost incredible."[33]

The charges ignited an anti-Chinese firestorm. As the suspects were taken from the jail to the courthouse, a crowd of about 350 people assembled. They began jostling one another to get a glimpse of Ding and Ya, making threatening statements against all Chinese. By ten o'clock, the mob had swollen to a thousand men and boys who shouted "Hang them!" and "String them up!" The next day, two thousand assembled in front of the courthouse, where they were disappointed to learn that police had already transferred the suspects from the jail secretly, overnight. Frustrated, one man after another took to a soapbox and harangued the throng with anti-Chinese rants. No longer able to contain its rage, the crowd marched down to Grand Avenue and then proceeded eastward, hurling rocks and smashing windows at the laundries of Sam Lee, Sun Chong, Mon Wing, and Sun Sing. They headed up Second Street and destroyed Wing Sam's place. Then they moved on to Third Street, where they vandalized the laundries of Sam Quong and John Ching. The violence continued until virtually every Chinese laundry in Milwaukee and its surrounding suburbs was attacked. The *Oshkosh Daily Northwestern* reported this sensational story on its front pages.[34]

The outraged Chinese ambassador demanded that the United States make restitution, but when he asked Sam Ring Kee to estimate the damages, Kee had difficulty complying, as so many of his terrorized countrymen had fled the city. Overnight, the number of Chinese laundries dropped from thirty-one to thirteen. Kee himself left not long after, following a police raid on his laundry and a $30 fine for alleged opium sales.[35]

How Charley Toy Succeeded

Charley Toy was born in Gum Ping Village, On Fun Section, Sun Ning District, China, in 1860 and came to America as a young man.[36] According to family lore, his only possessions were a small bundle of clothing and a rough piece of wood marked with the Chinese proverb, "Honesty Endures."[37] A photograph taken in 1894 shows a clean-shaven, well-dressed gentleman with short-cropped hair, a direct gaze, and perhaps a twinkle in his eye. His tailored, western-style suit and overcoat top a white shirt trimmed with one of the stiff, detachable collars popular at the time. He wears a dark tie fashioned into a heavy Windsor knot and ornamented with a gold stick pin. His derby hat is set at a slight angle—a picture of late-nineteenth-century masculine confidence and prosperity.

Toy arrived in the United States just prior to the passage of the Chinese Exclusion Act, at a time when anti-Chinese agitation was intense. After a brief stay in Portland, Oregon, he moved to Chicago and then to Appleton, Wisconsin, where his kinsman, Sam Wah Kee, who had arrived in the 1870s and was among the first Chinese in that part of the country, ran a laundry and a Chinese import shop. Toy joined the firm, and the Chinese population grew slowly over time.[38] By 1900, 212 Chinese were scattered across forty-seven different Wisconsin counties.

In addition to Sam Wah Kee, Moy Hee—variously identified as Toy's uncle, cousin, and brother—moved to Oshkosh in about 1888 to assist another uncle at the Hop Chong laundry. Shortly thereafter, Toy joined Hee and another colleague, Sam Wing, in Oshkosh as partners in the Mee Lee Yuen Chinese and Japanese import company. In the 1890s, Moy and Wing bought Toy's share and Toy started his own import business a few blocks away.[39]

Toy appealed to his neighbors' cosmopolitan fascination with the exotic goods he imported from China and Japan. He filled his bazaar floor to ceiling with hundreds upon hundreds of the most astonishing objects. He stocked teas, spices, rice, dried mushrooms and seafood, barrels of salted fish, and bottles of sauces and spirits. Inexpensive trinkets, lanterns, and firecrackers sat next to costly and exotic hand-carved ivory elephants and figurines, beautifully wrought porcelain bowls and tea sets, and elaborately decorated lacquer ware. In a corner, silk fabric, clothing, and tableware were neatly folded and stacked. Not an inch of either shelf or floor space was wasted, and there was barely room for three or four visitors at a time.

FIGURE 4.3. Toy Building. Milwaukee, Wisconsin c 1920. Author's collection.

Toy sat behind a narrow counter, next to a pot of tea and a stack of little cups. He greeted his visitors politely, offered them tea, and displayed his latest treasures. When they made selections, he ran up the sums on his abacus, used his camel-hair brush and pot of ink to enter the transaction into his account books, and weighed the tea and spices on his ivory and thread balance. Customers never questioned the accuracy of his scale. Toy and the other Chinese merchants were known for their honesty.[40]

Toy cultivated an identity that defied ugly stereotypes concerning the Chinese by pursuing personal friendships with open-minded members of the community. He befriended *Oshkosh Daily Northwestern* editor Colonel John Hicks, and Hicks, sensing a good story, wrote about Toy's peculiar but charming ways. He reported on the Christmas gifts Toy selected from among his imports. One year, a recipient mistook Toy's gift of a Chinese lily bulb for a cocktail onion which she would have boiled and served with butter had Toy not gently dissuaded her.[41] The flower bulb, like many articles from Toy's shop, frequently required explanation. After telling his neighbors he was a prominent member of a Chinese band, they invited him to play the Chinese flute at a public concert. He "contrasted so strangely" with the other performers, a reviewer wrote, that it "afforded much amusement to the audience."[42] Toy was one of the first Oshkosh residents to purchase a bicycle—a flashy maroon one no less. Hicks had his reporter cover the story. The reporter described Toy as he was touring the city, calling out greetings to his neighbors. "Everybody looked at him, for a Chinese bicyclist is not an everyday spectacle." The story continued, using language that expressed affection for Toy and his colorful personality:

> It is true that he has not reached that stage of proficiency where he can salute friends on the sidewalks without endangering his equilibrium, and it is hardly probable that, even were it his custom, he could raise his hat to a lady without immediately disgracing himself by tumbling off his 'bike.' Nevertheless . . . he is a very presentable rider and can adroitly find his way in and out among the teams on the rough pavement of Main Street.[43]

In 1900, when China's Boxer Rebellion prompted many Chinese Americans to return home to their families, the *Daily Northwestern* cheered. "As a rule," it opined, the Chinese "constitute an undesirable class of citizens. [F]our-fifths of the Chinese in this country could 'vamosse' and never be missed." But it did allow for some exceptions, "our own Charley Toy being a good example," suggesting that Toy had endeared himself to the local population to such an extent that he was able to elide such racist attitudes.[44]

As the legal and bureaucratic processes regulating Chinese immigration became increasingly restrictive, Toy needed all the goodwill he could garner. The Geary Act of 1892 renewed the Exclusion Act for another ten years and required Chinese living in the United States to obtain residency certificates so that they could be tracked and counted. The next year, regulations were further tightened to require Chinese merchants wishing to visit China to obtain affidavits from credible white witnesses before their departure (the assumption was that the trip would be for sinister purposes).[45] Observing the new rule, Toy secured backing from some of Oshkosh's most prominent citizens, including mayor William Dichmann, city clerk Dan Witzel, city treasurer R.A. Spink, furniture manufacturer William Spikes, and *Daily Northwestern* editor and recently-retired U.S. minister to Peru, Colonel John Hicks.[46]

Restrictions on the Chinese continued to tighten. In 1897, hoping to win the support of organized labor, President William McKinley appointed Terrance Powderly, former head of the Knights of Labor, as U.S. Commissioner-General of Immigration. Powderly was "one of the most vitriolic and vituperative of the labor movement's Sinophobes."[47] Once in office, Powderly lost no time in devising new hurdles to Chinese entry. He based administrative policy on the most anti-Chinese of the various court decisions emerging from litigation and authorized illegal enforcement when he judged the rules too lax. He rewarded zealots like James R. Dunn, head of the San Francisco Immigration office, who was a Powderly favorite. Dunn used delay, expense, incarceration, and gratuitous investigations to make Chinese entry as difficult and expensive as possible. Even Chinese merchants with good credentials were increasingly refused the right to land.[48]

In 1898, news of his first wife's death prompted Toy to return to China. During his trip, he visited his mother and children, married a second time and selected a large stock of goods for export to his Oshkosh store.[49] Toy and his family then proceeded to the American Consulate in Hong Kong to arrange for their entry into the United States. Unexpectedly and without explanation, the consul summarily rejected Toy's marriage and paternity documents and denied his family entry. Though his Oshkosh supporters protested on his behalf, Toy was forced to return alone.[50]

More trouble awaited Toy upon his arrival in San Francisco. There, immigration agents found fault with his documents and threw him into the Pacific Mail's detention shed to await further investigation. That one-story building, not much bigger than an ordinary cottage, held 357 persons on the day a local reporter visited.[51] Many detainees remained for weeks on end. One man's imprisonment lasted more than half a year. Toy was finally set free a month after landing, when a strongly worded letter from Oshkosh mayor James H. Merrill and Wisconsin congressman James O. Davidson persuaded immigration officials to release him.[52] A few years later, after he had risen within the ranks of the Republican Party and while serving as Envoy Extraordinary and Minister Plenipotentiary to Chile, Colonel Hicks used his influence to gain admission for Toy's wife and children.[53]

As he had done in Oshkosh, Toy cultivated the friendship and patronage of Milwaukee's elite. Shortly after he opened the Shanghai, he hosted a special celebration with a guest list that included a judge, the president of the state normal school, a customs collector, a court commissioner, an assistant district attorney, and a large contingent of Milwaukee newspapermen who described the feast in delicious detail for the many community members who had not been invited. A few years later, when his former Oshkosh patron James O. Davidson became Wisconsin's governor, Toy invited him to the Shanghai, and Davidson accepted. The next morning his constituents awakened to the headline: "Governor Eats Chop Suey."[54]

Chop suey's popularity and acceptance had far-reaching influence on Oshkosh's culinary style. The Pueppkes remodeled their Imperial Restaurant, adding palm trees and ceiling fans, updating the menu, and renaming it the Palm Garden. "Try the New Place," they urged their neighbors.[55] Down the street, the Little Cozy restaurant added chicken chop suey to its list of "Special Dishes," placing it ahead of the Welsh Rarebit and the Golden Buck.[56] Oshkosh diners were on their way to becoming the pluralistic culinary omnivores they are today.

FIGURE 4.4. Pueppke's Restaurant. 5 Otter Street, Oshkosh, Wisconsin, 1903 and 1912. Before: Imperial Restaurant. After: Palm Garden. Courtesy of the Oshkosh Public Museum.

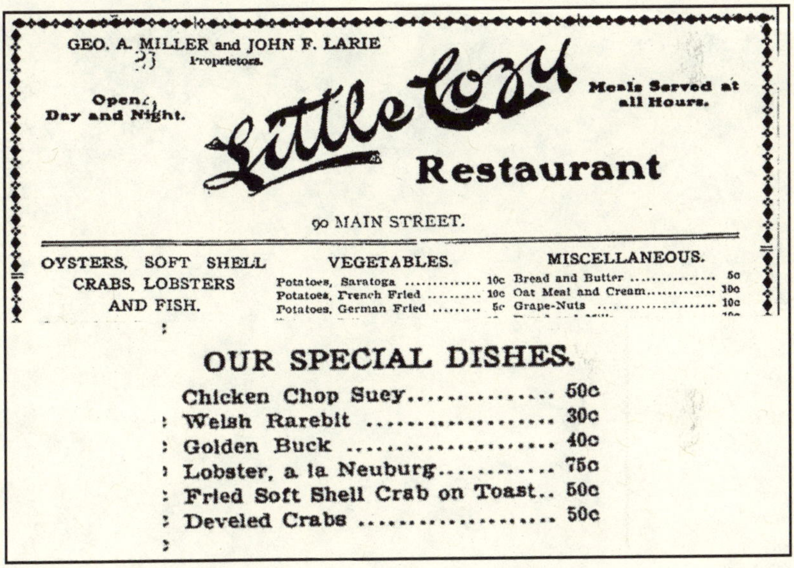

GEO. A. MILLER and JOHN F. LARIE
Proprietors.

Open
Day and Night.

Little Cozy
Restaurant

Meals Served at
all Hours.

90 MAIN STREET.

OYSTERS, SOFT SHELL CRABS, LOBSTERS AND FISH.

VEGETABLES.

Potatoes, Saratoga	10c
Potatoes, French Fried	10c
Potatoes, German Fried	5c

MISCELLANEOUS.

Bread and Butter	5c
Oat Meal and Cream	10c
Grape-Nuts	10c

OUR SPECIAL DISHES.

Chicken Chop Suey	50c
Welsh Rarebit	30c
Golden Buck	40c
Lobster, a la Neuburg	75c
Fried Soft Shell Crab on Toast	50c
Develed Crabs	50c

FIGURE 4.5. Little Cozy Menu, Oskosh Wisconsin, 1905. *Oshkosh Daily Northwestern*, Oshkosh, Wisc., Oct. 28, 1905, p. 15. Digital copy provided by Newspapers.com.

CHAPTER 5

From the Art of Dim Sum to the Art of Sculpture

Master Chef Kai Tai Chan and His Dough Evolution in New York

CLARENCE CHAN AND
TING MAN TSAO

What do we do now? For the first time in his life, Master Chef Kai Tai Chan (陳啟泰) reluctantly turned to his teen son, Clarence (coauthor of this essay), for a solution. This happened on the Lunar New Year Eve of 1979. Instead of enjoying the annual reunion dinner at home in Hong Kong, the family was lost in the middle of an airport at which they had not expected to land. Carrying a "high-skilled worker" permit, Chan was taking Seu, his wife, and Clarence to settle in New York. However, he did not speak English and misunderstood the flight connection process. The family disembarked the Pan Am jet without even retrieving their carry-ons. They found themselves in San Francisco International Airport and did not realize their mistake until they spotted a pile of their luggage lying there instead of being sent directly to their destination, New York. To this day, Clarence still vividly remembers how his usually overconfident father, a renowned chef in Hong Kong and Macao, counted desperately on him for an answer when he, only thirteen then, knew just as little about this strange land.

The master chef's desperation persisted even after Clarence helped him straighten out the connecting flight. Upon their arrival in New York the same evening, relatives with whom Chan had planned to launch his culinary business simply dropped the family off at 2 East

Broadway, the site of the family restaurant where he was now supposed to work. Little did he know that the basement of that restaurant—stocked with raw meat, fresh vegetables, soy sauce, and the infamous rats—would become his family's first home in the United States, the "Beautiful Country" that was America. The dim sum master was also unprepared for the shattering of his culinary dream, which was ten years in the making, and with it, the loss of his life savings. He had withdrawn all of his money and had sold his flat in Macao in order to invest in a dim sum restaurant and purchase machinery and equipment for the establishment of a fresh noodle factory in New York. But his relatives' restaurant did not serve dim sum, and the chef was reduced to a multitasking kitchen assistant there and a part-time salesman at a nearby seafood store, which was also owned by his relatives. Several weeks later, a total of six container loads of noodle-making machinery and equipment arrived. Yet Chan's relatives, including his only sister, had not come up with any sort of startup plan, and the cargo was left unclaimed at the port, incurring formidable storage fees and penalties. Eventually, the shipping company auctioned off the goods to offset the expenses. Disappointed by his closest relatives, Chan was heartbroken. The master chef had lost every penny of his investment and every hope of reestablishing his career.

That is how Chan began his life in the United States: a turbulent beginning similar to those faced by many, many immigrants. Chan's story provides a unique look at a world-class chef whose pioneering efforts helped Chinese food in America transition into a culinary art form in the post–chop suey era. Dating back to the 1980s, this era has seen an increasing number of restaurants—particularly located around quickly expanding middle-class Chinese immigrant enclaves in or near big cities such as Los Angeles, New York, and San Francisco—providing more "authentic" dishes to meet the exacting demands of customers. Hailing from hometowns that boast relatively high standards of living, these middle-class Chinese immigrants continue to enjoy Hong Kong–style roast pork and egg tarts, Lanzhou hand-pulled noodles, and Shanghai steamed pork buns, all of which have become conveniently available in their new neighborhoods in America.[1] They understandably detest chop suey and other Americanized dishes, and complain that these early forms of Chinese food are "inauthentic," if not outright inedible.[2]

These kinds of consumer complaints have been documented by studies about the globalization of Chinese food. Some of these studies even provide analyses of the composition and work of kitchen and wait staff of Chinese restaurants in America.[3] Yet few focus on the fascinating transplantation of the Chinese kitchen to a foreign country—in situation in which a traditional work space must come to terms with a new environment, new potentials, and, with them, new constraints. Chan, like many other gifted immigrant chefs of the time, knew very little English and could not promote his culinary art as today's celebrity chefs can. He could not boast of books, TV shows, interviews, or websites to record his professional experience for posterity, although his innovations within the realms of Chinese cuisine and food art could certainly rival the accomplishments of any contemporary celebrity chef.[4]

This essay explores how Chan, an immigrant chef, boldly experimented, adopted new methods and ingredients, innovated, and brought his culinary art to new heights while staying true to authentic Chinese taste and artistic style. In his pursuit, he grappled with—albeit unintentionally—an important dilemma in food studies, from a chef's point of view: authenticity. He wanted his restaurant customers and art patrons in America to enjoy the best traditional southern Chinese food and artwork possible. However, just as his *sifus* and ancestors had "for centuries absorbed ingredients and methods that came from far corners of the globe,"[5] Chan was also quick to adopt the best of what the West had to offer: modern culinary practices, different management styles, new ingredients, and even innovative scientific breakthroughs. The master's behind-the-scenes creativity and flexibility, together with his commitment to excellence, consistently yielded an unsurpassed dim sum menu and, later in his career, a revered catalogue of dough sculptures. His customers and patrons instantly recognized his food and art as representative of southern Chinese culture, but few knew that the production process was mixed with "foreign" elements. The narrative that follows rescues from obscurity the daring master chef and dough artist's journey in New York in the 1980s and 1990s. Like other Chinese immigrants before him, Chan was able to overcome seemingly insurmountable limitations and challenges during this journey, particularly in the culinary realm, rendering his story a remarkable addition to the Asian experience in America.

Inspired by Switzerland

By the time he set foot in New York, sixty-year-old Chan had over four decades of professional experience as the "royal" dim sum chef of the Hong Kong and Macao elite, including casino tycoons who had ordered his moon cakes for the annual Mid-Autumn Festival. He had also managed such exquisite restaurants as Macao Palace, a floating casino in the inner harbor of Macao. Chan had been honing his culinary and artistic skills since the age of sixteen, learning from various top chefs and a dough sculpture master in different restaurants in Guangzhou and, after the Second World War, in Hong Kong.[6] The first major breakthrough of this promising dim sum chef's career, however, did not happen in any of these hubs of Cantonese culture. Instead, it was in Switzerland, where Chinese cuisine was virtually nonexistent, that Chan revolutionized how dim sum was made and delivered to diners.

The dim sum revolution happened in 1969 (a decade before his move to New York), when Chan was invited to participate in the Hong Kong Food Festival organized by Swissair, Peninsula Hotel, and the Hong Kong Tourist Association.[7] The festival, which took place in three busy Swiss airport restaurants in Zurich, Geneva, and Basel, opened Chan's eyes to European haute cuisine. In stark contrast to the greasy kitchen to which he had grown accustomed, Swiss kitchens were modern, spacious, and sparklingly clean. These kitchens, with their European professional cookware and culinary tools, left the master chef in awe (figure 5.1). Moreover, the facilities were specially modified to accommodate Chinese utensils such as woks, roasting ovens, and steamers so that Chan and his colleagues could prepare their dishes according to routine (figure 5.2).[8] All of the conversions were made of state-of-the-art shiny and unblemished stainless steel. Chan found that this elaborate attention to detail could not be matched by any of the best restaurant kitchens he had seen in Hong Kong or Macao.

Chan was also captivated by the level of professionalism of the Swiss personnel, ranging from the managers to the cooking crew, from the PR department to the wait staff. He was impressed by their effective organizational structure and knowhow in managing upscale, fast-paced restaurants. This was an awe-inspiring experience for a chef who had come from a Chinese culinary environment where the majority of the staff belonged to a lower socioeconomic class with little to no formal education, and where restaurant management was a hit-or-miss affair.

The management of the food festival, which was located in the Swiss transportation hub of Zurich, was impressive. Collaborating with the Hong Kong Peninsula Hotel, the Zurich airport restaurant designed a unique system to serve Chinese food to diners hailing from all over the world. Since Chan and the other three chefs only knew Chinese, a trilingual menu in German, English, and Chinese was printed.[9] A member of the Swiss wait staff would take orders from customers by checking items on the list and Chan and his colleagues would understand the orders from the corresponding Chinese characters.[10] To create an authentic atmosphere, the management put a Chinese page boy[11] at the entrance to welcome guests and four "graceful" Chinese hostesses[12] inside the restaurant to teach diners how to use chopsticks.[13] The event was well publicized in European and Hong Kong magazines and newspapers.[14]

This new hybrid Chinese-Swiss culinary system enabled Chan to revolutionize how dim sum was prepared, ordered, and served. In restaurants or tea houses such as those in American Chinatowns and Hong Kong, dim sum is traditionally cooked in bulk, carted out by wait staff, and selected by patrons. A long-standing Cantonese tradition, this dim sum delivery system was considered unsuitable for exquisite European dining. Not only is it noisy, but the continuously steamed or boiled dim sum can also become overcooked and soggy. Supported by a modern kitchen and an efficient ordering system, Chan and his colleagues prepared dim sum, probably for the first time in Cantonese cuisine, in a made-to-order fashion. Raw dim sum would be quickly steamed, boiled, or fried upon receipt of the order.[15] Served this way, the quality of each order of dim sum would be guaranteed, as its dough would be fresh, hot, and crispy. However, the historical significance of Chan's pioneering contribution to dim sum production cannot be fully appreciated without noting that steamed-to-order (即叫即蒸) dim sum only became widely available in Hong Kong's upscale restaurants in the 1980s, more than a decade after Chan's Swiss experiment. Although such an order system is commonplace even in mid-priced restaurants in Hong Kong today, it is still uncommon in Chinatown restaurants in North America.

Better Dough, Better Dim Sum, Better Pastry

The one-and-a-half month Swiss experience in 1969 broadened Chan's horizons and inspired him to improve the quality of dim sum, particularly its main ingredient of dough, by taking advantage of European culinary management and technology. He hoped to implement some of these new ideas by managing a dim sum restaurant and establishing a fresh noodle factory in New York. However, as described in the introduction of this essay, Chan's dream crashed in 1979 when he arrived in the Big Apple.

Formerly a top chef who commanded teams of chefs and staff, Chan was now reduced to poverty. He had lost everything, including his dignity and his successful career. He strolled the alleys and streets of Chinatown where everyone seemed to have a destination, and he could not help but ask, "What am I if I'm not a dim sum chef?" Fortunately, one day he chanced upon one of his former apprentices from Hong Kong, who was about to open a small café-style restaurant, later known as the Fortune Restaurant, on 68 Mott Street in the spring of 1980. He immediately hired Chan as the head dim sum chef. This marked the rebirth of his career in America, where the master chef could finally try some of the ideas inspired by his Swiss food festival experience. He could now explore ways to improve his dishes by taking advantage of Western methodology and ingredients.

Master Chan immediately began to refine his dim sum and dough production. He discovered that there was a wide range of high quality flour available in the United States that was not accessible in Asia at the time. He began to combine traditional methods with these new ingredients. His first success was a sweet pastry not usually found on traditional dim sum menus, the sweetheart cake (or old wife cake). Chan loved sweets himself, and was impressed by the Western infatuation with candies and desserts; thus he found the sweetheart cake to be an ideal way to connect sweet and savory. Through the chef's innovations, East and West met. His experiments with flour to enhance the dough quality, and his remarkable manual skills in dough preparation, which enhanced the freshness and flakiness of the crust, began this (r)evolution. Although Chan had intended to serve his new pastry as a dessert to compliment savory dim sum dishes, patrons began consuming it as an alternative to donuts, muffins, and cookies. Lines began forming in front of the restaurant before noon, and customers waited patiently to purchase this freshly baked pastry. Through Chan's careful management of production and sales, the Fortune Restaurant's sweetheart cake—a traditional pastry with Western flair—became a household name in New York's Chinatown.

While he was busy reinventing traditional pastry at the Fortune Restaurant, Chan did not neglect other dim sum staples. Since the restaurant was small, the chef took the opportunity to abolish the use of dim sum carts. Instead, the wait staff used trays to take the dim sum, freshly cooked in traditional bamboo steamers, to the dining area. The chef made only what he estimated would be enough dim sum for the breakfast and lunch rush. He also strictly forbade the staff from serving diners any leftovers, which would be kept in the steam cabinet near the entrance solely for take-out orders. Although he was departing from the made-to-order way of serving dim sum he pioneered at the Hong Kong Food Festival in Switzerland, Chan felt this delivery system was the best option given the conditions. Undoubtedly, the chef's strict quality control measures limited supply, but he was determined to maintain excellence even at the expense of profits.

Building on the initial success of the small café, the owners of the Fortune Restaurant seized the opportunity to secure a larger, more visible space in the heart of Chinatown. The Fortune Restaurant expanded into larger quarters and, in the mid-1980s, became the Grand Fortune Restaurant on Canal Street. Chan continued to manage the development and production of dim sum at this new location. With significantly more space in the dining room and kitchen, Grand Fortune aimed not only to serve dim sum for breakfast and lunch, but also to become the premier restaurant for traditional Chinese dinner parties, feasts, and banquets. These parties often celebrate special occasions, such as weddings, birthdays, and the birth of children, and are usually extremely lavish, demanding the highest quality of service and food.

At Grand Fortune, Chef Chan continued to refine the use of flour and sugar to develop his dessert menu. The next two delicacies that Chan transformed were *shaqima*—a soft flour cake which originated in the Qing dynasty court—and *hup toh soh*, or walnut cookies, another ancient royal court favorite. Chan improved these two desserts by refining the delicate balance of flour, sweeteners, and shortening. Pork is the most popular meat in China, and lard is the traditional shortening of Chinese pastries. However, Chan learned that adding butter to the dough in a carefully measured quantity yielded a very different texture and taste. He also experimented with various natural sweeteners, such as cane molasses, maple syrup, and maize starch. Using these Western ingredients, Chan discovered new combinations with magically sweet results. He was literally like a kid in a candy store, eager to mix and match different sweets to satisfy his own insatiable appetite.

Chan's production of *shaqima* required a careful mixture of flour, sweeteners, shortening, and special flavors that were kneaded into the dough when it rose to the proper "lightness." The dough was then hand-cut into small strips, in the exact same size, prior to frying. After cooling overnight, the small crispy strips of fried dough were molded into a large cooking pan with a special blend of sweeteners. After being heated to an extremely high temperature for consistency and caramelization, this required overnight cooling. The entire pan of nearly ready "flour cake" was then cut into individual square blocks. This labor-intensive, golden, light, airy, sticky bite-sized dessert was then ready to serve as a final treat after the savory dim sum. Many of Chan's delicate desserts, including *shaqima* and *hup toh soh*, also found their way onto the dining tables of Grand Fortune's banquet parties.

Better Dough, Better Art

Chan also took advantage of the Grand Fortune kitchen as a "studio" to rediscover his lifelong love affair with dough sculpture. Weddings and birthday parties soon became a major platform for him to demonstrate his pastry art. Early in his apprenticeship in Foshan during the 1930s, Chan took up an unrelated interest of sculpting figurines out of bread dough, a traditional folk art from the streets of old China. While shopping for the restaurant, he watched street artists making all kinds of mythical characters on wooden sticks. Often admired by children, these folk artists' dough sculptures were crude and small in scale. Nevertheless, little animals and famous folklore characters, such as the Monkey King from the classic *Journey to the West* and the Eight Immortals, were brought to life in every crowded Chinese food market.

An aspiring artist himself, Chan was curious about this art since he had a passion for all beautiful things. He did not know that it would later play a significant role in his culinary career. His *sifu* never inspired him to go beyond the making of dim sum, and did not pay much attention to Chan's artistic curiosity. The old man probably scolded the apprentice for wasting his time on a childish amusement rather than learning how to become a good chef. Regardless, Chan maintained his interest in dough sculpture throughout his career. When he became the chief dim sum chef in Hong Kong, he was commissioned to make the Three Gods of Fortune, the Five Creatures of Longevity, and the Eight Immortals for the Manchu-Han Imperial Feast, the most elaborate banquet in Chinese cuisine.[16] As the general manager of Macao Palace, Chan would also occasionally present his beloved characters as gifts to select patrons. Yet deep down inside, he knew that someday he would be able to combine his love of food and art through the common medium of dough.

The chef's sculptural art made great progress in Grand Fortune's kitchen studio. Chan started to experiment with decorating dessert platters for banquets with colorful small dough sculptures such as roses and chrysanthemums. In fact, the revival of Chan's dough sculptures was in no small part aided by the tremendous palette of food coloring available in America. It did not take long for the Chinatown public to become aware of the restaurant's unique offerings. Combining delicious desserts with the delicate decor of its platters, Grand Fortune became the place to be for banquets and special events, large and small. Chan was thus encouraged to experiment with dough sculpture and further its development in both size and scope.

Chan's pastry and dough sculptures were also commissioned for local restaurant openings. Restaurant owners were proud to decorate their grand-opening celebrations with Chan's sculptures, including the Dragon and Phoenix, the *Fuk Luk Shou* Gods, and the Buddha.

However, he would not agree to offer any support unless the establishments were worthy of his presentations, thus ensuring the exclusivity of his artwork. It was through this relentless pursuit of excellence and strict quality control that Chan's dough sculptures expanded into new territory.

By the late 1980s, Chan was recognized as the only master who could provide such culinary artistry in New York City's Chinatown.[17] During those years, two important breakthroughs defined Chan's evolution in dough sculpture. The first was the blending of ingredients that comprised the dough. The second was the incorporation of the wireframe endoskeleton structure. Both developments came out of his dissatisfaction with the inherent limitations of edible dough materials.

Dough as Ceramics?

In the streets of China, where dough figurines were small handicrafts made to please children, their durability was never a high priority. Like this folk art, Chan's early sculptures were small fragile statues used to ornament dishes. He did not expect them to last any longer than the freshly cut flowers found on the serving tables next to his sculptures. Despite hours of painstaking work with fine-scale detail, his early sculptures could not withstand the test of time. While customers were extremely impressed with the work that went into the figurines, they were disappointed by their quick disintegration.

In Hong Kong and Macao, Chan attributed the short lifespan of his sculptures to the heat and humidity. He was aware that dough usually turned moldy or sour within a week. But since New York is less humid and cooler, he could no longer blame the climate. Recognizing this limitation, Chan was determined to find a method to preserve his precious art. One early experiment involved baking the finished product. However, this process was tedious. He decided against using a conventional oven to bake the dough because the cost was high and the temperature was difficult to control. Instead, he created a baking device out of a metal drum using an infrared lamp as the heating source. His intention was to bake the sculpture in the drum to evaporate its moisture, a method likely borrowed from pottery makers and other dough artists.[18]

While this heating technique was successful in driving out the moisture and increasing the dough figurines' shelf life, Chan found that it led to another problem. The sculptures dried up so quickly that they would shrink and deform beyond recognition. Worse still, many of the baked sculptures would prematurely crack after only several weeks. Chan used trial and error to find the best combination of heating intensity and duration in order to make his artwork last longer. Although he experienced some initial success with this process, he was far from happy with the result. He insisted on finding a better, more reliable means of preservation.

The next step in his quest for long-lasting dough sculptures was the addition of a protective coating. Drawing inspiration from dough sculpture's closest relative, pottery, the master chef studied ceramics. He learned that the glossy coating of ceramics was what gave it its luster, and also helped preserve and protect the porcelain. Since his dough sculptures were decorations for his dim sum and pastry, he preferred to use only edible coating media. Chan's first attempt was to coat his sculptures with egg whites, but he also experimented with various kinds of oil, butter, and sugar-based glazes, all of which could be traced back to his dim sum roots. However, each of these coatings presented its own set of problems, including microbial growth and pest attraction. These experiments nonetheless became a stepping stone to a permanent solution to the edible dough preservation dilemma.

The master chef's biggest discovery in dough improvement was not something he had learned from ceramics. Rather, it was his innovative preparation and combination of ingredients. Chan eventually created a stable, long-lasting dough that, after air-drying and natural hardening, could last for years and even decades without the need for additional baking or coating. What was the secret? Salt and sugar.[19] After months of exhaustive attempts to control the dough, Chan found that the most effective means was actually combining what he knew best. Namely, the ingredients for his favorite savory and sweet dim sum. He discovered that this modified version of dim sum dough could significantly lengthen the lifespan of sculptures.

By the beginning of the 1990s, Chan was no longer occupied with the daily routine of dim sum making and serving in the restaurant.

Those tasks were delegated to a team of chefs and a crew led by his disciple. Other than preparing a few items that he insisted on making himself, such as glutinous rice dumplings, sesame seed rolls, and coconut pulp cakes, a good portion of his time was devoted to dough sculptures. Now that he had found the formula for long-lasting dough, Chan felt that he had mastered his craft. As his excitement and confidence grew, his artistic repertoire expanded accordingly. Still, questions persisted. What else could the artist do with this art form? How could he improve on the subject matters and themes? Who else could enjoy this culinary art? Where else could he showcase his art?

With the end of the twentieth century came a rising global interest in Chinese culture, and Chan wanted to use this to expand his dough sculpture beyond the streets of New York City's Chinatown. One of the most popular themes that emerged during that period was the Chinese zodiac, which was composed of a dozen animals representing the twelve-year cycle of the lunar calendar. Chan saw this as a wonderful way to represent Chinese culture and his own artistry. Departing from his usual human subjects, Chan took on the challenge of designing animal figures. He knew a few of these animals, such as the rat and the snake, would not be appropriate for the restaurant setting. He therefore minimized their representations in his dough sculptures, and instead emphasized the rooster, ox, dragon, horse, and goat.

Chan gathered photographs and diagrams of these animals in their natural forms to serve as references. He started with small pieces of dough and gradually expanded to larger sculptures similar in size to his human figures. He experimented with different poses in different positions, but to his dismay, he failed to capture the characteristics of the animals. After months of struggling with the simplest creatures like the rabbit, he still struggled to represent their essence. What makes a monkey look like a monkey? The artist was puzzled.

Reluctantly, Chan turned to his son, a biology major in college and an avid animal lover and painter. Clarence looked at his father's rudimentary animal sculptures and remarked, "Animals do not pose or stand around!" The essence of an animal in art is to represent it in motion. "Animals exhibit their natural spirits when they move," his son explained. To bring the animals to life, his father should capture their unique movement patterns. For example, showing a monkey jumping from, or reaching for, a tree branch is far more expressive and interesting than making a monkey stand still next to a tree. The old master was not convinced. Clarence took some of the leftover dough materials and created three vivid zodiac animals without adding any color to highlight their features. He gave his father a snake coiling up from a stable base and extending its head in a ready-to-strike position. There was a small puppy crouching with a bushy tail wagging high up in the air. The young man also showed his father what a rat looked like when curling up into a fur ball with only a pair of long ears and a wrinkly tail showing. Not only was the chef pleasantly surprised by the simplicity and dynamism of the little creatures, but he was also amazed by how well his son could put several pieces of dough together and instantly create those lively figures. "I never taught you that!" wondered the old man. In fact, he had never wanted his son to go near the kitchen or play with dough at all.

Chan realized he was no longer the only one in the house who could make dough sculptures. With much ambivalence, he began to share his dough sculpting table with Clarence. He even gave his son a set of ivory sculpting tools as an acknowledgment of his craftsmanship. From time to time, he shared ideas and techniques with Clarence, and even teamed up with him to create some of the most elaborate combinations of human and animal displays for different venues.

Yet, Chan knew there was more to learn. The challenge of making animal figures gave him the idea for his next breakthrough. Never settling for second best, the artist took his son's suggestions and expanded them—literally. He decided to make larger and more dynamic sculptures. This ambition brought new difficulties. A larger statue required more dough, and more dough meant a heavier structure, which in turn entailed higher labor and material costs, more preparation time, and, above all, a more solid supporting base.

To overcome the increased weight, Chan immediately resorted to the method of using a tightly coiled newspaper core as the center of his statues. The paper core was light, relatively sturdy, and extremely economical. It could be made in any size and held up well when dough was molded around it. This method proved to be highly effective in supporting Chan's human figures. However, it was a different story for the animal characters. Unlike his human figures, which were typically standing upright with their extremities held closely to the body, the animals were dynamically posed, with extremities extending out in different directions. Animals such as the ox, horse, and goat had four very thin legs holding up a very heavy torso. There were also long arms and legs for the monkey, a pair of very thin and bony legs for the rooster, and the long, slender body of the snake and dragon.

Chan saw the need to improve the core structure, and borrowed his son's vertebrate zoology textbook. He studied the musculoskeletal structures of animals, and, fascinated by the forms and functions of animal anatomy, he acquired art reference books for different creatures. Unlike invertebrates such as the lobster, snail, and butterfly, the artist found that the defining characteristics of vertebrates are their vertebral columns and appendicular skeletons. Chan decided that his animal figures must have a skeleton of sorts. Popsicle sticks and barbecue skewers were too rigid to mold and too weak to support the heavy dough, so he turned to metal wire. Chan discovered the perfect combinations for the various animal skeletons after spending months twisting and tying copper and steel wires of different gauges together (figures 5.3 and 5.4). He could now create running horses, monkeys swinging from trees, and dragons flying through clouds (a common image from Chinese mythology).

As his proficiency in making wireframe animal structures improved, Chan began to scale up his design. Many of the dough sculptures reached several feet high. Furthermore, the master incorporated this structural concept into his once static and upright human figures, making them more dynamic through poses such as standing on one leg or wielding a sword. He created a series of mythical human figures based on the stories of the Eight Immortals (figure 5.5), molded in dancing or fighting poses. The grand master was now poised to take his dough sculptures beyond the confines of the restaurant.

From Chinatown Kitchen to Mainstream American Media

Chef Chan retired in 1993 after a long and illustrious restaurant career in the Far East and the United States, leaving the production of his popular sweet and savory dim sum to his apprentices in Chinatown. Well into his retirement, Chan continued his work with dough in the basement of his home, which he shared with his son's family. No longer did he have to wake up at 4:30 a.m. every morning to catch the subway to Lower Manhattan to prepare fresh dim sum dough for the morning rush. Instead, he devoted a large portion of his day to practicing and honing his dim sum and dough sculptures. He converted his basement into a mini Chinese-restaurant kitchen, and family and friends became the retired chef's new "customers." After cooking food during the day, Chan spent countless evenings trying out new themes and characters for his sculptural art. In addition to zodiac animals, he incorporated other popular characters such as the panda and the *Ao*, a mythological sea creature (figure 5.6), two quintessential Chinese symbols of good fortune and good will. He gave them as Lunar New Year gifts to relatives and friends.

Even though he was no longer working in Chinatown, Chan remained a prominent figure in the community. He and his son were invited as featured guests to the 1997 Hong Kong Dragon Boat Festival in New York. Held in Flushing Meadows–Corona Park annually, this event gave Chan an opportunity to show his dough sculptures to the general public (figure 5.7), which rivaled their counterparts in China. The festival brought back memories of Chan's youth, watching and admiring the old dough artists in the street markets. Decades later, he, too, was bringing joy to curious children. The success of the Dragon Boat Festival introduced Chan's legacy to a wider world. Master Chan and Clarence were commissioned by the Walt Disney Company to be the featured artists at the New York première of the animated feature *Mulan*. This performance marked the pinnacle and, at the same time, the summation of Chan's artistic career with dough sculpture.

For ordinary folks like the Chans, the *Mulan* première was an evening of Hollywood extravagance and celebration. For Disney, however, the première was part of a deliberately restrained campaign since the company had "so overhyped its [previous] animation [openings] that the public had grown cynical."[20] Therefore, instead of occupying Central Park or Times Square, Disney held the *Mulan* opening in the historic Roseland Ballroom in the summer of 1998.[21] The company, which "has built-in mechanisms for cross-cultural referencing," hired Asian and Asian American artists to give the movie "a Chinese touch."[22] Regardless of Disney's motives, Master Chan saw the opportunity as the affirmation of his accomplishments. He and Clarence spent over two months preparing exhibits and literature to describe the history and development of this ancient Chinese folk art. The team created numerous large-scale sculptures based on the film's characters, such as Mulan and Mushu, a cute dragon who is Mulan's closest companion. They brought along some of Chan's most popular sculptures, including the Chinese zodiac and other mythical figures, and a host of Disney cartoon characters (figures 5.8 and 5.9). As part of their agreement with Disney, the two artists made fifty small replicas of Mushu on wooden sticks as giveaways. That evening, Clarence showed young guests huddling around the display table how the Mushu figure was made. This time, the old master witnessed how his son shared the joy of the artwork with the children. Chan saw that his legacy might very well be continued by his own child.

The 1969 Swiss experience gave Chan the idea of bringing his expertise to the West. He began his legacy by demonstrating his dough artistry with dim sum. Almost thirty years later, he completed the journey by displaying his dough mastery through an American media giant. Ironically, it was the Disney event that reminded him of his limitations. Despite the popular acclaim he received for his live demonstrations during the première, Chan's language barrier also became a barrier for his art. He had immense experience and expertise in culinary aesthetics. However, his English, limited to "hello" and "thank you," rendered him incapable of explaining his craftsmanship to the curious audience. Perhaps he finally realized that none of his accomplishments and accolades could change the fact he would never be able to break through the glass ceiling. He saw his son conversing with children and their parents with ease, while he could only sit at the back, quietly making his dough sculptures.

Dough Lessons

What can we learn from Chan's decades-long experimentation and refinement of dough for dim sum and sculpture? Although he maintained his cooking and artistic work according to tradition, the chef/artist was very receptive of what was available in the West—Switzerland and the United States—in terms of methodology, knowledge, and ingredients. In fact, many of Chan's culinary and artistic breakthroughs resulted from his daring incorporation of European and American processes and materials. Thanks to Swiss management and a modern kitchen, Chan revolutionized the way dim sum was produced and consumed by preparing it in a made-to-order way in 1969. More than three decades later, this made-to-order system is still the gold standard for dim sum restaurants; connoisseurs and picky customers alike would not settle for anything less. However, most diners do not know that this system originated not in Hong Kong, the Gourmet Heaven, or Guangdong, the culinary hub of South China, but in Switzerland.

Chan was equally bold in improving traditional pastry by integrating unconventional ingredients from Western cuisine. For instance, the chef did not hesitate to replace lard with butter in order to enhance his sweet dim sum's taste and crispiness. Nor did he hesitate to experiment with the new types of flour, food coloring, and flavoring available in New York. As an artist, he was open to Western science, and his acquired knowledge in anatomy enabled him to create more elaborate, larger, and longer-lasting animal and human dough sculptures than what existed in China, the country from which this art originated.

Yet, like countless thousands of first-generation immigrants, the master chef had his limitations: he could not communicate with the general public beyond Chinatown. He first learned this "English lesson" when he landed at San Francisco International Airport as an immigrant. Decades later, he learned it again during the *Mulan* première. It was a hard lesson. Perhaps for that reason, Chan's final years were dedicated to teaching and mentoring the next generation of Chinese chefs. He also insisted that they had to develop their language competence and social acumen.

Chan's last student was a young man who had just come from China and wanted to become a dim sum chef. He apprenticed in the restaurant in the early 1990s, and stayed with Chan until the master retired. Chan passed on a considerable amount of skill and knowledge about dim sum to this up-and-coming chef. He continued his training in Chan's basement kitchen until the old master could no longer cook. Chan taught him the art of dough sculpture as well. But most importantly, he told him that the future of Chinese food in America lies outside of Chinatown, and that he must learn English and mingle with people from a wider social circle. He reminded him that mastering culinary skills is not enough; he must be able to present his mastery to a larger audience. Chan's life lessons also include craftsmanship in food preparation, excellence in quality, professionalism in delivery, innovation in development, and beauty in presentation, all of which he impressed on his apprentice and his son before his passing in 2004. The young chef left Chinatown the following year and became the head dim sum chef in a restaurant located in the West Village neighborhood of Manhattan. Master Chan would be very pleased with his achievements.

Food writers and scholars have long documented the spread of Chinese food all over the world, or what they call "the globalization of Chinese food."[23] Transplanting his career to America in the 1980s, Chan was undoubtedly an important player in the post–chop suey phase of this transnational movement. One of the key issues of this global force is the question of authenticity. Diners, especially first-generation immigrants, are concerned with the authenticity of Chinese food available in their communities and lament that Western incarnations are inferior adaptations of the food they ate in China.[24] Often influenced by cultural and postcolonial theories, scholars, on the other hand, have a more complicated take on the matter. They believe that "ethnic" or immigrant food in America is a social construct perceived as different from mainstream "all-American" food because of its foreign origin. However, as Martin Manalansan argues, some mainstream American foods, such as pizza, were once regarded as "ethnic." Therefore, the question about the authenticity of an ethnic food is "not intrinsic to the cuisine or particular criteria but to the dominant/mainstream and marginal/non-mainstream food choices and tastes that are constantly shifting."[25]

For Master Chef Chan, as for many skilled immigrant chefs sweating in the steamy kitchen to satisfy the insatiable appetites of customers, this sort of academic talk is irrelevant. Chan never questioned the authenticity of delicacies made possible by the combination of skills, recipes, ingredients, and habits that originated from the greater Guangdong region. He was, for instance, always proud of his dough-mixing and -kneading skills, which he had learned from his *sifus* since his apprenticeship in Foshan (figure 5.10). Moreover, he did not hold what may be called an essentialist view of the Cantonese culinary tradition; he did not pretend that this tradition had not changed or had not been influenced by other cuisines and cultures. For this master, then, the use of foreign ingredients and processes were means to produce the best food and art for his customers and patrons—Chinese, European, and American alike.

For Chan, the question of authenticity paled in comparison to questions of quality and innovation. As Yong Chen, J.A.G. Roberts, and other scholars point out, affordability and convenience have increased the popularity of ethnic foods, such as Indian and Chinese, in the West.[26] From the perspective of an uncompromising chef and artist like Chan, this was an unfortunate trend. He was philosophically and practically opposed to making food and art cheaply and quickly, at the expense of culinary and aesthetic quality. The master would instead charge higher prices and limit supply to ensure that his products were consistently appealing to both the discerning palate and eye. In other words, Chan's culinary and artistic modifications for Western markets were by no means substandard versions of what he made in Macao and Hong Kong. They were innovative improvements driven by the desire for excellence. Change, for Chan as for other overseas Chinese master chefs, is not only a necessity in their kitchen—now transplanted to a new environment—but also a positive force in their professional growth.

Let us conclude with the philosophy behind Master Kai Tai Chan's career. He once observed, "Every once in a while, we find ourselves drawn into something so compelling that a world of fascinating discovery would unfold and unfold, and we can't help but indulge in it even more deeply."[27] This sums up the life-long journey Chan undertook to pursue culinary and artistic perfection. Every challenge he met was a door which, after opening, led to others. The master opened these doors in his kitchen studio, no matter where he found himself: southern China, Zurich, or New York.

FIGURE 5.1. Master Kai Tai Chan and his Swiss colleague are showcasing a steamer of dim sum delicacies at the Zurich airport restaurant kitchen. Photo from Clarence Chan's Family Collection.

FIGURE 5.2. Master Chan and his colleagues are busy preparing dim sum while the Swiss staff and chefs are observing. Photo from Clarence Chan's Family Collection.

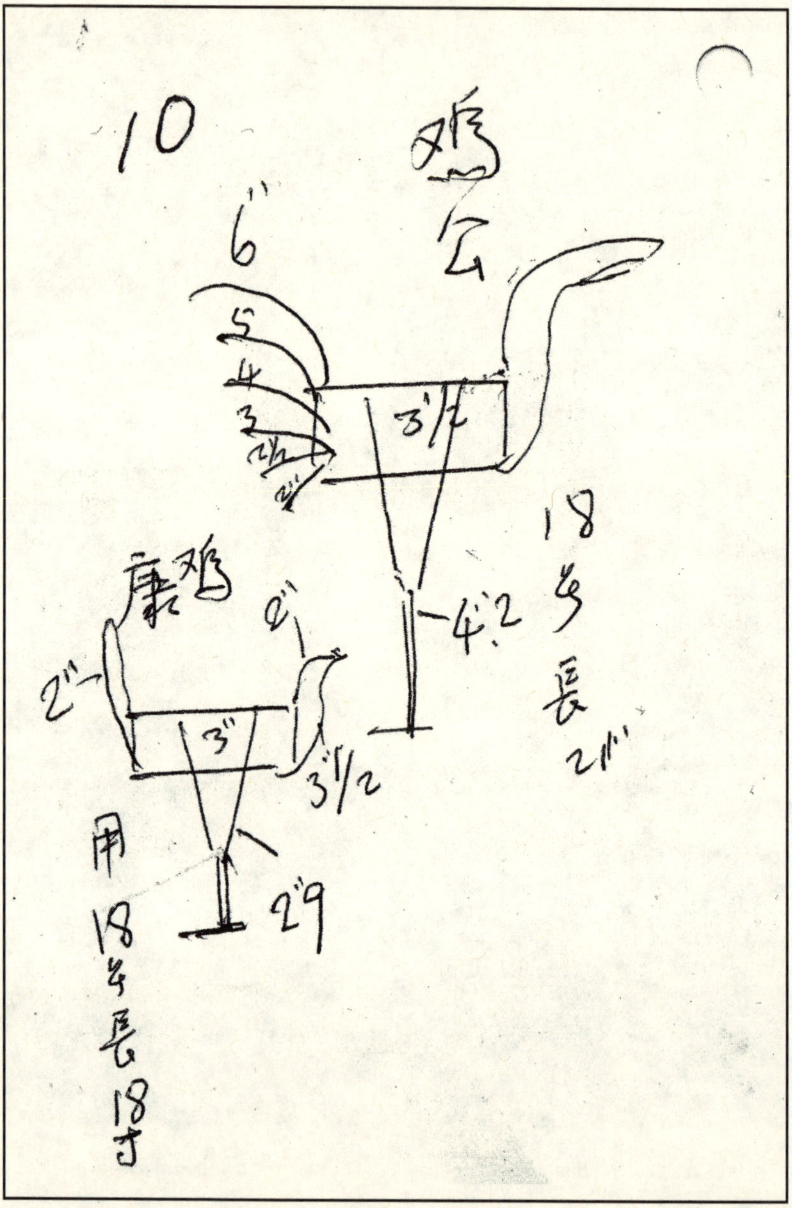

FIGURE 5.3. Master Chan's sketches of wireframe chickens. Photo from Clarence Chan's Family Collection.

FIGURE 5.4. A rooster dough sculpture created by Master Chan. Photo from Clarence Chan's Family Collection.

FIGURE 5.5. A collection of the Eight Immortals Master Chan made to celebrate the opening of a restaurant. Photo from Clarence Chan's Family Collection.

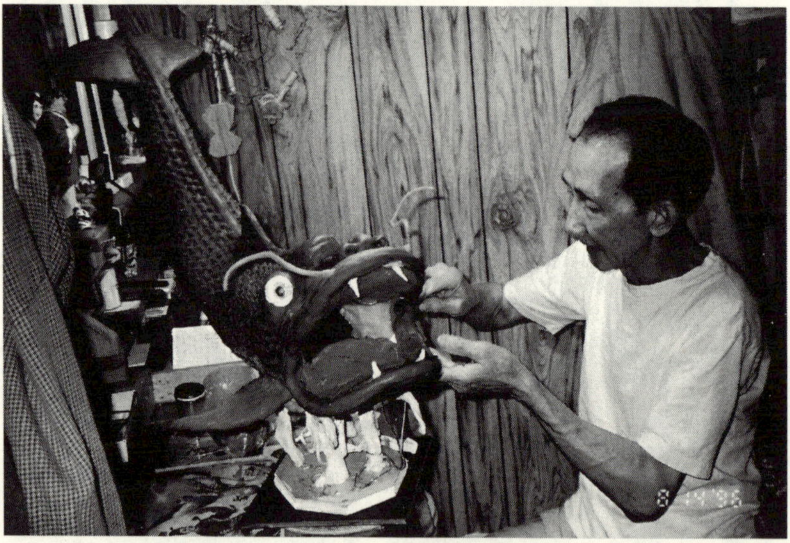

FIGURE 5.6. Master Chan is completing an *Ao* sculpture. He is working in his basement kitchen studio. Photo from Clarence Chan's Family Collection.

FIGURE 5.7. Master Chan is making a dragon sculpture at the 1997 Hong Kong Dragon Boat Festival in Flushing Meadows–Corona Park, New York. Photo from Clarence Chan's Family Collection.

FIGURE 5.8. Master Chan at the Mulan première at the Roseland Ballroom. Photo from Clarence Chan's Family Collection.

FIGURE 5.9. Master Chan's dough sculptures have lasted decades. This is a recent picture of a Hua Mu Lan sculpture made by Master Chan some seventeen years ago. There are visible cracks, but the sculpture is still intact thanks to the sugar and salt dough and the wireframe. Photo from Clarence Chan's Family Collection.

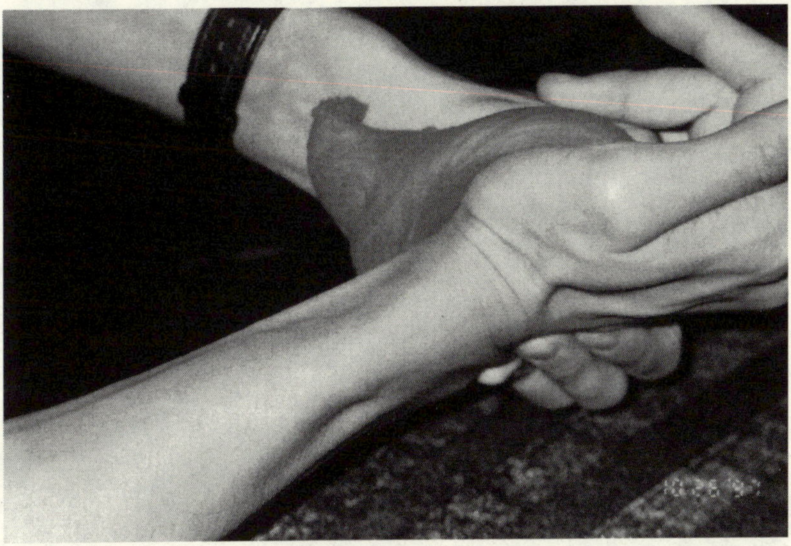

FIGURE 5.10. Master Chan is demonstrating his dough kneading skills. Photo from Clarence Chan's Family Collection.

CHAPTER 6

When Little Island Cuisine Encountered Chinese Food

The Evolution of Taiwanese Cuisine in New York City's Flushing Neighborhood, 1970–Present

CHUNGHAO PIO KUO

In the twentieth century, there was no large-scale immigration of Chinese (broadly speaking, including Taiwanese) to New York City (NYC) until the 1970s.[1] Like many other immigrants who would group together within cities for the purpose of mutual assistance, Taiwanese settled in Flushing, Queens, where they started up small businesses, including groceries, laundries, and of course, restaurants. When China's Cultural Revolution came to a close around 1980, and even earlier, when Chinese leader Deng Xiaoping promoted "the Policy of Reformation and Opening" in 1978, a large number of Chinese Mainlanders started immigrating to the United States. Culturally diverse NYC quickly became home to many of them, and in the 1980s and 1990s, Flushing, with its Taiwanese restaurants, was known as "Little Taipei."[2]

After 1980, two groups of Chinese immigrants moved to New York, sometimes legally and other times illegally. The first group consisted of Wenzhou immigrants from Zhejiang Province, who settled down in Flushing chiefly because Taiwanese immigrants in the neighborhood had already established a viable, quite self-sufficient ethnic-Chinese community there. The second group, Fuzhou immigrants from Fujian Province, initially set up residence in downtown Manhattan's East Broadway area (next to the original Chinatown) and, when the Broadway site became saturated, moved to Eighth Avenue in Brooklyn, effectively establishing the third Chinatown in NYC (Flushing being the second). Gradually, Wenzhou immigrants and other non-Taiwanese ethnic-Chinese immigrants in Flushing began establishing their own businesses. Both the numerical preponderance and the business savvy of these immigrants began to threaten the previously unchallenged commercial interests of Taiwanese immigrants in Flushing, especially Taiwanese restaurants. These shifting circumstances are the subject of this essay.

Against this historical background, I will discuss the evolution of Taiwanese restaurants in Flushing and, more specifically, explore how Taiwanese cuisine has encountered significant challenges from the massive non-Taiwanese ethnic-Chinese immigration to the neighborhood since the 1990s. To undertake this exploration, I conducted fieldwork, which led me to interview restaurant owners, and analyzed specific primary sources, such as menus. In short, I have found that there are four trends emerging among Taiwanese restaurants in response to challenges from Chinese immigrants who run restaurants in Flushing. The first trend can be seen in some owners' effort to integrate such non-Taiwanese cuisine as Sichuan and Hunan cuisines into existing menus in order to attract more customers from China. The second trend, by contrast, is some owners' decision to serve only authentic and refined Taiwanese cuisine. The third trend rests with a handful of restaurants that adopted Taiwan's very own "Mainland Chinese" cuisine. The fourth trend can be seen in some Taiwanese restaurants' efforts to satisfy customers' demand for healthy food.[3]

A Brief Background of Taiwanese Immigration to Flushing

My interviewees suggested two central reasons for Taiwanese immigrants' decisions to settle in Flushing. The first reason has its roots in 1964, when the New York World's Fair was held there. Many Taiwanese business representatives visited the fair to promote their commercial interests and were immediately impressed with NYC. The second reason has to do with the presence of a sizable Japanese immigrant community in 1960s Flushing. In general, Taiwanese and Japanese were on friendly terms with each other largely because the legacy of Japan's colonization of Taiwan was perceived as distinctly positive by many Taiwanese. Thus, early Taiwanese immigrants in NYC decided to set up home in Flushing.

The majority of Flushing's Taiwanese residents between the 1970s and 1990s emerged from two streams of immigrants: (1) Taiwanese businessmen and their families, whose exposure to the New York World's Fair convinced them to relocate to the city, and (2) Taiwanese overseas students who, in pursuit of material success and political freedom after graduation, decided to settle down in NYC (Flushing became one of their first choices because they could have easy access to social networks there).[4] It is worth noting that in the 1970s most real estate in Flushing was quite cheap and inhabited predominantly by Italian Americans and Jewish Americans.[5] As noted earlier and by several of my interviewees, the first wave of Chinese immigrants who moved to Flushing by the 1980s were, in general, initially from Zhejiang Province's Wenzhou area and later from different regions of China. During the 1980s, the percentage of Flushing's Asian population that was Japanese significantly declined as some Japanese residents relocated to White Plains, New York, and Fort Lee, New Jersey.[6] In addition to ethnic-Chinese immigrants, immigrants from South Korea settled in Flushing at this time, though in greater Flushing, not in downtown Flushing. By 2000, more and more Chinese immigrants were moving to Flushing, and quite a few Taiwanese immigrants, seeking to improve their station, moved to Long Island and New Jersey.[7]

Flushing's Taiwanese Cuisine—From Its Inception to Its Golden Age

Occupying an area developed by the Dutch in the seventeenth century and more formally structured by the British (with a city hall and a city council) in the eighteenth century, Flushing is currently known as one of the biggest Chinatowns in North America. How did Taiwanese immigrants to Flushing draw its "culinary map"? According to my interviewees, before Taiwanese immigrants began inhabiting Flushing *en masse* in the 1970s, one would have looked in vain for commercial signboards featuring Chinese characters anywhere in the neighborhood. During the 1970s, Taiwanese immigrants moved to the United States in response to two pivotal events: the withdrawal of the Republic of China from the United Nations in 1971 and the U.S. government's passage of the Taiwan Relations Act (1979), which resulted in a cessation of formal diplomatic relations between the United States and the Republic of China. Seeking a more stable and prosperous place in which to raise families and earn a living, these Taiwanese immigrants regarded Flushing in New York City as one of their best choices.

In the 1970s, when more Taiwanese immigrants moved into Flushing, they opened basic stores like groceries, barbershops, and laundries to fill their needs, and then began engaging in real estate transactions, chiefly on Fortieth Road, but also at the intersection of Main Street and Roosevelt Avenue. After encountering legal issues related to leases, investments, and real estate, Taiwanese residents in the area organized the Taiwan Merchants Association of New York in 1976 and then the Flushing Chinese Business Association in 1982 to promote the commercial development of Flushing. It was during these early years that Taiwanese cuisine made its first appearance in Flushing.

Strictly speaking, the term "Taiwanese cuisine" lacks a precise academic definition, but culinary historians of Taiwan generally accept Taiwanese cuisine to be a food culture consisting of Zhejiang–Jiangsu cuisine, Sichuan cuisine, Japanese cuisine, Hakka Taiwanese cuisine, and Fujian Taiwanese cuisine.[8] This working definition reflects Taiwan's long history of intercultural encounters and ethnic diversification. Restaurants run by Taiwanese all over the world, whether serving Fujian, Hakka, Chinese Mainlander cuisine, or American-Chinese cuisine, are essentially serving Taiwanese cuisine.[9] However, the definition of Taiwanese cuisine varies depending on which historical context is being considered.

According to my interviewee Mr. Mingsen Lu (i.e., Morris Lee), prior to 1980, there were only two Cantonese-run restaurants in Flushing: the first one was named Datong (大同), which sold American-Chinese fare, and the second one was named Linshi (林市), which sold authentic Cantonese cuisine. Both were located in downtown Flushing. From the early 1980s to the late 1990s, the growing population of Taiwanese immigrants and the booming commercial development in Flushing prompted more and more East Asian–themed restaurants in the area to open.[10]

According to Mr. Lu, three groups of ethnic Chinese (Cantonese, Taiwanese, and Chinese Mainlanders) have operated, amongst themselves, four categories of restaurants in downtown Flushing. The restaurants belonging to the first category have sold American-Chinese food and Cantonese cuisine and have been run by Cantonese entrepreneurs. These restaurants included Datong (大同), Hong Kong Building (香港樓), and Fu Ji Restaurant (富記). The restaurants belonging to the second category have sold northern Chinese cuisine and Sichuan cuisine and have been run by Chinese Mainlanders. Examples of these restaurants were Qi Hai (七海), Jinshan (金山), Lee Xiang Village (荔香村), Zhonghua Building (中華樓), and Zhuangyuanlou (狀元樓). The third category comprises restaurants specializing in Fujian-Taiwanese cuisine and Japanese-Taiwanese cuisine. Run by Fujian Taiwanese, these restaurants included Spring and Autumn Pavilion (春秋閣), Huawang (華王), Lobster House (龍蝦屋), Huaxiang (華鄉), and Foliage (紅葉). The fourth and final category of restaurants is known for mixed Chinese cuisine such as buffets, various types of buns, Cantonese cuisine, and Shanghai cuisine. Qinxiang Number One Building (清香一品樓) and Pine and Bamboo Garden (松竹園) were two restaurants representative of this category. It is telling that for diverse reasons including market competition, unaffordable leases, and the dissolution of partnerships, all of the above-mentioned restaurants have closed.

Mingsen Lu pointed out that, by the 1980s, the greater NYC area boasted restaurants serving Cantonese cuisine, American-Chinese cuisine, Shanghai cuisine, Sichuan-Hunan cuisine, and northern Chinese cuisine, but no authentic Taiwanese cuisine.[11] Aware of this discrepancy, Mr. Lu opened a Taiwanese-Japanese restaurant named Foliage in July 1983 on Thirty-Eighth Avenue. Foliage reflected Mr. Lu's response to the growing Taiwanese population in Flushing and his desire to promote Taiwanese cuisine there. He hired chefs from Taiwan to prepare Foliage's traditional Taiwanese cuisine, which he referred to as "high-end elite cuisine" (酒家菜).[12] In addition, he frequently held singing competitions at Foliage: Taiwanese patrons would sing Taiwanese songs not only for fun but also to promote Taiwanese identity. Mr. Lu's engagement in Foliage was all-consuming: he single-handedly designed his restaurant, including its seafood stall, piano bar, spacious dining areas, snack stand, and live-band and karaoke setup. Mr. Lu did concede that running a Taiwanese restaurant in Flushing was risky because the size of the area's Taiwanese immigrant population was relatively small. He was not the only restaurateur to hold this view, and many Taiwanese immigrants seeking to open profitable Chinese restaurants in the 1980s felt the need to serve various regional Chinese cuisines to attract non-Taiwanese customers.[13] Foliage thus stood out for its combination of Japanese and Taiwanese cuisines.

The evolution of Flushing's Taiwanese cuisine took a marked turn in 1987, when a collective of Taiwanese immigrants established Taiwan Center–New York with the intention of promoting Taiwanese identity. Taiwan Center is located on Northern Boulevard in downtown Flushing and promotes Taiwanese culture, education, and the arts. The Center also serves as a location where pro-Taiwanese politicians conduct fundraising and carry out political campaigns in the greater NYC area. Operating directly adjacent to the Center in the 1980s and 1990s was the increasingly popular Taiwanese restaurant, the Flavor of Chinese (華香). The restaurant's chef, known simply as "Chef Wang,"

FIGURE 6.1 Mingsen Lu (left) receiving a business award on June 18, 1985 (photograph courtesy of Mingsen Lu) and 6.2 (right) with the author in 2016 (photograph courtesy of Chunghao Pio Kuo).

hailed originally from Taiwan and was skillful at cooking traditional Taiwanese cuisine. Very soon, Flushing's Taiwanese community became well acquainted with the Flavor of Chinese. An assistant chef at the restaurant (identified to me as a "Mr. Lin") later ran another well-known Taiwanese restaurant in Flushing, Main Street Imperial Taiwanese Gourmet (北港台菜). This growth in restaurants was possible largely because Taiwan Center's hosting of numerous fundraising events, conferences, and group meetings brought more and more Taiwanese to Flushing, in turn triggering the establishment of more and more Taiwanese restaurants in the neighborhood.

My interviewee Mr. Chenghui Chuang attested to the growth experienced by Flushing's Taiwanese restaurants in the 1990s. As an example, he cited Ku-Shiang Restaurant. Run by Mr. Nanyang Huang (黃南陽), the restaurant opened in the 1990s at an excellent location near downtown Flushing's number 7 train terminal station and quickly thrived. In fact, Ku-Shiang Restaurant has steadily operated in Flushing's fiercely competitive restaurant market ever since.

The term *ku-shiang*, or 故鄉, is Mandarin for "hometown," has given voice to many Taiwanese immigrants' homesickness. In Taiwan itself, the term expresses the melancholy experienced by Taiwanese who, since the 1960s, have moved to the greater Taipei area from neighboring areas in search of work in the capital city. Taipei has been the center of Taiwan's extraordinary economic growth since the 1960s, when industry superseded agriculture as the island's largest contributor to the gross domestic product.

Outside Taiwan, *ku-shiang* expresses the intense homesickness felt by so many Taiwanese immigrants responding emotionally to the massive geographical distance between their homeland and their new land. Before the 1990s, the term had particular significance for Taiwanese immigrants residing in Flushing: between the 1950s and 1980s, many of these individuals lived in Taiwan where they opposed the Taiwanese KMT government's coercive martial law. In retaliation, the government exiled them, barring their return to Taiwan until martial law was lifted on July 15, 1987.[14] For these exiled pro-democracy Taiwanese, the term *ku-shiang* harbored multifaceted meanings, including deep homesickness for Taiwan, a yearning for loved ones back home, and an overall sense of loss in the United States.[15] In this regard, Ku-Shiang Restaurant has been much more than a simple Taiwanese eatery in Flushing—it has become a way to, at least vicariously, revisit home.

Just a short walk from Ku-Shiang Restaurant is 66 Lu's Seafood (六六海之味). Enjoying a fine reputation for seafood prepared Taiwanese style, this Taiwanese restaurant has operated since the 1990s. Another well-known Taiwanese restaurant is Main Street Imperial Taiwanese Gourmet (北港台菜館). Located along the perimeter of Flushing's downtown, this restaurant is run by the same Mr. Lin from the Flavor of Chinese (adjacent to Taiwan Center). According to my interviewee Mr. Chenghui Chuang, Chef Lin learned his cooking skills under Chef Wang at the Flavor of Chinese and eventually decided to open a Taiwanese restaurant of his own, the aforementioned Main Street Imperial Taiwanese Gourmet. Known for its diverse Taiwanese dishes, this restaurant's Taiwanese cuisine has earned a considerable reputation in the greater NYC area.[16]

In addition to these three Taiwanese restaurants, which sell Fujian-style cuisine, restaurants run by Chinese Mainlanders who immigrated from Taiwan to Flushing have also gained prominence in the neighborhood. Located in downtown Flushing until it closed in 2015 upon its owner's retirement, No. 1 East Restaurant (人人江浙海鮮小館) offered Jiangsu and Zhejiang cuisines to draw in customers who were fond of these regions' gastronomy. It is true that most Taiwanese Islanders prefer Fujian-style cuisine. However, this restaurant owner's different preferences stemmed from his background: Chien-hong Lin had fled from Mainland China to Taiwan with Chiang Kai-shek's KMT army around 1950 but never abandoned his native Chinese identity, which was rooted in Jiangsu and Zhejiang, the two coastal provinces surrounding Shanghai.

According to my interviewee Mr. Chenghui Chuang, the period dating from the 1980s to the 1990s was the golden age of Taiwanese cuisine's development in Flushing, and there were two reasons for this phenomenon. First, the idea of Taiwanese identity experienced a surge in popularity and legitimacy inside Taiwan, specifically when the island's first democratically elected president, Teng-hui Lee (李登輝), took office in 1996 and then when the main opposition party's presidential candidate, Shui-bian Chen (陳水扁), took office from

2000 to 2008. President Chen was Taiwan's first leader unaffiliated with—and indeed opposed to—the KMT, and he effectively ended its dictatorial reign of almost fifty years on the island. Of importance here is the fact that the Taiwanese community in Flushing took pleasure in both Taiwanese-identity promotion and then the liberalization of Taiwanese politics. In this regard, the consumption of Taiwanese cuisine became both a metaphorical and a literal manifestation of these trends. The second reason for this golden age of Flushing's Taiwanese cuisine is that despite China's proclamation of its Policy of Reformation and Opening in 1978, the population of immigrants from Mainland China to the United States remained a fledgling demographic category in the 1980s. In other words, Taiwanese cuisine at that time had not yet encountered fierce competition from any sizable Mainlander-Chinese (i.e., non-Taiwanese) network of Chinese-food businesses.[17]

Facing New Challenges in Flushing

Since the 1980s, Chinese immigrants, legally or illegally, started flooding into the United States to pursue studies in higher education, to make money, to participate in immigrant-investor programs, and perhaps to realize the fabled American dream. According to my interviews with Chenghui Chuang, James Huang, Patrick Huang, Borcheng Hsu, and Mingsen Lu, after the 1980s, the first wave of Chinese immigrants to Flushing were Wenzhou immigrants from Zhejiang Province and later, Chinese immigrants from an array of regions.[18]

Like the preceding Cantonese immigrants who in the nineteenth century had introduced the United States to a variety of Chinese foods (most notably chop suey), Fuzhou immigrants who settled in NYC in the 1990s were known for establishing Chinese groceries and Chinese restaurants.[19] Among the aforementioned Wenzhou immigrants in Flushing were entrepreneurs who, according to Mr. Chuang, opened small groceries in the 1990s but who, in the 2000s, responded to the large number of Wenzhou immigrants settling in Flushing by purchasing supermarkets from earlier Taiwanese owners or by simply buying up real estate and buildings in order to open brand-new supermarkets. Likewise, Wenzhou immigrants bought existing restaurants from their previous Taiwanese owners. Wenzhou immigrants acquired capital for such investments by, for example, amassing monetary donations from weddings. Interestingly, Mr. Chuang described both Fuzhou immigrants and Wenzhou immigrants as being similar to Jewish Americans insofar as many of them have generally proven adept at harnessing their own communities' social networks to mutually assist one another.

According to Mr. Chuang's own experiences, his service as chairman of Flushing's Business Improvement District and his ceaseless promotion of culinary activities in Flushing have prompted many of Flushing's Wenzhou immigrants and many of East Broadway Chinatown's Fuzhou immigrants to invite him to their wedding parties. At these events, Chinese immigrants have not only acquired investment capital by gratefully *receiving* monetary donations in "red envelopes," but have also elevated their social status by publicly *giving* monetary donations with the specific amount announced. Mr. Chuang was surprised to learn that through wedding parties alone, new Chinese immigrants could collect enough money to open an American-Chinese restaurant.[20]

My interviewee Mr. Lu acquired significant experience as the director of the Flushing Chinese Business Association and as an entrepreneur overseeing commercial enterprises based in Flushing. This cumulative experience helped him analyze the differences between Wenzhou immigrants in Flushing and Fuzhou immigrants first in Chinatown's East Broadway area and then in Brooklyn's Eighth Avenue area. In general, entrepreneurial Wenzhou immigrants run supermarkets, engage in real estate, and are skillful at market analysis, whereas Fuzhou immigrants struggling to survive in New York rely heavily on cooperation among family members.[21]

Mr. Chuang has also observed the strategies deployed by Fuzhou and Wenzhou immigrants to run their restaurants and supermarkets. A core strategy of these immigrants has been to engage in price-cutting competition, whose guiding principle is that the lower the price of goods or services, the greater the number of customers. According to Mr. Chuang, however, the "price-cutting competition" strategy, though effective, has had a downside: the strategy might benefit a particular business in Flushing while simultaneously degrading Flushing as a community. In fact, Mr. Chuang argued that price-cutting competition benefits, most of all, individual customers who prefer to consume inexpensive foodstuffs, and he added with a tinge of frustration that the competition had significantly dampened the quality of many businesses, including restaurants, in Flushing.[22]

By the 1990s, the development of Taiwanese restaurants in Flushing was encountering two serious challenges: first, the neighborhood's increasing number of Chinese restaurants serving Cantonese, Fuzhou, and Wenzhou cuisine instead of Taiwanese cuisine; and second, a pronounced shortage of Taiwanese chefs. Indeed, with economic growth and political liberalization taking place in Taiwan during these years, fewer and fewer Taiwanese immigrated to the United States or were willing to stay after arriving. Owners of Taiwanese restaurants became hard-pressed to find skilled chefs from Taiwan and started turning their attention to chefs who came from China. In the absence of a Taiwanese chef, the first choice would be a chef from Fuzhou, since much Taiwanese cuisine originated there. However, because Taiwanese cuisine had come to constitute a regional Chinese cuisine whose evolution rested on a unique multi-faceted mix of Dutch, Han Chinese, colonial Japanese, and KMT dietary traces within different historical contexts, chefs from Mainland China struggled to grasp the essences of Taiwanese cuisine.

Nevertheless, mastering another culture's culinary arts is not impossible: usually all that is needed is a modicum of talent and an investment of time and effort. In the case of Flushing's Taiwanese restaurants, the biggest obstacle was the management of chefs, as noted by Mr. Chuang, who had borne witness to criticisms emanating from other Taiwanese restaurants. Approaches to running these Taiwanese restaurants can be divided into two categories. The first approach is the family style of management, typified by Ku-Shiang and 66 Lu's Seafood. An advantage of the family style of management is that some family members, including the founder and later generations, usually have backgrounds working as chefs, meaning that the family members are familiar with the actual preparation of dishes and simultaneously oversee the business of running the restaurant itself. However, many of these Taiwanese restaurants have had to hire chefs from outside the family, and as Mr. Chuang stressed during my interviews with him, the quality of chefs who came from China was a mix of good and bad.

Indeed, even some chefs skilled at cooking Chinese and Taiwanese cuisines exhibited less than professional behavior while on the clock. Some chefs who were fond of gambling between the lunch and dinner rushes consequently neglected the business of prep and line work. By contrast, some Chinese chefs were attentive to their duties but for various reasons were unable to grasp the subtle differences between Chinese cuisine and Taiwanese cuisine, with the result that customers were distinctly unsatisfied with the given restaurants' offerings.

The second approach to running Flushing's Taiwanese restaurants is the non-family style of management. Taiwanese restaurants employing this approach have included Foliage, run by Lee Mingsen, the Flavor of Chinese, which has played a crucial role in promoting the development of Flushing's Taiwanese cuisine, and Fuhao Seafood Restaurant, Ice over Fire Banquet, and Taipei 101, all run by Mr. Chuang. Unlike restaurants adopting the family style of management, those adopting the non-family style of management have encountered countless problems with their hired chefs.

Mr. Chuang's considerable experience in restaurant management helped him form several preferences regarding chefs' work at Taiwanese restaurants in Flushing. First of all, Mr. Chuang preferred to hire chefs from Taiwan rather than from China, because he deeply believed that managers could more easily communicate with the former than with the latter regarding food preparation. The common cultural backgrounds of Taiwanese managers and Taiwanese chefs made communication a simple affair—certainly much simpler than what Taiwanese managers would generally experience with Chinese chefs, many of whom, according to Mr. Chuang, had grown up during the Cultural Revolution (1966–1976), which had more or less inculcated in them a commitment to class struggle. Put simply, the Cultural Revolution created generations of Chinese who held a sometimes fanatical distrust of employers.[23]

Another matter of concern to Mr. Chuang specifically and to other owners and managers of Flushing's Taiwanese restaurants generally was the tendency of some chefs to use their cooking skills as a bargaining chip when negotiating salaries. These skilled chefs would threaten to work for another Flushing-based restaurant if the ownership or management refused to meet their demands for increased pay. In response, some owners would submit to or compromise with chefs. Owners who rejected outright any salary demands would run the risk of angering the chefs, who might surreptitiously sabotage the restaurant by, for example, preparing excessively salty or otherwise unpalatable dishes. Such tactics had the effect of turning away regular customers. A no less serious form of payback was the effort by some resentful chefs to instigate pay disputes between waiters and owners, and frequently these disputes escalated significantly.[24] According to Mr. Chuang, many Taiwanese restaurants in Flushing have closed their doors and gone out of business because of the deleterious consequences of such labor problems.

In addressing Flushing's dearth of amenable chefs skilled in Taiwanese cuisine, Mr. Chuang, to little avail, frequently petitioned culinary schools in Taiwan to train chefs who would relocate in NYC and work as chefs in Taiwanese restaurants. Though culinary schools in Taiwan were graduating a large number of well-trained chefs, few showed a willingness to come to NYC to work in the field. Mr. Chuang added that, in contrast to governments in Asian countries such as South Korea, Japan, Thailand, and Malaysia, the Taiwanese government had no plans to facilitate the training and relocation overseas of chefs skilled in Taiwanese cuisine.

The Transformation of Taiwanese Restaurants in Flushing

By the 1990s, Chinese immigrants were pouring into Flushing not only from Fuzhou and Wenzhou, but also from northern regions of China such as Greater Beijing and the three northern provinces of Liaoning (遼寧), Jilin (吉林), and Heilongjiang (黑龍江). Taiwanese restaurants in Flushing were encountering fierce competition from Chinese restaurants that had opened for business in response to these immigrants' demand for Chinese, not Taiwanese, food. In addition to this competition, Flushing's Taiwanese contended with unusually daunting difficulties related to the hiring and managing of chefs. Some Taiwanese restaurants would meet the chefs' salary demands to survive in the food industry, whereas other Taiwanese restaurants would experience seemingly endless trouble in search of reliable, long-term chefs—trouble that would often prove terminal for the restaurants. However, when facing the fierce challenges posed by Chinese restaurants, the owners and operators of Flushing's Taiwanese restaurants transformed their businesses along four distinct lines, all in the hope of ensuring smooth, ideal, and solvent business operations.

The first type of transformation resulted in Taiwanese restaurants whose menus incorporated Mainland Chinese cuisine, such as Sichuan. The objective here was to attract customers who were interested in something other than Taiwanese cuisine. By contrast, the second type of transformation resulted in Taiwanese restaurants that emphasized the significance of Taiwanese cuisine. Despite the decline in Taiwanese immigration to Flushing, the owners and managers of these Taiwanese restaurants subscribed to the operating principle that "rare things are precious," and demand for Taiwanese cuisine was, indeed, increasingly rare. The third type of transformation had to do with a handful of restaurants' adoption of mostly Jiangsu–Zhejiang cuisine. The fourth type of transformation resulted in Taiwanese restaurants that featured healthy Taiwanese cuisine: that is, less salt, less oil, and, most prominently, no MSG. In order to realize how Taiwanese restaurants specifically amended their menus to counter new challenges from diverse Chinese restaurants, in the following discussion I will analyze the menus created by Taiwanese restaurants in response to new demands.

The Transformation of Taiwanese Restaurants' Menus

Taiwanese restaurants in 1990s Flushing had to figure out how to survive. To attract more customers from among the neighborhood's Chinese immigrants, Taiwanese restaurants had two choices: promote Taiwanese cuisine or revise the contents of their menus in favor of Mainland Chinese cuisine, which would appeal to Chinese immigrants with little knowledge of or desire for Taiwanese cuisine. In other words, these Taiwanese restaurants, to appeal to a demographically evolving clientele, had to modify their product.

Although not part of the first wave of Taiwanese restaurants to have emerged in Flushing, Ku-Shiang is widely known in the

Taiwanese community for two things: its well-designed signboard, which expresses the previously discussed specific meaning of homesickness, and its menu, which conveys a unique perspective on Taiwanese cuisine. As for the menu, Ku-Shiang sought to appeal to Flushing's Chinese immigrants by revising the menu's cover, inscribed on which are four Chinese characters, "正宗川味," literally meaning "authentic Sichuan flavor." Directly below this declaration are more Chinese characters noting that the restaurant serves Taiwanese cuisine, nutritious vegetable dishes, and a lunch special. Clearly, the declaration of "authentic Sichuan flavor" on the cover of the Ku-Shiang menu strongly suggests that this restaurant has incorporated the dishes of Sichuan cuisine as a selling point capable of drawing in and retaining new customers from China.

Inside the menu, not surprisingly, are many well-known Taiwanese dishes covering soups, appetizers, standard cuisine, house specials, and vegetarian meals. Indeed, because Taiwanese cuisine remains the most significant selling point of Ku-Shiang, the restaurant's menu features a section entitled "Taiwanese Cuisine." In terms of ingredients, the Ku-Shiang menu uses glutinous rice for the preparation of such dishes as "Sweet Rice with Mushroom and Meat," one of the more famous dishes both in southern China and in Taiwan. Particularly in Taiwan, glutinous rice is regarded as a dish signifying the auspiciousness of such celebrated events as childbirth or a couple's engagement. Other dishes in the "Taiwanese Cuisine" section include bouillon noodles with pork, stinky tofu, fried pork rolls, oyster pancakes with egg and vegetables, and steamed squid.[25] The "House Special" section features many typical Taiwanese dishes that emphasize the significance of Taiwanese cuisine. Among these dishes are "Spicy Squid Taiwanese Style" (五柳花枝), "Chicken with Basil in Casserole" (三杯雞), "Squid with Basil in Casserole" (三杯花枝), and "Sautéed Intestine with Ginger" (薑絲炒大腸).

Interestingly, Ku-Shiang's menu also offers Sichuan dishes ranging from appetizers, noodles, pork, beef, and poultry to spicy fish. The menu features many dishes that, though associated with Sichuan, are perhaps not purely Sichuan cuisine: stand-outs include "Spicy Sliced Beef Stomach and Tendon" (夫妻肺片), "Wonton Sichuan Style" (紅油抄手), "Dan Dan Noodle" (擔擔麵), "Double Sautéed Pork"

(回鍋肉), and "Sliced Beef in Fresh Hot Pepper" (水煮牛). Another section in Ku-Shiang's menu is entitled "Sichuan-style Rice with Meat and Vegetables," offering convenient meals for customers seeking to dine in or to carry out. In order to appeal to potential Chinese customers, Ku-Shiang has strategically revised its menu. According to my interview with Mr. Chuang, amending the contents of menus to attract more customers has been a prevalent trend in Flushing's Taiwanese restaurants. Reflecting this trend is the fact that almost one-third of Ku-Shiang's dishes are prepared in the Sichuan style.

Like Ku-Shiang, 66 Lu's Seafood is another celebrated Taiwanese restaurant in Flushing. Having opened on August 15, 1992, the restaurant encountered fierce competition from the neighborhood's Chinese restaurants. However, unlike Ku-Shiang, 66 Lu's Seafood has maintained a deep tradition of Taiwanese cuisine: in other words, the restaurant has refrained from adopting menu changes that would meet the demands of Flushing's growing Chinese population for Chinese cuisine. Inside the menu, a brief glance at the list of snacks reveals a set of Chinese characters in traditional Chinese referring to "Ancient Tainan Style Snack" (台南古都風味小吃) followed by the names of each snack. Almost all of these items are staples at restaurants in Taiwan.[26]

The range of these snacks is broad, featuring many famous Taiwanese local foods including "Minced Pork on Rice with Egg" (魯肉飯), "Steamed Sweet Rice" (筒仔米糕), "Taiwanese Hamburger" (割包), "Pork Roll" (雞卷), "Stinky Tofu" (臭豆腐), "Oyster Pancake with Eggs" (蚵仔煎), "Sweet Rice Sausage" (糯米大腸), "Meat Ball" (肉圓), and "Taiwanese Sausage (香腸)."[27] In Flushing, these snacks reflect Taiwanese heritage for the restaurant's Taiwanese customers but, for non-Taiwanese customers, may have too strong a flavor. In other words, the "Ancient Tainan Style Snack" section of the menu at 66 Lu's Seafood is apparently designed to appeal to Taiwanese customers.

The menu also covers Cold Appetizers, the Chef's Special, Lu's Special, Homemade Noodles, Special Soups, and Special Rice Dishes, many of which showcase the culinary culture of Taiwan. Under the category of Cold Appetizers, a dish called "Taiwanese Pork Leg" (萬巒豬腳) is closely associated with auspiciousness in Taiwanese culture.[28] For many Taiwanese, Taiwanese pork legs, more commonly known as Wangluan pork legs in Taiwan, refer not only to the location of Wangluan, which is a Hakka village in Taiwan renowned for its pig-feeding practices and pig-hoof production, but also to Chiang Chiang-kuo (蔣經國, 1910–1988), whose father, Chiang Kai-shek, exercised authoritarian rule over Taiwan between 1950 and 1975. While himself president of Taiwan in 1981, Chiang Chiang-kuo visited a restaurant named Haihong (海鴻飯店) in Wangluan Village and took a photo with the establishment's owner. This photo, after countless media showings in newspapers, magazines, and on television, actually had the effect of promoting Taiwanese pork legs.[29]

Among the special dishes on the menu at 66 Lu's Seafood are several reflective of Hakka cuisine. As the second largest ethnic group in Taiwan (the largest ethnic group is associated with Fujian immigration), Hakka Taiwanese immigrated to Taiwan during the late seventeenth century, after the Fujian immigration, which itself took place during the early seventeenth century. The Hakka brought to Taiwan their own distinct cultural heritage. Known for their assiduousness and frugal spirit, the Hakka people have reflected these characteristics in their preparation of culinary dishes. In the Qing era, Hakka Taiwanese spent much time performing agricultural labor: planting rice, tending crops, and preparing agricultural products. This labor required abundant energy day after day. Thus, the Hakka people relied heavily on sauces (soy sauce, wine, ginger, and sesame oil), which would lend a pronounced, appealing flavor to otherwise bland ingredients like rice, thus promoting more consumption of rice, which translated into more nutrients for the body. Over time, Hakka cuisine has preserved this characteristically heavy, rich flavor.

Many dishes on the menu at 66 Lu's Seafood are closely associated with such Hakka culinary characteristics. Examples of these dishes are "Ginger Vegetarian Chicken" (素三杯雞), "Eggplant with Basil" (客家茄子), "Pork and Dried Bean Curd in Hakka Style" (客家小炒), "Chicken with Ginger and Basil" (三杯雞), and "Ginger Basil with Squid" (三杯小卷). The dishes share not only a prominent richness of flavor but also underlying cooking methods and ingredients. For example, to prepare these dishes, one typically uses soy sauce, ginger, garlic, and sesame oil as basic seasonings and then incorporates them into chicken, vegetables, clams, and squid during the cooking stage of the preparation. Before serving the dishes to customers, one adds basil to generate even more potent savory flavor. These ingredients yield the characteristically rich flavors that nicely accompany rice and that, not surprisingly, are quite popular among Hakka people.

The rest of the dishes on the menu at 66 Lu's Seafood are diverse and include many dishes from other Chinese regional cuisines, such as Sichuan. However, unlike Ku-Shiang, which emphasizes Sichuan cuisine both on the menu's cover and in the menu's description of the dishes, 66 Lu's Seafood restaurant strongly identifies itself as an authentic Taiwanese-cuisine restaurant by serving many Fujian- and Hakka-style dishes, as well as by creating a specific category of appetizers entitled "Ancient Tainan Style Snack," all of which give expression to the rich characteristics of Taiwanese cuisine.

Located in downtown Flushing and owned by the previously mentioned Chien-hong Lin, No. 1 East Restaurant closed its doors to business in 2015. Lin belongs to a segment of the Taiwanese population that settled in Taiwan in the late 1940s and early 1950s, after the Fujian and Hakka segments of the Taiwanese population had established themselves there.[30] Lin's Taiwanese demographic group belongs to the much wider demographic group known as *waishengren* (外省人); that is, Chinese Mainlanders. In present-day Taiwan, *waishengren* comprise one of the four basic ethnic groups.[31] Thus, I situate No. 1 East Restaurant under the category of Taiwanese restaurants because the establishment served a particular, though historically recent, component of Taiwanese cuisine: Taiwanese "Chinese Mainlander" cuisine.

Interestingly, compared with 66 Lu's Seafood and Ku-Shiang, No. 1 East Restaurant suffered little from the challenges posed by the growing number of nearby Chinese restaurants. This resiliency was due largely to No. 1 East Restaurant's cuisine, which was rooted in regional Chinese cuisines and was easily accepted by Flushing's new Chinese immigrants. The content of No. 1 East Restaurant's menu epitomizes Taiwan's "Chinese Mainlander" cuisine in Flushing and deserves a detailed examination, particularly in comparison to other ethnic-Taiwanese cuisine in Flushing.

No. 1 East Restaurant's menu differed from the menus of 66 Lu's Seafood and Ku-Shiang in terms of its representation of Taiwanese cuisine. Interestingly, neither the cover of No. 1 East Restaurant's menu nor the menu's content suggested any close affinity with Fujian Taiwanese cuisine or Hakka Taiwanese cuisine. In terms of dietary principles, Fujian and Hakka Taiwanese cuisines differ from Taiwan's "Chinese Mainlander" cuisine, even though all of them play one role or another in Taiwanese cuisine as a whole. Unlike both Fujian Taiwanese cuisine and Hakka Taiwanese cuisine, which have long emphasized seafood, glutinous rice, bouillon, and rice flavors derived from southern China's culinary heritage, the cuisine that accompanied the Chinese Mainlanders to Taiwan was as diverse as the regional cuisine in China itself. The Mainlanders hailed from multiple provinces, the four most prominent being Zhejiang, Jiangsu, Shandong, and Sichuan. Before Chinese Mainlanders' immigration to Taiwan, cuisine there rested largely on the *fan-cai* principle (see endnote 25), whereas after 1950, flour-based foodstuffs gained prominence in Taiwan, enriching the population's consumption of food.

No. 1 East Restaurant offered customers a host of dishes found at neither 66 Lu's Seafood nor Ku-Shiang. A prominent example was No. 1 East Restaurant's Chinese-style breakfasts, which included salty and sweet soybean milk, toasted sesame cakes, deep-fried cruller, glutinous rice rolls, fried buns with chives and eggs, steamed buns with meat balls, fried pork Shanghai cakes, and Shanghai-style wonton soup.[32] It is difficult to judge precisely these breakfast items' geographical origin in China, but they more or less combine the essences of breakfast styles across China. The most prominent ingredients in these items are flour, wheat, barley, and soybean, all of which are rarely used by Fujian Taiwanese and Hakka Taiwanese for the preparation of breakfasts.[33] Apparently, the Chinese-style breakfasts at No. 1 East Restaurant were one of its major selling points for both Taiwanese and Chinese customers.

The menu contained a "Snacks" section. The term "snacks" can be misleading, as each item in the section could constitute a meal in itself: take, for example, steamed spinach dumplings, soup noodles with spicy braised beef, soup noodles with pork chop, fried rice, rice noodles, and sautéed rice cakes.[34] Among these snacks, soup noodles with spicy braised beef (otherwise known as beef noodles soup) is worth mentioning for it is one of the most popular foods in Taiwan. According to Taiwan historian Yaodong Lu (逯耀東), the Taiwanese version of beef noodles soup (typically centered on beef braised in a soy-sauce mixture) originated in Gangshan (岡山), a district located in Kaohsiung City and the site of Taiwan's Air Force Academy. For this reason, many military dependents' villages can be found in Gangshan District.[35] An accurate and empirically verifiable explanation of how and why beef noodles soup was created in Gangshan District remains sorely lacking, and future research in Taiwanese food studies would do well to fill in this gap. Nevertheless, current research has suggested that KMT veterans created beef noodles soup on the basis of a prepared ingredient known as "broad bean paste with chili" (辣豆瓣). Essential in the preparation of Sichuan beef noodle soup, this chili paste is a sauce that KMT veterans, according to Yaodong Lu's account, combined with beef local to the Gangshan area. Eventually this recipe spread to other areas in Taiwan. Though unconfirmed, this account is quite reasonable because before 1950, beef dishes were rare in Taiwan, a region where both ethnic-Fujian Taiwanese and ethnic-Hakka Taiwanese worked alongside oxen on farms and felt deep sympathy for the animal. In fact, beef dishes were rarely seen on Taiwanese tables until the KMT's mass withdrawal to Taiwan. Today, beef dishes, especially beef noodles soup, are popular throughout the island, and the soup dish can be ordered at five-star restaurants as well as from ordinary street-food vendors. Not surprisingly, then, beef noodles soup is a mainstay item at each Taiwanese restaurant in Flushing, with some of these restaurants making it their signature dish.

In the menu section entitled "Special Cold Dishes," No. 1 East Restaurant presented a slew of dishes prepared in Shanghai styles.[36] Among these dishes were "Chicken Marinated in Wine" (醉雞), "Black Mushroom with Gluten Puffs" (烤麩), "Shredded Jelly Fish in Garlic Sauce" (海蜇皮), "Smoked Fish Fillet" (燻魚), and "Light Salt Duck" (鹹水鴨).[37] The following clues make it easy to ascertain that these dishes derive from the Shanghai area. First, Shanghai is close to the ancient city Shaoxing (紹興), known for its historical production of a specific wine called Shaoxing rice wine (紹興酒), which led to the incorporation of wine into dishes like chicken marinated in wine. Most aspects of Shanghai cuisine reflect dietary characteristics from the adjacent areas and cities, such as Suzhou, Hangzhou, Shaoxing, and Yangzhou. Second, compared with other regional cuisines in China, Shanghai cuisine has been celebrated for its preparation of seafood, which reflects the location not only of Shanghai but also of adjacent cities in the lower Yangtze River region, historically an abundant source of seafood, whether of the freshwater or saltwater variety.[38]

Because we know that Jiangsu and Zhejiang cuisines are known for their seafood dishes, it is not surprising to see that the seafood section in No. 1 East Restaurant's menu was the dominant section. The menu listed such Jiangsu and Zhejiang items as "Sautéed Shrimp with Wine Sauce" (清炒蝦仁), "Steamed Shrimp with Fresh Garlic" (清蒸蒜蓉蝦), "Any Styles Crabs" (各式螃蟹), "Sea Cucumber with Shrimp Eggs" (蝦子大烏參), "Fish in Vinegar Sauce" (西湖醋魚), and "Sweet and Sour Yellow Fish" (糖醋黃魚).[39] Crabs, shrimp, sea cucumbers, large yellow croakers, and small yellow croakers all can be caught on the coastlines of Jiangsu and Zhejiang Provinces, where people have acquired an appreciation of seafood dishes. This heritage of seafood preparation and consumption came to Taiwan with the KMT's exodus from Mainland China and then was disseminated to overseas Chinese communities. No. 1 East Restaurant's Taiwanese "Mainland Chinese" cuisine is thus an important category of Taiwanese cuisine in Flushing.

When encountering the commercial challenges of nearby Chinese restaurants, some Taiwanese restaurants in Flushing have adopted a novel strategy: rather than revise their menu's content to attract Chinese-immigrant customers, these restaurants have promoted healthy eating. A key example of this trend is the Taiwanese restaurant known as OK Ryan (福冕台菜). Compared with the three previously discussed restaurant types specializing in variations of Taiwanese cuisine, OK Ryan boasts several innovations in terms of the menu's design and its promotion of healthy food choices. Appearing on the cover of the menu are the four Chinese characters "福冕台菜," meaning Fu-Mian Taiwanese Cuisine. This shares space with the ardent declaration that the restaurant's dishes contain "NO MSG" (monosodium glutamate), which originated in Japan, but which became very popular among the Chinese, who tend to prefer "pan-fried" (i.e., stir-fried) cooking in which MSG enhances the flavor. The downside to MSG is that people regard it as unhealthy, even though researchers have uncovered no definitive proof to this effect. In this era of healthy dining, a growing number of Asian restaurants boldly pronounce their "no MSG" policy on menus.

Unlike the menus of the other three Taiwanese restaurants discussed here, OK Ryan's menu features a "Beverage" section. It passes over carbonated beverages such as Coca-Cola and Pepsi for "Vital Juice" (freshly squeezed juice) and fresh bubble milk tea. The former beverage is popular in Taiwan among health-conscious people, whereas the latter beverage, which admittedly is tastier than it is healthy, remains one of the most famous beverages to hail from Taiwan.

OK Ryan's menu denotes Taiwanese dishes (as distinct from non-Taiwanese dishes) by placing a little "thumps up" icon in front of those items associated with the island's cuisine. The icon impresses upon customers the dishes that are, so to speak, "hometown cooking." Examples of these menu items are "Braised Pork Rice" (魯肉飯), "Stew Chicken with Rice Wine" (燒酒雞), "Sesame Oil Chicken" (麻油雞), "Taiwanese 3 Cup Chicken" (三杯雞), "Taiwanese Style Salt and Pepper Chicken" (鹽酥雞), "Hakka Style Stir Fry" (客家小炒), "Spicy Stinky Hot Pot" (麻辣臭臭鍋), "Taiwanese Thin Rice Noodle" (台式炒米粉), "Taiwanese Style Lo Mein" (台式炒油麵), and "Beef Stew Noodle Soup" (紅燒牛肉麵).

Some of these dishes are common in Taiwanese restaurants, but others are quite unusual and are nowhere to be seen on the previous three menus discussed here. Perhaps most interesting among these unique dishes is the "Mini Hot Pot." Actually, the consumption of hot pots (火鍋) is nothing new to the Chinese, who have long appreciated the relative ease of placing myriad ingredients into a single pot along with a sauce for both the cooking and serving stages. However, the mini hot pot first emerged not in China but in Japan. Perhaps Japanese people observed Chinese people's consumption of hot-pot dishes in China during Japan's military occupation of parts of Mainland China in the late-nineteenth century and the first half of the twentieth century, bringing the idea of the hot-pot dish back to Japan. Once there, the dish became part of Japanese culinary culture while undergoing an evolution of sorts. Eventually, the mini hot pot was born, reflective of both a Chinese heritage and Japanese modifications.

The reason underlying Japanese people's preference for the mini hot pot, however, remains an unexplored topic but might have something to do with the Meiji Restoration's emphasis on individuality, efficiency, and hygiene as promoted by Western culture. Thus, unlike the Chinese, who generally preferred to consume a hot-pot dish while seated at a circular table and chatting for a long time, post–Meiji Restoration Japanese generally preferred individual dining to group dining, and presumably the mini hot pot emerged under these circumstances. Moreover, Taiwan was a colony of Japan (1895–1945) during this time period, and thus there should be little surprise that the Taiwanese likely duplicated the Japanese version of the Chinese hot pot.

The case of OK Ryan reveals an interesting fact: the concept of healthy dining (no MSG, less salt, and less oil) has become popular with restaurant-goers who frequent Taiwanese restaurants in NYC, including Flushing. Clearly, customers, owners, and managers are increasingly attracted to healthful eating, and OK Ryan is a pioneer in shaping the dishes that Taiwanese and Chinese restaurants serve in Flushing.

When Taiwanese Cuisine Encounters Chinese Cuisine in Flushing

If we were to take a walk in Flushing today, we would feel as though we were strolling along a city street in China, with a seemingly endless stream of distinctly phenotypical Chinese people passing by us, the sounds of local Chinese dialects crowding our ears, business signboards featuring Chinese characters instead of English lettering, and of course, restaurants selling different sorts of Chinese food. Indeed, Flushing, home to immigrants from Taiwan and China, has developed into the biggest Chinatown in the northeastern United States. In Flushing, immigrants have come and gone, but their culinary heritages have left a lasting mark. Today we can see an almost complete accounting of China's regional cuisines here, including Taiwanese, Hong Kong, Cantonese, Sichuan, Jiangsu-Zhejiang (i.e., Shanghai), northeastern Chinese, Hunan, Shandong, Fuzhou, and even Chinese-Muslim (Uyghur) cuisine.

In this study, I have identified the vicissitudes of Taiwanese restaurant cuisine in Flushing from the 1970s to the 2010s by conducting interviews with prominent restaurateurs (Chenghui Chuang, Patrick Huang, Borcheng Hsu, Mingsen Lu, James Huang, Sam Lin, Cheng San Lee, James C. Shau, and Suqing Yang) and by analyzing the menus of four Taiwanese restaurants (Ku-Shiang, 66 Lu's Seafood, No. 1 East Restaurant, and OK Ryan). On the whole during this period, Flushing's Taiwanese restaurant cuisine experienced an unmistakable rise and fall in popularity.

With the decline of Taiwanese immigration to the United States since the 1990s and with many ethnic-Taiwanese residents of Flushing moving out of the downtown area, the task of running a restaurant that offers only Taiwanese cuisine has become increasingly difficult. Many Taiwanese restaurants in Flushing have closed and many Chinese restaurants specializing in non-Taiwanese cuisine have been flourishing. Endeavoring to survive in the face of fierce competition from nearby Chinese restaurants, some of Flushing's remaining Taiwanese restaurants have struggled with the additional problem of how to hire and retain conscientious chefs. Indeed, as Mr. Chuang stressed frequently in my interviews with him, the business of chef-recruitment has been an extremely pesky problem. The simple fact is that fewer and fewer Taiwanese chefs are available and willing to work at restaurants in Flushing.

Flushing's Taiwanese restaurants have deployed various marketing strategies to meet the challenges posed by nearby Chinese restaurants. For example, Ku-Shiang added to its menu's cover the declaration "Authentic Sichuan Cuisine," a direct approach, if there ever was one, to winning over customers interested in Sichuan cuisine. Several have incorporated popular non-Taiwanese Chinese dishes, essentially giving customers, including the growing number of customers from Mainland China, not only more choices but also choices that are more in keeping with Mainland Chinese people's cultural and culinary backgrounds.

Another of Flushing's surviving Taiwanese restaurants, 66 Lu's Seafood, has preserved its adherence to authentically Taiwanese cuisine. Despite offering some famous non-Taiwanese Chinese dishes, the menu privileges the culture of Taiwanese cuisine, which is itself the foundation of a certain market strategy: a restaurant that remains faithful to a menu of almost uniquely Taiwanese cuisine can stand out from Flushing's many competitors that offer dishes reflective of a broad range of Chinese cuisines.

No. 1 East Restaurant represents a specific component of Taiwanese cuisine: Taiwan's "Chinese Mainlander" cuisine which, in Flushing, caters to the tastes of the neighborhood's Chinese Mainlanders who came to Flushing not from Mainland China but from Taiwan. Flushing's restaurants that serve Taiwanese "Mainland Chinese" cuisine have a built-in marketing strength: they can appeal to Flushing's rapidly growing population of immigrants from Mainland China because these immigrants are familiar with the restaurants' cuisine. Thus, the restaurants' owners need not adapt their menus and business strategies. As for No. 1 East Restaurant, it is no longer in operation: its doors closed in 2015 mainly because its owner had reached the age of retirement.

OK Ryan is a Taiwanese restaurant new to the fierce competition among Chinese restaurants in Flushing. Recently, OK Ryan has been devoting itself to healthy Taiwanese dishes both by banning MSG from dishes and by selling well-known Taiwanese health beverages, as exemplified in the menu's offering of "Vital Juice." Innovation in the direction of physical health and popular contemporary Taiwanese restaurant items has helped OK Ryan appeal to a discerning population of prospective customers, but the restaurant never forgets to cook up the tasty foods one would expect from an esteemed Taiwanese eatery.

According to my interviews with some of Flushing's ethnic-Taiwanese community leaders who have witnessed the vicissitudes of Taiwanese cuisine there since the 1990s, the cuisine's fusion principle has threatened the cuisine's survival. As I stressed earlier, Taiwanese cuisine is a historical combination of Fujian, Hakka, Japanese, Chinese Mainlander, and other cuisines. Whether pan-fried or steamed, Taiwanese cuisine is known for its rice-made foodstuffs, noodles, snacks, pickled food, meat products, and seafood. My point is this: fusion cooking, despite being one of the selling points of Taiwanese cuisine, is also a drawback because it offers no consistent culinary theme that can serve as a strong selling point for diners interested in a particular Chinese cuisine. For example, if ethnic-Chinese customers in Flushing intend to consume seafood, they would likely go to Cantonese and Hong Kong–style restaurants, which are famous for seafood dishes suitable for weddings and other celebratory occasions. If these customers intend to consume flour-based cuisine, they would go to northern Chinese restaurants for Shandong cuisine rather than frequent Taiwanese restaurants. If customers are in the mood for spicy Chinese cuisine, they would likely venture to Sichuan and Hunan Chinese restaurants, not Taiwanese restaurants—not even one like Ku-Shiang, which sells Sichuan dishes that, though impressive, would fail to meet a purist's criteria for authenticity. Under these circumstances, Taiwanese restaurants in Flushing still have their work cut out for them: they must identify, explore, and cultivate competitive ways to survive economically. The four Taiwanese restaurants I have discussed in this essay have embraced these market challenges and have made positive choices along the way.

From the 1970s to the present, Taiwanese restaurant cuisine in NYC's Flushing neighborhood went from a fledgling marketplace presence, to achieving a golden age, to struggling for economic survival. In recent years, restaurants selling authentic non-Taiwanese Chinese cuisine have opened in Flushing, bringing customers more choices for dining out and drawing quite a few of these customers away from Taiwanese restaurants. Moreover, a decline in Taiwanese immigration to New York since the 1990s has resulted in fewer chefs skilled at cooking Taiwanese cuisine. But perhaps the greatest challenge is that Taiwanese cuisine is not simply a regional cuisine: it is a product of the culinary heritages of different historical periods. The culinary hybridity of Taiwanese cuisine prevents Taiwanese restaurants from establishing a powerful selling point in NYC these days, especially in Flushing, because both Chinese and non-Chinese customers seeking "authentic" cuisine have trouble perceiving the restaurants as pure and, thus, as attractive or professionally operated. For this reason, many Taiwanese-associated restaurants have embraced the twin pillars of simplification and practicality. Consider Sam Lin's Coco Bubble Tea and Iris Bakery and James Huang's famed Vivi Bubble Tea and Chi-Ken Taiwanese Popcorn Chicken Store. These eateries focus on specific food and beverage items that, while conveying images of Taiwan, shy away from comprehensive Taiwanese cuisine. This new breed of specialty Taiwanese restaurants, in fact, rejects *comprehensively Taiwanese* cuisine in favor of *niche Taiwanese foods and beverages* associated with the island's culinary culture. Almost all of my interviewees stressed the point that when encountering the challenges of Chinese immigration, Taiwanese restaurants interested in successfully selling Taiwanese cuisine in NYC must take advantage of Taiwan's unique historical gastronomical heritage by focusing only on a very few specific culinary factors, such as Taiwanese beef noodles, Taiwanese-style boxed meals, and Taiwanese street food. Only these refined and simplified selling points can attract customers, whether in Flushing or other NYC neighborhoods.

CHAPTER 7

Chop Suey

A Personal Legacy of Cantonese Chinatown Cuisine

RAYMOND DOUGLAS CHONG

Chop suey—the Cantonese cuisine that captivated the palate of Americans since the Gold Rush—is part of the forgotten legacy of the early immigrants from China to "Gold Mountain," California. Chop suey is an American dish meaning "little bits." It reached its zenith between 1896 and 1965 when at chop suey joints in Chinatowns and urban downtowns, Americans casually glimpsed the exotic world of China—the Middle Kingdom—as neon chop suey signs brightly lit ethnic neighborhoods.[1] As this personal reflection will convey, for the early Cantonese, chop suey was a cherished fragment of their cultural fabric as pioneers on Gold Mountain. In America, my family's (Zhang and Yue) ties to chop suey stretches from 1917 to 2006, and extends geographically from Central Square in Cambridge, Massachusetts, across the country to San Francisco's Chinatown, and then down the West Coast to Los Angeles's Little Tokyo and Santa Barbara's Chinatown.

During the nineteenth century, Chinese sojourners immigrated to the United States mostly as miners, laborers, and farmers, and to escape a chaotic litany of disasters and wars. Pioneers from the Siyi (Wuyi) region of Kwangtung (Guangdong) came from four counties in the Pearl River delta—Toishan (Taishan), Hoyping (Kaiping), Yanping (Enping), and Sunwui (Xinhui)—near the South China Sea. In 1849, the first waves of Chinese pioneers arrived at "Gold Mountain," California, the site of the Gold Rush, including Cuen Zan Chung

(Zhang Chun Zan), my great grandfather. The second wave occurred from 1865 to 1869, mostly to labor on the Transcontinental Railroad, from American River in California, through the Sierra Nevada, to Promontory Point in Utah. This wave of immigrants included Bein Yiu Chung (Zhang Bin Yao), my great, great grandfather.

Chinese immigrants brought their native foods; in San Francisco and beyond, restaurants flourished in Chinatowns, and Chinese enclaves and ghettos grew due to rampant racial discrimination.[2] Cantonese (Yue), one of the most famous of the Eight Culinary Traditions of Chinese cuisine, was brought by immigrants to the United States, and this culinary landscape also came to include Sichuan (Chun), Shandong (Lu), Fujian (Min), Jiangsu (Su), Hunan (Xiang), Anhui (Hui), and Zhejiang (Zhe) cuisines. Cantonese, however, is arguably the most refined and celebrated cosmopolitan cuisine of China, and involves shallow frying, stir frying, deep frying, sautéing, braising, steaming, and roasting. The flavors are well balanced with minimal spices and herbs. Subtle, simple dishes with natural and clear flavors, lightly infused with garlic, ginger, and scallion, with seasonings of soy sauce and other sauces and pastes, are the hallmarks of this cuisine. Roasting meats is popular, as are delicately tender and slightly sweet flavors. Popular sauces include hoisin, oyster, plum, and sweet-and-sour. Chop suey, a dish made up of meats (chicken, fish, beef, and pork), eggs, and vegetables (bean sprouts, cabbage, celery, onion) mixed in a starchy sauce, grew out of this Chinese culinary tradition.[3] It is typically served with steamed rice or fried mein, which conformed well to the palate of nineteenth-century America, with its European sensibility.

Due to widespread racism, including the infamous Chinese Exclusion Act of 1882, Chinese men were trapped in Chinatowns across America without their wives and children—a grim bachelors' society. One means of survival was to turn the chop suey joints they had established to feed American miners and other laborers into full-fledged businesses so they could acquire coveted merchant status. In these restaurants, the Chinese savored their Cantonese dishes, and adapted them to the American market. Chinese restaurants began to dot downtown streetscapes as Americans "slowly and eagerly" consumed Cantonese dishes.[4] Americans were mainly lured by the exotic flavors, generous portions, and cheap prices. Restaurant cooks used fresh produce from Chinese farmers and fishermen, as well as preserved Chinese ingredients. Chop suey became so popular that urban legends even began to grow about its origins. The most notable legend allegedly occurred in 1896, during the state visit of Hung-chang Li (Li Hongzhang), Viceroy of Liangguang (provinces of Guangdong and Guangxi) of the Qing dynasty, to America. Shrewd Chinatown entrepreneurs supposedly served the viceroy chop suey and used the trip to promote their cuisine, leading to the "chop suey craze" that swept America in the early twentieth century.[5]

Chop Suey Enters Mainstream America

In New York and other cities, chop suey jazz restaurants and nightclubs became part of the urban scene of the Roaring Twenties. In 1923, Shanghai Low in San Francisco's Chinatown, with its hardwood dance floor and orchestra, offered chop suey and other Cantonese-style dishes. On December 22, 1939, the golden age of swanky Chinese nightclubs began with Charlie Low's Forbidden City near Chinatown, with its dining, drinking, dancing, and erotic entertainment. Inside such chop suey joints, Cantonese entrepreneurs furnished interiors to reflect the exotic Orient and to captivate the senses of Americans, and they became quite successful at it.[6]

During the 1920s and 1930s, newspaper and magazine cooking columns with chop suey recipes became the fashion, as did Chinese cookbooks. The first, *Chinese Cookery in the Home Kitchen* by Jessie Louise Nolton, was published in 1911. However, it was Mei-Mei Ling's *Chop Suey: A Collection of Simplified Chinese Recipes Adopted for the American Home* (1953) that introduced chop suey cooking to middle-class America. In her work, she described the advent of Cantonese cuisine via sojourners from the Siyi region of Guangdong. Her recipes presented cooking techniques and food ingredients to the American "housewife," and gave general directions for preparing, cooking, and serving while using fresh vegetables, especially scallion and ginger. Meats and vegetables, she advised, should be fried quickly and then combined with various sauces. Techniques included barbecuing, braising, deep fat frying, dicing, kneading, marinating, mincing, pan frying, parboiling, roasting, sautéing, simmering, and steaming. Essential ingredients were soy sauce, peanut oil, cornstarch, and bouillon cubes, and her menus were geared towards American eating patterns of the era (dinner, luncheon, early supper, and late supper).[7]

Around the same time, in 1947, Jeno Paulicilli, the "King of Frozen Food," also helped mainstream Chinese food in America. That year, the Italian American established Chun King, a line of chop suey dishes in cans and frozen packages, mostly using recipes with bean sprouts, celery, and Italian herb mixtures. With Stan Freberg, a radio comedian, he sponsored "Chun King Chow Mein Hour" to celebrate Chinese New Year. The Chun King brand was phased out in 1995, when bought out by ConAgra; however, its cultural impact is immeasurable. La Choy, another brand of canned and packaged Chinese food, which included a chop suey dish, was also instrumental to the mainstreaming of this cuisine. In 1922, Ilhan New, who was Korean, and Wally Smith began selling canned bean sprouts. They sold their products to middle America while also promoting the La Choy book of Chinese Recipes, which grew into a major industry. Their famous slogan was "La Choy makes Chinese food swing American," and La Choy successfully continues to sell Chinese food ingredients today.[8]

Chop Suey and My Family (Zhang and Yue)

The culinary legacy of chop suey in America has waned and faded with the onslaught of other Chinese cuisines, especially since the Immigration and Nationality Act of 1965, when Chinese from other regions began to immigrate to America. The ubiquitous Panda Express Chinese Kitchen and P.F. Chang's China Bistro now thickly dot the downtowns and shopping centers of America, beyond Chinatown, and beyond Cantonese-style cuisine, but for me, chop suey has never lost its personal and cultural significance.[9]

My Zhang and Yue forefathers in America hailed from Kaiping in the Guangdong province, and immigrated during the California Gold Rush and the building of the Transcontinental Railroad. Between 1917 and 2006, many made their living in the chop suey trade in Boston, Cambridge, San Francisco, Los Angeles, and Santa Barbara. Moi Chung (Zhang Xi Shou), my grandfather, who arrived in San

Francisco in 1912, moved to Cambridge, Massachusetts, in 1917 to serve as a manager at the Imperial Restaurant, which was along the Charles River between the Massachusetts Institute of Technology and Harvard University. James Ott had opened the Imperial Restaurant in 1915 as an elegant venue for the finest Chinese cuisine, with service from 11:00 a.m. to 12:00 a.m. Moi Chung's father, Pui Lan Chung (Zhang Pei Lan), my great grandfather, who arrived in Boston around 1892, was a silent partner.

After he managed to raise $500, Moi Chung became partner and manager of the Royal Restaurant at 19 Harrison Avenue/1 Oxford Place in Boston's Chinatown, between Quong Shue Lung Company (a grocery store) and a noodle company. Royal Restaurant opened with $15,490 in capital, raised from forty-one silent and five active partners. Thus, it was a true community venture, like many immigrant restaurants in that time period. Within the brownstone that housed the restaurant, they seated 100 patrons and served American and Chinese food, with $6,000 in monthly receipts, for which Chung earned $90 a month. Boston's Chinatown was the center of the Chinese community in New England, and amidst laundries, restaurants, and stores, a bachelor society of men engaged in vices at gambling halls, opium dens, and brothels. Tong Wars (i.e., gang wars) between the On Leong Tong and Hip Song Tong factions were also fought on the streets and alleys of Boston's Chinatown during this era.

In 1923, Moi Chung became a partner in the Imperial Restaurant for $700. This restaurant seated 170 customers in two dining rooms and a cellar for high-end dining in the Block Building. The Imperial Restaurant started out with $13,000, raised from thirty-three silent and seven active partners. It served Chinese and American dishes, especially chop suey, with $4,000 in monthly sales, for which Chung earned $100 a month as manager. The Imperial Restaurant was widely advertised in the *Cambridge Sentinel* and *The Chinese Students Monthly*, a nationally-distributed magazine for Chinese university students in the United States, and became a favorite locale for those studying in the Boston-Cambridge area.

Gim Suey Chong (Zhang Bao Shen), my father, arrived in Boston in 1932. After World War II, he became a partner (1946–1950) of Eddie Pond's Kubla Khan Theater Restaurant. A nightclub and bar which served Cantonese-style Chinese and American dishes, it was located at the entrance of San Francisco's Chinatown. The Kubla Khan occupied the Dong Toy Building, which had previously housed the Mandarin Café, with its Peking Forbidden City décor, which went out of business during the Great Depression. During the golden age of Chinese nightclubs, hundreds flocked to Kubla Khan and other establishments. San Francisco's Chinatown became the largest Chinese settlement in the United States since days of California Gold Rush.[10]

Their signature dish was the Kubla Khan De Luxe. It came with various relishes, egg flower soup, almond chicken, fried prawns, egg foo young, chicken chow mein, and steamed rice. Desserts included Chinese candies and fortune cake or sesame cookies, accompanied by tea or coffee. The price was three dollars. Single entrees included chop suey, chow mein, fried rice, chow yuke, and wonton. Kubla Khan's special chop suey included boneless chicken, white mushrooms, water chestnuts, bamboo shoots, vegetables, bean sprouts, with sesame and the chef's special sauce. Kubla Khan's chow mein was comprised of vegetables, water chestnuts, lotus seeds, white mushrooms, bamboo shoots, finely-sliced chicken, chopped almonds, fried noodles, and the chef's special sauce. Egg foo young was prepared with bamboo shoots, water chestnuts, white mushrooms, green onions, bean sprouts, and eggs, while chow yuke included water chestnuts with meat sauce. The fried rice contained either chicken, barbecued pork, or crab or shrimp, and the wonton was filled with chicken. Kubla Khan also offered a fine assortment of imported and domestic beverages, including champagne, red and white wine, beer, mixed drinks, after-dinner rum, Scotch whisky, bourbon whiskey, Irish whiskey, gin, and liqueur to whet the appetites of its patrons.

The menu cover was colorful, with a giant devilish Kubla Khan positioned in a fierce stance. The dragon and linear decorative motif on the top and bottom edges were stereotypical. Kubla Khan's history, on the last page of the menu, was told in an overly dramatic style, for entertainment. In the kitchen, a Cantonese cook prepared chop suey dishes, and after dinner, patrons danced, couples held each other tightly in intimate embraces, and Bill Oetke and his Rumberos Latin band played nightly with loud percussion instruments. Latin music was in vogue, and the dancers heard mambo from Cuba. Eddie Pond played with the Latin band and was dubbed the Chinese Demon of the Maracas. Chinatown nightlife catered to the vaudeville and burlesque sensibilities of Americans, and Kubla Khan did three shows a night. Ivan Paul, the Nite Club Editor of the *San Francisco Examiner* wrote: "No need to travel to China for the spell . . . the mystery . . . of the Orient. Ankle Chinatown way to the KUBLA KHAN . . . there it is."[11]

The Far East Café

Gim Suey Chong, my father, worked as a quality assurance inspector for the Lockheed Aircraft Corporation from 1950 to 1979. But on weekends, he proudly served as a waiter for twenty-four years at the Far East Café in Little Tokyo, Los Angeles. Five Zhang village cousins opened the Far East Café after they had moved from Mason City, Iowa, where they had a hand laundry. The Far East Café was known in the Nikkei community for its "China meshi" cuisine, a Japanese version of Cantonese food.[12]

The storied Far East Café on 347 East First Street in Los Angeles evokes sentimental nostalgia among many Chinese, Japanese, and non-Asian L.A. patrons. For fifty-nine years, this famous chop suey joint served diners in the landmark Far East Building alongside other China meshi restaurants such as Lem's Café, San Kow Low, and Yet Quong Low Chop Suey Café (aka Nikko Low). From 1935, during the Great Depression, to 1994, the Jeong (Zhang) clan from Guangdong Province happily served their customers. The Far East Café was a unique place for the Nikkei and others; there, they gathered for weddings, birthdays, graduations, parties, and funerals. Memories of chop suey, historical red-colored wooden booths, and iconic neon signs are etched in the hearts of four generations of Americans.[13]

The Far East Café showcased its cuisine through a number of signature dishes. Chicken and duck dishes were popular, along with the ubiquitous chop suey, chow mein, rice noodles, fried rice, and eggs. Family-style dinners were available with or without beer, sake, and wine. Almond duck was pressed boneless duck, flattened for easy deep-frying, then garnished with almonds. Hom yu was salted fish from China that was placed on fatty pork hash. Cha shu was lean pork baked with a secret sauce. Chow mein was pan fried and topped with bean sprouts, celery, and onion in a sauce. The menu of "Far East Café—Famous Food" was written in English, Japanese, and traditional Chinese. For $1 per person, one could have feasted on soup, fried chicken, fried shrimp, almond chicken, chow mein, chicken fried rice, egg foo young, chop suey, and roasted spare ribs. Window slogans read, "Famous Chinese Food," "Try Our Real Chinese Dishes," and "Served in Complete Family Style Dinner at All Hours."

The Chinese cooks of the Far East Café bought their meats from Wai Sang Meat Company on 700 North Spring Street in L.A.'s New Chinatown. Frozen shrimp and abalone were from Mexico, and the frozen lobster was from Cuba. Later on, they bought fresh local fish. Vegetables and other cooking ingredients were from the Kwong Dack Wo Company grocery store on 702 North Spring Street. This included bean sprouts, onions, celery, bok choy, water chestnuts, and Chinese peas, which always had to be fresh for a crispy texture. They used canned mushrooms (fresh mushrooms spoil quickly), and cooked in vegetable and peanut oils. They bought 100-pound bags of long grain rice with the usual condiments of soy sauce and mustard sauce. The Peking Noodle Company, Hong Kong Noodle Company, Eastern Noodle Company, and Quon Yick Noodle Company of Los Angeles provided their mein, egg-flour noodles, and wonton skins.

Jimmy's Oriental Garden Restaurant

James Yee Chung (Yee Yak Kan), my Yue uncle, arrived in America in 1922. He eagerly sought better business opportunities and opened the Friendly Café on 718 State Street in Santa Barbara, California, in 1936. In 1940, he opened Jimmy's Oriental Garden Restaurant at 330 West Cabrillo Street along the West Beach. In 1942, he moved his restaurant to 320 West Cabrillo Street and then in 1947, to 126 East Canon Perdido Street in Santa Barbara's Chinatown, across from the Presidio. This landmark restaurant was well-known for the finest Cantonese cuisine, its gigantic egg rolls, and the powerful mai tai's from the bar. Tommy Yee Chung, James's second son, started to work for his father in 1967 and assumed management of the restaurant from 1970 until its closure. Julie, his wife, operated the kitchen; Esther and Pearl served the patrons; Sal provided support; and Willie, the bartender, mixed high-octane drinks at the bar.

Tommy served chop suey dishes, with steamed white rice, vegetables, pork, beef, chicken, shrimp, almonds, and black mushrooms. Popular Cantonese-style dishes were pan-fried noodles mixed with pork, beef, chicken, or shrimp, almond chicken, mushroom chicken, tomato beef, and subgum. They also had family-style dinners, as well as "American" dinners, including steak and chicken meals. Tommy operated Jimmy's Oriental Garden Restaurant as a comfort station and watering hole for the eclectic local community until July 26, 2006.

My Chop Suey Legacy

On June 7, 2008, that beautiful sunny Saturday reunion morning when I arrived, excited and anxious, at the Far East Café, I retraced my father's footsteps walking along East First Street. I looked at the neon signs on the building's façade proudly proclaiming "Chop Suey" and "Far East." In front, two stone Chinese lions now stood, protecting the Far East Café from evil spirits, and *En To Low*, Chinese for the Far East Building, was still etched on the glass front door, as it had been since 1935. For Saturday reunion lunch, my guests and I savored and devoured the classic chop suey dishes of the Far East Café: tofu seaweed soup, a lighter version of the pork-based seaweed soup we grew up with, yet still very tasty with its ribbons of seaweed, swirls of egg white, cubes of tofu, and the crunchiness of Chinese peas. The cha shu, sliced one-quarter inch or thinner and served wet with a sweet and salty sauce, was great spooned on the rice. Baby bok choy with black mushrooms was a very generous portion of whole black mushrooms, firm baby bok choy, and a light clear sauce. The chop suey was nothing like the overcooked and bland versions of the past. This one was brightly colored with oranges and greens, and seasoned just right. The sweet-and-sour pork was dressed in electric-red sauce with pineapple chunks and green and red peppers. This sweeter dish helped round out the meal, even though it was not my grandmother's version of pork on the bone. Her dish had a bit more vinegar and was made without the artificial dye. Many people considered the almond duck the best dish served that day. It was formed into an oblong patty and made of duck meat, flour, cornstarch, and spices, deep-fried and cut into squares, and served over a bed of lettuce. It arrived topped with gravy and chopped almonds. Hom yu was also served, a large patty with cilantro accents that had more pork than fat, some salted fish, and salted egg.

A Chinatown legacy of chop suey is forever embedded in the cuisine and culture of America. Once upon a time, in the old Chinatowns and downtowns of America, neon signs glowed vividly in the city streets to lure hungry patrons to chop suey joints. Because of my Zhang and Yue forefathers, I deeply cherish such chop suey joints: the Imperial Restaurant in Cambridge, the Kubla Khan Theater Restaurant in San Francisco, the Far East Café in Los Angeles, and Jimmy's Oriental Garden Restaurant in Santa Barbara. As chop suey neon signs fade away and the exotic aromas drift into the past, we should cherish the fragments of the golden age of chop suey in America, for they represent the struggles and triumphs of generations of Chinese immigrants in the United States.

CHAPTER 8

The Sour Side of Chinese Restaurants

JOHN JUNG

Over the past century, Chinese restaurants have become one of the most popular types of eateries across the United States, Canada, and beyond. The primary business of Chinese immigrants in North America in the late nineteenth century was hand-wash laundries, but more Chinese began to open Chinatown cafes by the end of the nineteenth century. Whereas laundries relied primarily on non-Chinese customers, cafes served Chinese laborers, mostly bachelors, with dishes familiar to their village roots. Gradually, these eateries gained acceptance and patronage by non-Chinese customers, although the menu offerings had to accommodate non-Chinese tastes as well. In subsequent decades, they increased rapidly in number, spreading to regions with few Chinese. By the early 1920s, restaurants overtook laundries as the most prevalent form of self-employment for Chinese. As one observer wrote, "Nowadays the entire public is eating Chinese dishes and thinks nothing of it."[1]

Chinese restaurants range from small family-run establishments, generally located in or near residential neighborhoods, to larger ones in Chinatowns with hired employees. Whereas small restaurants often operated with the help of family members, and perhaps a few employees, the larger ones that served banquets typically required investments from many partners and hired managers, cooks, waiters, and other staff to handle actual operations. For example, fourteen Chinese formed a voluntary association to finance the opening of a restaurant in New York's Chinatown in 1900. By 1916, it was making $20,000 annually, a considerable amount for that time.[2]

Despite the popularity of Chinese eateries, Chinese restaurateurs faced many daunting problems that were not apparent to the dining public. Financial success was by no means a certainty, and many failed. Moreover, some problems were largely beyond their control, such as public ignorance, fear, and distrust of an unfamiliar cuisine. These attitudes prevented acceptance of Chinese restaurants for decades. Additionally, Chinese restaurants often faced government regulations and health issues related to business operations. Furthermore, problems such as poor management, inexperience dealing with non-Chinese patrons, and personnel issues were often due to inept business skills and decision-making. Taken as a whole, these problems added a decidedly sour taste to the operation of Chinese restaurants.

Social Prejudices against the Chinese

In the earliest days of Chinese restaurants, whites were generally disdainful towards Chinese food, which was foreign to them and often contained unfamiliar ingredients. Thus, the earliest Chinese restaurants were frequented almost entirely by Chinese patrons. The bill of fare featured dishes that appealed to the Chinese, such as salted fish, webbed duck feet, pig stomach, intestines, and fish heads. Before the late nineteenth century, a handful of adventuresome whites explored and came to appreciate Chinese food, but their efforts to persuade other whites to venture into Chinese restaurants were generally unsuccessful. Further discouraging the acceptance of Chinese restaurants among non-Chinese was the commonly held view that the Chinese ate dogs, which was actually true in parts of China.

Chinese restaurants did not initially attract "foreign" customers for other reasons: they were "not located on the ground floor, like solid American restaurants, but set up two or three flights of stairs, and there were no menus, and the smells seemed awful, but it was all this that made them exciting for the young of the 'gay nineties.'"[3] A typical negative viewpoint expressed in a Philadelphia newspaper in 1890 described the atmosphere of a Chinese restaurant with its offensive odors and "queer viands" as follows: "The visitor ascends a narrow, uncarpeted stairway to the second floor. He is not half way up before his nose tells him that he is in peculiar quarters. It is impossible to describe the smell of a Chinese restaurant. It is something like a mixture of burnt wool, strong tobacco and black tea. It is almost always offensive at the first, but the visitor soon becomes accustomed to it." The writer continued by describing the "suspicious" food in the same condescending tone that was common at the time: "This is a sauce, which you are supposed to pour into your soup. What its ingredients are is a mystery not given to Occidentals to know." In relating a dish that contained pieces of meat, he asserted, "This meat is alleged to be beef or veal. What it really is there is no need to inquire, as it is toothsome," suggesting that while it was "toothsome" or tasty, like the sauce, what he was actually consuming was a mystery. While the reporter passed on some items on the bill of fare, his attentive host assured him that they too were "purty good."[4]

The unexpected popularity of chop suey among white patrons at the end of the nineteenth century was a major turning point in the mainstream acceptance of Chinese restaurants. One explanation for this interest originated in the gold-mining regions of the West. In this version, drunken, hungry, white miners descended upon a Chinese restaurant late one evening demanding food. The cook had run out of food by the end of the day, but being resourceful, he gathered all the leftover vegetables and meat and quickly stir-fried them to create "chop suey," which the miners enjoyed and continued to order in the future.[5] A different explanation emerged on the East Coast, and centered on an unlikely event in 1896. That year, a prominent Chinese diplomat, Li Huang Chuang, visited the United States. One evening, tired of American banquet meals, he expressed a desire for Chinese food. Similarly, the local Chinese restaurant had run out of food by the end of the day, and the cook quickly improvised a meal by tossing together a stir-fried concoction of odds and ends left over from the preparation of earlier dishes. The diplomat enjoyed the dish, and when asked for its name, he was told "chop suey" (a translation of "odds and ends"). Newspaper accounts of this dish kindled curiosity among whites, and it became an overnight sensation that led many young white businessmen and professionals to venture into "unsavory and dangerous" urban Chinatowns for a firsthand taste. Newspapers referred to these excursions of groups of young whites into dark and mysterious Chinatowns as "slumming."[6]

By 1901, "chop suey joints," as these restaurants were called, became popular, especially with "bohemians." As one *New York Tribune* reporter lamented:

> The cooks are invariably true Celestials [natives of China] . . . the food is prepared, therefore, according to the most approved methods of the Middle Kingdom, with the result that in cheapness and savoriness (if you like it) it can easily outclass similar places run by American cooks. Moreover despite appearances, the food is prepared in an extremely cleanly manner. . . . There is also a free and easy atmosphere . . . which attracts many would-be Bohemians as well as a goodly share of a class below the lowest grades of the city's many graced.[7]

Although newspaper accounts acknowledged the increasing popularity of chop suey, they also invariably found something to criticize. In 1912, a writer complained: "It is true that the average Chinese cook becomes as inscrutable as the Sphinx when asked by a 'foreign devil' for a recipe, and even when, under exceptional circumstances, he is induced to part with one, he generally leaves out a vital ingredient, so that the American seldom really obtains the true Chinese dish."[8] Criticism of Chinese restaurants reflected the general anti-Chinese sentiment and pervasive suspicion held by whites. In fact, the Federated Trades and Labor Union boycotted Chinese restaurants, charging that Chinese restaurateurs in Chicago conspired to keep their food prices high by creating a "chop suey trust," so that "You pay or you don't eat."[9] Similar accusations of price fixing were expressed across the country and were used to discourage patronage at Chinese restaurants, which were starting to become serious competitors with white establishments.[10]

Fears of interracial sexual encounters also arose from the growing popularity of Chinese restaurants.[11] Chop suey houses were portrayed as hangouts for riff-raff where whites and Asians mingled freely. They allegedly served whiskey and beer to soldiers and sailors, and permitted the presence of girls as young as sixteen years of age. A crackdown on immoral behavior in New York City led to a series of raids on chop suey joints. In one instance, police questioned over 1,000 patrons about why they were at objectionable restaurants late at night and detained 119 men and 68 women.[12] In 1915, one Chinese man was charged with luring two young girls to his chop suey joint and assaulting one after giving her whiskey.[13] In 1921, two Chinese men were arrested for allegedly enslaving two white girls in Chinese dens in New York, reinforcing fears of white sexual slavery and opium dens that were already circulating in society.[14] The same year, investigators raided a Chinese restaurant in Philadelphia, where they arrested a Chinese man and his white wife, who were found with a quantity of opium valued at $1,000.[15] Widely publicized incidents such as these cast suspicion on all Chinese restaurateurs, who were not only seen as economic threats, but also racial, social, and criminal ones—true "yellow perils," as Asians were commonly stereotyped in America.

While these concerns have dissipated over the last century, with Asians transforming from the "yellow peril" to the "model minority," discriminatory laws against the Chinese still hamper the operation of Chinese restaurants in the United States, especially in terms of hiring employees from mainland China. Over a hundred years after the Chinese Exclusion Act of 1882, restaurateurs complained in 1988 that Immigration and Naturalization Service (INS) restrictions made it difficult to hire cooks, wait staff, and other workers, all of whom were not considered to be skilled enough to merit visas. Chinese restaurants in Washington, D.C., also reported difficulty in finding employees because of the 1986 Immigration Reform and Control Act, which criminalized the hiring of illegal immigrants and placed stricter rules on bringing in temporary workers. Moreover, the INS fined some owners for failing to complete employment forms accurately.[16] Owners also complained that INS raids at their restaurants harassed legal as well as illegal workers, an inconvenience which hurt their businesses.[17]

Over the past few decades, concerns about high fat and high sodium in Chinese food have also had an adverse impact on the Chinese restaurant business,[18] as has monosodium glutamate (MSG), which was used in Chinese restaurants as a flavor enhancer until the 1960s, when concerns about its health risks arose.[19] A reader's letter in the *New England Journal of Medicine* in 1968 about symptoms of numbness at the back of the neck, weakness, and palpitations after eating at Chinese restaurants was dubbed the "Chinese Restaurant Syndrome."[20] However, Chinese food includes numerous components—including food dyes, preservatives, histamines in fermented sauces, salt, cooking wine, and the allergenic proteins in crustaceans, fish, peanuts and fish—that can cause sensations and symptoms like those attributed to MSG. Glutamate is an amino acid present in many foods including mushrooms, tomatoes, and cheese, ingredients that exist in many other cuisines. Yet, few complain of hot flashes after eating spaghetti, for example, which also contains glutamate. Despite the lack of definitive studies demonstrating the ill effects of MSG, the belief is so persistent that many Chinese restaurants no longer use MSG and make efforts to assure customers, especially on menus, that it is not used in their food preparation.

Other Dangers for Chinese Restaurants

Robberies, assaults, and even homicides, far too numerous to cite, have occurred in Chinese restaurants, with no end in sight. A few examples serve to illustrate these dangers. In 1907, an Omaha restaurant keeper was robbed of $100 and brutally killed with a meat cleaver.[21] In 1910, another Chinese restaurant owner was robbed, murdered, and incinerated when his building was set on fire in Domingo, New Mexico.[22] Today, the violence continues. In 1980, a restaurant owner in Queens, New York, tried to prevent a midnight holdup by pulling a gun from behind his counter, but the robbers shot and killed him.[23] Similar incidents have occurred all over the country for decades and continue to be a risk for Chinese restaurateurs. However, violence in Chinese restaurants is not always directed towards the restaurant owner or staff. Gun battles have also occurred between rival gangs inside restaurants. A horrific incident in 1977 involved a late-night retaliatory ambush of a Chinese youth gang in San Francisco's Golden Dragon restaurant. This attack killed five innocent bystanders, including two tourists, and wounded eleven, which sharply reduced restaurant patronage in Chinatown for many weeks.[24]

Many Chinese restaurants provide home food delivery, but it is a service that is very taxing on delivery personnel who must rush, sometimes on bicycles, to impatient customers before their food gets cold. Not only do they receive low pay and often poor tips for long working hours in dangerous traffic and bad weather, but they are also easy targets for robbery, and in some instances, violence and even death. An illustrative incident in North Andover, Massachusetts, in 2009 involved the robbery and killing of a Chinese man delivering a food order late at night to an isolated address. The location proved to be unoccupied and the fake order was traced to a throwaway cell phone.[25] Conflicts also exist between restaurants owners and delivery personnel regarding working conditions and wages. The latter charge that they are given demanding schedules and fined if they are late in their deliveries. When demand is high, such as in cold weather, they must work even if it is their day off, or risk being fired.

Restaurant owners also face the threat of extortion by Chinese youth gangs. Unable to compete with better-educated American Born Chinese (ABC) youth, the new or Fresh Off the Boat (FOB) youth arriving in the late 1960s found it difficult to survive in the United States, as they lacked English language proficiency and the skills and training required for employment. Some turned to gangs that exploited Chinatown businesses, and in the 1970s, these predatory groups routinely threatened unpleasant consequences for restaurant owners unless they paid protection money. Moreover, they demanded food from restaurant owners and also robbed illegal gambling establishments.[26] Around the holidays, especially Chinese New Year, the gangs expected "lucky money" from merchants. Some even demanded that merchants buy goods from them at outrageously inflated prices, while others stole goods or ate and left without paying.

Chinese restaurant operators also face insulting and demeaning treatment from customers, such as not leaving tips and racial epithets. One Chinese owner described such racial abuse:

> Most were racial slurs, terms like "Chinamen," "chinee," and "chink" directed at us. On the whole most customers were OK; however, it was during the time of the Sonoma County Fair which ran for about a week then, when we would get the fair crowd who were most abusive. The worst incident was . . . when one of the customers threatened one of my sisters physically. They had order[ed] multiple dishes, and tried to hide a few of the emptied dishes after eating, and argued about the bill. My sister saw the hidden dishes and pointed them out and that is when one of the party got up and threatened her. I asked my sister to

> come in, the customer followed, so I turned up the fire on the oil wok and had my sister get behind me. I told the fellow if he came into the area, I'd toss hot oil on him; he backed down, paid the bill in full, and left.[27]

Telephone prank take-out orders also present an annoying and time-wasting nuisance for Chinese restaurateurs. Some pranksters even record and upload their fake take-out orders on YouTube, speaking in mock Chinese or placing orders using fabricated Chinese food names.

Chinese restaurants have earned recognition for serving delicious food at low prices. However, they also have a long-standing, dubious reputation for questionable sanitary practices, although this situation is by no means limited to Chinese restaurants. In 1912, the Health Department in New Orleans closed several Chinese restaurants for unsanitary conditions that presented a health nuisance.[28] Such stereotypes persist to the present day, and Chinese restaurants are often criticized for rude, inattentive, or slow service, with most customers overlooking the fact that some restaurant staff are recent immigrants and have a poor command of English or knowledge of Western restaurant practices. Moreover, after working long hours and multitasking, members of the wait staff often do not have the time or energy to indulge the sometimes frivolous demands of patrons.

The success of small Chinese family restaurants has owed much to the decreased operating costs of low rent locations, little or no advertising, and minimal decor and menu planning. Many offer the same items that other local Chinese restaurants have on their menus. This approach makes sense, as most customers do not venture into ordering unfamiliar items, especially since menus often lack adequate descriptions of ingredients and preparation methods. Moreover, wait staff do not have the time or in some cases, adequate English skills, to explain menu items in detail to customers. Too many menu items may also lead to low inventory turnover, resulting in losses from spoilage. Family labor has also contributed to the success of Chinese cuisine restaurants in the United States. Traditionally, children were not paid for working in family eateries, but were expected to contribute their labor in return for room and board. While many children might have preferred not to work in family restaurants, most realized that their participation was essential for survival. Children had little recourse but to obey parental orders. However, some of the work was dangerous for children, who occasionally suffered injuries, especially in the kitchen.

Family-operated Chinese restaurants have not been immune from problems such as disputes over operations and finances. For example, brothers Ken and Henry Ng operated the successful Hu Shang Restaurant in Portland, Maine, in the 1980s. Like many Chinese restaurants during that era, they accepted cash only, a method that made it easy to underreport income, allowing the older brother to skim over close to $2 million dollars between 1979 and 1985 without his younger brother's knowledge; however, he later went to prison for income tax evasion.[29] In some instances, if the opportunity arises, partners may decide to go their separate ways. Partner conflicts often arise when one accuses the other of questionable accounting practices or business operations, or when personal disagreements over family matters, for example, interfere with restaurant management.

Early Chinese immigrants had difficulty acquiring loans from American banks and had to rely on capital pools from partners and family members, especially when opening larger restaurants with banquet facilities and dance floors. These large restaurants attracted a wide range of employees including Chinese immigrants or contract chefs with little or no education and almost no knowledge of English, foreign-born Chinese students, American-born Chinese, and if necessary, non-Chinese as cashiers, wait staff, busboys, and dishwashers. Most Chinese restaurants did not provide much in the way of job training or advice concerning customer relations. Usually, staff members were left to learn on their own, so it is not surprising that a frequent complaint about Chinese restaurants has always been poor customer service.

Perhaps the biggest challenge for any restaurateur is how to find and retain good cooks. Chinese restaurants usually recruited cooks through employment agencies in Chinatowns or through referrals from friends, relatives, or current employees. Chefs were notorious for working a short while and leaving at the slightest sign of unhappiness or conflict at work. Moreover, rival restaurants would often "steal" good chefs. Hiring Chinese wait staff and cooks in areas located far from Chinese communities is still difficult because there is little for them to do when they are not working. For example, Chinese restaurant owners have gone to New York City to hire workers to work in remote areas like Vermont and New Hampshire. However, cultural isolation created mental-health problems for these workers, so work schedules had to allow them to return to New York City's Chinatown, by bus, every few days.[30]

Exploitation, such as working long hours with few or brief breaks, has also been a problem for Chinese restaurant employees. In 1915, a Chinese restaurant owner in Duluth, Minnesota, was fined for requiring two white women employees to work seventy hours a week, and today the situation is not much better, especially in family-owned restaurants.[31] Moreover, employees of Chinese restaurants generally receive no overtime pay or health benefits. They typically receive only one day off each week. They are often expected to share tips and in some cases, their tips are treated as part of their salary. With the influx of more Chinese immigrants since 1965, the supply of workers has far exceeded the number of jobs, so owners pay lower wages. In some cases, employers owe back wages to workers, but restaurant employees have few means of seeking redress. They lack English skills and have no funds to hire attorneys. Complaining also increases the risk that owners might fire them, or report them to immigration authorities.

Traditionally, Chinese workers did not form or join labor unions, but in 1978 at one New York City high-end Chinese restaurant, Uncle Tai, about half of its employees protested working conditions by creating a union with the help of Local 69 of the Hotel and Restaurant Employees Association. However, the white union leaders proved to be largely ineffective in helping the Chinese restaurant workers, prompting them to form the Chinese Staff and Workers Association. In 1980, workers successfully fought a large restaurant, the Silver Palace, over their policy of forcing wait staff to share a large portion of their tips with other employees. Management retaliated by hiring new wait staff to replace some of the dissidents, but picketing forced the restaurant to rehire them.[32]

In 2007, wait staff and other workers filed a lawsuit accusing a Chinese restaurant chain in New York, Ollie's, of paying below the minimum wage. Some employees reported that management retaliated by cutting their work hours.[33] In 2010, four former employees filed complaints over wage abuse at the Grand Buffet Restaurant, maintaining that it owed each of them tens of thousands of dollars for regular and overtime wages. They charged the restaurant with violations of child labor laws, which require work permits and restrict hours for youth under eighteen. Workers also reported that they were exposed to hot oil, poor air circulation, toxic cleaning products and wet, slippery floors.[34]

A 2010 report based on interviews with 433 workers, augmented by independent observations in 106 San Francisco Chinatown restaurants, found instances of wage theft, sub-minimum wages, and lack of overtime pay. Working conditions were often hazardous, with employees suffering burns, cuts, and falls, and a lack of adequate safety precautions and training was common. Almost half of the employees reported that their supervisors, coworkers, or customers yelled at them. About half of the workers had to pay out-of-pocket for their medical care, and only three percent of them received healthcare coverage. Although San Francisco requires mandatory paid sick leave, the survey found that 42 percent of workers had pay deducted if they took time off sick. Moreover, most workers did not receive paid vacation time.[35] In 2012, the California Labor Commission fined San Francisco's Tsing Tao Restaurants $339,716 for unpaid minimum wages and overtime pay, as well as failure to provide itemized payroll statements for twenty-eight workers at two locations.[36] In 2013, the Washington State Wage and Hour Division of the Department of Labor investigated two restaurants, Super China Buffet and Great Dragon. Around thirty of the restaurant employees were paid in cash off the record, and no time and pay records were kept or they were inaccurate, incomplete, or falsified. Some wait staff were paid as little as $10 a day and worked more than forty hours a week. Kitchen staff received a straight monthly salary with no overtime for work over forty hours per week. The Department sued the restaurants for minimum wage, overtime, back wage, and record-keeping violations, and forced them to sign agreements for future compliance with the law.[37]

Operating a Chinese restaurant has always been a difficult way to make a living in the United States. Clearly, they face many challenges beyond the task of serving good food. Chinese restaurateurs are hemmed in by rising costs of supplies, rent, and labor on one hand, and the pressure to offer low prices to meet customer expectations and compete with other restaurants on the other. Other common problems include long working hours for employees, uncertain customer patronage, stiff competition, health and sanitation issues, unreliable help, physical danger, and demanding customers. All of these factors have contributed to the sour taste of operating Chinese restaurants in the United States.

CHAPTER 9

"Foreign, Brackish, and Exotic"

Japanese Food in the American Press, 1853–1918

FRANK JACOB

Sushi is a tremendously important part of global food culture. There is almost no country in the world where one cannot order this symbol of Japanese food globalism.[1] For a long time, however, Japanese food was rather unpopular, especially in the United States, where fear of growing immigration from Japan bred mistrust in the food culture that originated from that island.[2] Hawaii, however, was one of the major spots for the initial fusion of different food cultures,[3] described as "a small-sized melting pot" by the *Topeka State Journal* in 1911: "More than 40 per cent of the population of Hawaii is Japanese," and "the Japanese element of the population increases far more rapidly than any other," which facilitated this culinary exchange.[4]

As a U.S. territory, Hawaii was certainly one of the largest importers of Japanese food until the second half of the twentieth century.[5] Large ships brought several different "foodstuffs and liquors" to the islands.[6] These products were sold to Japanese settlers who were impatient to be resupplied with "homemade" products. After the Russo-Japanese War (1904–1905), which made Japan a great power—especially when compared to Great Britain or France—and underscored its status as a "civilized" nation, Japanese food became more popular in the United States, even if the main consumers of Japanese food were members of the Japanese diaspora.[7]

Food is usually able to serve as a cultural bridge, but there are always factors that decide if there is interest in the food of a different culture. One is availability: one can only try new food if it is available. Another one is taste: one will only try what is said to be tasty, and one will only continue to eat it if that is true. The third is familiarity: if one does not know about a certain food, the opportunity to taste it is even more diminished. The steady import of food from Japan, the growing number of Japanese settlers in America, and the increase of general interest in Japan after its victories against Russia and its role as an ally of Britain and the United States during the First World War all led to the spread of Japanese food culture in the United States, with newspapers playing an important role in this process.

This chapter will analyze the period between 1853 and 1918, when, with the influence of the American press, Japanese cuisine in the United States was introduced, evaluated, and finally accepted. Special focus will be placed on the development of the American public's attitude toward Japanese food, especially as conveyed through newspapers. Three historical periods will be taken into consideration during this discussion: the impact of the opening of Japan in 1853 and imports to Hawaii; developments during and after the Russo-Japanese War, which will illustrate how the successful war against Russia stimulated an American interest in Japanese culture, especially its food; and changes up to the First World War (1914–1918), including the perception of Japanese restaurants in the American print media. Comparing images of Japanese food in the American press during these three periods will also reveal how, at the time, new foodways were adopted, and how an unknown food culture was transformed and reevaluated using the factors of availability, taste, and familiarity.

The Opening of Japan and the Meiji Restoration

In 1853, Commodore Matthew C. Perry arrived in the Bay of Edo with his "black ships" to open up Japan as a possible spot for the coaling stations sought by U.S. whalers. The government of the Tokugawa shogun was unable to resist Western demands because military progress had been interrupted by the almost total seclusion of the country since the early seventeenth century. Consequently, the ruling elite was compelled to accept American demands.[8] Following the success of the U.S. mission, more and more diplomatic emissaries arrived from all major and minor Western powers, aiming to establish trade relations that would favor them by signing unequal treaties. The first foreigners to arrive in Japan also made contact with the habits and food culture of the island country.[9] In most cases, however, the foreign adventurers, missionaries, salesmen, diplomats, and soldiers seemed to dislike Japanese dishes.[10] In 1868, the emperor was reinstalled and the Meiji Restoration began. This was a long process of reforms and modernization-oriented measures by the new government through which all of Japanese society was changed.

The opening of Japan led to the hiring of foreign specialists to assist in its modernization process. These "hired foreigners" (*o-yatoi gaikokujin*) would be the first to provide detailed reports to Americans on Japanese culture, including its food.[11] With the pursuit of modernization, more and more people from abroad, including the United States, started to visit Japan, some simply for vacations, and others to experience the culinary differences. As a traveler reported in the *Grange Advance of Minnesota* in 1877,

> During the whole of our journey of fourteen days from Kioto to Tokio, we lived on Japanese food, with the exception of four small pots of Liebig's extract of beef, and some spirits and tobacco. Eggs and rice are always to be obtained, and occasionally fish, with other dishes, the origin of which the European traveler would do well not to ask. If accepted on trust, some of them are by no means bad.[12]

While the taste was judged to be "by no means bad," the report would not have stimulated an interest in mysterious food that was possibly not even as good as canned meat.

Clearly, there was still substantial resistance to the unknown culinary "Other." Many travelers seemed unwilling to trust Japanese cuisine, especially since it used numerous unfamiliar ingredients. The fact that bread and milk, essentials of the Western diet, were not widely eaten in Japan engendered distrust of the "oriental" way of eating. On the other hand, there was also discussion in Japan about the westernization of food, particularly when intellectuals suggested the consumption of milk as an indicator of a civilized diet.[13] Nevertheless, it would take a few more decades until Western foodways began to enter the diet of the Japanese masses.

Another important factor that influenced the negative image of Japanese food in the United States was taste. At the time, American cuisine was centered around the use of butter, cream, red meat, and salt and pepper. Thus, Japanese food must have been a shock for many American visitors. Its soft texture, the lack of spices and red meat, as well as its emphasis on seafood contributed to the negative image of Japanese food brought back by early American visitors. However, it was not solely the taste of Japanese food that shaped its public image in the United States. Most American newspaper readers had never eaten, and would never eat, Japanese food because it was simply unavailable. Moreover, reports about the blandness and brackishness of Japanese food were also mixed with ideas of racial superiority. The same resistance to another foreign diet (Hawaiian) was also reported for Japanese immigrants to the United States:

> The Japanese immigrants in Hawaii are suffering from the scarcity of suitable food . . . the Japanese emigrants to Hawaii carry with them all their household requisites, as though they were going to establish new homes there, and they expected to get Japanese food and live in Japanese houses. . . . The question of food, especially, must have caused them great dissatisfaction.[14]

Despite contact between white American and Japanese settler communities on Hawaii, the culinary culture of Japan was still depicted as foreign in the U.S. and Hawaiian press. To "live upon Japanese food exclusively" was described as unhealthy and unpleasant.[15] Yet, this negative impression of the island's Japanese food culture did not stop the importation of foodstuffs from Japan. The only interruption came when the Hawaiian Board of Health temporarily prohibited imports, claiming fears of contamination. Japanese importers protested this limitation on their business, and ultimately, such measures did not prevent the triumph of Japanese food culture in Hawaii, even though critics were not immediately persuaded.[16] Japanese workers who quit their jobs to open the first restaurants, which were initially only patronized by Japanese customers, were harshly criticized. Stereotypes dominated public opinion, as expressed in Honolulu's *Hawaiian Star* on August 15, 1900:

> Many of the Japanese have quit labor altogether and have opened small stores all over the country. These stores are fitted up with a shelf or two on which are a few cans of doubtful salmon, some yellow soap, some cards of matches, some Japanese food dainties of powerful odor and a back room. These places are, almost without exception, gambling dens and illicit liquor joints.[17]

In general, the Japanese seemed unwilling to adopt American foodways. No matter where they went or worked, they preferred their traditional food, which was also a part of their culture. On the steamer *Kaga Maru*, which was docked in the United States, Japanese "sailors eat Japanese food, which is prepared for them in their own galleys. Rice and fish are the staples which they enjoy three times a day."[18] It is therefore not surprising that "the goods brought to the islands from Japan are made up almost wholly of Japanese foodstuffs."[19] Far from home, the prices for such imported traditional cuisine were high, and fluctuated in response to events on the Japanese mainland. For example, floods in 1910 were responsible for price increases on Hawaii.[20] Regardless, the Japanese settler community on Hawaii continued to follow their culinary habits and honor their food culture. By doing so, they also secured the availability of Japanese food on U.S. territory, which provided the possibility for non-Japanese, who had read or heard about this particular Asian cuisine, to try it. Clearly, the existence of a Japanese community led to a culinary exchange with members of non-Japanese communities on the island.

While a blending of different food cultures seemed as impossible as a blending of Western and Japanese culture in general, the chance of future interest in Japanese cuisine was encouraged by its availability. Adoption, however, was delayed by racist stereotypes and the belief in "food superiority" on both sides. It was not only food that was critically commented on, but also interracial marriages between Japanese and non-Japanese: mixed marriages were rarely successful, especially when the bride was "the other." A case was reported in which "the European daughter had to abandon her European custom, to adopt Japanese dress for herself and her child, to sit on the floor and live principally on Japanese food."[21] The mother-in-law was unwilling to accept foreign European food as part of her daily diet. Similarly, there was also a suspicion of the foreign wife who, the Japanese believed, would change the heritage and customs of the family (microcosm) and perhaps of the nation (macrocosm). Food, after all, was a symbol of Japanese identity; the Meiji era even produced national emblems for Japanese food (e.g. *washoku).*[22] This kind of stereotypic evaluation continued on both sides until the Russo-Japanese War between 1904 and 1905, which eventually changed the image of Japan in the West and opened the door for the acceptance of the island empire as an equal member of the "civilized world community."

The Russo-Japanese War and Beyond

When Japan attacked the Russian fleet at Port Arthur on February 8, 1904, nobody believed that Japan would be able to defeat a great European power such as the Czarist Empire.[23] The expansion of the latter into Manchuria and towards Korea, however, had forced the Japanese government to accept that there was just one solution to its security problem: to take an offensive position. Regardless of its status as the "underdog" in the war, the Japanese won battle after battle, beating the Russian forces on land, and annihilating the Czarist fleet in the Battle of Tsushima.[24] Russia was at its military nadir in 1905, so Japan was depicted as the gallant victor in a fight between an Asian David and an Eastern European Goliath.

The war itself had a tremendous impact on Japanese expansionist ideas, international relations, military and naval strategies, and the global reception of Japan in general.[25] While the Japanese immigration to Hawaii and California might have increased the availability of Japanese food on U.S. soil, the Russo-Japanese War stimulated a genuine interest in Japan, and especially in the food of the island nation. In fact, many saw food as an essential part of Japanese military success. By this point, bread, red meat, and milk had been incorporated into the diet of the Japanese imperial army, and was being seen as a reason behind its sudden prowess. As conveyed by the *Saint Paul Globe* (Minnesota),

> Something has made the Japanese soldier brave and strong beyond the belief of the world. . . . Is that something fish? . . . Certain it is that the soldier of Japan has shown himself brave and strong in battle—and his ration, the emergency supply of

food provided by his government, is a small fish, hard and dry, which lasts him seven days when he is too busy for the commissary department to keep up with him in the field. The whole nation is one of fishermen and fish-eaters.[26]

According to the *St. Paul Globe*, in addition to traditional provisions such as fish, Japanese soldiers were also consuming Western products, and dairy in particular was having an impact on their fighting prowess. Few other newspapers would venture so far, but they did, however, see a relationship between diet and the general effectiveness of the Japanese army.[27] Although Japanese cuisine was partially responsible for success on the battlefield, it was still depicted as something that could not be adopted by the West. Various papers in Virginia made it clear that not much had changed since the opening of Japan in 1853 and the first visits by Western tourists and travelers:

> That Japanese food can be eaten only by the Japanese, with a few rare exceptions, is a fact painfully well known to those who have traveled in Japan . . . with the exception of a few hotels conducted expressly for foreigners, it is impossible to obtain bread, butter, milk, meat, poultry, beer, wine and coffee, and even fresh fish is rare, and one is indeed fortunate if he can subsist cheerfully on eggs, rice and tea and now and then a vegetable devoid of taste.[28]

The same author recommended that prospective travelers take proper precautions, and to be prepared to take sufficient Western food with them since "it takes long and constant practice to eat and digest Japanese food." As the article implied, there were connections between race and food, and East and West were as incompatible as oil and water.

A number of articles published in the American press during the Russo-Japanese War provided a general survey of Japan's culture, including the varieties of food that were on offer.[29] On August 11, 1905, one feature in the *Nebraska Advertiser* focused on the "Fisheries of Japan," using the opportunity to outline the ways in which Japan was a "fish country": "So important are water products and so numerous are their kinds and the methods of preparation, that I venture the assertion, from what I have seen of domestic life in Japan, that every day in every Japanese family some form of fishery food is served—I am almost ready to say at every meal."[30] However, despite Japan's growing international position, the stereotypes that existed regarding Japanese cuisine did not vanish; racist statements and cultural arrogance remained constant themes. The *Baxter Spring News* in Kansas provides just one example:

> As to Japanese food in general, travelers are rarely enthusiastic. . . . The food of the middle class Jap at home is about as follows: Breakfast consists of rice and some kind of flavoring, fresh or pickled vegetables, salted fish and eggs, and green tea, taken without sugar. At the second meal, the principal one of the day, there may be fresh fish, a little beef or chicken cut up and cooked with vegetables in a stew, and the inevitable rice.[31]

The differences between the common Western (American) diet and the diet of the Japanese were emphasized quite often. Newspapers in different states still claimed that the insurmountable differences between American and Japanese food cultures made it impossible for travelers to rely solely on the food provided in Japan.

> Japanese food is so different from American food that it takes the visitor some time to acquire a fondness for it, more time than the tourist usually has at disposal. With the masses rice is the staple article of diet, and it is the most palatable native dish that the foreigner finds here. . . . Milk is seldom used except in case of sickness and butter is almost unknown among the masses.[32]

The assumption of "food backwardness" was obviously not ready to be overcome just yet. It took two more years until the *Spokane Press* could finally and victoriously announce that the Japanese in the United States and its territories were adapting to American foodways. The victory was, of course, sold as evidence for American cultural superiority. The decrease in imports of Japanese foodstuffs made it obvious why the "Japs [were] adopting our food."[33] Other articles pointed to the same fact from another angle, stating that for those who have "been used to Japanese food all one's life, the meats and sauces of the Americans are a terrible thing to tackle."[34]

The image of insurmountable differences, however, lingered in the minds of readers and writers for years. Five years later in 1913, a description of the typical Japanese food box (*bentō*) was published across the United States in several different newspapers. It described, in detail, the traditional meal of Japan: "The bento may contain in neat separate compartments prawn fish, chicken, rice, preserved ginger, johnnycake, omelette, a broiled mushroom, a slice of radish, glazed beans, kind of sweet pickle, tripe, a slice of cooked chestnut, licorice, etc. The bento is inviting to the eye, is garnished in green, in neatly wrapped."[35] The description itself might have been more favorable, but the author also emphasized the difficulties Americans would face consuming this food:

> "Japanese dishes fail to satisfy American cravings;" says an officer in the United States army. "Imagine a diet without milk, bread, butter, coffee, salad or any sufficient quantity of nicely cooked vegetables without pudding, stewed fruit and with comparatively little fresh fruit. The European vegetarian will find as much difficulty in making anything out of it as the ordinary meat eater.[36]

The Japanese diet thus seemed unsuitable for Europeans and Americans, which was another reason for hostility towards Japanese cuisine in the United States. While interest in Japan had been growing since the Russo-Japanese War, cultural arrogance by no means changed in inverse proportion. On August 21, 1913 a "round the world tour" was organized in Edgefield, South Carolina, where guests at a large banquet had the chance to experience several different food cultures in one evening. Events like this would stimulate the availability of Japanese food for American consumers, but the press was not yet willing to encourage interest in this particular cuisine. The *Edgefield Advertiser* supported the event, promoting it the week before. Yet, despite the fact that the event itself was described as "must-see," descriptions of Japanese culture was still dominated by prejudice:

> Here you will be met by little Japanese girls and young women, a veritable Island home in miniature. You will be served by Japanese and talk to Japanese and eat Japanese food. They say they eat dried bearings in Japan, but fortunately for the tourists that is not all they eat, and in order to gratify the American appetite, the Japs will "temper the wind to the shorn lamb" and give you something you really like.[37]

Japanese cuisine was obviously not enough to satisfy Americans. The stereotypes thus proved durable, and during the First World War, the same characterizations of Japanese food would again be recycled in the U.S. press, regardless of the fact that the Japanese were allies in the war.

The First World War and Japanese Food

Imports of Japanese food were interrupted during the war, since ships were needed elsewhere to serve as troop transporters. This led to a shortage of Japanese food in the United States, especially in San Francisco, where the "Japanese in this city are suffering, owing to the shortage of Japanese food. Japanese rice, shou and miso are the principal food products among local Japanese, and as no steamer has recently arrived from Japan the prices have jumped."[38] The shortage led to increased contact between the Japanese and American food culture, but as a consequence of a lack of alternatives. Of course, in other parts of the country like Seattle, Japanese food was still available, albeit only from specialty stores with high prices.[39] In Hawaii, Japanese churches tried to organize food sales to keep a sense of unity within the Japanese community, even if the amount of available food steadily caused problems.[40]

The Japanese government, in contrast, was no longer interested in maintaining a positive image of Japan's cuisine. Ironically, during the war, Japanese officials exploited the myths of the non-adjustable food habits of its soldiers to explain to the American public why Tokyo, in contrast to Washington, was not sending troops to the battlefields in Europe. Ambassador Ishii Kikujirō (1866–1945) explained to the U.S. public that

> From a tactical point of view, it is impossible to send Japanese troops to France. . . . It is because of the difference in climate and food and the language. You send American troops to France and they can eat the foods produced there. Japanese must have Japanese food. Their food could not sustain the long voyage and it would be rendered useless passing through the tropics.[41]

The myths about food incompatibility had finally come full circle, but it was not only Japanese soldiers who felt uncomfortable with foreign food. As described in "Quite Another Story," published in the

Maui News on December 7, 1917, when U.S. troops were able to choose their own lunch in Honolulu, instead of trying Japanese food from the local food and fruit stands, the men "secured their favorite dish—pie and sodawater."[42] Soldiers on both sides were not interested in each other's food, regardless of its availability, a fact that suggests the influence of the press.

Soldiers in both countries had not yet overcome stereotyped images of each other's food culture. However, during the First World War, some journalists began to recognize the value of Japanese food, signaling a slow shift in attitudes. In an article published by the *New-York Tribune*, Mary Alden Hopkins underscored that "Japanese food, as sampled in restaurants, is delicious, esoteric and aesthetic. I feel as guiltily gross when I consume it as if I were destroying madrigals and rosebuds."[43] She might have been influenced by orientalist ideas in her article, but at least she suggested engaging with the "other" food culture. In Columbia, Missouri, the University of Missouri's Rothwell Gymnasium became a "Corner of Nippon" where guests were "seated in the far way of Japan." There,

> the guests will be met at door by two Japanese students of the University garbed in the dress of their native lands. The waitresses will wear Japanese kimonos. During the banquet, ten newsboys, dressed in the newsboys costume of Japan, will distribute the "Made-in-Japan" extra of the *Daily Missourian*. Everywhere will be Japanese decorations, Japanese food, Japanese costumes, and Japanese souvenirs.[44]

While the setting reinforced numerous stereotypes, for a change, the food was not presented in a hostile way. Nevertheless, there was little intellectual interest in Japanese food, and Americans' opinions remained ambivalent during the First World War. Because Japan was a U.S. ally, there were occasional reports on its foodways, but most of them were orientalist in nature, focusing on "curious" aspects of its cuisine, and not encouraging the consumption of the food itself. For example, the *Free Trade-Journal* of Ottawa, Illinois, published an article on the "Use of Chopsticks in the Orient," explaining how the Japanese used sticks to eat their exotic dishes.[45]

Almost all articles on Japanese culinary culture during the First World War were still biased. Thus, the war did not change much.

While newspapers reported on the East Asian ally and its foodways, the general perspective of western "food arrogance" did not disappear. The rice-based diet, the lack of milk or bread, as well as the way Japanese ate—small dishes with several components of a meal, using chopsticks—were perceived as odd and uncivilized. It would take many more years until Japanese cuisine became an accepted part of American culture.

Japanese Restaurants in the U.S. Press

During this period, the perception of Japanese food in the U.S. press was always related to Japan itself, but usually not to Japanese restaurants in North America. This is because the places where Japanese food could be consumed were culinary meeting points for the Japanese immigrant community, and not points of exchange between American and Japanese culinary culture. They remained safe spaces for immigrants and did not, in contrast to restaurants today, become cultural exchange zones. This was mainly due to the negative coverage that American Japanese-cuisine restaurants received in the U.S. press.

For starters, Japanese restaurants were usually depicted as dens of criminal activity and illegal gain. In 1908, a report of an official raid of a Japanese restaurant on Hawaii conveyed that the Japanese restaurant owners were trying to make money illegally by selling beer and liquor without permission.[46] A year later, another Japanese restaurant owner made the front page of the *Pacific Commercial Advertiser* for a similar crime.[47] The owner, named Take, had sold beer and sake without permission as well. The police officer who was responsible for bringing the criminal to court, a man called Fennell, expressed that Take's was not an unusual case, since "the Japanese restaurants are growing very careful, and . . . sake, and even beer, is being sold in teapots, the proper receptacles being too risky."[48] Japanese restaurants were consequently labeled as sinister, something that further stimulated suspicion regarding their foodways and anti-Japanese feelings in western states.

Japanese restaurants were, much like their Chinese counterparts, accused of unhygienic practices. In 1916, a member of the Tuberculosis Bureau of Hawaii's Board of Health stated in the *Honolulu Star-Bulletin* that the only way to force restaurant owners to maintain hygienic standards was to take away their Red Cross certificates. To give a vivid example of this procedure, he mentions a particular case of one Japanese restaurant owner: "In one instance the proprietors of a Japanese restaurant came to us crying to get their certificate back. They have lived up to the regulations ever since."[49] More important, however, was the continued problem of illegal liquor, especially during the 1920s. Japanese restaurant owners were well-known for their lack of interest in following prohibition orders and on April 25, 1922, the *Semi-Weekly Maui News* named two Japanese restaurant owners who were involved in such criminal activities. While one "appears unable to keep clear of the law . . . (and) was arrested on Sunday for alleged violations of the prohibition law at his place of business," another Japanese man was named "an alleged offender against the prohibition laws" and was "accused of transporting booze and is alleged to have been delivering the stuff to a Japanese restaurant."[50]

In Hawaiian newspapers, Japanese restaurants were spaces of criminal activity, not culinary delight. The food that was offered in the restaurants was not described, as most of the articles focused on how these eateries were fronts for illegal gain. In 1907, there was one incident when a Japanese restaurant in San Francisco received some national fame, not for its cuisine, but for being destroyed by angry white men.[52] The case was related to the immigration crisis in California, where Japanese students were excluded from primary schools for racist reasons. Since the Japanese restaurant owners in the city had established their own union and only served Japanese customers, there was usually no contact with other ethnicities in the restaurants, which became enclaves for the Japanese immigrant community.[53] However, due to the wave of anti-Japanism in 1907, even restaurants could become battlefields of the immigration war. It was the "Expulsion of Two White Men from a Japanese Restaurant in San Francisco . . . followed by an Attack on Japs by Citizens" that captured headlines.[54] However, the eruption should be seen not as an isolated incident but as part of the widespread anti-Japanese sentiments that year.[55] A more detailed description of the events was published in early June in the *Pacific Commerical Advertiser*:

> Shortly after they [the two white men and their friends] had entered the restaurant some one threw a brick through the front window. From then on a regular fusillade of bricks and stones

> shot through broken windows. After the Japanese in the restaurant had made their escape, the mob proceeded to destroy the Folsom-street Baths, a bathhouse also run by a Japanese, directly opposite the restaurant.[56]

The case was perceived as an example of mob violence that had been stimulated by the anti-immigration movement in California and an expression of anti-Japanese feelings by the white population of the state.[57] In short, this case demonstrates that Japanese restaurants in the United States at the beginning of the twentieth century were, for the most part, not spaces of culinary exchange, but rather political spheres in which racist resentments could lead to violence.

The food of a society reflects its wider capacity to integrate elements from different cultural backgrounds. With regard to Japanese cuisine, the United States was not very successful in this respect during the years between the forced opening of Japan and the end of the First World War. While the Russo-Japanese War stimulated a general interest in the Asian country and its culture, its food remained something that was "indigestible" for the American stomach. The first signs of change occurred during the First World War, when writers and intellectuals started to praise food from the East Asian country, even if it remained incomparable to the "superior" American diet. However, this minority was not able to shift the public image as a whole.

Nevertheless, it was mainly white American consumers who paved the way for the success of Asian food in the United States. A growing interest in Japan and its culture had been stimulated by Japan's military successes in East Asia, eventually leading to publications on Japanese food, Japan's economy, and Japanese culture during the Russo-Japanese and First World Wars. Japanese food, however, was only of interest when it was related to Japan itself, and not to Japanese restaurants in the United States, which were mostly described as spaces of illegal activity. Unfortunately, in that era, nationwide press coverage was only achieved when Japanese restaurants were involved in scandal. The acceptance of Japanese food as a part of the U.S. diet would occur decades later, after World War II, when, eventually, food enthusiasts would report on the broad variety of Asian food in general, and Japanese food in particular, encouraging Americans to try this cuisine in earnest.

CHAPTER 10

The Problem with Persistence

The Rise of Tucson's Japanese Cuisine and the Fall of Its Nikkei Community

BRUCE MAKOTO ARNOLD

In 1954, while Sue Tilton (née Suzue Fujita, b. 1921) was working at Yokota Air Base's gift shop, she met her husband, Homer, an Air Force electronics engineer.[2] It was love at first sight and the couple married that year. After he was unable to secure work in Japan post-discharge, Homer received an offer from the newly-established Hughes Missile Systems, which had broken ground in Tucson, Arizona, in 1951. Tucson was a rather alien environment for the daughter of a samurai-cum-teacher and a native of Hokkaido, Japan. The heat, dust, and western Americanness of the burgeoning city of just under 200,000 people was foreign indeed. Although a handful of Nikkei (those of Japanese heritage) lived in the area, most worked as farmers and few, if any, congregated in the city as a group. Sue's only Nikkei contact was a Japanese military bride at Ft. Huachuca, in Sierra Vista, some seventy-five miles away.[3] If Sue wanted to experience Japanese culture in Tucson, she was going to have to supply it herself.

Not surprisingly, Japanese foods were difficult to come by in the western desert city. In 1955, an Asian grocery selling some Japanese foods existed near downtown (perhaps in Tucson's second Chinatown bounded by Meyer, Main, McCormick, and Broadway and demolished in the 1960s) where Sue found the rudiments of her native palate such as tofu and some canned Japanese goods, but she only went "once

FIGURE 10.1. The last remnants of Tucson's second dedicated Japanese restaurant, Sakura-ya, featured in a 1977 photograph on the front page of the *Tucson Citizen*, with the caption "As the sun slowly sinks . . . an oriental arch lends a touch of the Far East to a typical Western sunset. Actually, the arch is all that remains of a sign that advertised a now-defunct Japanese restaurant at 8455 E. Speedway Blvd." (Photo used courtesy of and by permission of the *Arizona Daily Star)*.[1]

or twice," because the area around the store was such a "wild place" in the mid-1950s that she could never venture there without accompaniment. The only sure outlet for her tastes were occasional trips to Los Angeles that allowed her to buy Japanese foods in bulk.

In the meantime, Sue had to settle for meals at American-cuisine restaurants, but within this confine she found someone who understood her dilemma and endeavored to make the desert cow town feel a little more like home. A friendly elderly lady ran a small corner restaurant in downtown Tucson and she understood Sue's need for the familiar. "I can fix anything you want," the proprietor told her, "just tell me what it is." Sue acquired a little formal cooking experience before she left Japan, but for the next six months, she went to the hole in the wall, told the owner the characteristics of the food she sought, and the kindly old woman cooked it for her as best she could. Through this collaboration, Sue not only found a welcoming place, but a better understanding of the foods with which she had grown up. Eventually, the Tiltons opened the first and second dedicated Japanese restaurants in an area commonly known as Southern Arizona.

A count of restaurants in Tucson reveals that there are almost forty non-chain eateries that identify as Japanese directly by their names, with another twenty or so claiming to serve some sort of Japanese food (usually sushi) in addition to their primary non-Japanese fare. Indeed, the Tucson area boasts more Japanese restaurants per capita than restaurant-friendly metropolitan areas such as Boston, Chicago, Austin, and Atlanta. In a metropolitan area of just over one million people with around 1,100 people of Japanese descent, there are obviously many individuals eating Japanese cuisine who do not trace their ancestry to the Land of the Rising Sun. Roughly one-half of Tucson's Japanese cuisine restaurants are owned by Nikkei, particularly surprising since Latinos and increasingly Koreans—two of the largest groups of Japanese cuisine restaurateurs—are numerous in the metropolitan area.

This examination of Tucson's early Japanese restaurants illustrates the determined steps undertaken to educate the public about Japanese cuisine in smaller urban areas with few Nikkei. When the area's first Japanese restaurants started to appear in the 1960s and 1970s, relatively few people knew about Japanese culture beyond World War II, James Clavell's *Shogun,* compact cars, and electronic consumer goods. In this environment, Japanese restaurateurs were responsible for informing the public about the intricacies of Asian delicacies ranging from the nearly familiar (teriyaki) to the near-repulsive (sushi).[4] By examining these early restaurateurs, we can thus understand the ways in which minorities made inroads into American society through person-to-person contact and education, without the benefits of ethnopoles and concentrated ethnic communities.[5]

This study also reveals that the popularization of Japanese food in the desert community had drawbacks that directly affected its Nikkei. When Japanese restaurants were few, they acted as semi-formal community centers for Tucson's small population of Nikkei. Eventually, these restaurants served the Japanese American community by providing Tucson's Nikkei with a forum to express their heritage and to strengthen their ethnic and cultural bonds. One large eatery took on the mantle of becoming Tucson's *de facto* Nikkei community center, serving as an ethnopole of sorts. However, as the numbers of Japanese restaurants increased, so did the competition for Nikkei and non-Nikkei loyalty.

This weakened the ability of this restaurant-cum-community-center to serve the small Nikkei population, gradually leading to its demise. Moreover, as Japanese food became increasingly popular, Nikkei owners, who had been the sole proprietors in the region, began to face competition from non-Nikkei. The end result was that they lost their dominance of the Japanese restaurant industry in Southern Arizona.

The Wilmot Inn and the Formation of Southern Arizona's Japanese-Cuisine Culture

Millions of service members were stationed in Japan after 1945, yet most Americans still knew very little about the country's culture or foodways in the immediate postwar era. In a 1958 article series entitled "Orienting Your Diet," the *Stars and Stripes, Pacific* recommended that its readers familiarize themselves with Japanese food, first through sake and through the then-uncommon soy sauce, which was "as basic in Japan as salt and pepper." If readers felt adventuresome, they could try "it for tangy extra flavor in many standard Occidental dishes" and then advance by moving on to "powdered essence of seaweed," an "iodine-rich . . . protein source . . . used by the Japanese to enhance flavors in everything from breakfast fruit juices to salads." The three foods it suggested included sukiyaki, which was comprised of "thinly sliced lean meat with green onions, mushrooms, and bamboo shoots and seasonings" and often eaten "from the same pan." The second dish recommended was shrimp tempura, a Japanese delicacy easily westernized into a "do-it-your-self [*sic*] adventure for party guests!" Tempura, the article claimed, should be served with a mixture of soy sauce, white wine, water, sugar, and powdered ginger. The final recommended dish was teriyaki-marinated meats, another "easily prepared Japanese dish." Although the article focused on chicken, the intrepid eater could use "the same sauce . . . for steak or hamburger teri-yaki." These "big three" Japanese dishes presented in the series—teriyaki chicken or steak, sukiyaki, and tempura (usually shrimp)—while traditional, constituted a small portion of the Japanese diet.[6]

Although the Chinese restaurants in Tucson's Chinatowns probably served some form of food that was common to both Chinese and Japanese cultures, the first restaurant with dedicated Japanese dishes in the

Old Pueblo was the restaurant at the Wilmot Inn. The Inn was built in the 1940s as a dude ranch, but within twenty years was converted to a year-round resort that provided its guests with a swimming pool and "relaxation and sunshine" in combination with "lovely gardens, friendliness, exceptional food, and patio rooms." Eventually, the Inn was purchased in 1960 or 1961 by Bernard J. Sloan and his spouse, Mary. The son of a naval commander, Bernard spent part of his childhood in Yokohama, even attending Yokohama High School in the late 1940s, where he courted his wife. By 1962 the Sloans, who had "learned the art of native [Japanese] cookery," offered Japanese food at the Inn "on occasion." Guests were given kimono (women) or "hari [*sic*], or happy coats" (men) and were seated "on cushions around a low table" while the "haunting music of the Orient" played through the "hifi."[7]

The *Tucson Citizen*'s columnist served double-duty not only by acting as a food critic, but also as Tucson's resident educator on the intricacies of Japanese food, including the use of its unfamiliar dinnerware, chopsticks. Guests were served a fixed course over the span of about two hours by a "gracious" waitress named Kazuko, a "Japanese girl from Yokosuka."[8] The menu included *suimono* (described as "a clear broth of fish and seaweed"), *mukozuke* ("wafer-thin pieces of raw fish, dipped in a sauce of soya and horse radish"), *sunomono* ("crabmeat and cucumber, marinated in vinegar, soya sauce and ginger"), tempura ("mouth-watering shrimp, hunks of squash, egg plant, green beans, parsley and fresh spinach, dipped in a batter of beaten eggs and then deep fried"), and finally, sukiyaki, ("bacon-thin diagonally sliced beef, diagonally sliced green onions and celery, bamboo shoots, water chestnuts, shirataki [noodles], bean curd, and mushrooms, cooked in soy sauce, sake wine and soup stock"). Kazuko, ever gracious, kept the patrons' "glasses filled with icy Nippon beer and . . . cups filled with heated sake." By the end of the meal, the columnist and the other non-initiated at the table found that there was "nothing to eating with chopsticks" and handled them "like old pros."[9]

It is difficult to determine how often the Inn offered Japanese service, but such evenings were encouraging enough for the Sloans to incorporate them on a full-time basis. "WANTED," a Wilmot Inn ad began in late September 1965, "customers for polite and beautiful service of authentic Japanese food." On October 1, 1965, the Bamboo

Room opened and began taking reservations for "dinner and [parties]." The service must have not lived up to the hopes of the Sloans to bring a full-time Japanese restaurant to Southern Arizona, and by the end of November, the advertisements dried up and the Bamboo Room faded into the desert landscape.[10]

The Tiltons Bring Dedicated Japanese Cuisine to Tucson

While the Wilmot Inn was probably the first restaurant to offer a Japanese menu in the Old Pueblo, the Tiltons' was the first to bill itself as an "authentic" standalone Japanese restaurant. Sometime in late April or early May 1964, Sue and Homer opened Tokyo Sukiyaki on Tucson's west side. An examination of this restaurant demonstrates the troubles faced when such an exotic cuisine is served in an isolated corner of the desert Southwest. It also demonstrates a continuing attempt by the Tiltons to introduce Americans to the foreign taste of Japanese food and, by extension, a large part of its culture.

The restaurant, located a mile north of Mission Road on Ajo, served "sukiyaki, tempura, teriyaki, and many other fine dishes . . . in an authentic Japanese style" as well as drinks on Sundays from 11:00 a.m. to midnight and on weekdays, except Tuesdays, from 5:00 to 11:00 p.m. Advertising these three foods was no coincidence, as they were arguably the most well-known Japanese dishes at the time. The first week was a "gratifying success," according to an open letter from Sue and Homer to patrons published in the *Tucson Citizen* on May 7, 1964. The letter encouraged Tucson residents to celebrate Mother's Day at the restaurant in order to "treat the family to a new taste sensation," imploring them to call ahead to reserve a space in the restaurant's tatami room.[11]

In 1964, there was a great deal of interest in Chinese cuisine, but Japanese food simply was not *en vogue,* forcing Tokyo Sukiyaki to change its public image within just a few short months.[12] It is clear from advertisements that Tokyo Sukiyaki relied more and more on its liquor license than the fact that it was Tucson's only Japanese restaurant. While the restaurant still stressed its "authentic Japanese food," atmosphere, and "Japanese delicacies," it was now open from 11:30 a.m.

to 11:30 p.m. daily (except for Tuesdays) and offered "special Japanese lunches" served with their customers' "favorite Japanese or American cocktails." Tokyo Sukiyaki even offered "special party rates" to large groups.[13] The Tiltons also suggested that Tucsonans "be different" by celebrating New Year's at the restaurant, which opened at noon.[14] Eventually, Tokyo Sukiyaki's hours were changed back to evening hours on weekdays (5:00 to 11:00 p.m.), the list of authentic Japanese foods was curtailed or left out altogether, and advertisements prominently told customers that cocktails were available "At All Times."

By April of 1965, Tokyo Sukiyaki went on the offensive, telling their potential customers that they should "Yen for the Best" by dining at the "resplendent Tokyo Sukiyaki." Not only was the restaurant "authentic" with "Tokyo style" food served by "kimono-clad Japanese waitresses" in the main dining and tatami rooms, where patrons would sit at "low tables" topped by "glowing lamps," but the Tiltons had also set up several tables shabu-shabu style, where "sukiyaki dinners [were] cooked at tables." Potential patrons were still told that cocktails were a main feature of the restaurant, and were encouraged to order the "famous Saken-San Lotus Blossom" cocktail.[15] American food was also prominent in the ads, with "charcoal broiled steaks" (which is actually also an Asian way to prepare beef) being offered to pique Western palates. However, it was clear that authenticity was not going to drive customers to their door, and from the end of 1965 to the restaurant's closure around February 1966, ads were simple. Except for the name of the restaurant, only cocktails were advertised.

Despite their failure, the Tiltons were not deterred. A decade later, they encountered another opportunity to open a Japanese restaurant by way of some friends who enjoyed Sue's Japanese cooking and knew of a location that needed a commercial tenant. When friends provided approximately $10,000 in seed money, the Tiltons once again agreed to try to introduce Japanese food to the city. The property near Camino Seco and Speedway was actually a large house containing a commercial kitchen, several rooms, and an unused (but filled) swimming pool—a far cry from the small hole-in-the-wall that had housed Tokyo Sukiyaki. Sue, an accomplished painter, decorated the restaurant's walls with murals that resembled classical Japanese *mokuhanga* and created an entrance that looked like a Shinto shrine. She also hand-painted the new restaurant's name, Sakura-ya (Cherry Blossom House), in kanji. Once again, early advertisements for the restaurant downplayed liquor and emphasized cooking, but later ads stressed cocktails, banquets, and catering.

Sakura-ya, which opened in the first weeks of February 1973, featured a limited menu, as had Tokyo Sukiyaki. As more Japanese, and

FIGURE 10.2. Advertisement from 1973

FIGURE 10.3. Advertisement from 1976

those who had lived in Japan, came to Southern Arizona, Sakura-ya began to offer a larger selection. Sue acquired as many of her ingredients from local suppliers as she could. It was only the fish and Japanese-specific ingredients that she had to order from Japanese Food Corporation, a Los Angeles–based supplier. Original menu items such as teriyaki beef and chicken were soon joined by miso soup, *sunomono* (cucumber vinegar salad), *yakizakana* (traditional grilled Japanese fish), shrimp tempura, and eventually a few simple types of rolled and *nigiri* sushi. She did not attempt to educate her customers, as most patrons who ordered the more traditional Japanese foods were either Nikkei or clients who had lived in Japan.[16]

Sakura-ya was one of the few non-agricultural businesses in Southern Arizona where someone of Japanese heritage could work for a Japanese owner. Around a third to a half of the restaurant's employees at any one time were Nikkei, and the Tiltons used them to add to the authentic, and perhaps exotic, atmosphere by requiring staff members to wear Japanese *happi*. Nikkei tended to prep in the morning and then cook for the lunch crowd after the restaurant opened. As the day wore on, more non-Nikkei, particularly boys from the local high school, began to work as short-order cooks and on the cleanup crew. A few years later, the restaurant advertised "Japanese dancing," giving Nikkei women a chance to perform "Shizoko-san-do ["Shizoko's way/method"] style Japanese dances on Friday and Saturday evenings." There were at least two dancers: Shizoko, who worked at IBM during the day, and Emiko, who usually helped Sue prep and serve at the restaurant. Shizoko and Emiko actually danced in "yakuza style," which is an informal style of dance consisting of traditional *odori* dance forms combined with individual interpretive movements.

Sakura-ya fared much better than Tokyo Sukiyaki, most likely because of its location on Tucson's then-more-affluent east side, the area's larger population, support from Tucson's growing Nikkei community, and an increasing awareness of Japanese cuisine among locals. Sue's proudest moment came in 1974, when after a vetting by around twenty Caucasians (mostly women), Sakura-ya was awarded the Gold Plate Award by the Southern Arizona Restaurant Association and the Pima County Health Department on October 10, 1974 for "consistently excellent standards of cleanliness and sanitation."[17]

Homer received a lucrative employment offer in 1975 from a former supervisor who had moved to Fort Hood, Texas, and decided that it was too good to refuse. Thus began the downfall of Tucson's second Japanese restaurant.[18] Sue found a buyer for the restaurant and explicitly warned him about the perils associated with the local food inspector, whom she described as a "real mean fellow." She had learned the intricacies of the inspection system and the quirks of the inspector, but the new owner paid little heed and the Japanese restaurant, Tucson's only one at the time, closed within months, sometime in early 1976.

Post-Tilton Japanese Restaurateurs

Southern Arizona had to wait another decade before the next Japanese restaurant was built, but in the interim, a Japanese-owned establishment took up the task and began offering traditional cuisine. The Driftwood Restaurant and Lounge, located just outside of the gates of Davis-Monthan Air Force Base, was purchased by the Kakishita family. Momoko (b. 1934, Tokyo), came to the United States in 1957 via an arranged marriage to a Nikkei, Kazuo, who had been living in North Carolina and working as a chicken sexer. Like Sue Tilton, Momoko Kakishita also had to learn to cook Japanese food as a housewife, using local ingredients or those ordered from Chicago. Eventually, the Kakishitas relocated to Tucson. After the local chicken farm shut down, they purchased the Driftwood, a steakhouse, in 1974. The Driftwood was already a successful staple for the airmen and women who worked at Davis-Monthan, but the Kakishitas hoped to add Japanese food to the menu as well (initially, their only Japanese selection was sukiyaki). However, they had difficulty cooking steaks to suit their customers' palates (they were accustomed to specific inter-mountain Western recipes) and within a year, the Kakishitas filled the large dining room with pool tables and converted the Driftwood to a part-time grill restaurant and full-time bar.

Momoko, who had worked at Sakura-ya for a few months before purchasing the Driftwood, enjoyed being in the kitchen and was determined to share Japanese food with her customers. The establishment was perpetually slow on Wednesdays and Thursdays, and perhaps offering something different on one of these days would help bring in a mid-week customer base outside the bar crowd. Within a couple of years, the Driftwood became the only restaurant in Tucson serving Japanese food. In order to save on cost, control inventory, and take advantage of once-a-week air deliveries to Tucson, "Momoko-san," as she affectionately became known to her customers, decided to offer Japanese food only on Thursdays, which was ideal for freshness, since the shipment from the Japanese Food Company came in on Wednesday nights or early Thursday mornings.[19] In another cost-saving measure, the menu was not printed and could vary from week to week. Common staples, such as teriyaki and sukiyaki, were always on offer, but so, too, were the wholly exotic and unknown (to non-Nikkei palates, at least) *tonkatsu*, sushi, octopus, and squid. In order to add to the ambiance, the jukebox was loaded with Japanese songs and played continuously.

The once-a-week Japanese menu was designed to introduce non-Japanese patrons to Japanese foods and to bring in members of Tucson's growing Nikkei community. Consequently, the Driftwood set the stage for the next phase of Tucson's Japanese restaurants. While non-Nikkei generally ordered the familiar, on Thursdays the kitchen help and wait staff were Nikkei women. In addition to helping "Mrs. K" prepare most of the day, they were instructed to ensure that no matter what they ordered, customers fully understood what they were going to consume. Momoko-san and her compatriots also educated customers on how to use chopsticks and eat meals properly, and perhaps how to disguise unfamiliar tastes with teriyaki sauce.

Advertising was always word-of-mouth, and in the beginning, it was mostly regulars who ordered Japanese food. However, once they learned of these Thursdays nights, "homesick Japanese students" from the University of Arizona began to stop by so they could enjoy familiar meals cooked by "mama-san."[20] Another Nikkei group who came were Nikkei professors who appreciated congregating as an ethnic lot. A third group consisted of patrons who wanted to purchase sashimi meat, which Momoko would sell at cost so that her fillets—sometimes as large as three feet or more—would not go to waste. In between were servicemen and women from Davis-Monthan who had served in Japan and longed for the Asian tastes they left behind. Dinners were soon well-attended affairs, sometimes with waitlists, especially after the *Tucson Citizen* profiled the Japanese night in May 1977. Although Kakishita enjoyed serving her native cuisine and liked interacting with her Nikkei workmates and customers, the all-out Thursday cooking marathon was physically and mentally taxing, and after about two years, Tucson, once again, lost its only Japanese restaurant.

During their relatively short runs, Sakura-Ya and the Driftwood established the paradigm for Japanese restaurants in Southern Arizona by not only providing Nikkei with a space to congregate—ethnopoles, albeit small ones—with familiar foods, sounds, and atmosphere, but also by educating the dominant culture about Japanese cuisine—a cuisine that would become faddishly popular within the next two decades. Other proprietors of Japanese restaurants who opened their establishments in the 1980s and early 1990s reported having to undertake the same painstaking task of educating their clientele. For Michiko Maggie Grace (b. 1953), a native of Okinawa who opened her restaurant in nearby Sierra Vista, authenticity was paramount. At her restaurant, Tanuki, she hired only Japanese-trained sushi chefs, made her own sauces, and would throw out any fish that did not meet her high standards, preferring to lose money rather than customers.[21] She noticed from her pre-Tanuki venture, a Chinese restaurant that sold a limited Japanese menu, that "maybe more than ninety percent . . . of people never ate Japanese food." In order to educate them, she offered free samples of Japanese food and two-for-one specials to encourage experimentation. Grace emphasized the taste, freshness, and health benefits of Japanese food to her customers, many of whom were Southern Arizona retirees who were on a limited budget and distrusting of new dishes. Her first success came with *bento* lunches where ingredients were presented together on a plate rather than in individual compartments like in a *bento* box, thus taking on the external appearance of familiar Chinese dishes.

The Tokyo Restaurant

In early 1980, Tucson acquired a new traditional Japanese restaurant and would never again find itself without one. Isidro Sanchez, a Latino American, and his Nikkei wife, Michiko, opened the Tokyo Store, which within two years would become Tokyo Store and Restaurant, on East Twenty-Second Street. The original restaurant was described by Tucson food critics as a "little market . . . laden with exotic goodies" such as "packages of seaweed, rice crackers, sauces, and all kinds of fish."[22] Probably sensing the need for prepared Japanese foods in Tucson, the Sanchezes eventually carved out a small portion of the store for a restaurant that met the void left by the Driftwood. The restaurant was described as an "unromantic . . . little hole in the wall . . . [with] an L-shaped sushi bar in one corner of the room and . . . six or seven small tables." The decor was also rudimentary, "with metal napkin holders on the tables and the sounds of both radio and television intruding from the store." Those who remember eating there recall seeing Isidro behind the sushi bar but rarely his wife, who cooked in the back. Nevertheless, the Tokyo Store served a larger selection of Japanese food than the Tiltons' restaurants or the Driftwood. The Sanchezes no doubt took advantage of the air cargo deliveries that had made the Driftwood's once-a-week Japanese fare possible. They were open every day except Mondays, and offered a full menu of the big three, *nigiri*, *maki*, and *chirashi* sushi, *sashimi*, sake, and Japanese beer.

By 1982, the Tokyo Store and Sushi Bar became the Tokyo Restaurant and Sushi Bar, and moved to a larger location about a block west. The store was gone, replaced by "one dining room, with a partition dividing it into two smaller areas." The restaurant sported two *chabudai* (traditional low tables) surrounded by cushions and a sushi bar in the back. The same food critics who reviewed the original restaurant were greeted not by Isidro, but by a Nikkei waitress named Kazuko (whether she was in kimono or not is unclear). Surprised by this formality, the reviewers were worried that the restaurant "had become more of a commercial venture than a family business inspired by the chef's love of good food." They found this not to be the case, and described their experience in Ezra Vogel–like terms, writing that it was "simply a manifestation of the widely observed talent of the Japanese for incorporating Western marketing techniques into their traditional pursuit of precision and aesthetics." The new menu was even more complete and was expanded to include *chirinabe*, *gyoza*, and even green tea ice cream.[23]

The Rise of King Sushi

In John Hughes's popular teen dramedy, *The Breakfast Club* (1984), the "Princess," a rich, virginal, suburban high school student played by Molly Ringwald, prepares her *bento* box while the "Criminal," an underprivileged, poorly-behaved student from the wrong side of town played by Judd Nelson, is taken aback. "What is that?" he asks in a disgusted tone. "Sushi . . . raw fish, rice, and seaweed," replies the Princess. Unable to resist a jab against both the prissy coed and her unappetizing tastes, the Criminal responds, "You won't accept a guy's tongue in your mouth and you're going to eat that?" In a 1988 episode of the popular legal drama *L.A. Law* entitled "Hand Roll Express," one of the firm's senior partners is ordering at a sushi bar for the first time. As a sushi neophyte, he asks a comely woman sitting next to him if he should order the "giant clam" or the "red snapper." The woman advises him that those dishes cost $40, and in the end, he agrees to a "hand roll" for $20. At that point, she informs him that he has been busted for soliciting a prostitute and he is hauled away in cuffs. Both scenes represent the state of sushi in the United States at the time: foreign, suspicious, yet entertainingly dangerous and, for many, irresistible.

By 1980, Los Angeles, New York, Chicago, and other large cities had already accepted Japanese food and were well in the middle of a "sushi-eating trend."[24] This trend most likely began in the late 1970s in Southern California, already home to a large number of Japanese Americans, when Angelinos began to see an "open-mindedness toward foreign cultures," healthy eating, fresh ingredients, and the California lifestyle as being synonymous. But in smaller cities like Tucson, Japanese restaurateurs had to educate the local populations about the intricacies of raw fish. Many avoided it because in inland areas, "fish [has] a bad reputation" owing to "the distance from the sea," which "usually means that the fish arriving . . . took a wrong turn into a net days or weeks ago."[25] Although the lack of fresh fish was certainly a factor, sushi was simply "so foreign" that most Americans reacted in disgust, just as Judd Nelson's bad-boy character did. In Escondito, California—described as a "conservative farming enclave steeped in traditional American values"—the owner of the Katsu Restaurant began offering courses on the basics of sushi at the local community college. He was criticized by college officials who believed that "the course would never go," but was surprised to find that his six-week classes soon had waiting lists of up to eighty people; one student even flew in regularly from St. Louis, Missouri.[26] Classes were primarily comprised of Caucasian females, but restaurateurs were also interested in learning how to prepare sushi.

In May 1984, the *Tucson Citizen* ran an article that introduced Tucsonans to sushi, a dish that was "simple to eat and pleasing to the eye." The *Citizen* instructed its readers in the basics of the food's components, how it is prepared, and how one should eat it. The article also provided an ingredients list, cooking instructions, and preparation tips for its more adventuresome readers.[27] "Sushi," read the article, "though it requires a minimum of cooking, is complicated in ways that make home preparation difficult."[28] The "trick" to sushi, stated the author, was in "the presentation" of the "mixture of raw fish, cold rice and dried seaweed" in a "small package about the size of a large thumb." Probably not familiar with sushi herself, the author concentrated on the "presentation" of sushi and not on its potential health benefits or taste.

While Japanese food slowly gained recognition, sushi was still several steps behind. Michiko Maggie Grace and her employee Hideko Espinoza (b. 1941, Hiroshima, Japan) both remembered that customers had to be educated "slowly, slowly, slowly! Educate all the time!" They would start by explaining the food, and then would introduce customers to California rolls, which was actually a type of sushi that contained no raw fish and was developed in Los Angeles in the 1970s. Customers "asked all kinds of questions!" and proprietors had to "have a lot of patience to answer them." In the next stage, they could introduce customers to *tekka maki* (tuna rolls), then advance on to more complex sushi such as *unagi* (eel), *hamachi* (yellowtail tuna), and *hotegai* (raw scallops). In order to make this possible, Grace had to ensure that quality remained paramount, or she could not only turn a patron off to sushi, but also lose them as a customer forever.[29]

The Japanese Kitchen: A Restaurant and Ethnopole

The Tokyo Restaurant was popular for a time as the city's only Japanese eatery, but the Old Pueblo's burgeoning market attracted the attention of the owner of the Japanese Kitchen and Steakhouse, a chain of western *teppanyaki* restaurants modelled after the successful Benihana. Once the Kitchen arrived, it attracted both Nikkei and non-Nikkei alike, while the Tokyo Restaurant maintained a primarily smaller, mostly Nikkei clientele. Although the Tokyo attempted to regain its non-Japanese customer base by stressing its "authentic Japanese cuisine" and its "traditional setting of naturalness and tranquility" featuring "kimono clad hostesses," it never regained them in mass numbers. Soon, the Tokyo Restaurant began to lose its Caucasian customer base to the Kitchen, with its larger menu and made-to-entertain atmosphere. Also, as a chain, the Kitchen appeared to have a better pipeline to fresh seafood, and most subjects interviewed for this study who visited the Tokyo Restaurant at the time clearly remembered that sushi was not served consistently due to the constant shortage of fresh fish.

Although the exact history of the Japanese Kitchen has been somewhat obscured by time, the chain was formed sometime in the 1970s, and restaurants opened in Albuquerque, Denver, Colorado Springs, Fresno, and Scottsdale. The Japanese Kitchen's ambiance was modeled after Benihana, which took its cooking style from post-war Japanese *teppanyaki* steakhouses and its external appearance from Japanese Buddhist temples.[30] The Kitchen's slogan, "Ah, So Good!" was backed with the taglines "continuous entertainment," "it's a meal in a show," and "a show to see again and again." The Kitchen touted its entertaining, *teppanyaki*-style cooking in which up to eight patrons would sit around three sides of a common table that housed a large, flat-griddle, under-heated cooking surface approximately one-and-a-half meters squared. Once guests ordered their meals, they would receive *oshibori* (hot towels) from a kimono-clad waitress (Nikkei, if at all possible) to clean their hands, and hot green tea, if desired. Moments later, a chef sporting a smart uniform (including a very distinctively shaped tall hat) brought all of the ingredients to the table using a cart, lit the under-surface burners, and proceeded to cook each meal directly in front of the patrons. It is through this preparation method that Japanese steakhouses like the Kitchen left their impressions, as the food was not simply cooked but was theatrically prepared with flair and panache. Chefs were specifically trained to perform, cooking with flailing knives, food flipping and flying through the air (even onto patrons' dishes), "volcanoes" made of sliced onion rings, running narratives about the meal to come, and even the occasional joke. John Jennings, a food critic from the *Tucson Citizen*, probably echoed the concerns of many patrons when he wrote that "as fast as those knives are moving . . . you worry that although you may have ordered seafood, you will end up with steakfingers."[31] In addition to the entertainment, the restaurants sported *torii*, a Japanese garden-style bridge, a koi pond, a non-*teppan* dining area, and a sushi bar. The spacious interiors were furnished with touches such as *shoji* and exposed, brown-painted wood.

The Kitchen opened in Tucson sometime in early to mid-1981 and became popular due to its entertaining format and its more diverse menu, which appealed to both Nikkei and non-Nikkei alike. The Kitchen even included a children's menu featuring simple, minimally-spiced meals of chicken, steak, or shrimp that included ice cream or sherbet desert. To make the atmosphere as inviting as possible, the Kitchen was spacious and housed common rooms as well as private meeting/party rooms. Tucson newspapers' advertising sections were replete with announcements for graduation parties, wedding receptions, organizational outings, and family reunions held at the Kitchen. As the Japanese Kitchen rose, the Tokyo Restaurant slowly fell, even among Nikkei patrons. In 1983, a two-room restaurant, Maiko, was opened by Hawaiian Japanese Americans, but its small size, limited menu, and proximity to the Kitchen doomed it from the beginning and it remained in operation for less than two years.[32] Only in 1986 did two more restaurants open, and their distance from the Kitchen and their intimate atmosphere were the primary characteristics that allowed them to flourish.

The Japanese Kitchen's appeal with Nikkei was also due to its direct attempts to connect with the Japanese community in Tucson. The owner of the Japanese Kitchen, Takeshi Ishihara, hailed from Japan and made it a point to hire as many Nikkei as possible, only resorting to chefs of other ethnicities (particularly Mexican Americans) if he could not find anyone else. In addition, the Kitchen began to promote cultural events that interested patrons of Japanese ancestry. On a once- and then twice-monthly basis (seemingly on Sundays beginning in 1983 or 1984), the Kitchen sponsored "Japanese Night" and invited the area's two local Japanese dance troupes (one from Tucson and the other from Sierra Vista, some seventy minutes away) to dance in a large open area of the restaurant on a purpose-built wooden floor. Unlike Sakura-Ya's dance performances, the Kitchen's were specifically designed to attract Nikkei clientele and provide them with a sense of home and community. After dancing and dinner, the Kitchen staff would set up an eight-track *karaoke* machine and keep the restaurant open until liquor laws mandated its closing at 1:00 a.m. Most interviewees remember between thirty and fifty patrons on average. Additionally, many groups of students and formal and informal Nikkei groups, such as the professors who had gone to the Driftwood, began to meet regularly at the Kitchen.

As the Kitchen grew in popularity with the Nikkei community, its managers realized that it was turning into a bona fide community center and sought to engage the Nikkei population of Southern Arizona even further. The Japanese Kitchen was built on the outskirts of town at 8424 E. Old Spanish Trail where land was relatively inexpensive. Because of this, its parking lot was large, unbroken, and could serve as the site of cultural events.[33] The timing of the Japanese Kitchen's first festival, the *Ohigan Matsuri* (also known as the Fall Festival; it changed to *Aki Matsuri* the following year), was held from 5:30 to 9:30 p.m. on September 26, 1982.[34] Not only were Nikkei invited to attend (wearing "Japanese dress" if possible), but the general public was also encouraged to discover Japanese culture for themselves. Mari Kaneta (who had just moved to Tucson before the 1984 *Aki Matsuri*) described it as "a small-scale Buddhist church [festival] . . . with a *yagura* (a scaffolded bandstand common at matsuri) and booths that sold food." Florence Misako Azeka-sensei, a traditional Japanese dance *natori* (one ranked as a professional and bestowed with a stage name), and her *odori* group, the Minyo Dancers, were invited to dance by the festival's organizers, the Japan-America Society of Tucson. Those wishing to learn the traditional Japanese festival dances (done in large circles during the festival so everyone could enjoy themselves) were invited to the Kitchen's parking lot the prior Thursday and Friday. Ishihara-san even brought in decorations from his Albuquerque Japanese Kitchen, along with that area's *taiko* drum group to help bolster the festival's atmosphere.

Finally, several booths were set up by groups with at least tangential relationships to Japanese culture.[35]

The first Fall Festival went better than planners had hoped. Although it was "not a huge success from the dollar standpoint," the festival attracted a "larger . . . crowd" than had been expected, which made it a sure-fire "cultural success."[36] The Society thanked the many employees of the Kitchen (both from Tucson and Albuquerque) for their help and even recognized the Tokyo Restaurant for providing a "sushi booth" that added to the cultural atmosphere. The *Aki Matsuri* the following year was moved to October 30 (most likely to take advantage of the cooler weather) and blended the "two traditions" of Halloween and the *matsuri* together. Children were encouraged to either dress in traditional Japanese garb or in costume and they were allowed to show off their wares for the judges during an 8:00 p.m. parade. They were judged and prized for costumes that were the "most original," "prettiest," scariest," "authentic ethnic," and "funniest."[37] Koreanna Shop (a Korean grocer), McDonald's, and Jack in the Box donated prizes. A "special category" was even held for "senior citizens . . . 60 yrs. and older . . . who would like to get in on the fun." Another new event was a karaoke competition, held just after the parade. Booths included food/confectionaries (with the Kitchen providing tempura and *yakitori*), "arts and crafts" (e.g. origami, *sumi-e,* and *shodō* [calligraphy]), and a "flea market" that sold goods donated by those wishing to support the Japan-America Society.[38] The Minyo Dancers (*odori* style) from Sierra Vista and Albuquerque's taiko group appeared along with "two rickshaws with rides for everyone."[39]

The Japanese Kitchen also began to host the Japan-America Society's Oshogatsu (New Year's Celebration) and closed on New Year's Day so that it could host traditions such as *mochitsuki* (in which rice is pounded into a traditional pastry used in *ozoni*), *koto* (Japanese harp playing), *ikebana* (flower arranging), and *cha-no-yu* (a tea ceremony). The menu was fixed by the Japanese Kitchen and was a traditional multi-course meal that included *kamaboko* (fish cake), *gomame/tatsukuri* (dried anchovies), *datemaki* (a type of Japanese omelet), *kuromame* (black beans), *maguro shashimi*, *kinpira gobo* (a type of simple stir-fry vegetable dish), *gomi goshoku* and *namasu* (both traditional New Year's dishes), *kikka kabu* (turnip), and *ozoni* (mochi soup).[40] Each year, around two hundred people celebrated the event.[41]

Popularity and Dissolution

The Fall Festivals were increasingly popular, with a headcount in the hundreds for the 1982 inaugural event, but eventually, the *matsuri* became the harbinger of the problems faced by Tucson's growing fascination with Japanese culture and food. The growing popularity of Japanese food and culture ironically began to create business opportunities that led to the Kitchen's downfall and overwhelmed Tucson's small, temporary, but notable ethnopole. In the case of the latter, in just its second year, the festival drew over 800 (probably closer to 1,000) participants—what was just two years old was becoming too large (partially thanks to the Japanese Kitchen's large overflow parking lot) and the Japan-America Society began to struggle to find the resources necessary to continue it.[42] During that year, the Society estimated that at least thirty booths would participate and by October (the festival was held on November 4), the Society was still calling for volunteers. Their sign-up sheet indicated that fewer than 50 percent of the needed volunteers were secured.[43] The third annual *Aki Matsuri* was similar to the previous two, and included demonstrations on origami (by Sam Ciulla, a noted practitioner of the art), martial arts, and music (such as the *koto*). The following year, the Society was "desperately" in need of workers for that year's *Aki Matsuri* and its projected thousand-plus participants. It told its members that "the workers have more fun than anyone there!"[44] Fun it may have been, but the entreaty did not elicit the full-fledged help the Society needed, and the *Aki Matsuri* of 1985 was the last held at the Japanese Kitchen, due to "labor problems, costs, lack of returns commensurate to the work involved, etc."[45] Smaller festivals were subsequently held at a home donated to the Society for a few more years, but they were never the popular affairs that took place in the Kitchen's parking lot (New Year's celebrations were also held at the new location, and did not meet the same numbers as those held at the Kitchen).

Similarly, the success of the Japanese Kitchen marked a turning point in the evolution of both the Japanese-cuisine restaurant in Tucson as well as the city's Nikkei community. Tucson's denizens finally came to appreciate Japanese dining in the early late 1980s, and were ready to have more options. The Tokyo Restaurant and Japanese Kitchen's policy of hiring Nikkei, when they could, created a local pool of talent who were versed in the restaurant business and ready to leverage their skills in the open market. Potential restaurateurs realized that headlining popular and genuine Japanese dishes combined with "authentic" atmospheres were huge selling points for the Tucson public. Beginning with fits and starts in 1986, Tucson's Japanese restaurants began to grow in number, as others began to open new establishments and hire the cooks and sushi chefs that the Japanese Kitchen and Tokyo Restaurant and Sushi Bar had so carefully trained over the years. Sometime in 1985, the Fuji Restaurant and Sushi Bar, whose ads touted an atmosphere "beautifully decorated in Japanese custom decor" with "kimono clad waitresses," opened in Tucson's Catalina foothills. A year later, Michi's Express opened near the University of Arizona, and in 1988, Shogun Japanese Restaurant and Sushi Bar, which offered "the finest in traditional Japanese dining" opened on the northwest side of the city. This was followed by the Yamato Japanese Restaurant about a mile north of the University of Arizona.

One example of this trend is the Yamato Japanese Restaurant, whose proprietor, Nobu Nakajima (b. 1953, Matsumoto, Japan), worked at his uncle's restaurant in Japan, trained as a *teppan* chef at the Japanese Kitchen in Colorado Springs for eleven years, and eventually transferred to Tucson. Although he was unsure if opening his own restaurant was the right thing, after a phone call with his father who suggested that he "stand up on his own," Nakajima decided that conditions were right for an attempt. He originally copied his former employer's successful formula in the more populous Phoenix area, but quickly tired of the commute and found an available space on Grand Avenue and First Street in one of the oldest strip malls in the city that was all but abandoned. Nakajima realized that the location, albeit tired from age and neglect, had two upsides: its proximity to the University of Arizona and its distance from the Japanese Kitchen. The Yamato was outfitted with *shoji*, *chochin* (Japanese paper lanterns), and a full-length sushi bar. In 1988, when the Yamato opened, Nakajima offered all-day sushi, and his business immediately "boomed," particularly on the weekend, when it was "packed."[46] Over the course of its existence (it was still in business and owned by Nakajima and his wife, Mari Kaneta, at the time of this study), the Yamato stressed consistent, fresh, and healthy cuisine. The menu has remained relatively traditional and has maintained a steady and loyal customer base since its founding.

Over the next few years, the number of Japanese restaurants continued to grow in Tucson. Bunbuku, Fujiya, Tai Pan's Teriyaki Grill, and five restaurants serving *gyūdon* (beef bowl), among others, brought more varieties of Japanese cuisine to Tucson. None, however, changed the landscape of Tucson's Japanese restaurants and its Nikkei community as much as Sakura, a *teppanyaki* steakhouse on Tucson's east side "restaurant row" that was established by a Korean immigrant, Kwang C. An (b. 1940, Korea). Hailed as a "business genius" by a Southern Arizona Japanese restaurant owner, and a "household name and one of Tucson's most recognizable faces" by the *Arizona Daily Star,* An saw an opportunity in the Japanese Kitchen.[47] At the age of thirty-one, An and his wife moved from Korea to El Paso with $800 in their pockets so he could take a job as a civil engineer. His journey towards becoming one of Tucson's most successful Japanese restaurateurs began with a brush with fame sometime in the mid-1970s when he met President Jimmy Carter. The world leader came through the El Paso airport where An was working as a construction supervisor and shook hands with him; their picture appeared in the next day's newspaper. Fortuitously, someone in Tucson who needed a construction supervisor saw An's photo and called to offer him a job.

Once in Tucson, An excelled at his job and eventually quit to start his own company, but found the city's Asian fare lacking.[48] Dining out on one occasion, An found that "everything that night was bad—the food, the service, the cleanliness." Although he had no restaurant experience, he purchased a small Italian establishment near Davis-Monthan, expanded it, changed its menu, and renamed it the Great Wall China.[49] The Great Wall flourished, and it did not take An long to realize that if Chinese food was so poorly represented, then there was probably business to be found in Japanese food, still a fairly underrepresented cuisine in Tucson. In the late 1980s, An sold the Great Wall and opened a *teppanyaki* restaurant within two years.

An had no intentions to reinvent the wheel and chose to emulate Tucson's standard-bearer restaurant, the Japanese Kitchen. By the end of 1990, his restaurant, Sakura, opened on East Tanque Verde, and the only thing it lacked, according to this study's interviewees, was a koi pond. Although not near the downtown area or the University of Arizona, it was in a location closer to the heart of the city than the Japanese Kitchen and took advantage of the growing traffic flow down Grant Avenue towards the eastern foothills. Additionally, An hired some of the Kitchen's Nikkei staff with greater pay.

Soon, the owner of the Japanese Kitchen began inquiring whether or not other restaurant proprietors wanted to purchase his business, but even a cursory examination of the books revealed deep-seated problems with few solutions. After the *Aki Matsuri* ceased, "Japanese Night" kept going for several more years. However, after Sakura opened and hired away most of the Kitchen's Nikkei staff, the latter was forced to hire non-Nikkei in their place. The nights, no longer a priority for the non-Nikkei staff, sputtered out and stopped altogether. Nikkei students and professors from the University of Arizona began to go to establishments near campus, and the Japan-America Society met at Yukari Sushi, in Tucson's eastern foothills. Furthermore, the Arizona Diamondbacks professional baseball team, which trained in Tucson during the off season, made Sakura their unofficial after-hours hangout. "I think I ate there every night for spring training," exclaimed Luis Gonzalez, the MLB superstar who drove in the championship-winning run in the 2001 World Series.[50] An grew to know him so well that he considered Gonzalez his "No. 1 son" and featured him in his restaurant commercials. Perhaps fittingly, sometime during 1996, both the Tokyo Restaurant and the Japanese Kitchen closed for good, while the Sakura still soldiers on in its original location (albeit without Mr. An's ownership).

Conclusion

Early vendors of Japanese food had a lengthy uphill battle to find non-Nikkei customers as they had to rely on the area's Caucasian and Latino populations to serve as their primary clients since the number of Japanese who lived in the area remained relatively small. Few of these customers were familiar with Japanese food and proprietors were forced to educate their patrons about Asian food. Most settled on Japanese food that was easily adaptable to Caucasian palates, such as teriyaki chicken or beef, and only slowly introduced more uncommon meals, such as tempura and sushi.

Japanese restaurants in Tucson grew slowly after the first, single-owner restaurant was founded in 1964. In time, a few more restaurants opened here and there in the Tucson area, but the city's Asian fare was still primarily the sort of Chinese food that had been familiar to the American palate for almost a century (e.g., chop suey and chow mein). People simply knew very little about Japanese cuisine, and Japanese restaurants had difficulty staying open because of this knowledge gap. Nikkei proprietors' efforts to educate their customers slowly gained traction and progressed when the nation, as a whole, became more interested in Japanese culture and business practices in the mid- to late 1980s. As Japanese cuisine increased in popularity, Nikkei, many of whom were employed by Tucson's Japanese restaurants, began to realize their dreams of business independence and opened restaurants of their own. Thus, Tucson's Japanese restaurant boom began.

However, there is a bittersweet story surrounding all of this success. As Tucson's Nikkei population grew, they yearned for a place to express their Japanese identity, and Nikkei-owned Japanese Restaurants provided these venues. Eventually, one of Tucson's early Japanese restaurants was so large and accommodating that it became the *de facto* Japanese ethnopole for the city. Formal meetings and informal get-togethers were soon punctuated by monthly "Japanese nights" and seasonal *matsuri*. For a few years, the Japanese of Tucson had a common community center they could call their own. The success and growth of Japanese cuisine and the subsequent expansion of Japanese restaurants depleted the resources and thinned the customer base of this restaurant, slowing reducing its relevancy and eventually forcing it to close.

Arising from this was a diverse array of restaurants that gave their owners fiscal independence and its customers choice, but at the cost of Tucson's only Nikkei ethnopole. This can be taken as a warning about the dangers of capitalistic cultural appropriation. As Japanese food became more popular and lucrative, those of non-Nikkei origin could open Japanese cuisine restaurants and profit on a cultural staple that was not their own. Although the true numbers stretch beyond the scope of this research, a non-statistical sampling indicates that the majority of Japanese restaurants, particularly outside of large Nikkei population centers (e.g., Los Angeles, San Francisco, and Hawaii) are not Nikkei-owned. Initially, half of the restaurants contacted for this study were either owned by people of Korean (the majority) or Latino origin. However, Nikkei have never claimed Japanese restaurant ownership for themselves and, at least for the Nikkei restaurateurs who were interviewed, those who do take pride in their restaurants believe they have inroads to a more authentic Japanese taste and dining experience. One interviewee was proud of their ability to attract and retain customers from the dominant culture with "real" Japanese cuisine, as well as their ability to attract a loyal Nikkei clientele (as was also the case with Yukari Sushi, the current Nikkei-owned meeting place of the Japan-America Society).

However, this study also demonstrates that even in "cow towns" such as Tucson, the United States offered ample room for cultural acceptance. Restaurants may, in part, provide opportunities for the dominant culture and those of minority status to interact and learn from one another. As Nikkei restaurateurs gently poked and prodded their customers toward a greater understanding and appreciation of their ancestral cuisine, proprietors also gained an appreciation for the values of their customers. While Japanese food may have been comfortable and familiar, it was also healthy and fresh, something many clients from the dominant culture valued. In time, "exotic" Japanese food allowed Nikkei restaurateurs to turn extraordinary, fanciful sets of ideas into something real and tangible—prosperous and popular establishments. In doing so, Nikkei restaurateurs were successful, at least in some small measure, of changing attitudes concerning Japanese food from a conceptualization of the "other" to a connection between individuals.

CHAPTER 11

From Asian Fusion to Asian Hipster Cuisine

Consuming Cosmopolitanism and Authenticity

SHOON LIO AND MEGAN BOTT

Asian hipster and street cuisine has generated tremendous excitement among foodies, food writers, and food critics.[1] The chefs and the restaurants who are most identified as part of this culinary trend, which includes Momofuku's David Chang, Mission Chinese Food's Danny Bowien, Kogi BBQ's Roy Choi, Pok Pok's Andy Ricker, Ivan Ramen's Ivan Orkin and Talde's Dale Talde, among others, have challenged and redefined notions of authenticity, cultural capital, and haute cuisine in American culture. This essay argues that the popularity of these Asian/Asian American hipster restaurants and the Asian fusion restaurants that preceded them can be understood alongside the emergence of contested spaces within which the chefs and their restaurant customers/patrons construct their cosmopolitan identities and acquire cultural capital and status through their food practices.

The concept of culinary capital builds on Bourdieu's discussion of how cultural tastes reinforce class hierarchies.[2] As Johnston and Baumann, and Naccarato and Lebesco, argue, food and food practices are markers of social status.[3] Foodies are individuals who distinguish themselves from others based on their knowledge, taste, and food practices. Johnston and Baumann characterize foodies as cultural omnivores who eschew "high culture" and cultural snobbery and are open to experiencing a diversity of culinary cultures and practices.

Their markers of distinction have shifted away from the consumption of fine dining and haute cuisine to eating that valorizes border-crossing cuisines that are new, "authentic," and "exotic," such as Asian street food or cuisine.[4] However, this is not to say that consuming dim sum or Chinese takeout from restaurants in Chinatowns, or slurping ramen from noodle shops in the Little Tokyos and Japantowns, or eating authentic rotis from Indian restaurants will automatically confer cultural capital and social status. The way that certain foods and food practices are valued and legitimized in omnivorous culinary discourse is still constituted within a hierarchy of taste and distinction. We argue that the popularity of Asian hipster and street cuisine constitutes culinary capital for foodies.

Food-related television shows and the increasing use and accessibility of social media platforms, smart phones, and global positioning applications have become important tools in self-formation and the construction and circulation of culinary capital.[5] Food-related television programming, such as Food Network or Cooking Channel shows like *No Reservations*, *Top Chef* and *Iron Chef*, have constituted culinary capital for their viewers by creating cultural knowledge of what is trendy, which allows them to claim enhanced status.[6] Many of the Asian hipster chefs and their restaurants have been featured on various cooking shows, especially food ventures/travels shows such as *No Reservations* or programs on the Travel Network. Asian hipster chefs like Dale Talde, Beverly Kim, Leah Cohen, and Stephanie Izard have also been contestants on Bravo TV's competitive cooking show *Top Chef*.

Social media platforms such as Twitter and Facebook, photography and video platforms (e.g. Instagram, Vine, Snapchat), food blogs, and business and food review websites (e.g. YELP, Urbanspoon, Eater, Chowhound, and MobiMunch) have been instrumental in creating a connection between producers and consumers of culinary capital.[7] Food blogs and social media communicate to a localized audience the latest culinary trend and are used by chefs and food vendors to communicate to their customers their real-time location and daily menu items.[8] The meaning of Asian hipster or street food as cosmopolitan and adventurous was, as we will also argue, constructed online, forming the basis of culinary capital for millennials just as Asian fusion cuisine had done for the previous generation of American culinary consumers.

A Brief History of Asian Fusion Cuisine

The term "fusion cuisine" was coined in 1988 by Florida chef Norman Van Aken to refer to combinations of flavors and culinary techniques from two or more cultures. Early on, Asian fusion cuisine typically referred to the blending of Asian ingredients and cooking methods with French or other European culinary techniques. The term Asian fusion has also been used to describe restaurants with Pan-Asian menus. There is considerable debate over the origins of Asian fusion cooking. Some point to the nouvelle cuisine of the 1970s, which combined French and Japanese cuisines. Others, such as Joyce Goldstein, see its origins in California Cuisine.[9] Richard Wing, the late owner of the five-star Imperial Dynasty restaurant of Hanford, California, is considered to be one of the pioneers of Asian fusion cuisine with his "chinois" cooking, which he described as "French cooking with a Chinese accent." In 1958, Wing opened Imperial Dynasty next door to his family restaurant in Chinese Alley in Hanford, California.[10] Wing introduced French culinary techniques that he had learned during his stint in the army serving as the personal chef of U.S. Army five-star general George Marshall during World War II.[11]

In the 1970s and 1980s, fusion, especially Asian fusion cuisines, became celebrated as the cuisine of choice for young urban professionals (Yuppies) for its ability to confer a cultural cosmopolitan identity.[12] However, the popularity of fusion cuisine must be understood in light of several social trends and conditions, including globalization, increasing cultural flow through media and travel, high-income gentrification in global cities such as New York, Los Angeles, London, and San Francisco, and the rise of celebrity chefs. High-income young urban professionals found value in what they perceived as "authentic" international experiences, while chefs saw an opportunity to market "Asia" to this highbrow clientele by crafting a haute "cuisine" with Asian flavor, in contrast to the Asian restaurants that just served cheap Chinese or Japanese ethnic "food" to the working class.

On the West Coast, Wolfgang Puck, a major pioneer of fusion cuisine, opened the Chinese- and French-inspired Chinois on Main in Santa Monica in 1983. The official website for Chinois on Main described the eatery as the "first and best" example of American fusion cooking with its "bold menu of Asian dishes made with California fresh products using French culinary techniques." Chef Mark Miller celebrated fusion cuisine's inventiveness. According to Miller, Chinois took "Chinese things, cooking them in an Italian oven, and putting French sauces on them. It was a mastery of multiplicity, fashion, form, design, flavor, everything."[13] In 1987, Nobuyuki "Nobu" Matsuhisa opened his first Peruvian-Japanese restaurant in Beverly Hills. Nobu introduced nouveau-Japanese cuisine, which was Japanese cooking with "North and South American influences."[14] At Chaya Brasserie in Los Angeles, Italian-trained Shigefumi Tachibe combined Japanese, French and Italian ingredients in dishes such as his Italian carpaccio with sashimi, fettuccine with prosciutto and shiitake mushrooms, and his famous tuna tartare. In 1982, the Asian fusion trend reached Chicago with the opening of two new restaurants. Yoshi Katsumura, a classically French-trained chef from Japan, opened his French-Japanese fusion restaurant Yoshi's Café, while Jackie Shen opened Jackie's, which served nouvelle French seafood with Chinese influences.[15] In 1987, Susanna Foo opened her restaurant Susanna Foo Chinese Cuisine in Philadelphia, which garnered acclaim for its fusion of Chinese and French cooking.

In the 1990s and early 2000s, chefs Nobu Matsuhisa, Ming Tsai, Jean-Georges Vongerichten, Floyd Cardoz and television celebrity and model Padma Lakshmi became the face of Asian fusion cooking.[16] In 1998, Ming Tsai opened the Blue Ginger restaurant and hosted his *East Meets West* and *Ming's Quest* cooking shows on the Food Network. Ming Tsai defined successful East–West cooking as a "harmonious way to combine distinct culinary approaches."[17] In 1992, Jean-Georges Vongerichten opened Vong in New York, where he created a menu that pushed "the boundaries of French and Thai cuisines."[18] At Vong, patrons were introduced to the fusion of Southeast Asian and French dishes such as soup dumplings stuffed with *foie gras*, shrimp satay stuffed with coconut mousse, and a French interpretation of the Vietnamese pho made with roasted marrow bones and seared steak. Many of the chefs associated with fusion or Asian hipster cuisine have worked in one of Vongerichten's restaurants.

From Asian Fusion to Asian Hipster Cuisine

By the mid-2000s, Asian fusion cuisine had become so ubiquitous that critics began to view the combinations of flavors as being haphazard, "inauthentic" and "uncool."[19] Historian Felipe Fernandez-Armesto has described fusion cooking as "Lego cookery" where restaurant kitchens become assembly points for the mixing and matching of highly processed elements.[20] Chris Cipollone, chef of the Korean and Italian restaurant Piora in New York City, stated that the term fusion conjures up images of "sesame-crusted tuna with wasabi mashed potatoes . . . and it's next to a Caesar salad."[21] Bill Kim, the Korean American chef of UrbanBelly restaurant in Chicago considers the term "fusion" to be an "abrasive and impersonal word."[22] Susanna Foo rejected the term completely by asserting that she was "truly a Chinese cook. I don't cook fusion. I don't like it. There's no base to connect to."[23] Anita Lo, chef of Annisa, felt that fusion signified an "emboldening of the American palate that was catalyzed by a collective embracing of other cuisines."[24] However, perhaps due to less-skilled chefs,

> the word fusion came to have negative connotations; it began to signify a diluting of clarity within flavor profiles. Now we need another word to describe what is, in essence, all cuisine. There are no true borders in food. Each cuisine has been affected by another, be it Vietnamese with its French and Chinese influences; French Alsatian with its German influences; or South African with its Dutch and Indonesian influences.[25]

Chefs and restaurants that would have formerly been labeled "fusion" quickly distanced themselves from the term.[26] Chefs began to describe their food as "globally inspired," "contemporary American," "mashups," or "Asian influenced small plates."

New York Magazine declared 2012 the "Year of the Asian Hipster Cuisine," or the year when Asian hipster cuisine had replaced the popular Asian fusion cooking of the 1990s.[27] In the article, Mary Jane Weedman describes Asian hipster chefs as a new "restaurant tribe" that found its calling through passion, not ancestry. Their cooking shared the "inspiration, ingredients, and attitude—a legacy, many of them say, of Momofuku's David Chang—and also engage[d] in perennial debates about ownership, appropriation, authenticity, and the F-Word (fusion), not to mention who can (or should) cook this often irreverent food."[28] Weedman named Mission Chinese Food's Danny Bowien, Danji's Hooni Kim, Pok Pok NY's Andy Ricker, Baohaus's

Eddie Huang, Pig and Khao's Leah Cohen, and Talde's Dale Talde as the vanguard of this new Asian Hipster cuisine.

Adam Platt, food critic for *New York Magazine,* also declared that 2013 would be the year in which the Asian hipster culinary revolution that began with David Chang's Momofuku Noodle Bar reached its "improbable zenith."[29] Like Weedman, instead of defining the characteristics of this new culinary trend, Platt listed several restaurants as its exemplars, including Danny Bowien's Mission Chinese Food, Leah Cohen's Pig and Khao, Masaharu Morimoto's Tribeca Canvas, Hooni Kim's Hanjan, Jason Wang's Biang, and Ed Schoenfeld's RedFarm, among others.[30] Platt described Danny Bowien's restaurant Mission Chinese Food as a small faux-carryout space mobbed by "hordes of lumberjack-shirted hipsters."[31] Platt recommended Ed Schoenfeld's RedFarm as a restaurant where diners could sample chef Joe Ng's "New Age dim sum" stuffed with ground lamb, crispy duck, pork, and steamed lobster.

Georgia Kral, food editor for *amNEWYORK*, argues that what distinguishes Asian hipster cuisine from regular Asian takeout "is more than just price, though the cost difference can be quite noticeable. The quality of the ingredients is one thing; whether the food is buzzed about on blogs and on social media is another. But the main difference is culinary adventurousness."[32] Like Weedman and Platt, Kral named David Chang's Momofuku, Danny Bowien's Mission Chinese Food, Greg Hugunin's Pho 66, and Andy Ricker's Pok Pok as exemplars of Asian hipster cuisine. However, most of these chefs eschew the Asian hipster and Asian fusion labels. When Weedman's article went live, Dale Talde, one of the eight chefs Weedman had called an "Asian hipster chef," tweeted that he was not a hipster.[33]

David Chang, the Big Brother of Asian Hipster Cuisine

David Chang has been described as one of the most influential chefs in the United States and the forefather of the Asian hipster cuisine trend.[34] Historian Alison Pearlman argues that the ascent of Chang signaled a major transformation in gourmet dining:

> Noodle Bar and Ssäm Bar have hybridized the high and the humble by turning out exceptional renditions of everyday foods. By boutique sourcing, carefully crafting, and creatively tweaking the likes of ramen, fried chicken, and pork buns, Chang and his chefs de cuisine, Tien Ho and Peter Serpico, have garnered the sort of praise once reserved for haute cuisine.[35]

Chang defied categorization as a Korean or Asian American chef serving high-end Asian inspired food.[36] He also tried to avoid being labeled a fusion chef. In fact, he jokingly referred to his food as "bad pseudo-fusion cuisine."[37] Chang insisted, in several interviews, that he was a "regular dude chef" and that his restaurants served delicious "American food."[38] Chang even featured a quote from Wolfgang Puck on Momofuku's website in an attempt to describe his cuisine: "Ethnic crossovers also occur when distinct elements meet in a single recipe. This country is, after all, a huge melting pot. Why should its cooking not illustrate the American transformation of diversity into unity?" Kevin Pang, food writer for the *Chicago Tribune*, argues that David Chang was trying to expand the boundaries of American food to include kimchi and dashi. In a 2013 profile of Chang written for *Vogue* magazine, John Powers described Chang as "America's most relevant chef" whose "street food shares the table with haute cuisine and deliciousness matters more than décor."[39]

David Chang's first restaurant venture, Momofuku Noodle Bar, started off as a ramen shop that "serve[d] food made with integrity at an affordable price."[40] The noodle bar's original menu offered ramen with pork and a poached egg, spicy noodles, rice with chicken and egg, and the dumplings and edamame typically expected at a ramen joint.[41] The restaurant's experience with near bankruptcy liberated Chang and chef Joaquin Baca from the conventions of running a regular ramen shop and led them to be more adventurous in what they were cooking. For example, they began serving bowls of tripe, fried veal sweetbreads, and a Korean-inspired burrito. Chang also took advantage of green/local market sources, which allowed him to tap into the emerging locavore culture.[42] Momofuku Noodle Bar's pork-belly buns became such a cultural sensation that they began appearing on Asian restaurant menus across the United States.[43] Many of these restaurants referenced Momofuku while acknowledging the pork bun's Asian origins.[44]

Momofuku pork-belly buns, like Chang's ramen and the food served in his restaurants, were a sophisticated and innovative take on "low cuisine."[45] Greg Morabito, editor at *Eater*, argued that

> Although Dave Chang did not invent the pork bun, he created a very specific and somewhat luxe version of this dish that everyone went crazy for, and his kitchens have served it the exact same way every single service since its introduction. It also inspired countless imitators across the country, even entire restaurants devoted to buns in the very specific David Chang style. Pork buns are now a part of our modern American restaurant vernacular, and it's all because of this dish.[46]

Similarly, journalist and culture critic, Rachel Cooke expressed:

> He is probably the only chef in the world who can put kimchi—the spicy, fizzy, sweet-sour fermented cabbage he adores—on the same menu as his own riff on red-eye gravy. He makes these juxtapositions seem not just daring, but elegant, too. He turns out dishes of astonishing creativity and tastiness, but they are also, very humble, at least in origin. Chang's chicken wings, for instance, look like anyone else's chicken wings. Only when you stick one in your mouth, at which point you think: Jeez! How in God's name did he make these bits of gristle taste so good.[47]

Chang's Momofuku empire consists of fourteen restaurants, including Momofuku Milk Bar and Fuku, a fried-chicken sandwich shop which opened in 2015. Many food writers have compared Fuku to a high-end version of Chick-fil-A, an American fast food restaurant that specializes in chicken sandwiches.[48] In January 2016, Chang opened Momofuku Nishi, which is his and chef Josh Pinsky's deconstruction of Italian food: "There are Italian words on the menu but we're not trying to make Italian food. We're not trying to make a Korean restaurant. We're trying to do something that we've never done at Momofuku. We're inspired by Italy but we're not using any Italian ingredients. . . . This is like writing a paper. Our thesis right now is: How do we find certain patterns in food through cultures?"[49] Chang has conveyed that the best dishes at his restaurants are those that merge disparate ingredients, and "If people want to call it fusion, well fuck you. It is fusion. Tell me what food isn't fusion."[50] Clearly, Chang's creative renditions of everyday street food such as ramen, fried-chicken sandwiches, and pork-belly buns have redefined what is haute cuisine in the United States.[51]

Psychedelic Mission Chinese Food

Danny Bowien, chef of Mission Chinese, attained rock star status for his idiosyncratic and "revolutionary" interpretation of Sichuan cooking through dishes such as Kung Pao pastrami, mapo tofu and cumin lamb. His long orange hair and clear-framed glasses also helped define him as one of the "piety-smushing hipster chefs favored by today's influential eaters."[52] Moreover, his take on Chinese food has been described as "David Chang-inspired," "electric," "psychedelic," "hallucinatory," and consisting of "cross-cultural flavor detonations."[53] Pete Wells, a *New York Times* food critic, raved that "Mr. Bowien does to Chinese food what Led Zeppelin did to the blues. His cooking both pays respectful homage to its inspiration and takes wild, flagrant liberties with it. He grabs hold of tradition and runs at it with abandon, hitting the accents hard, going heavy on the funk and causing all kinds of delicious havoc."[54] According to John Swansburg, a more apt analogy would be to compare what Bowien did with Chinese food to what the indie-rock group Pavement did to rock music—Bowien was "a virtuoso with the mien of a slacker."[55] Bowien, on the other hand, described his cooking as "Americanized oriental food" or "weird Chinese food." Lessley Anderson, senior editor for the food website *Chowhound*, characterized the menu at Mission Chinese Food as reaching "deeper into a broad Chinese-food lexicon, interpreting dishes like Mapo tofu and sizzling cumin lamb as spicy, rich, full-frontal assaults."[56]

Mission Chinese Food began as a Guatemalan food truck that was sublet by Anthony Myint to serve his "PB&J" sandwiches stuffed with pork belly and jicama, as well as other specialty sandwiches, once a week in San Francisco.[57] The Mission Street food truck was tremendously successful due in part to publicity it had gained through social media. After the food truck was shut down by a local developer, Anthony Myint and his wife, Karen Leibowitz, opened its next incarnation as a pop-up restaurant within an existing Chinese hole-in-the-wall eatery in San Francisco. Danny Bowien joined Mission Street Food and cofounded Mission Chinese Food in 2010, where he served signature Sichuan dishes such as mapo tofu, salt-cod fried rice, and Kung Pao pastrami. Alan Richman and the editors of *GQ* magazine listed Mission Chinese Food as one of the ten best new restaurants of 2011. Richman described the cuisine as "mostly Chinese, somewhat American, occasionally spicy, a bit unorthodox, absolutely brilliant."[58] In 2012, Danny Bowien opened Mission Chinese in New York City. The original Mission Chinese location in New York, on Orchard Street, was similar to its San Francisco restaurant—it was defined by its low-budget décor, with wooden chairs and a paper dragon hanging from the ceiling, and young staff members who were almost indistinguishable from the patrons. The menu featured the same signature neo-Sichuan dishes—Kung Pao pastrami and thrice-cooked bacon—with Mission Chinese's mapo tofu exemplifying Bowien's interpretation of Chinese cooking. Rather than using the ground meat typical of the dish, Bowien uses braised pork shoulders, Japanese kombu, cilantro and fish sauce, transforming this Chinese dish into a cross between a ragú and Texas chili.[59]

In December 2014, Mission Chinese, NYC reopened in a new location on the edge of Chinatown. Although the Kung Pao pastrami, thrice-cooked bacon, and salt-cod fried rice are still being offered, the décor and significantly expanded menu pay homage to "old school" Chinese restaurants and banquet halls.[60] Bowien and executive chef Angela Dimayuga went beyond the Sichuan-inspired spicy signature dishes, drawing on a variety of Chinese regional cuisines as well as other Asian and Pacific Islander influences. Adam Platt described the "new, gentler recipes" as embodying the "Filipino combination of lightness and good old-fashioned heft."[61] When asked about the seemingly new direction the restaurant was taking, Dimayuga stated, "I am so not a Chinese chef. This is beyond that. It's about being able to have a fluid concept and then bring it in whatever direction that Danny and I want. We could use under this guise of Mission Chinese Food anything that's vaguely Asian."[62] Case in point: Dimayuga introduced her Filipina grandmother's recipe of stuffed chicken with raisins, olives, and soft-boiled eggs to the expanded menu. In his review of the new Mission Chinese Food, *New York Times* food critic Pete Wells described menu items such as steamed Napa cabbage in almond milk and saffron, and the nori-sprinkled red cabbage salad as "nuanced": "All of these are smart, layered and vibrant enough to win over anybody who shows up thinking that Mission Chinese Food is still in the business of knocking your head against the wall until you smile or pass out or both. It's easier to taste the quieter flavors now."[63]

Culinary mashups, such as the pairing of their interpretation of Japanese Koji fried chicken with Hainan chicken rice, are also on the new menu. Bowien and Dimayuga have reworked the daikon turnip cake, a staple in Chinese dim sum restaurants, into a staggered column of daikon turnip cake cubes topped with shaved bonito and steeped in peanut milk. The new Mission Chinese Food, NYC includes pizza ovens in the front bar area where it makes cheese pizza, bread, and two *prix fixe* options. On Christmas day in 2015, Bowien and Dimayuga introduced a weekend dim sum lunch to the menu at Mission Chinese, NYC. However, as one would expect, it was anything but ordinary. As Bowien commented, "We're gonna have dim sum carts going around, but not with traditional dim sum. . . . It's gonna be Mission Chinese Food: little plates of Mapo tofu, and scrambled egg and tapioca dumplings."[64] According to Platt, Bowien's culinary genius was in creating a "grand sense of occasion." Platt went on to posit that Mission Chinese, NYC's new location provided Bowien with the "proper New York stage" for his "theatrical" culinary experiments.[65]

Roy Choi's L.A. Street Food

In 2008, Roy Choi launched the Korean tacos fad and food truck boom with his Kogi BBQ-To-Go food trucks.[66] In its first year, flash mobs of hundreds of people appeared at a location posted on Kogi's Twitter feed, waiting in line for several hours to order Kogi Korean short rib tacos, kimchi quesadillas, and kimchi-covered Kogi dogs.[67] According to *Newsweek*, Kogi had transcended its roots as a "gourmet gastromobile" to emerge as America's "first viral restaurant."[68] Choi, who grew up in East L.A., was trained at the Culinary Institute of America and had cooked for Le Bernardin in New York City before Mark Manguera approached him with the idea of putting Korean barbecue on a taco.[69] Choi talks about his food as his "graffiti" and characterizes himself as a "sort of post-Abstract Expressionist food artist."[70] Choi's ethnic-fusion cooking had been characterized as a culinary distillation of Los Angeles.[71] In fact, Choi described Kogi tacos as embodying the cultural geography of Los Angeles on a "plate" or in a "bite": "Maybe it wasn't everyone's L.A., but it was mine. It was Koreatown to Melrose to Alvarado to Venice to Crenshaw crumpled into one flavor and bundled up like a gift. The elements looked like city blocks. The flavor tasted like the streets. And the look said home."[72]

Choi has asserted that his street food has broad appeal, catering to everyone from the *cholos* (gangsters) in white tees, to club kids, college students, and hipsters.[73] Choi's Kogi food trucks and later gourmet or haute-cuisine food trucks inverted the traditional meaning and function of *loncheras* or Mexican food trucks. *Loncheras* have long provided cheap and "authentic" food for Latino working-class clientele by going where workers are located—factories, construction sites, plazas, and soccer fields.[74] On the other hand, haute-cuisine food trucks, such as Kogi BBQ, go where culinary tourists, seeking cosmopolitan and new ethnic culinary experiences, are located—farmers markets, cultural events, and gentrified urban hotspots.[75]

In 2010, after the success of his Kogi BBQ food trucks, Choi opened his first sit-down, brick-and-mortar restaurant, Chego. Jonathan Gold, food critic for the *Los Angeles Times* describes the food at Chego as "a fount of culinary postmodernism" and typical of Choi's "cross-cultural mash-up" cooking.[76] Choi's riff on the ubiquitous rice bowl was the central concept at Chego: "Taking a short break from the streets to chill and cheer from the sidelines, this happy, humble little LA-in-a-rice bowl restaurant full win and the color orange set out to reinvigorate the rice bowl. Slow roasted prime rib with creamed horseradish? Check. Sticky-sweet slabs of Berkshire pork belly over hot rice and fried egg? Done. A jukebox of feelings and L.A. youth piped in through the speakers? It's been Chego Man approved."[77]

During its first five years in business, Choi's A-Frame restaurant served "urban picnic" entrees of beer-can chicken, pickle plates and green-curry coconut-milk clam chowder. Choi brought in executive chef Johnny Yoo who transformed A-Frame into a Hawaiian-themed restaurant that served "Hawaiian blue collar cuisine" for the mainstream diner "without sacrificing its soul."[78] Choi defines the A-Frame cuisine as "True ono grindz" which is Hawaiian pidgin for "tasty local eats": "If you took Zippy's," a fast-food-casual restaurant chain in Hawaii, and "mixed it with some L.A. OG Kush [*sic*], and you mixed it with the breeze from Venice pier and our attitude, and our whole style here in L.A.—if you mix those things together and created a child, that's what this is."[79] As with his Kogi BBQ food trucks, Chego, and other restaurants, Choi weaves a narrative about the food at A-Frame as embodying Los Angeles culture. As Choi describes his overall philosophy on the A-Frame webpage:

> Whether it's the Caribbean with Sunny Spot or POT with second-generation Asian Americans or Kogi on the streets or Chego to stoners or Commissary to vegetarians or Alibi Room to Westsiders or 3 Worlds Café to the community. . . . I never try to do something unless I understand a culture and feel we can represent it and respect it, but also have the courage to push it like a DJ would a song. I wouldn't do anything unless the people from these cultures know we are real: no matter how different it may have been twisted, it still feels like home.[80]

Jonathan Gold has designated Choi's "culinary postmodernism" as "using the tricks of fine dining to elevate street food," whether it is the Chubby pork-belly rice bowl at Chego or the Kogi short rib tacos.[81]

The Authentic Inauthentic Asian-American Cuisine of Dale Talde

A veteran chef of Vong Chicago and Buddakan NYC, former *Top Chef* contestant Dale Talde proudly proclaims his food to be "inauthentic."[82] His eponymous restaurant's website describes the effortless blending of "the tastes, ingredients and nuances of Eastern and Western cuisines and techniques."[83] Talde's menu includes pretzel pork and chive dumplings, Korean fried chicken, and his interpretation of the Vietnamese dish *cha ca la vong* prepared as a fish taco with a roasted branzino inside a banana leaf in a tomato turmeric jam. He serves a "phot roast," which is a pot roast stewed in the ingredients of a Vietnamese pho. As a nod to his Filipino heritage, his menu includes Filipino sausage sliders with garlic-vinegar mayonnaise. Another example of this cultural appropriation and (re)mix is his take on the Filipino dessert *halo-halo*, which is a shaved ice sundae with condensed milk, coconut, and tapioca—Talde's version is topped off with the cereal Cap'n Crunch. Talde describes his cooking as being "for members of Generation Steamed Bun":

> These are the masses who were raised on takeout pad thai and egg rolls, who will travel two hours for real-deal Sichuan, and who would just as soon eat some dope pho as they would dine at Alinea. These are some Momofuku-loving, pork bun-eating motherfuckers. My food, though is different from my peers' food. Some of the chefs making waves cook food meant to transport you—to Northern Thailand or Sichuan Province, to Vietnam or Tokyo. My food is meant to remind you that you're home.[84]

The greatest influences on his cooking are his memories of his mother's Filipino cooking while growing up in Chicago as well as the gyro shops, diners, Polish delis, *taquerias*, burger joints, Chinese BBQ restaurants, *bodegas*, and other "food meccas" of his "American landscape."

Culinary Capital, Place-Making and Cosmopolitan Asian Hipster Foodscapes

Over the past couple of decades, culinary markers of distinction have shifted away from the consumption of fine dining–haute cuisine to include a broader range of locally sourced ethnic street food. The rising popularity of Asian hipster and street food coincides with these cultural processes, which include the emergence of cosmopolitan foodscapes where individuals can engage in status displays through the consumption of hip ethnic and exotic cuisine.[85] Chefs such as Roy Choi, David Chang, and Dale Talde have participated in this paradigmatic transformation by characterizing their cuisine as "good local street food" that gives people a sense of "home." Dale Talde describes his menu as having always been influenced by the local neighborhood: "I walk to Chinatown in Brooklyn, and you could be in mainland China. You can't help but be inspired by the live fish and whole pigs. . . . We say the restaurant is Asian-American, but what does that mean in Miami? We want to do a riff on a Cuban sandwich in a bao, with roast pork and pickles."[86]

Stephanie Izard, an "Iron Chef" and the winner of season four of Bravo's *Top Chef*, opened her Chinese-inspired restaurant Duck Duck Goat in 2016. The restaurant has been described as "part ode to Izard's childhood memories of Americanized Chinese Takeout, part deeply-researched riffs on the cuisines of Chengdu, Beijing and Shanghai."[87] The website of AvroKO, the design firm behind Duck Duck Goat, conveys that their design was supposed to evoke an

> "everytown Chinatown"—a dream-like version of the stores and shops that can be found in all quintessential Chinatowns in America. The outdoor/indoor style of these neighborhoods is brought to life via each dining room entryway that's envisioned as a store front. 1960s saturated cinema played a significant role in the use of color leading to a vibrant and over-saturated palette evoking the eclectic irreverence and curious chaos found in most American Chinatown communities.[88]

Andy Ricker, chef and owner of the Pok Pok restaurants, described his eateries as "neighborhood restaurants." The design of one of the dining rooms of Pok Pok PDX evokes the food stalls and open-air restaurants of Thailand. Moreover, the foods he serves at Pok Pok are approximations of the dishes he encountered during his food travels and road trips to Thailand.[89] On the other hand, John Nguyen, the chef at Hanoi House NYC, wanted his food to remind diners of Orange County, California, which was where he grew up. At the time of the restaurant's opening in January 2017, Nguyen related: "Some people from Orange County came in and said, 'It tastes just like O.C. . . . I just smiled, that's all I want.'"[90] According to Nancy Matsumoto, a food and culture writer, this new cuisine had

> been filtered through the multiethnic influences of their upbringings: taco stands, fast food joints, barbecue shacks, hip hop and graffiti. Theirs is not the "fusion" cooking of the late '70s and '80's, effete creations of European-trained masters who melded cultures with delicacy and nuance. . . . This new wave of chefs is dishing up what I call Asian Soul Food: a gutsy, high-low mash up of street food and haute cuisine, old country flavors and new-fangled cooking techniques.[91]

Leah Cohen, owner and chef of Pig and Khao, moved to Southeast Asia for a year and worked at several restaurants, including Bo Innovations in Hong Kong. At first she only wanted to cook Thai food, but her mother urged her to incorporate her Filipino heritage and culture into her restaurant: "You can't just do Thai food. You're half Filipino, you have to incorporate some of your heritage and your culture."[92] Chef Thai Dang of the Chicago-based restaurant Embeya described his cuisine as representing all of his professional experience: "The kitchens I came out of and the chefs I learned from. They inspire me. Then I add nuance of Southeast Asian flavors and textures. But truthfully I lean more toward my Vietnamese background but refining. It's inevitable, because I'm Vietnamese."[93]

"Local" also has another social and deeply political meaning—food and its raw materials are locally "sourced," "farm-to-fork," and demonstrate the chef's commitment to a "green market sensibility."[94] Chefs Cory Lee and David Chang, and restaurants such as the Red Egg, rely on relationships with local producers. Here, heritage also assumes another meaning as well, referring not only to the cultural influences on the chefs' menu but also to the pedigree of the meat that they serve. Even Danny Bowien, who once dismissed the importance of the pedigree of meat, lists "heritage pork" as one of the ingredients in his mapo tofu.

Although some Asian hipster restaurants are offering their (re)imaginings of Asian or ethnic street food, many of these chefs have extensive training and experience in some of the top culinary institutes and restaurants in the country such as Boulad, Vong, or Thomas Keller's Per Se. Official websites and restaurant reviews of, and interviews with, Asian fusion/hipster chefs emphasize the culinary pedigree of European, especially French, techniques blended or infused with Asian flavors or influences. Michael Schulman, the executive chef at Buddakan NYC, is described as serving modern Asian cuisine with French techniques and ingredients.[95] Baoburg in Williamsburg, Brooklyn, serves a "modern twist on French cuisine by adding multicultural influences from Spanish & Asian—most notably Thai—culinary traditions."[96] Suchanan Aksornnan, the chef at Baoburg, graduated from the French Culinary Institute and began her training at L'école in New York City, followed by Jean-George Vongerichten's Mercer Kitchen and Bar Boulad, and her dishes reflect her background. For example, her sushi rice is thickened with cream, parmesan, butter, and chicken stock, and worked into a velvety risotto. On the other hand, the food at the Aviary in Portland, Oregon, is "roughly built around the idea of pairing Asian flavors with European techniques."[97]

Corey Lee, the chef at San Francisco's Benu restaurant, is often described as using western techniques with distinct Asian flavors and textures to create cross-cultural blends. Lee's experience cooking for Thomas Keller for eight years, and his four years as *chef de cuisine* at the French Laundry, are mentioned in every restaurant review and article about Lee and his restaurant. In his foreword to Lee's cookbook, David Chang describes Lee's biography as the story of the modern American chef:

> It is, for one thing, an immigrant story. Corey came to Western food as a stranger, but fell in love with the grand cuisine of France. He studied it ferociously, and to his practice of it he brought the Korean flavors of his heritage. When he discovered the brilliance of Chinese cooking, he hungrily immersed in that, too. As a result, people have mislabeled his food with a number of descriptors in various permutations—French, Chinese, Korean, modernist, classical—but the simple fact is that his cooking is his own. . . . he merges his encyclopedic command of both Asian and French cooking with modern techniques. And yet, miraculously, the technique remains in the shadows, almost invisibly supporting what he does.[98]

Lee describes his cooking at Benu as exploring "how Asian flavors, ideas and aesthetics can harmonize with Western ones. In that way, I think it reflects my bicultural background as well." He has also argued that while establishing an identity for his restaurant, he also discovered his own "self-identity."[99]

Performance and Authenticity

The creative (re)imagining and (re)interpretation of Asian/American food has raised questions about authenticity. Anthony Bourdain asks of Korean American chefs: "As a chef, what are your responsibilities to your family heritage? What is authentic and do I owe anything to this notion of authenticity at all? People ask David Chang how does he describe his food, he says 'tasty food.'"[100] Korean American novelist Alexander Chee views "authenticity" as a "bourgeois value posing as an aesthetic one."[101] Moreover, Asian hipster restaurants and their chefs—Dale Talde, Danny Bowien, and Andy Ricker—interrogate the notion of authenticity as the faithful replication of "traditional," "national," or even regional cuisines. Even Bourdain concedes that "authenticity" and "cultural appropriation" have become quaint and irrelevant notions because chefs such as David Chang and Danny Bowien are "changing, redefining, and defining forever what 'American cuisine' really is."[102]

Many Asian hipster chefs (e.g., Dale Talde, Leah Cohen, Stephanie Izard, and Beverly Kim) have been contestants on Bravo TV's *Top Chef*, whereas others (e.g., David Chang, Danny Bowien, Eddie Huang, and Roy Choi) have been featured on culinary-tourism television shows such as Anthony Bourdain's *No Reservations* and his *Parts Unknown*. Moreover, the early success of Mission Chinese Food, Eddie Huang's Baohaus, and Roy Choi's Kogi Korean tacos, among others, have been directly linked to foodies and their use of social media (Facebook, Twitter), food blogs, and other Internet-based platforms. Such resources have not only facilitated a more personal connection between chefs and patrons, but have also constituted a form of culinary capital for both groups.

Foodie or hipster culture has played a major role in reorganizing urban spaces and spurring the redevelopment and gentrification of less affluent neighborhoods.[103] Thus, for foodies, once-low-income neighborhoods such as Williamsburg, Brooklyn, the East Village in Manhattan, San Francisco's Mission District, and Portland's Alberta Art District, add to the appeal of hipster restaurants. Asian hipster restaurants constitute the foodscapes where chefs perform the roles of culinary and cultural rebels and artists, and also define a certain authenticity based on the personal experiences and narratives that have shaped these chefs.

Chefs, restaurants, and patrons have participated in the production of Asian fusion and Asian hipster/street cuisines and their foodscapes. The chefs have been creating a vision of the world with their food, and in consuming this food, customers support that particular vision one bite at a time. Asian hipster chefs and the foodies that follow them are choosing a specific worldview when choosing a meal and often signal those choices to others through the (social) media. When Asian fusion was popular, the message was that haute cuisine did not have to be exclusively French or European, but could include food from another culture. Today, with the advent of Asian hipster/street cuisine, that message has changed.[104] Those who consume this cuisine display their credentials as cosmopolitans who possess insider knowledge. In other words, they are individuals who value exotic and "authentic" ethnic street food, often searching for adventure in a gentrified urban terrain.[105] At present, culinary capital is no longer solely derived from fine dining; in fact, connections to the "street," the neighborhood, and the local are currently valorized over other forms of high culture.

Nevertheless, this seemingly more democratic cuisine is still constituted within a class-based hierarchy of taste. Both Asian fusion and Asian hipster cuisines constitute a form of class distinction, providing status for those who produce and consume it. The gentrification with which these cuisines are associated came at the expense of the working class, who left gentrified neighborhoods because they could no longer afford them (and their cuisines). While bloggers and online reviewers confirm the cosmopolitan character of their neighborhoods by writing about these food establishments, those who identify with street cuisine—chefs, patrons, and restaurant owners—are simultaneously destroying the diversity of the street, for Asian hipster cuisine ultimately excludes those without the cultural and economic capital to consume its products.

CHAPTER 12

"Stirring the Pot"

Asian Foodways in American Eating Places

CARMEN BIRKLE

In an episode from the American situation comedy *How I Met Your Mother*, Barney Stinson and his friends are looking for "The Best Burger in New York."[1] However, since Marshall can no longer remember where he ate this burger, the friends discuss other options for dinner. To each suggestion, Barney replies: "I don't like Chinese." Finally, his friends give up and tell him that Mexican food is *not* Chinese, but that does not make any difference to Barney. Barney Stinson's conflation of Chinese, Indian, and Mexican food not only reveals his own cultural ignorance but also the blurring of ethnic specificity, and of culinary difference.[2] However, my argument is that foodways do give access to precisely such cultural and historical difference, a difference, however, which is challenged in a cultural contact zone.[3]

In the following essay, I will emphasize the representation of spaces of food production and consumption, most frequently the public space of the restaurant and the private space of the kitchen and dinner table but also the public realm of the street, since space is fundamental in communal life both as the physical real as well as the imagined or even utopian space of nostalgic longing.[4] Food spaces, therefore, become heterotopian places of the Other, spaces in which ethnic identity is recovered, imagined, and negotiated.[5] Furthermore, these culinary spaces often "become metonymic of an ethnic group."[6] Therefore, their representations not only run the risk of being conform with what Edward Said has called "Orientalism,"[7] but also of practicing what Lisa Lau terms "Re-Orientalism" or what Ruth Maxey calls "Self-Orientalizing,"[8] that is, an Orientalism "propagated [. . .] ironically enough, by Orientals, albeit by diasporic Orientals."[9] I will look at the representations of the restaurants in Frank Chin's novel *Donald Duk* (1991) and M. Elaine Mar's autobiography *Paper Daughter* (1999), at the use of the private dinner table as public eating space in Amy Tan's novel *The Joy Luck Club* (1989), and at the streets of New York City in Elizabeth Wong's play *Kimchee and Chitlins* (1994) as public culinary contact zones that foster ethnic hybridization.

"Stirring the Pot": Appetizers[10]

When Ralph Ellison's protagonist in *Invisible Man* declares: "'I yam what I am!,'" we are not looking at a typo, but at a cultural, ethnic, and political statement emphasizing the African American preference for yams to an extent that these become a cultural and ethnic marker and a political declaration for equality in difference and self-confident identity politics.[11] Eating, the preparation of food, and the sharing of this nourishment go far beyond a merely biological satisfaction of hunger, but reveal a complex semiotics, the analysis of which strongly contributes to a better understanding of cultures in contact at a time of increasing immigration processes.

Since ways of cooking differ according to cultures, Claude Lévi-Strauss proposes that "'the cooked is a cultural transformation of the raw, whereas the rotted is a natural transformation.'"[12] Thus, the cook's culture determines the transformation of what is considered to be natural. Diasporic life presents significant challenges for both immigrants and hosts and, as I will show, it is via foodways that some major concerns of (im)migration are processed, tasted, and digested. It is not by chance that food metaphors such as *the melting pot* and *the salad bowl* have served as prominent models of life in cultural contact zones. Ever since Roland Barthes's influential essay "Le bifteck et les frites,"[13] cultural studies has been aware of the intimate connection between food and national as well as ethnic identity. As Barthes points out, "la frite est nostalgique et patriote comme le bifteck. [. . .] la frite est le signe alimentaire de la 'francité'" (chips are nostalgic and patriotic like steak…chips are the alimentary sign of Frenchness).[14]

Consequently, the analysis of food seems to be particularly rewarding with respect to the widespread Asian foodways of North America.[15] The history of Asian foodways in the United States, starting with the mid-nineteenth-century Gold Rush, reveals, as Wenying Xu points out, that "[t]here is nothing natural or culturally predetermined about Asian Americans' vital relationship with food. Harsh circumstances made such work one of the few options available to them."[16] Because running one's own restaurants facilitated self-nourishment, the preservation of one's own culture, and a certain degree of independence, Asian cooking and Asian restaurants gradually began to emerge at the turn of the twentieth century, in particular around the time of the Chinese Exclusion Act of 1882. Ever since the late nineteenth century, "the restaurant trade has continued to be the economic mainstay of Chinese immigrants."[17] Ultimately, as Wenying Xu insists, "food and eating occupy a significant place in the formation of Asian American subjectivity."[18]

It is, therefore, no surprise that quite a number of Asian American writers in the twentieth and twenty-first centuries have made food—the preparation and consumption thereof—and their respective eating-places central to their literary production.[19] Literary and cultural representations of Asian foodways in fictional and autobiographical narratives can serve as indicators of multi-, inter-, and transcultural life, shedding light on ethnic relationships in the United States, but they can also be "an index of psychic struggles."[20] "Eating," as Mervyn Nicholson points out, "is a *metaphor*,"[21] which is intimately related to the formation of identity and identity-building processes, as Donna Gabaccia's book's title, *We Are What We Eat*, clearly expresses.[22] In addition, how and what we eat are always also embedded in specific locations such as the home or the restaurant. As soon as eating is more than just the intake of food in order to ensure survival, it is often a social activity, even if taking place at home. While restaurants undoubtedly are public places, I will argue that social eating events at home can take on some of the functions and qualities of eating out in restaurants, among them negotiations of inclusion and exclusion of different ethnic groups from an in-group. Foodways, including their locations, therefore, have particular social characteristics and aim at specific effects or goals in a social community.

First, as a sign system, as "a system of communication, a body of images, a protocol of usages, situations, and behavior," foodways can metaphorically mirror multicultural coexistence, a living together of ethnic groups side by side.[23] This model of cultural pluralism, as Horace Kallen described in the early twentieth century, seems to allow for what Michelle Cliff calls the creation of culinary "home[s] away from home."[24]

Second, in these "homes," whether private or public, immigrants perform "rituals of cultural belonging"[25] that frequently reject the inclusion of other ethnic groups. This "invention of tradition"[26] has to be seen as a strategy for survival on physical, psychological, and cultural levels:

> Traditional foods and ways of eating form a link with the past and help ease the shock of entering a new culture; thus many struggle to hold on to them despite pressures to change. Immigrants open restaurants so that it is more convenient to get certain foods that take a long time to prepare; they open stores so that ingredients are available; they grow otherwise unavailable vegetables and herbs in their backyards.[27]

Third, discursive foodways can also point to moments of inter- as well as intra-cultural interaction. They may highlight attempts at assimilation on the part of the (im)migrants by either adjusting their own food habits as much as possible to those of the host country,[28] or by catering to the latter's stereotypical expectations of one's own tastes, a practice which Frank Chin has called "food pornography." As the editors of *Eating Culture* explain, this is the attempt "to make a living by exploiting ethnic foodways so as to gain a foothold in a white dominated society."[29] Questions of authenticity are discussed with reference to "imagined communities" of belonging.[30]

Fourth, ingredients can be mixed differently and combined into new dishes; foodways, just like ethnic identity, never remain static but are processes in flux: "Food as a semiotic system, a marker of ethnic identity, symbolizes this idea of fluidity on several levels. Food incorporation and assimilation is flux, an opening of the body for foreign matter which is transformed into self. Food points to the fact that the body is a process, constantly being re-built and altered."[31] Foodways can be steps in a process of transculturation,[32] that is, the creation of a culture that is new and independent as a kind of Thirdspace in Edward Soja's sense.[33] Overall, the semiotics of foodways, that is, the preparation and eating of food in specific social contexts, located in private and public places, give insight into ethnic relationships and psychological frames of mind throughout the history of ethnicities, regions, and nations.[34] Moreover, the qualities of restaurants such as the choice of food, the service, and the exchange of food and service for money, can be transferred to private places where money is mostly replaced by simply social relationships of family and/or friends.

Whether foodways take place in the family's home or a more public space such as a restaurant, the specific place creates atmosphere, identity, and community. Chinese immigrants opened up restaurants to find work and create forms of home away from the place of origin. These eating places metaphorically try to recreate the Asian past and are meant to offer a home free of ethnic discrimination. However, these places are never devoid of tension and often witness generational conflicts and the revelation of devastating secrets repressed in the past and returning in the present with a vengeance. At the same time, they are places that often cater to ethnic stereotypes in the attempt to make a living. It is "the mainstream customer [. . .] who has the power to decide what is agreeably authentic and what is unthinkably outlandish. As a result, ethnics in the food trade often find themselves forced to play up to stereotypes of their own group."[35] In short, these private or public restaurants are, as Lily Cho points out, the "settings in which human drama unfolds."[36] The restaurant is part of a development which Donna Gabaccia describes in the following words: "Chinese restaurants that catered to tourists moved upstairs, to differentiate themselves from the simple shops serving Chinese food to Chinese bachelor workers at street level."[37]

Chinese Restaurants and the Performance of (In)Authenticity

A most central experience for some Chinese immigrants is their life and work at Chinese restaurants. First-generation immigrants move to places where family and friends have already taken root and, in many cases, have opened up restaurants as a means for survival. This is the case in Frank Chin's novel *Donald Duk* (1991) and M. Elaine Mar's autobiography *Paper Daughter* (1999), both of which I will discuss in the next two sections respectively. Although Frank Chin (b. 1940) "as a creative writer seems bent on disavowing all affinities with Asian American women's writing,"[38] he shares with them the focus on the relevance of ritualistic foodways.[39] *Donald Duk* offers the reader the story of a young Chinese American boy and his coming-of-age in San Francisco's Chinatown.[40] It is the aim of Chin's narrative, as Eileen Chia-Ching Fung suggests, "to create a positive masculine identity" through the boy's "father's participation in food preparation, festivity, and storytelling."[41]

In contrast to a traditional Western allocation of spheres according to gender norms, Chin's cook is Donald's father, King Duk, who is in control of the kitchen as well as the connected dining-hall. These two locations are linked by "swinging doors,"[42] which the Asian Canadian writer Fred Wah (b. 1939) in his autobiographical text *Diamond Grill* (2006) associates with the hyphen as part of ethnic identity,[43] as a state of in-betweenness where people constantly move from one side to the other, from the private to the public sphere, from the cooks to the customers, from the past to the present, and, by implication, from one ethnic group to another. Fred Wah's term for the restaurant where this mixing takes place as well as for the food that is cooked in such a space is "*mixee grill.*"[44] As Cynthia Sugars points out, "for the narrator, the swinging doors of the Diamond Grill function not just as a border between 'Occident and Orient,' but as the hyphenated divider and connector between multiple identity markers."[45]

In Chin's novel, on the evening of a large family dinner "on the first night of the first day of the new year," "Dad," that is King Duk, prepares a special dinner that not even the Chinese have tasted before; at the same time, he says, "I will restore ways that have become abandoned and recover knowledge that has been lost."[46] Restoration and recovery as the key terms indicate a connection to a forgotten past, which, however, has shaped Chinese identity and can be perceived in the preparation of food. In the absence of the mother, the kitchen becomes the realm of the ethnic and masculine father who is aware of tradition and history but who also invents new types of food that integrate Chinese and American foodways:

> Now Dad cooks up meatless originals mixing the common items of many cuisines into things wonderful, strange and tasty. Fettucini Alfredo with shark's fin. Poached fish in sauce made with fruit and vegetables. Olives on toast that taste like rare thousand-dollar caviar. Chocolate, bananas, yellow chili peppers, red chili oil and coconut milk go into one sauce over shredded chicken and crabmeat to be eaten rolled up in hot rice-paper pancakes with shredded lettuce, green onions and a dab of plum sauce.[47]

In Dad's cooking, the aim no longer is the preservation of old style, but the integration of what is offered by the new surroundings. The father is in charge, and the movements in the kitchen are presented as "a warm rhythm, as if everyone in the kitchen is a player in a well-tuned orchestra and Dad is the conductor, moving in and out of the steam of his woks, finishing and starting one dish after another."[48]

These two quotations, taken from the same moment described in the novel, evoke and discard images of the melting pot, but then also of a form of cultural pluralism and transculturation. While the food's origins are multiple, it is combined in new ways; it by no means loses its original character, and its ingredients are clearly visible and do not melt with each other. Yet, in their combination they form something new, something that no one has ever eaten before. The chef is compared to the conductor of an orchestra, and everyone else is a player in that orchestra. Not only does this metaphor open up associations with Horace Kallen's (1882–1974) cultural pluralism, but also with art and performance. Cooking juxtaposes each (ethnic) ingredient; together, they form a unity, an *e pluribus unum*. Simultaneously, cooking is an art form based on performance; it needs a stage, players, and an audience. The kitchen, the cooks, and the eaters participate in this performance. Kallen discusses cultural pluralism in *Culture and Democracy* "as a coöperation of cultural diversities, as a federation or commonwealth of national cultures," "a multiplicity in a unity," and, ultimately, as the "orchestration of mankind."[49] Such an orchestra needs a conductor, that is, leadership that steers and shows the way. In the case of Chin's *Donald Duk*, King Duk orchestrates the culinary incorporation of ethnic diversity and cooks transculturated food.

His role model is Chiang Kai-shek's restaurant with Cantonese cooks who "could cook everything—Italian, Greek, French, Spanish, Brazilian—they did it all. I asked them, Why? And they said, Chiang never entertains other Chinese, only Europeans, who can stand to eat only one Chinese banquet a month. And Chiang wants all his foreign visitors to feel at home, in their noses, palates, and taste buds." While phrasing the intention for this style of cooking as an attempt at making Europeans, and Americans by implication, feel comfortable and "at home," Chin subtly implies the loss of authentic Chinese food in favor of a culinary hybridity that caters to the expectations of a white majority—however ethnically mixed that majority may be—that seems to rule the world, as "the most nationally powerful men in the world."[50] In short, these cooks, including King Duk, perform ethnic authenticity and, thus, implicitly deny/erase performance and authenticity in the juxtaposition of performance and authenticity.

Ethnicity as performance and the integration of Chinese and American cultures are two leitmotifs in the novel. Right from the beginning, the reader learns from Donald Duk's perspective how much he, the son, hates being Chinese and, by implication, he does not want to be associated with Chinese food. But he also hates the unwillingly, or ignorantly, caused funny effect that his and his family's names cause, Donald Duk, King Duk, Daisy Duk; these names are evidently allusions to the Donald Duck cartoon characters: "Donald Duk does not like his name. Donald Duk never liked his name. He hates his name. He is not a duck. He is not a cartoon character. He does not go home to sleep in Disneyland every night."[51]

Through Donald as the focal character, the reader understands that Donald's hatred for his own ethnic background comes from the confrontation with the stereotypes that the children throw at him. As a twelve-year-old boy, "Looking Chinese is driving him crazy!," and so does living in Chinatown.[52] He simply does not want to be funny. As the father points out, "I think Donald Duk may be the very last American-born Chinese-American boy to believe they have to give up being Chinese to be an American." In contrast, the new immigrants do not give up anything, but "add on. They're including America in everything else they know. And that makes them stronger than any of the American-born, like me, who had folks who worked hard to know absolutely nothing about China, who believed that if all they know was 100 percent American-made in the USA Yankee know howdy doodle dandy, people would not mistake them for Chinese."[53]

These statements evoke the discourse of assimilation in his parents' and perhaps grandparents' generations. Upon arrival, those Chinese who did not leave the United States again worked in the gold mines and later for the railroad companies or opened up their own laundries and restaurants. They tried hard not to draw attention to themselves because the general atmosphere of anti-immigration sentiments and the visible otherness of Asians turned them into the "yellow peril." Thus, they felt the need for the erasure of difference in order to survive. And yet, they did gather in their own communities and built Chinatowns. Later generations, such as King Duk's, recognized that being 100 percent American included being ethnic and integrating American and Chinese cultures. Yet, generational attitudes do not progress linearly, as Donald Duk's resentment of anything Chinese shows. At the same time, his sisters are perfectly able to live in both worlds and, or perhaps through, the world of the media.

Performance in various media seems to be a key issue in the life of the Duk family. For Daisy Duk, the mother, it turns into the accusation of being inauthentic because she was born in the United States and because of "her theatrical impersonations of performers in American cinema (i.e., Greta Garbo and Katherine Hepburn), which further reinforces her distance from Chinese traditions and culture. She represents the 'white-washed' generation of Chinese Americans."[54] Similarly, the twin daughters, Penny and Venus, are closely associated with TV or cinematic personalities and American mass media. Uncle Crawdad Man accuses Mom (Daisy) of not being able to understand Chinese stories: "Everybody knows it. Ah-Daisy, you're born here, your folks are Christians. You don't hear the Chinese stories like Chinese children. That's why you don't understand more of the opera."[55] Everyone is involved in performance in different ways: some of them star in operas such as Mom, and Dad "stars" in the kitchen where he has the power to give instructions.

Donald Duk dreams of dancing like Fred Astaire, his role model: "Donald Duk wants to live the late-night life in old black-and-white movies and talk with his feet like Fred Astaire, and smile Fred Astaire's sweet lemonade smile." While Fred Astaire, Rita Hayworth, and Barbara Stanwyck as film celebrities date the novel's plot (1940s and 50s), they also manifest an American culture that is prominent in San Francisco's Chinatown. Donald Duk's desire to be like everyone else, however, is doomed to fail because "Who would believe anyone named Donald Duk dances like Fred Astaire?" Fred Astaire, the image of the perfect white entertainer seems to be, from a white American point of view, incompatible with Chinese culture. Like Pecola in Toni Morrison's *The Bluest Eye* (1970), Donald Duk desires what he cannot have, that is, the looks of the dominant ethnic group. Although he knows how to tap-dance, he will never be Fred Astaire; he could only, like his teacher, become "'The Chinese Fred Astaire.'"[56]

Chinese New Year is a time of frustration for Donald Duk. Not only does everyone in his surroundings celebrate anything Chinese, "Donald Duk's father's old opera mentor, Uncle Donald Duk, is coming to San Francisco to perform a Cantonese opera."[57] Readers will immediately understand why the boy is named Donald Duk and that the cartoon figures never stood as models for this naming process. Readers will also consider Cantonese opera in San Francisco an attempt to cater to Chinese feelings of (be)longing, nostalgia, and ethnic unity. Memories of the past are as celebrated as family and ethnic relationships and friendships.

The prominence of performance suggests ethnicity as performance, or, at least, as changeable, not fixed, and subject to interpretation. Both the culinary and theatrical performances present multiple cultures in interaction and break apart the fixed definitions of ethnicity. At the very end of the novel, politics and food are joined in a personification of power: "it begins and ends with *Kingdoms rise and fall, Nations come and go*, and food."[58] By associating only men with the preparation of food, masculinity is attached to kingdoms and nations, thus "restoring masculinity to the Asian American male subject."[59] Furthermore, King Duk is often addressed as "sifu," "which means simultaneously a maestro chef and a kung fu maestro." As Wenying Xu concludes, "[m]etaphors of war and martial arts thus dominate the descriptions of King and his kitchen, a semiotic site where the enjoyment of masculine assertion colludes with that of cooking and eating."[60] Ultimately, as Xu argues,

> Cuisine and appetite in Chin solidify rather than dismantle a transcultural paradigm of patriarchy by equating cooking with martial arts, by relegating women to the positions of consumers and charity cases, and by converting the feminine into food matters that fuel the masculine subject formation of Asian American males.[61]

However, Chin's novel is also a perfect example of the very different ways of dealing with intercultural encounters. The desire for complete assimilation fails because of visible and invisible markers of ethnicity that do change but do not or should not disappear since they are important constituents of personal, cultural, and collective identity. Nevertheless, the contact zones, and the kitchen and the restaurant are two of them, allow for mutual influences that gradually change everyone and everything involved. Cooking is the perfect literal and figurative activity to represent this form of transculturation through active performance from which something new emerges that does not erase its constitutive components.

Chinese Restaurants as "Voluntary Ghettos"

M. Elaine Mar (b. 1966) is three years old when her father leaves the family for the United States in search of better working and living conditions. It is only three years later that his wife and daughter can follow, in 1972, to join him in Denver, Colorado. Their life, however, is far from being improved, because they live in one small room in their relatives' basement. The whole family, including Mar's parents, has to work as cooks, kitchen help, and wait staff in the restaurant that the relatives run for the owner, who trades "kitchen space for a percentage of the food receipts."[62] Long working hours, especially on the weekends, make family life difficult and prevent both parents from learning English or doing anything to integrate into American society.

While the parents live for and work in the restaurant that is called "Casey's Palace—Annie's Castle Restaurant & Lounge,"[63] to make ends meet, Mar has to go to school, where she learns English, which is her first step to move away from family, relatives, and restaurant. English becomes a "code" for her and her cousin, "moving us closer to the majority culture, further marginalizing our parents and memories of our past."[64] However, the process is difficult since family and community are central for Mar's parents. Aunt Becky tells her: "You're no one without your father's name."[65] Her parents' inability to speak English and their work in the restaurant are constant irritations for Mar who oscillates between American society in school and Chinese life at home. She hides her background; she starves in order to spend her food money for a T-shirt the school sells, and she begins to falls in love with one of the American busboys in the restaurant. This, together with the work she does in the restaurant, reconciles her for a while to her life in poverty.

The kitchen of the restaurant and its entrance door are the best-lit and most-frequented spaces, so that even customers confuse it with the actual entrance to the restaurant.[66] With the restaurant's name already alluding to some of the glamor Las Vegas is associated with, gambling is equally connected to this place, and, as Mar tells her readers, "the rumor was that organized gambling accounted for the restaurant's success."[67] The young Elaine is significantly shaped by the restaurant's life when she begins to work there: "Its sights and sounds, its scent, its very essence seemed to become a part of me. My sleep and hunger patterns adapted around the restaurant's hours."[68] Her parents hardly ever eat the food they prepare at the restaurant because it is just meant for American taste buds, but then Mar is shocked to see that her mother eats the leftovers: "The family never ate the same food as the customers, and I was curious." Mar does not like the food but "tasting it behind the kitchen, I imagined magic. I suddenly understood how it felt to sit in the dining room, to command rather than serve."[69]

For Mar, the food served and consumed at the restaurant represents the power relations between "commanding" and "serving." Mar and her family can only "taste" this food in secret; they become, as Mar claims, "vultures, bottom feeders"[70] who feel betrayed by their own poverty which they experience as twice as hard because they serve food to their customers that they cannot afford themselves unless as leftovers. While at home in the basement, Mar's family lives excluded from any American social contacts, the restaurant gradually becomes a location where both cultures meet. Not only does it become Mar's "preferred home," but also a "'middle kingdom' [. . .].

It was a country where my family and the rest of America coexisted. It forced my parents to form relationships with the non-Chinese. There, I didn't feel like the solitary mediator between two worlds, isolated by my dual affinities."[71]

Just like in Chin's novel *Donald Duk*, Mar, too, perceives the restaurant as a multicultural location, however, with separate spaces clearly allocated to the respective ethnic groups. The food itself crosses the threshold between ethnic groups, and so do the waiters who carry the food from the Chinese kitchen to the all-American dining room. The overall impression for the diners is that of authentic Chinese cuisine, whereas the Chinese know it is fake. As in *Donald Duk*, performance is at the center of daily activities. The difference, however, is that Mar does not suffer from this performative life but even temporarily enjoys its in-betweenness, where she feels at home as someone who constantly has to oscillate between her Chinese family and ghetto and her American school surroundings. The restaurant becomes a contact zone where food is exchanged. However, any real permanent contact does not take place. It is a location where the customers' demands are satisfied by the pretense of authenticity.

After a fight with Uncle Andy, who officially runs the restaurant, Mar's father loses his job but is temporarily hired at another restaurant in a different section of Denver, the Dahlia Lounge, a lower-scale location. He eventually returns to the old location and the old job at Andy and Becky's restaurant. For Mar as a teenager, this place is where she falls in love for the first time. It begins to represent the changes in her life as well as in society, because black dishwashers and female bus staff have replaced the "all-American boys."[72] Mar internalizes life at the restaurant. It becomes the most essential identity marker against which she rebels: "I slept and woke according to the restaurant's schedule. But now I hated it, I felt consumed by it, and I worked out to purge its influence the only way I knew how—by denying food."[73] Food becomes for her a *pars pro toto* of the restaurant, a part of the whole that determines her life and takes away the little control she has over who she is and wants to be: "I hated the way food controlled my life. I resented having to spend every weekend at the restaurant, thinking about food, waned about the lack of business. I was disgusted by the vats of food, obscene quantities that we couldn't sell, the way its odor crept into our clothes, our hair, our skin. The way its presence signaled failure."[74] Consequently, refusing to eat is Mar's only way of rejecting this life that dominates time, space, body, and mind and instills in her a fear of the future because there is never enough work or money for the family.[75] Mar's body image is equal to food that is at the same time Chinese and non-Chinese, family and the trouble with family, failure and success. Food equals her life in between cultures and, thus, the instability of identity that is constantly shaped by outside forces that seem to run counter to Mar's own desires and visions. However, the restaurant is also the place where she, through her resistance, begins to understand who she is and what she wants from life.

The Chinese restaurant, for Mar's family, is a transplantation of their home in China to the United States, although her parents had never been involved in the restaurant business before their migration. The "voluntary ghetto" of the Chinese community offers stability but also means confinement.[76] The individualism that Mar gets to know at school has no place in the daily life of her family. However, the preparation and distribution of food at the restaurant are anything but authentically Chinese, since they cater to non-Chinese customers who would never recognize "authentic Chinese" food even if served and who, instead, prefer Americanized Chinese food. The restaurant keeps changing and becomes less and less Chinese while the Chinese family suffers from the pretense of authenticity and their need for performance. The young girl, teenager, and adult Mar breaks the boundaries of the culinary confines and moves away from Denver to the East coast, first to Cornell University and then to Harvard with scholarships. The restaurant remains a constant reminder for her of the ethnically exclusive ghetto, and her parents' poverty that strongly contrasts with the stereotypical label of the "model minority," which Mar considers a lie:

> For the better part of my life, I have struggled to live up to the image of the "model minority," a stereotype that has long been used to describe Asian Americans. I wanted to dispel the stereotype, because I know from experience that it is not true. [. . .] I wrote this book because I needed to reveal these truths about myself: that at my core I am more "minority" than "model"; that

as an American I continue to lie if I perpetuate the myth of a classless, integrated America.[77]

The restaurant endorses a fake Chinese life and the performance of inauthenticity that both preclude actual understanding between different ethnic groups.

Of Culinary Homes as Spaces of Ethnic Encounter

While *Paper Daughter* and *Donald Duk* offer insights into Chinese immigrants' lives in restaurants both as a work and a living space and, therefore, merge the private and the public space, Amy Tan's (b. 1952) novel *The Joy Luck Club* depicts the life of two generations of women, of mothers who left China in 1949, four years after the end of the Sino-Japanese War (1937–1945), and of daughters who are born in the United States, and situates the dinner scene to be discussed here in the private space of a family's home, however, with a public function.[78] First- and second-generation immigrants have to come to terms with the otherness of American society but also their own otherness within that society. While the mothers desperately cling to traditional rituals and nostalgic memories of their homes and create "homes away from home," their daughters have to struggle with their lives in between cultures, lives determined, on the one hand, by their ethnicity and their parents' reinforcement of it, and, on the other hand, by the Americanness of American society clashing with traditional Chinese notions of behavior, style, language, and gender roles.[79]

Rituals are part of the mothers' traditions and offer moments of stability through repetition. A "[r]itual therefore serves the function of integrating the individual more closely into the social whole. Taking this theme further, ritual may also be seen as a response to threats to the community. Ritual activity intensifies in the face of social change or during other periods of social instability."[80] The game of mahjong and meals are such rituals, which are visible in Jing-Mei Woo's depiction of the preparations for a dinner at the Hsu family's house. The detailed description of each food item that is placed in abundance on the table creates an atmosphere of exoticism for the readers and evokes the characters' Chinese past. While the first generation performs the dinner rituals unconsciously, the daughter Jing-Mei perceives them as conduct that someone at some point must have invented: "Who started this ritual?" she wonders.[81]

Tan's depiction of food and eating rituals can be read in the context of Lévi-Strauss's understanding of these rituals as "a socially expressive language" and Roland Barthes's idea of "the meal as signifying society's deepest values."[82] Furthermore, the "preparation of food and its eating can be read as tropes signifying the hierarchical levels of class [or ethnic] structure in which an individual introjects—or re-jects—social identity."[83] As a consequence, "[e]ating is a communicative act of taking in 'the Other,' incorporating it into oneself."[84]

When Waverly Jong wants to tell her mother about her upcoming marriage to the American Rich Schields, she chooses the occasion of a family dinner. Although the place of the dinner is the family's home, it, like a restaurant, requires cultural knowledge to find one's position in the encounter of hosts and guests as groups of insiders and outsiders. For Waverly's mother, "cooking was how [she] expressed her love, her pride, her power," and, thus, a successful dinner with Rich would pave his way into the family.[85] However, as Waverly soon notices: "I couldn't save Rich in the kitchen. And I couldn't save him later at the dinner table."[86] Rich, in his attempt at doing everything right, commits every culinary ethnic blunder one can think of in spite of Waverly's tutoring. He brings the wrong present; he drinks and eats too much; he soils himself in his effort to eat with chopsticks; and he ignorantly criticizes Waverly's mother's cooking. Thus, he breaks all the rules of the culinary system; he cannot decipher the signs of this "ethnic feast,"[87] and remains an outsider:

> As is the Chinese cook's custom, my mother always made disparaging remarks about her own cooking. That night she chose to direct it toward her famous steamed pork and preserved vegetable dish, which she always served with special pride.
>
> "Ai! This dish not salty enough, no flavor," she complained, after tasting a small bite. "It is too bad to eat."
>
> This was our family's cue to eat some and proclaim it the best she had ever made. But before we could do so, Rich said, "You know, all it needs is a little soy sauce." And he proceeded to pour

> a riverful of the salty black stuff on the platter, right before my mother's horrified eyes.[88]

Here, foodways perform on a culinary level the exclusion immigrants experience in the host country. As Waverly's mother laments: "This American rules [. . .]. Every time people come out from foreign country, must know rules. You not know, judge say, Too bad, go back."[89] Rich does not just over-season the traditional Chinese dish and thus destroy its flavor, but, more importantly, he interferes with Chinese traditions which define and empower the Chinese family, disrupts the performance of their identification process, and ultimately, disempowers them.[90] As Robley Evans points out, "the dinner party has only hidden conflict and break ups, the shared table permitting expression of oral aggression." Rich's behavior at the table turns "the paradigm of meal-taking upside down."[91] Ultimately, as Mary Douglas argues in her essay "Deciphering a Meal,"

> If food is treated as a code, the messages it encodes will be found in the pattern of social relations being expressed. The message is about different degrees of hierarchy, inclusion and exclusion, boundaries and transactions across the boundaries. Like sex, the taking of food has a social component, as well as a biological one. Food categories therefore encode social events.[92]

But *The Joy Luck Club* also offers strong images of continuity, of bonds between mothers and daughters through ritualistic cooking and eating. When An-Mei's grandmother in China is about to die, An-Mei's mother returns, after having been excluded from the family, and attempts to save her mother. The young An-Mei (later the mother of Rose) watches or dreams about her mother "cooking a soup, pouring herbs and medicines into the steaming pot. [. . .] And then my mother cut a piece of meat from her arm. [. . .] My mother took her flesh and put it in the soup. She cooked magic in the ancient tradition to try to cure her mother this one last time."[93] In spite of the failure of this attempt, it shows the intimate relationship between mother and daughter, that "[y]our mother is in your bones!," as An-Mei later exclaims.[94]

With the offering of her own flesh as food for her mother, An-Mei's mother literally returns to her mother's womb. This is an attempt to return to a time when she was still an unborn child taken care of by her mother. The quasi-cannibalism that is involved in this mother-daughter relationship can be considered a form of sacrifice as well as communion that is characterized by the eating of the body of Christ. In both cases, the incorporation of human flesh is a symbolic act which is meant as a means of survival that, in this case, fails; but the ritual does indicate "that Necessity might have taken a peculiar and acutely distressing form in Asian American immigrant families,"[95] even before their arrival in the United States.[96]

The Joy Luck Club distinguishes between present-day rituals representing contemporary American culture's abundance, in which the Chinese also partake, and the rituals of the past evoked through memories of the scarcity of food and the threats to one's own life. While in the past, the flesh of the daughter's arm as food for the mother expresses the daughter's possible gradual disintegration as an individual and merging with her mother, the dinner party reveals the attempt to perpetuate the past into the present and to actually keep the body intact. Rich's inability to fully participate in the rituals and his disruption of the smoothness of the event, that is, his challenge to the rituals that keep the family tied to their past in China, expose the cultural constructedness of this particular preparation and incorporation of food in a domestic setting. The Chinese family clings to it because it represents their version of a past to which they can otherwise not return. It serves as a continuing line between past and present and cannot allow for any disruption. In the private space of this dinner, the family's history and, as a consequence, their identities are at stake, which Rich could easily destroy if they took him seriously. The daughter's story reveals irony and amusement, on the one hand, but also despair on the other, since she finds herself in between her family and her fiancé, the present and the past, America and China; thus, her location is inter-generational, inter-temporal, and international/inter-continental. While her parents are Chinese, her boyfriend is American; she is in the liminal space of in-betweenness where she has an either/or choice or needs to make the decisive and crucial decision for both at the same time.

New York City Streets and the Hybridization of Foodways

"America Was Born in the Streets," as the subtitle of the film *Gangs of New York* (2002) tells us. *Kimchee and Chitlins*, a comedy by Chinese American writer Elizabeth Wong (b. 1958), presents race relations in New York City and the media coverage of the 1990 black boycott of Korean-owned stores in Flatbush, Brooklyn. Here, Haitians and Koreans, as two immigrant groups of the late twentieth century, fight verbally and, to some extent, physically for the power over territory that serves as their means for survival.[97] From Chinese restaurants as places of separation and voluntary ghettoization via the quasi-public space of the family dinner table, the play opens up the cookbook as literary space for hybrid recipes that reveal that foodways, including restaurants, can become means of integration if cultures open up toward each other.

Although there seems to be an unbridgeable gap between the black Haitian and the Korean communities, foodways as in Korean kimchee and African American chitlins,[98] overcome the tension. Kimchee, as Grocer Mak explains, is "not just dead cabbage, kimchee is the heart of Korea. When I eat it, my homesickness says 'Adios.' [. . .] When I was a boy, my mother cut up Chinese cabbage, garlic, ginger, put in chili pepper, salt. That's kimchee. The trick is to pickle it for a long time. [. . .] Kimchee is like wonder drug."[99] The black Nurse Ruth Betty relates what her Grandpa would always say to her: "'You know, Ruthie, chitlins is our history. It come about because the slave master took the best part of the pig and left the slaves with the shit.' 'Life is like chitlins,' he would say. 'Someone gives you shit, but you make a banquet out of it.'"[100] The metaphorical "chitlins is our history" again aligns food with the past, this time not with the history of a particular nation but with that of an ethnic group that was thrown into slavery. African slaves who were transported via the Middle Passage to the New World did not feel connected to a nation but to a tribe. In slavery, they had to find ways of communicating with each other in spite of different languages, rituals, and tribes. This multiplicity of backgrounds, forcefully brought together in a new location and confronted with another culture, namely that of Americans, started a process of transculturation that would eventually produce something new. "Chitlins" is a type of food that was created in slavery and is ultimately connected with the hardship slaves had to suffer in this peculiar institution. Slaves had to survive on what was left to them, namely the "shit" of a pig. Because of slaves' ingenuity, the shit was literally turned into a feast, a banquet, with which they celebrated their survival. "Life is like chitlins" can again be read as a simile of survival that turns slavery into empowerment.

The food that is evoked here is not prepared in restaurants but is homemade and ripe with cultural implications. It is "the heart of Korea," thus a metaphor but also almost a metonymy which indicates the close association between this type of food and Korea. Via kimchee, Grocer Mak is transported back to his country of origin with which he connects familiar rituals and his own well-being in childhood. The mother, as the provider of nourishment, not only prepared this dish for him as a boy and obviously also passed on the information about its ingredients and the specific way of cooking it. Furthermore, Grocer Mak also attributes healing functions to this dish; for him, it becomes a "wonder drug" that can cure all kinds of ailments. Healing in both metaphorical and literal senses as curing people of homesickness but also of colds is an important function of immigrant, here Korean, foodways.

Similar ideas are evoked when the black Barber Brown eventually suggests a creative convergence through foodways:

> Well, I had this idea, see. I was eating your kimchee. I was sneezing my head off. Then for no reason, I put some of that kimchee into my chitlins, and wouldn't you know, it tasted good, AND it cleared up my sinuses. So, I got to thinking, I mean, you could sell the stuff in your store. In the food-to-go section *or* in your pharmaceutical department. Kimchee and Chitlins. The wonder *food* or the wonder *drug*. [. . .] What is chitlins? Next time you come in, I'll make you a mess of chitlins on a sweet soft bed of kimchee. I might even enter it into some kind of Betty Crocker cookbook contest.[101]

The first step that Barber Brown undertakes is that he tastes kimchee. Although its spices irritate his sinuses, he stirs the kimchee together with his chitlins and produces a never-experienced effect. He likes the taste of the new dish, *and* the tickling of his sinuses clears them up like medication would do. The literal and metaphorical combination of two ethnic foodways has a healing effect, that is, it cures sickness and eases the irritability between African (Caribbean) Americans and Koreans. Its multiple functions can even be turned into economic profit by selling it as a new product in Grocer Mak's store. No matter whether it is considered food or drug, the new dish is labeled a "wonder" and effects unheard-of bodily changes. Barber Brown, in a neighborly and conciliatory gesture, offers to prepare this dish for Grocer Mak to taste. In this instance, ethnic boundaries, which before seemed to have been fixed and insuperable, are made permeable. The home becomes a private restaurant where ingredients are reshuffled and served in a gesture of friendship.

Betty Crocker, a famous American cook who started a cookbook contest, is a representative of the culture that has emerged from immigration and subsequent transculturation and has merged into something new that is constituted by still visible different ingredients which are, however, no longer separable. The combination of kimchee and chitlins, or Korean and African, becomes American in the process and ensures ethnic survival in hybridity. What the two bring together here are not just the traditional foods of the respective ethnic groups, but different heritages, rituals, and pasts that are joined for a new purpose. The dishes bring peace to the conflict by being stirred into something new that is defined as "wonder food/drug." In both cases, food is not only a marker of identity and a part of the history of origin but has also become "ethnic history in the US,"[102] and, in this way, affirms the preservation of the old and the acceptance of the new.

Food has become the texture through which the text is turned into historiography. Foodways in *Kimchee and Chitlins* offer "alternative links between the living and the dead, thus ways to recover a forgotten narrative and reunite fragmented families, broken bodies, dislocated bones," as Nicole Waller argues in reference to Fae Myenne Ng's *Bones* (1993).[103] By entering the new dish into the all-American Betty Crocker cookbook contest, the process of transculturation will take its further course because of the acceptance of ethnic Otherness into American society and, thus, also into the public sphere of the restaurants. As a consequence, American society is always already

Other. Because all people are Other in the United States, consequently, Otherness is an inherent part of U.S. identity.

"Stirring the Pot": Desserts

"Stirring the Pot" of Asian foodways in the United States not only sheds light on the relevance of culinary fictions for an understanding of ethnic life in the United States, but, more precisely, reveals a number of phenomena in intra- and inter-ethnic relationships that challenge notions of home, community, and authenticity. In all examples, foodways are intimately connected to physical and psychological survival. The first-generation immigrants open up their own cafés, grills, or restaurants in the nostalgic but often futile longing for homes away from home. They take pride in and empower themselves through cooking and resist intrusion from outside. The authenticity of these public and private foodways is *imagined*, to speak with Benedict Anderson, *imaginary*, to use Salman Rushdie's term,[104] *invented*, as Hobsbawm and Ranger explain, or *performed*, as seen in Chin. Authenticity, as Tan shows, is performed through rituals as well as naming. Nostalgic memories and/or the exoticization of the respective Asian homelands may lead to ethnic self-empowerment but may equally well evoke the specter of re-Orientalism, that is, the re-Orientalization of the Orient by the Orientals themselves. Ultimately, foodways are always "a system of signification" that may prevent but also allow for communication.[105] As Wong and Chin show, acknowledging the ongoing changes in the culinary system of signification and with it "the symbolic power of food," will lead to new, hybrid, and, ultimately, transcultural dishes in the all-American Betty Crocker cookbook. "'If we are what we eat, who are we?'" will remain a question to be discussed.[106]

Furthermore, as the spaces for the preparation and intake of food, namely the home and the restaurant, have shown, both locations are simultaneously private and public. Chinese immigration, as shown in Chin's *Donald Duk* and Mar's *Paper Daughter*, often takes the immigrants to the larger family already established in the United States and to the restaurants which they run. Lack of knowledge of the English language does not allow for other forms of employment until, eventually, the next generations break the family bonds and leave the restaurants that have become their home and, in some way, their prison. Both Chin and Mar observe the increasing hybridity of the space and the food in analogy to their own insecurity about identity and belonging. Mar's family moves away from the restaurant run by relatives only for the father to work in yet another restaurant that keeps him fairly secluded in his ethnicity and his wife—Mar's mother—without any social contact whatsoever. It seems that this seclusion can more easily be undone in the private home if it is opened up—even if involuntarily, to others, such as Americans—as in Tan's *The Joy Luck Club*. The semi-private/public family dinner allows for temporary intercultural encounters and prepares the Chinese family for future intercultural negotiations. Finally, Wong's *Kimchee and Chitlins* takes foodways from the homes and restaurants to encounters on the streets of New York City, where foodways ultimately merge and find entry into more than just restaurants, that is, into the all-American Betty Crocker cookbook.

Let me conclude with Ralph Ellison's affirmation: "'I yam what I am'"[107] and where I am in this world of "'culinary citizenship.'"[108] The most recent culinary discovery in Asian African America, "Obama Sushi," is a sign of hybridization and diversity in foodways and, thus, in American identity.[109]

CHAPTER 13

"As American as Chop Suey"

The Chop Suey Joint in Classical Hollywood Film

ANDRÉE LAFONTAINE

The expression "as American as chop suey," in print as early as 1933, is semantically rich.[1] It translates at once the American pride in the nation's ability to reinvent itself but also in its aptness to appropriate foreign products, to "civilize" them, and to produce them better and cheaper. The chop suey restaurant, like the dish, comes to represent the "civilized" Chinese and, by extension, America's superiority as a civilizing force.[2] A Chinese American invention, chop suey emerged in San Francisco in the latter years of the nineteenth century, passing as authentic Chinese cuisine. Andrew Coe has detailed the dish's origins and the various myths regarding its paternity. Some people attribute the dish to Chinese migrant workers, others to specific chefs or diplomats. Coe, however, has traced a certain lineage to a similar dish from the Guangdong province town of Taishan, which immigrants tried to replicate using the ingredients found on the American West Coast, and which came to be known as *shap sui*.

The popular dish's use of unusual ingredients perpetuated the myth of its Chinese origin, while its relative blandness—compared to authentic Chinese cuisine—made the dish more amenable to the American palate. In a short lexicon of Chinese words in the journal *American Speech*, Kwei Chen defines the famous dish in haiku-like fashion—with what can only be tongue-in-cheek humor: *Chop Suey /*

Bamboo-shoots, bean-sprouts, mushrooms, and chopped meat,— / In one pan are fried together many ingredients. / This is a dish by the Chinese cook— / For Americans only.[3] By the end of the nineteenth century, non-Chinese "slummers" could be seen walking to San Francisco and New York Chinatowns, looking for adventure and exoticism on a plate.[4] Such slumming is the object of mockery in Henry King's 1925 film adaptation of *Stella Dallas.* To convey Stella's increasingly vulgar and hopelessly provincial manners, the title card indicates that while in town with her equally uncouth friend, the pair did "Chop Suey—Burlesque Show—Beer Garden—Stella and Ed missed nothing." Using images that would be familiar to the audience, the filmmakers appear to share an inside joke regarding unsophisticated "out-of-towner" slumming.

The craze for chop suey spread in Chinese restaurants throughout the United States between 1900 and 1920, and peaked in the 1950s. Soon enough, Chinese restaurants, owned and operated by Chinese Americans but attracting mostly non-Chinese customers, were thriving in various American cities outside of large cities' Chinatowns. Offering a variety of Chinese American fare scaled to suit the American palate, Chinese restaurants covered a broad spectrum from posh nightclub to chop suey joint. Higher up the echelon stood swanky nightclubs featuring "dazzling three-ring circus[es] with singers, chorus lines, dance teams and acrobats" and sometimes large orchestras.[5] Chinese American nightclubs and upscale restaurants, however, catered not only to celebrity and wealth, but also to white Americans from all social strata in search of elegant, elite, exotic, yet "safe," entertainment.[6] The social history of this popular Chinese American dish has been studied extensively, notably by Andrew Coe and Samantha Barbas, who show that "culinary preferences do not always correlate with racial and social attitudes."[7] For this reason, as Barbas posits, "ethnic restaurants may be more interesting and lively sites of cross-cultural exchange and interaction than scholars have traditionally assumed."[8] The author concludes by inviting scholars to pursue case studies to explore how specific foodways have shaped identities.

Focusing on the representation of chop suey joints in early classical Hollywood film, this essay constitutes one such case study.

Hollywood is understood as a national cinema, which I study using a functionalist approach. This approach treats film in terms of how it functions within the nation state and for its members.[9] Using Mikhail Bakhtin's "chronotope," I investigate the significance of the chop suey joint as an ideologically charged place that fulfills specific historical needs in the context of America's continual reimagining of its national identity. The chronotope is a valuable—though underused and undertheorized—concept for film studies, as it establishes a relationship between films and the society which creates them, while avoiding simplified causality or a mirroring effect. It is a way of understanding a concrete socio-historical period and its artistic output without resorting to banal sociological explanations that seek to reduce artistic productions to mere reproductions of reality under a different banner. More than a simple topos, the chronotope possesses axiological value, "colouring with emotions and values" the events depicted.[10] It is therefore a useful concept for understanding America's national imaginary. In this multidisciplinary approach, I use the tools developed by film studies, phenomenology, and food studies to investigate the significance of the chop suey joint chronotope in early-1930s Hollywood films. I aim to show that, because of the presence of food, the chop suey joint becomes a particularly powerful chronotope, conveying a sense of personal and national identity. Unsurprisingly, the chop suey joint becomes particularly important in narratives of belonging and exclusion.

The Chop Suey Joint as Chronotope

The *chronotope*, a term coined by Mikhail Bakhtin, literally means "time space."[11] Its significance, however, lies in the underlying idea (also formulated by Bakhtin) that artistic productions stem from a concrete experience of time and space, which in turn influences the type of characters and narratives generated. Although many interpreters have acknowledged the importance of the chronotope as more than a simple time/space coordinate for literary analysis, few have actually used the term to its full potential by posing it as the link between the on- and off-screen worlds. In their glossary to Bakhtin's *Dialogic Imagination,* Holquist and Emerson define the chronotope as "an optic for reading texts as x-rays of the forces at work in the culture system from which they spring."[12] The chronotope was conceived by Bakhtin as much more than a simple motif; it was thought of as that which links the creating and the represented worlds. Indeed, Bakhtin was preoccupied with the conceptualization of this link in a way that would not be a mere causal relationship. Although he stresses the importance of maintaining the difference between art and the lived world, Bakhtin describes the two as participating in a dynamic akin to dialogue.[13] Accordingly, the chronotope can be seen as a key point of entry into this dialogue and the central element of Bakhtin's "historical poetics."

As Michael Montgomery, Robert Stam, and Joy Ladin point out, the chronotope is best exemplified not in literature, but in film.[14] Because of its nature, every filmic image is inherently chronotopic: time is represented through space, and spatial representations unfold over time. As a series of fused time/space coordinates, film poses a unique challenge to a chronotopic analysis. In order to help determine whether a particular element in a film should be considered a chronotope or not, Ladin lists four conditions: (1) being organizing and foregrounding centers of key events and scenes; (2) repeating explicit, concrete markers (the language must call attention to the spatio-temporal dimension); (3) being well delineated (time and space must fuse in a distinct manner); and (4) providing physical metaphors for abstract ideas or elements.[15] To function in a significant way, chronotopes should combine some of these characteristics. Otherwise, these spatio-temporal knots "remain incidental chronotopes, which are neither visible nor functional as 'grounds' for narrative."[16]

The chop suey joint as chronotope makes unlikely appearances in a surprising number of early-1930s Hollywood films. Visually, these chop suey joints are generally free of many of the clichés and racial stereotypes often associated with Chinatowns in film. There are no red lanterns, "wonton fonts," traditional clothing, or references to Confucius and opium dens. Instead, the studios are aiming for verisimilitude, appealing to their audiences' familiarity with the urban institution but also displaying their own hipness. As seen in the exterior shot from *Young Bride* (1932), the restaurant's sign is in marquee lightbulb lettering. This inscribes the chop suey joint as an urban, nighttime locale associated with other forms of entertainment—namely theaters and dance halls. In fact, the chop suey joint is one of several lower-middle-class amusement venues featured in *Young Bride,* whose main protagonists also patronize a drugstore, a ferry, a pool hall, and a taxi dance hall.

The chop suey joint is featured early in the film as the location of the protagonists Allie (Helen Twelvetrees) and Charlie's (Eric Linden) blind date. Looking at the menu with bewilderment, Allie confesses that she "do[es]n't know what this all means, but it looks exciting." Over piano and dance music, Allie and Charlie daydream about travelling to Asia. It is in fact this shared dream of escape to exotic lands that seals the couple's future together. Beset by financial obligations after an all-too-early and ill-conceived marriage, the couple must abandon their plans to see the world. Charlie, moreover, proves to be a poor provider: conceited and obsessed with instant success and the high life, he refuses to lower himself to the daily drudgery of work. The only exoticism available to them is the one found on their plate at the chop suey joint. As in many other American films depicting forms of otherness, exciting and alluring exoticism quickly turns into threat and destruction. The chop suey joint becomes a place of excessive drinking, violence, financial ruin, and sexual misconduct. It stands as both the source of the couple's ill-fated marriage and its destruction. The hardboiled, late-night environment may have been fit for young, innocent folks looking for a cheap thrill while "slumming," but married people do not belong there, for they risked perdition. *Young Bride* is thus a cautionary tale designed to teach young women about the various dangers of modern urban living, including boys and quick marriages.

The chop suey joint is visually presented in *Blondie Johnson* in a similar way: devoid of overt Asian signifiers and with a "Broadway lights" exterior. The restaurant is elegant and simple, but it is again implicitly linked with the underworld, as it affords privacy to its diners, who can discuss their illicit activities freely. Blondie (Joan Blondell) and Danny (Chester Morris) use this space to elaborate on their plans to take over a criminal gang. Deploying the chop suey joint in this fashion implies a pejorative association with criminal activity. The year, however, is 1933, and the gangster is still a powerful cultural "hero," to quote Robert Warshow.[17] Blondie Johnson is, additionally, presented by Warner Brothers as a new type of gangster, revealing a certain truth about the era:

> When serious historians begin to piece together the picture of our modern times they will give particular thanks to four people, James Cagney, Edward G. Robinson, Paul Muni and Joan Blondell. These young players, more than any other, are supplying future generations with the true picture of our own hectic current problems by their work on the talking screen.[18]

Many have seen in the gangster story the universal quest of the individual for community.[19] The genre has consequently been linked with immigrants: the gangster, who comes from immigrant stock, represents in an indirect way the immigrant's quest for integration and acceptance within American society. As Martha Nochimson notes, at the core of the gangster film exists a tension "between immigrant reality and the deeply cherished central fable of modern democracies that promise immigrant (and other) outsiders that they can become social insiders."[20] Defined as an outsider who aspires to join the American capitalist and materialist middle class, the gangster is not a rebel, or an insider who makes him/herself an outsider and attacks society.[21] Blondie breaks away from this tradition, as she is not presented as belonging to an immigrant community. Rather, she is linked, in the first scene, with the tenements and the masses of poor people struggling through the Depression. The film establishes early on that Blondie has suffered injustice and rejection not only because of her socioeconomic status as a member of the working class, but also on account of her gender. In fact, she enters poverty and becomes ineligible for relief aid when she voluntarily quits her job after her boss's inappropriate behavior. As a downwardly mobile working-class woman, Blondie joins the outsiders and shares the gangster's longing to take part in the American dream. A quintessentially democratic space—chop suey restaurants would serve all social classes and racial groups—the chop suey joint certainly taps into a significant element of the American dream.[22] Incidentally, Blondie's fate will take a sharp turn for the better after her business meetings inside the chop suey restaurant.

A later example, from Ida Lupino's *The Bigamist* (1953), shows both continuity and change in the depiction of American Chinese restaurants. As its title indicates, the film features a man who loves, and comes to marry, two women. The second marriage results from Harry's inability to fulfill fully his marital role with his first wife. In a true film noir form, Harry (Edmond O'Brien) is a weak character, a failed husband—unable to conceive with his wife—and a fading entrepreneur. Eve Graham (Joan Fontaine), the first wife, is an industrious and business-savvy upper-middle-class blonde. Her entrepreneurial aptitude—far superior to that of her husband—is depicted in the film as a source of marital tension and distance, with Harry shrinking in his wife's presence, and Eve abandoning him to build their company. On a business trip to Los Angeles, left lonely by his wife's "executive mood," Harry meets Phyllis Martin (Ida Lupino). She invites Harry to dine at the "early Chinese American" Canton Café where she works. Stating what is already commonplace, Phyllis informs him that chop suey isn't really Chinese and that egg soup is the only authentic dish on the restaurant's menu. The restaurant, we surmise, is a tourist trap mocked by locals "in the know." Although the film adopts many tropes of the noir genre, it resists characterizing the two women using the Madonna/whore dichotomy: both characters are strong, smart, and independent. In fact, Harry is the only truly weak character.

The Canton Café, which reappears throughout the film, effectively serves to establish Phyllis's character as a smart and savvy, urban, working woman with Chinese American friends. Harry always meets her at the café, which, within the film's structure, detaches Phyllis from the domestic sphere. This also makes the Canton Café a dangerous space, especially for the sanctity of the home and family. In this early 1950s noir film, however, the restaurant is a failing rather than a thriving business, with the Chinese American cuisine craze having run its course. By the time of the movie's release, the mid-range "Cantonese" restaurant was already a remnant of an old fad. Yet here, it is unclear whether this signals an openness to more authentic Chinese fare, or an admission that the great American melting pot has failed.

It has been remarked that food scenes play paradoxical functions in gangster movies, as they express the gangster's opposing quests for community and the destruction of that community. Dining scenes, therefore, become imbued with tension and anxiety.[23] In all three films, the chop suey joint plays a similarly paradoxical role: it allows for intimate—but also dangerous and destructive—encounters. While in the first two films, the diners aspire to take part in the American dream, in *The Bigamist*, Harry desperately seeks companionship. Their quests for belonging, however, are thwarted in various ways, resulting in the characters' increased exclusion.

Dorothy Arzner's 1931 *Working Girls* also features a chop suey joint as a key setting, though this time one resulting in successful community belonging. The Paramount film follows look-alike sisters Mae (Dorothy Hall) and June (Judith Wood) as they settle into their new life in the big city. *Working Girls* is, above all, a movie about modern young womanhood—the young, independent, working woman facing the challenges of urban living—an exciting and popular topic for early-1930s moviemaking. Indeed, modern women—as secretaries, stenographers, entertainers, or taxi dancers—provided ample material for movies exploring the trials and tribulations brought on by fast-changing morals. In *Working Girls*, the two girls' respective attitudes towards modern urban life are contrasted, with Mae adopting demure behavior and June, a plucky, go-getter approach. In short, Mae follows traditional rules and respects boundaries, while June ignores them by putting herself and her needs first.[24] Consequently, Mae naïvely pursues an upper-class college man well above her social status, while June dates a bohemian jazz saxophone player before choosing Mae's former employer, Dr. Schrader (Paul Lukas). All three frequent a chop suey joint, typical of New York's bohemian scene.

As Coe and Barbas explain, chop suey joints became particularly popular with "bohemians"—young intellectuals and artists seeking to distance themselves from mainstream culture. Chinatowns and chop suey joints represented the liminal space between exoticism, puritanical morals, and the *status quo*. The strong aromas, loud noise of the diners' chatter, incomprehensible servers, and the absence of Western dining etiquette came to represent freedom, rebellion, and sensual liberty for many young Americans who felt constrained by social norms. Edward Hopper's 1929 painting, *Chop Suey*, depicts such an environment: two women wearing cloche-hats and makeup, sitting together without male companions, at ease in an urban setting.

In *Working Girls*, the chop suey joint is once again filmed in a rather matter-of-fact way, without the excessive kitsch often associated with American films (i.e., the moral depravity of the underground, exoticism, and the lifestyle of the lower rungs). Instead, the restaurant takes on the allure of a modest, functional diner. The choice of a chop suey joint for Schrader's and June's "date" marks the place as, if not on the outside, then on the social margin. In this atmosphere, both June and Schrader find themselves quite at home: June is a frequent customer, and Schrader is not only familiar with the items on the menu, but he orders in "Cantonese."[25] June's initial quest to make it in the big city is realized in this liminal space, where community is achieved within the margins and where the mainstream is undesirable.

In *Young Bride*, *Blondie Johnson*, *Working Girls*, and *The Bigamist*, the chop suey joint acts as a chronotope. Its centrality is emphasized, notably, by the characters' return to the location, and the importance it plays within the narrative for key scenes. It is, finally, linked to various abstract ideas regarding community, belonging and exclusion, and exoticism. Chronotopes, as the previous examples illustrate, should not be understood as "inert, discrete and a-temporal" motifs. They are, as Ladin reminds us, "dynamic, interrelated and highly temporal," and they must, first and foremost, be experienced as such by an interpreter.[26] The chronotope must be "lived through" by a historically situated interpreter, for one of its roles is precisely to establish a link between the world of art and that of the interpreter/reader/spectator.[27]

The chronotope, therefore, is not simply time/space, but *lived*—and, by extension, axiological—time/space, as it links together at least two bodies: that of the on-screen character and that of the off-screen spectator. The significance of the space would, therefore, not be completely deciphered without an analysis of its main attraction, the chop suey itself. Indeed, the case of chop suey is a curious and interesting one, given that food was not particularly present in early-1930s Hollywood films.[28] A phenomenological approach, one focusing on the activation of the spectator's senses, therefore seems compatible with a chronotopical analysis. As I will show, food is particularly well suited to establishing sensorial connections between the on and off-screen worlds, especially when it is linked to personal, ethnic, and national identity.

Film, Food and Identity

In "food films"—*Tampopo* (1985) and its American remake *Tortilla Soup* (2001); *Babette's Feast* (1987); *Like Water for Chocolate* (1992); *Eat Drink Man Woman* (1994); and *Big Night* (1996), among others—food preparation and consumption are intimately linked to ideas about national and ethnic identity. Dishes are carefully selected to quickly and effectively convey information regarding the film's characters, their socioeconomic class, and their stance towards their ethnic or national identity. A similar use of the signifying function of food is also evident in non-food-focused vehicles, for instance, in the television series *The Sopranos* (1999–2007)—where classic Italian American dishes regularly connote class and ethnicity—but also, perhaps more subtly, in films such as *Pulp Fiction* (1994). In the latter, Americanness is conveyed through American restaurants and the various foods consumed and invoked: the Denver omelet, blueberry and buttermilk pancakes, hamburgers, milkshakes, pork chops and sausages, doughnuts, blueberry pie, Pop Tarts, and Cap'n Crunch cereal. As Rebecca Epstein claims, *Pulp Fiction* defines national character through food, as is illustrated in Vince (John Travolta) and Jules's (Samuel L. Jackson) discussion of the different fast-foodways of Europe and America.[29] The Americanness conveyed in *Pulp Fiction* can, furthermore, be characterized as nostalgic and traditional, as the food celebrated is emblematic of the industrial postwar diet—a diet focused on red meat, starch, and processed foods.

A cultural marker, food often serves conservative functions, promoting traditional values and conceptions of national and personal identity and belonging. Chinese identity is reinforced in *Eat Drink Man Woman* by the preparation of decades-old forgotten dishes, as is Mexican identity in *Like Water for Chocolate,* and French culinary tradition in *Babette's Feast. Tortilla Soup*'s patriarch keeps the family together and asserts his position of superiority with the confection of elaborate traditional Mexican dishes for Sunday dinner. In these food films, food is used to either return to or reassert a waning ethnic identity. By establishing cultural continuity, food becomes a reassuring signifier. According to Helene A. Shugart, food acts in film as a concrete, stable, and consumable marker of personal, national, and ethnic identity. In fact, "ethnic film narratives seem more and more likely to involve the use of food as a key textual element."[30]

Food's relationship to personal and national identity is not simply cerebral and semiotic, however; it is viscerally anchored in the body. Since humans are omnivores who can eat anything, they run the risk of eating dangerous foods. This is what Paul Rozin describes as the omnivore's dilemma, which results in what Claude Fischler calls the omnivore's anxiety: the twin pull and oscillation between human beings' desire for new tastes and their fear of and resistance to change. As a species, humans have developed not only biological mechanisms, but also complex "cognitive competences and culturally constructed practices and representations" to resolve the paradox and attenuate this attendant anxiety. For instance, one identifies with members of a specific community by the food one eats and does not eat, and, conversely, perceives the foods eaten by members of their own community as safe.[31] Social anthropologists and psychologists have studied the symbolic purchase of foods as ways to code and decode not only belonging but also danger, contagion, and threat: "flavor principles" become economic ways for human beings to identify easily members of their own communities by their familiar foods, and foreigners by their foreign, and potentially dangerous, tastes.

One could follow Anne Bower and maintain that "filmmakers in *all* film genres turn to food to communicate important aspects of characters' emotions, along with their personal and cultural identities."[32] In *The Skin of the Film: Intercultural Cinema, Embodiment, and the Senses*, however, Laura Marks goes further by claiming that "memories that evoke the physical awareness of touch, smell, and bodily presence can be vital links to home for people living in diaspora from their culture of origin."[33] Diasporic memory, as Marks explains, often only consists of cultural sensoria: the particular smell of the ocean air, the taste of freshly harvested fruits, and the noises and aroma of the markets. Although Marks is concerned with the multisensory experience of film and video, some of her most compelling case studies involve diasporic food. Notably, foods reminiscent of home can be used in film to powerful effect in a transnational context. Indeed, food can be made to function as "haptic visuality," triggering, through visual imagery, memories of taste, smell, and touch, and establishing a direct link between the screen and the viewer's body. "The cinematic encounter," Marks writes,

> takes place not only between my body and the film's body, but my sensorium and the film's sensorium. We bring our own personal and cultural organization of the senses to cinema, and cinema brings a particular organization of the senses to us, the filmmaker's own sensorium refracted through the cinematic apparatus. One could say that intercultural spectatorship is the meeting of two different sensorial systems, which may or may not intersect. Spectatorship is thus an act of sensory translation of cultural knowledge.[34]

Chop Suey as Edible Identity

In *Sailor's Luck* (1933), Jimmy, a sailor on leave in San Pedro, complains of an upset stomach following an evening of "too much chop suey." Chop suey was popularly associated with sailors for various reasons: unable to cook, these bachelors would most likely spend the little money they have on girls and alcohol rather than food.

Boxed, take-out chop suey serves as such a symbol of easy, cheap grub in *Our Blushing Brides* (1930). The third installment in the Joan Crawford/Anita Page trilogy—the other two being the lavish *Our Dancing Daughters* (1928) and *Our Modern Maidens* (1929)—the film was presented as rendering on screen the pulse of a generation. Fashions and crazes were changing at an incredible pace in the late 1920s and early '30s, and movies often struggled to keep up. Popular culture also needed to appeal to a younger crowd, which proved an additional challenge to studios often comprised of old, out-of-touch men. Studios, therefore, devoted considerable effort and money to recruit writers, designers, actors and directors who could tap into the youth-crazed era. With each installment, the filmmakers sought to present the most up-the-minute portrayal of modern youth.

By the time work began on *Our Blushing Brides*, the *Dancing Daughter's* flapper insouciance, and her wasteful and excessive lifestyle, were most definitely out of style. The hardships of the Depression years were only just starting and the new popular girl on the screen was no longer a careless partygoer, with whom the audience could neither relate nor sympathize, but a working girl. For Hollywood, this was a new type of heroine: urban, independent, and street-smart. True to its goal of representing the young American woman "*au goût du jour,*" *Blushing Brides* turned heiresses into department-store employees boarding together. Nevertheless, continuity was maintained through character psychology, with Joan Crawford remaining the most sensible and levelheaded girl of the bunch. Indeed, in all three films, Crawford remains an example of moral correctness. In the last installment, thriftiness and home science are added to Crawford's character portfolio of moral rectitude. The most responsible of the trio, she takes care of her housemate much like a devoted mother would. Tellingly, however, come supper time, she does not slave away in the kitchen. Instead, she stacks on the table a series of boxed Chinese take-out dishes. Cheap and filling, chop suey was the sensible modern solution to an empty stomach on a tight budget.

In the context of the Depression, chop suey became a symbol of modern urban working-class thrift. In these cinematic representations, it is once again devoid of overt ethnic markers, even though the dish's "foreign" lineage remains distinctly in the background, as is evidenced in *Sailor's Luck* (Jimmy's difficult incorporation of the unusual dish), *Blushing Brides*'s prominent little boxes, and *Young Bride*'s exotic daydream travels. Yet, as one of the quintessential elements of modern American life, chop suey becomes primarily a signifier of Americanness. This is evidenced in our last example, *Man of the World* (1931).

In the film, William Powell plays Michael Trevor, an American con artist exiled in Paris. Forced out of the United States following a scandal, the gentleman racketeer now makes a living blackmailing American tourists who are visiting the French capital to conduct illicit affairs and rendezvous. For Trevor, Paris is no longer an attractive destination of glamor and adventure, but rather a land of imposed exile, of which he has grown weary and which he longs to leave. Entertaining fellow American tourists who long to see "the real Paris," Trevor takes them to Au Père Jules, a small bistro serving late night fare. Dining on onion soup, he reminisces about his old days as a newspaperman in America. After putting the newspaper to bed late at night, Trevor recalls, the reporters would go to "a small place on the corner for chop suey and" he pauses, unable to recall the second dish's name, "foo young," his companion interjects longingly. "Ah yes," Trevor slowly reveals the pleasant memory, "chop suey and foo young." "It's not the chop suey you miss," he explains, as if in a dream, "it's what it stands for: home, America, friends, fellows I used to know, *plain things without sauces.*"

The scene, running almost two minutes, is rather long considering the standards of the time and its placement at the beginning of the film. Length and placement indicate that the filmmakers saw this scene as playing an important role within the narrative, revealing key information about the film's protagonist. What triggers the mnemonic connection in the film is chop suey as not only a dish, but also as an institution—a "little place" to eat with the fellows at 1:00 a.m. The description of the dish itself is rather odd—"plain things without sauces"—since chop suey is notoriously viscous. One could venture to suggest that "plain things without sauces" corresponds more closely to an idea of how Americans liked to see themselves: unpretentious straight shooters.

Man of the World diverges significantly from the corpus of independent and experimental video and film from the eighties and the nineties analyzed by Laura Marks in *The Skin of the Film*. Chop suey, however, becomes in this film a powerfully evocative American diasporic food, establishing, in a similar manner, a connection between on- and off-screen bodies through the sensorial memory of home and cultural identity. Contrary to food films, where extreme close-ups of foods are used to entice visually an emotional bond and cultural connection, *Man of the World* does so through a fond description of chop suey's social function as a shared American locale and institution. It is interesting to note that, unlike other ethnic foods in film, chop suey does not serve to promote a traditional or conservative conception of national identity based on ethnic lineage. It is associated, rather, with American inventiveness, the ability to succeed despite hardship, and the quest for community belonging, especially for gangsters, working class men and women, involuntary expats, and failed husbands.

Contrary to other Chinese American films such as *Flower Drum Song*, the chop suey films of the early 1930s are populated by American characters who actively seek out the patronage of Asian American establishments. Moreover, the chop suey joints feels "homey" or even "American," offering only a flavor of safe exoticism. Usually, this space is devoid of visual ethnic markers. However, this is a double-edged sword: it is an example of co-mingling—Caucasians and Asian Americans unproblematically frequenting the same establishments, sharing a culture by meeting at a halfway point. Yet, it can also be seen as poaching—an appropriation of Chinese culture by emptying it of its ethnic markers. As Jennifer Jensen Wallach elucidates, Chinese food was discovered and ingested by Americans while racist and xenophobic stereotypes persisted, and consuming "Chinese" food was in no way a consumption or integration of Chineseness.[35]

De-ethnicized, the chop suey joint is, in *Young Bride*, *Blondie Johnson*, *Working Girls*, and *The Bigamist*, a central space for the redefinition of American mainstream identity as it negotiates a renewed relationship with the margins. It proves an interesting case study of the affirmation of American national identity through non-WASP food. It is, moreover, the expression of a national identity that encompasses various ethnicities, albeit at the cost of erasing their visual markers, and appeals to common socioeconomic struggles rather than reaffirming traditions. If we accept that food is "a nonverbal way of articulating ideas about what it [means] to be an American or an outsider," a "modern or a conservative," the chop suey joint in Depression-era Hollywood films proves a telling case study.[36] The national identity that is conveyed is one that—if not open to immigrants of Asian origin—then, at the very least, is open to newness. The chop suey's no-nonsense, pragmatic character (filling yet cheap during an era of poverty, and an alternative to the domestic drudgery of cooking) marks the dish as fundamentally American, despite its "ethnic" origin. This can certainly be seen as expressing ideas regarding the assimilation of Chinese immigrants within American society. However, given the quintessential whiteness of the characters associated with the dish in the films explored in this essay, we should also note that the reverse idea is at play: that to face the challenges of modernity brought on by the Depression, Americans had to open their minds—and mouths—to newness and otherness.

Filmography

Babette's Feast (*Babettes fæstebud*). Dir. Gabriel Axel. Perf. Stéphane Audran. Panorama Film, 1987.

Beauty and the Boss. Dir. Roy Del Ruth. Perf. Marian Marsh, David Manners, Warren William, Charles Butterworth. Warner Bros., 1932.

Big Night. Dir. Campbell Scott, Stanley Tucci. Perf. Marc Anthony, Tony Shalhoub, Stanley Tucci. Rysher Entertainment, 1996.

The Bigamist. Dir. Ida Lupino. Perf. Joan Fontaine, Ida Lupino, Edmond O'Brien. The Filmakers, 1953.

Blondie Johnson. Dir. Ray Enright. Perf. Joan Blondell, Chester Morris, Claire Dodd, Mae Busch. Warner Bros., 1933.

Central Park. Dir. John G. Adolfi. Perf. Joan Blondell, Guy Kibbee. Warner Bros., 1932.

Eat Drink Man Woman (*Yin shi nan nu*). Dir. Ang Lee. Perf. Sihung Lung, Yu-Wen Wang, Chien-Lien Wu. Ang Lee Productions, 1994.

Flower Drum Song. Dir. Henry Koster. Perf. Nancy Kwan, James Shigeta. Universal, 1961.

Like Water for Chocolate (*Como agua para chocolate*). Dir. Alfon Arau. Perf. Marco Leonardi, Lumi Cavazos, Regina Torné. Arau Films Internacional, 1992.

Man of the World. Dir. Richard Wallace, Edward Goodman (uncredited). Perf. William Powell, Carole Lombard, Guy Kibbee. Paramount, 1931.

Our Blushing Bride. Dir. Harry Beaumont (uncredited). Perf. Joan Crawford, Anita Page, Dorothy Sebastian, Robert Montgomery. MGM, 1930.

Our Dancing Daughters. Dir. Harry Beaumont. Story Josephine Lovett. Perf. Joan Crawford, Anita Page, Dorothy Sebastian, Johnny Mack Brown. MGM, 1928.

Our Modern Maidens. Dir. Jack Conway. Story, Josephine Lovett. Perf. Joan Crawford, Anita Page, Douglas Fairbanks Jr. MGM, 1929.

Pulp Fiction. Dir. Quentin Tarantino. Perf. John Travolta, Samuel L. Jackson, Uma Thurman. Miramax, 1994.

Sailor's Luck. Dir. Raoul Walsh. Perf. James Dunn, Sally Eilers. Fox, 1933.

The Sopranos (TV). Created by David Chase. HBO, 1999–2007.

Stella Dallas. Dir. Henry King. Perf. Belle Bennett. Samuel Goldwyn. United Artists, 1925.

Tampopo. Dir. Juzo Itami. Perf. Nobuko Miyamoto, Ken Watanabe. Itami Productions, 1985.

Tortilla Soup. Dir. Maria Ripoll. Perf. Hector Elizondo, Jacqueline Obradors, Tamara Mello. Samuel Goldwyn Films, 2001.

Working Girls. Dir. Dorothy Arzner. Screenplay, Zoe Akins. Perf. Judith Wood, Dorothy Hall. Paramount, 1931.

Young Bride. Dir. William A. Seiter. Perf. Helen Twelvetrees, Eric Linden, Arline Judge. RKO Pathé Pictures, 1932.

CHAPTER 14

Intergalactic Gastronomy

Orientalist Representations of Asian Food, Chefs, and Restaurants within Science Fiction Films

INGRID E. CASTRO

When considering the various ways society may be reimagined, re-explored, and reinterpreted, one particular genre that is linked to new ways of seeing, new ways of believing, or even new ways of knowing is science fiction (SF). SF has the potential to allow us to "go where no man has gone before" in reference to discussion, representation, and audience witness/experience of race and ethnicity within the United States and beyond. SF represents "future myths" which "are stories about where a society is headed or might be headed. Even though they can be outlandish, these visions are undoubtedly significant to society as hopeful projections, extrapolations, or warnings."[1]

Similar to the notion that SF is "feminist friendly," SF is also viewed, to a degree, as potentially race friendly.[2] According to Isiah Lavender III, SF is well-suited for race discussions given the inclusion of imagined exotic territories and transformed histories, which permits alternate ways of viewing our somewhat shared cultural past and allows us to revise history (or sometimes even change history).[3] Particular to the present research, "Asian Americans or figures of Asian descent often have played large parts in tales of alienation, or they conspicuously appear when interplanetary travel and galactic exploration take center stage."[4] However, the history of SF is unmistakably a history of whiteness. In fact, SF is above all referred to as a "universal white space" dominated by an "Anglo male perspective"—white male authors with long histories of catering to younger white male audiences consuming the genre.[5] Early SF writers penned stories that reflected "a fascination with the perceived need to recapture the so-called 'real man,' a figure who was not only white and heterosexual, but whose masculinity was unassailable."[6]

This essay addresses the intersection of otherness, whiteness, future, and representations of Asian food, chefs, and restaurants in SF. I have noticed for many years that SF tends to locate the future within the constructs of "Asian" food, "Asian" chefs, and "Asian" restaurants. Why do SF portrayals continue to depict the future of "other" food as Asian? Perhaps overrepresentation of Asian food, chefs, and restaurants in SF is due to the fundamental basis behind the use of orientalism. According to Edward W. Said, "In a quite constant way, Orientalism depends for its strategy on . . . flexible positional superiority, which puts the Westerner in a whole series of possible relationships with the Orient without ever losing him the relative upper hand."[7] Thus, using Asian cultural products, people, and locations through the portrayal of Asian food, chefs, and restaurants allot white heroes of SF films power through a negative relationship with these eastern-bound tropes and, in a further connection, Caucasian audiences are assured continuous power in imagined yet apparently static futures.

Early SF tales are concomitantly littered with an investment in spreading paranoiac beliefs of "yellow peril." In these stories, evil characters like Dr. Fu Manchu and Ming the Merciless highlight yellow peril sentiments; aliens/men/emperors/rulers whose terrible misdeeds, technological prowess, and mystical powers stood in stark contrast to these works' white male heroes. Due to the massive and imposing presence yellow peril had in early SF, the cultural anxiety engendered by these imagined villains is "impossible to disassociate from our conceptions of the Orient in science fiction."[8] Therefore, as a genre, SF has an unequivocally sordid past in portraying Asians as alienized "others." According to Said, otherness and Orientalism encompass a combination of politics, knowledge, power, theory, culture, media, production, history, geography, language, and ideology pertaining to the Orient and the East by reference of the West, colonialism, and modernism. Evident in yellow-peril messages, SF has a long history of employing Orientalism through the portrayal of Asians in a negative light, imaginings politically and economically motivated by xenophobic fears of Asia/Asian takeover. "As a genre preoccupied with speculations of the future, American science fiction has been engaged in a parallel discourse about the roles Asia and Asians will play in Western conceptions of the future, and has long entertained this question in explicit and implicit ways through orientalist figurations."[9]

The "Forever Foreign" Future of Asian Food

Seemingly sound logic that Asian food should be included as part of the fabric of widely available, and therefore average, food in America is held at bay through the persistent othering of Asians and their cultures. As commented on in numerous texts, Asian food and restaurants continue to embody exotic fare for the "average" (read white) American today. Theorists state that Asians remain "'forever foreign' through their phenotype and their food," whereby white Americans' framing of Asian restaurants as exotic is "a telling example of how difficult it is to overcome the marginalized image of Asian Americans as perpetual foreigners."[10] Characterizing Asians as embodying a particular brand of perpetual forever foreignness through exotic otherized food, chefs, and restaurants allows those in power to maintain clear evidence of Asian cultural inferiority.

While I have found two works that discuss the portrayal and use of food in SF generally, I am unaware of any published academic arguments pertaining to the incidence or purpose of portraying Asian food, chefs, or restaurants in SF specifically.[11] There is, however, some debate surrounding this phenomenon on internet websites—most of these commentaries offer ideas pertaining to food in the future, ruminations on what foods we will eat and how these foods are or will be represented in SF. For example, SF writer Elizabeth Bear indicates that Asian food represents a future where "trade and cultural exchange persist" and food fusion increases. Particular to Asian foods, Bear states that "noodles stick together well in a microgravity environment. So, for example, Asian-style cuisine is very convenient to adapt to the demands of space!"[12] From Bear's observations, we might assume the use of Asian food in SF is due to issues of practicality and not underlying racial and ethnic messages of domination and power. Martha Jay believes that "noodles are the symbol of globalization . . . noodles are the perfect food to demonstrate this mishmash of cultures."[13] Jay, similar to Bear, comments that Asian food works well in space, though Jay believes this is due to noodles being easily packaged, processed, and reconstituted, and not necessarily related to the complications of gravity in cooking mentioned by Bear. Regardless, both commentaries reiterate that the use of this culturally specific food in SF is twofold: the restraints associated with cooking in outer space demand Asian cuisine and the cultural globalization of food is best depicted through Asian cuisine.

Since the invention of the foodstuff "soylent green," SF has perhaps placed more attention than expected on food in the future.[14] Many SF films and television series depict cooking and eating scenes in restaurants with great attention to detail. Food editor and SF author Jason Sheehan states the following about the importance of the role of food specifically found in the genre:

> Food can (and should) be a powerful grounding element in science fiction . . . because it is something that is *common*—that we all do, every day. Something that we have done for all of our combined history. . . . Food can (and should) be used to define the world and the people in it; to delineate relationships and power; even just to pause the action for that second-most-intimate of all human endeavors: the sharing of a meal.[15]

As food is important to today's audiences and our everyday existence, so must it be important within the future world of SF where, assumedly, we will all in some form be present and hungry. What is particularly interesting about Sheehan's SF food theories is the link he makes between food and an indication of power differentials. In fact, "food helps illustrate the competing claims of past and present, nostalgia and progress, memory and desire, familiarity and difference."[16] The portrayal of Asian food, chefs, and restaurants in SF allows for the insertion of messages that powerless and poor "others" continue to be non-white in the future, similar to the present and the past. In addition, utilizing these three elements situates SF films within an "exotic hyperreality" where those who lose power (white Americans) are differentially located to those who take over (any other alien population, often a position occupied by and through Asians).[17]

Fear Asian Food, It's Alive!

The first method of employing Asian food in SF highlights the supposed otherness of the person attempting to eat the food; food which is deemed inedible, food to be feared and avoided at all costs. One such food scene takes place in the film *The Lost Boys* (1987), which certainly reflects the clear connection between Asian food, otherness/strangeness, and group belongingness/social distance.[18] Here, vampires have infested Santa Carla, a fictional coastal town in California, and set their sights on unsuspecting new resident teen Michael (played by white actor Jason Patric), who is attracted to the group via his romantic interest in near-vampire Star (played by white actress Jami Gertz). After being taken to the vampire lair, he is offered food by the vampire leader, David (played by white actor Kiefer Sutherland). The following conversation takes place between Michael and David over the offering of Chinese take-out:

> David: Chinese, good choice . . . guests first. You don't like rice? Tell me Michael, how could a billion Chinese people be wrong?
>
> [Michael appears to be eating white rice, but then the food turns into bugs.]
>
> David: How are those maggots? Maggots, Michael, you are eating maggots, how do they taste? Sorry about that. . . . No hard feelings though. Why don't you try some noodles?
>
> [Michael looks at the noodles and they begin to squirm around.]
>
> Michael: They are worms.
>
> David: What do you mean they are worms?
>
> Michael: Don't eat. . . .
>
> [David takes a bit of the worms/noodles.]
>
> David: They are only noodles Michael.

[Blood is presented in an 'oriental' style bottle.]

Michael: Drink some of this Michael, be one of us.[19]

In this exchange, Asian food is utilized as a tool to trick and ultimately infect Michael, while at the same time it highlights Michael's lack of "belongingness" to the vampire nest. The food is the vessel that causes Michael to doubt his sanity and popular membership; thus, Asian food is pitted against him for the gains of the larger infected vampire brood.

The animated SF film *Titan A.E.* (2000) also uses Asian (specifically Japanese) food to point out the otherness of the main character, Cale Tucker (voiced by white actor Matt Damon).[20] In the thirty-first century Cale is living on Tau 14, a space salvage station, after earth was destroyed by an alien population, the Drej. Setting the stage for Cale's otherness in comparison to a variety of aliens living and working on the station, his 'humanness' is repeatedly pointed out: he is told to wait at the back of lines, made fun of for his human head, called dirty, disgraceful, and unsanitary, and twice accused of being uppity. After waiting in line for food during his one-hour lunch break, Cale is served Akrennian Beetle Sushimi, a plate of what appears to be green wiggling worms and bouncing bugs (aka living Asian noodles). Cale is put off by the sushimi, stating to Tek (voiced by black rapper/actor Tone Loc), the alien who cared for him during his teen years, that he wants the mess-hall staff to kill his food before serving it to him. He continues on, passionately explaining that he does an honest day of work, for which he believes he deserves to be served food that is not alive; therefore, indicating he wants food cooked correctly for his human/white palate. Placing the Caucasian male as minority in the future may allow white populations of today to feel better about their own privilege in the present. This film emphasizes that, after all, Cale is an "everyman" whose privilege does not extend into the future, while at the same time it reinforces the American ideology of meritocracy by pointing out that he is not being given what he deserves, yet what he has obviously and "honestly" earned.

The bug-infested Asian food in both films foreshadows future perilous journeys for the white protagonists; in *The Lost Boys*, this food is the introduction to Michael's clash with the vampire clan and struggles with his own burgeoning vampirism. Similarly, as soon as Cale attempts to eat and eventually rejects his food, the Drej invade Tau 14, uprooting him from Tek to reluctantly join a band of space pirates in *Titan A.E.* The portrayal of Asian food as suspect and its connectedness with dangerous future outcomes in these two films is not surprising, given that all food is generally presented as "dishonest" in SF films.[21] Related, Asian food is frequently branded as "repulsive," "disgusting," and containing "suspicious ingredients" of "doubtful character," all of which "boil[s] down to a single overwhelming perception: the Chinese presence in America is first and foremost alien."[22] There is telling irony in that Cale is called some of the exact same words that are habitually used to describe Asian food. Serving Cale sushimi reinforces the fact that foreign, alien, Asian food is clearly and extremely different from human food (read white human food). In total, the use of Asian food in *The Lost Boys* and *Titan A.E.*, both tainted with live insects, further highlights the 'otherness' that Cale and Michael, as white men, must 'suffer through' in their new future, widely differing physical and social locations.

Fear Asian Cities, You Must Eat Asian Food in Asian Restaurants

A second way Asian food is consumed in SF is based as much on the food as the location. Here, setting is quite important, whereby populations continue to live on earth but in some distant future. Films like *Men in Black 3* (2012),[23] *The Fifth Element* (1997),[24] and *Blade Runner* (1982),[25] among other SF films, employ Asian food and Asian restaurants in a variety of ways to insert stereotypes about Asian otherness in the future.[26] In all three films, Caucasian men are primary characters and the otherness of Asian food in Asian restaurants is utilized to point out that these men are still powerful, in control, and decision makers of their own fates (in some ways divergent to the use of Asian food in films like *Titan A.E.* and *The Lost Boys*).[27]

According to the blog *Scouting New York*, the frequent use of Asian restaurants and food within popular film is meant to take moviegoers on a trip to another place, while at the same time reinforces stereotypes of otherness via orientalism. "I don't know anything about the history of Chinese restaurant décor in America, but I wouldn't be surprised if, early on, part of the draw was in presenting patrons with an EPCOT-like level of intense orientalism. Not only are you dining, you're also going on an exotic vacation."[28] Likewise, Said believes that "the orient at large . . . vacillates between the West's contempt for what is familiar and its shivers of delight in—or fear of—novelty."[29] Taking these statements in tandem, the Asian restaurant setting, along with the ordering of and process of eating Asian food from Asian chefs, is meant to draw out three distinct feelings in an audience: enjoyment, release, and ultimately fear. Fear of the unknown in SF is a basis for set and setting, whereby the storyline and accompanying visuals must convince the audience that the future is something strange and compelling, while at the same time dangerous and to be avoided.

Blade Runner and *The Fifth Element* both include lengthy exchanges that take place at Asian restaurants, scenes which further stereotypes associated with Asian men, Asian culture, and Asian food. Location is paramount; both films are set in U.S. future locations; but while *The Fifth Element*'s twenty-third-century future New York City is relatively "diverse," *Blade Runner*'s twenty-first-century future Los Angeles seems to have become "overrun" with Asians, displayed in the first few scenes when electronic billboards brim over with images of "exotic" Asian women. Of all the films discussed in the present work, *Blade Runner* is the most frequently cited in writings that span discussions pertaining to general SF, orientalism in film and popular culture, as well as the few works I found that analyze food scenes presented in SF film.[30] We must ask ourselves, what was the point of portraying *Blade Runner*'s Los Angeles as a dystopian Asian cityscape? After watching *Blade Runner*, were white Americans supposed to fear Asian takeover and assumedly act on it by "upping their games" in industry? Was *Blade Runner's* "city-speech," echoed two decades later in the film *Code 46* (2003), a warning for Americans to protect English as the (assumed) dominant global language?

Referencing *Blade Runner*, as well as several other SF stories set in Asianized futures, Timothy Yu states that "in their attempts to localize the operations of global capitalism, these portraits of the postmodern city expose the extent to which the imagining of postmodernism has been grounded in Orientalism and racial anxiety."[31]

To a certain extent, I believe Yu is correct in stating that hero Rick Deckard (played by white actor Harrison Ford) in *Blade Runner* and, by proxy, hero Corbin Dallas (played by white actor Bruce Willis) in *The Fifth Element* are marginalized as white subjects in future cityscapes overrun by global marketplaces. However, what I find a more potent outcome of exchanges with Asian chefs at Asian restaurants to eat Asian food in Asianized U.S. cities is that both Deckard and Dallas are initially threatened in and by their new orientalized worlds but eventually regain their identities and power as white men in a future imagined, yet strikingly similar, hierarchical structure.

While some may make the argument that "otherness" is a descriptor that could be used for most of the characters in *Blade Runner*, including those who are white, a clear delineation between residents of Los Angeles is evident through their physical placement within the new Asianized society. Here, locations of apartments and dwellings recreate racial and ethnic hierarchical separation.[32] In addition, traditional Japanese music and city-speech "cumulatively underscore the displacement of American hegemony in the film. It is against this backdrop of Asian 'otherness' that Rick Deckard's whiteness starkly reflects multiple points of crisis in American hegemony and cultural self-perception."[33] To this end, the Asians who Deckard and Dallas interact with are primarily low-income food or other service/blue collar workers, never gun-wielding heroes who save the day, the city, the world, or the universe.

Fear Asian Chefs Who Make Asian Food in Asian Restaurants, They Are the Reconstituted Fu Manchu

Third, Asia otherness is made obvious in SF films through interactions between Asian chefs in Asian restaurants and white male protagonists/heroes. For example, the primary eating scene in *The Fifth Element* takes place between Dallas and Mr. Kim (played by Chinese born Kim Chan), the operator/cook of an unnamed floating Thai restaurant boat. Stereotypes of semi-comprehensible language and foreign, alien culture abound in the floating restaurant scene, whereby Mr. Kim references his grandfather's Confucius-like advice that it does not rain every day. Following that remark, Mr.

Kim guarantees Dallas's newly arrived message is good news (betting the cost of lunch), but when Mr. Kim opens and reads the message, he tells Dallas he is fired. When Dallas looks to the bright side that he won lunch, Mr. Kim tells Dallas that he likes Dallas's philosophy of seeing the good in bad things. Mr. Kim says goodbye to Dallas, and upon leaving apparently throws him some cookies, stating that their good fortune will keep bringing him good luck in the future. During this exchange, the otherness of Mr. Kim is displayed through his accent and lack of English mastery, his impermanent location via the floating restaurant, and his mystical culture. Also, Mr. Kim is the one who brings Dallas the bad news (the messenger) and predictions for the future, a future which brings death and destruction to nearly all who surround Dallas later in the film.

A similar scenario starts the action in the film *Blade Runner*, where Rick Deckard is attempting to order food at an outdoor noodle bar, to no avail. The cook, Howie Lee/"Sushi Master" (played by Japanese-born Robert/Bob Okazaki) does not seem to understand the simplest of English, where Deckard is trying to order "four pieces" with noodles, but after multiple verbal exchanges and hand miming to Lee, Deckard ends up with "two pieces" with noodles. Deckard is approached by some policemen and the cook must translate their city-speech for him, telling Deckard that he must go with the men because, "He say you under arrest Mr. Deckard. . . . He say you Brade Runner."[34] Like Mr. Kim, we hear "broken" English from this Asian cook, along with Lee occupying both the position of the keeper of knowledge (understanding city-speech, unlike Deckard) and the bearer of bad news (Deckard is under arrest). Deckard's irritation with the cook during the ordering process extends later to his general contempt for rules, where Deckard is shown unceremoniously eating the rest of his noodle meal in the back of a police hovercraft.

Utilizing Asian men as the bringers of bad news for both Deckard and Dallas capitalizes on negative race and ethnic relations, where these ethnic minorities are changing the lives of white men and taking them on dangerous future-life courses. Mr. Kim and Lee function as "middlemen" in their restaurants—Mr. Kim, in particular, distributing and recycling his culture's wisdoms for white audiences.[35] In fact, "So far as the Orient is concerned, standardization and cultural stereotyping have intensified the hold of the nineteenth-century academic and imaginative demonology of 'the mysterious Orient.'"[36] The mysticism built into the exchanges between Deckard, Dallas, and their respective Asian chefs in *The Fifth Element* and *Blade Runner* is part of the postmodern reinterpretation and reaffirmation of orientalism in SF film, as Asian restaurants and food are connected to Westerners' enduring definition of Asian "culture as exotic and mysterious."[37] The otherness of the two Asian chefs further reinforces the future worlds of *The Fifth Element* and *Blade Runner* implying and, indeed, forewarning that Chinatowns have nearly taken over U.S. cities.

According to Robert Ferguson's analysis of media race representations, "the concept of the Other is used as a means of imposing meaning rather than negotiating meaning through dialogue . . . this has meant that the concept of the Other has become an ideological signifier of considerable discursive power."[38] The link between "the other" and mystical powers used against Caucasian male protagonists in these two films is profound. This mysticism is traceable to the future past imaginings of yellow peril characters like Fu Manchu and Ming the Merciless. Those men were seen as "ruthless mystics" who held "different or obscure knowledge" and embodied "the exotic, enigmatic and mysterious essence of Japanese particularism."[39] Asian restaurant chefs such as Kim and Lee appear to be founded on original yellow peril notions of a strange Asian otherworldliness, as well as fear of the supernatural, and potentially destructive, information Fu Manchu and Ming the Merciless used against white protagonists in early SF stories.

The portrayal of Asians as food-service and other low-positioned industry workers is not a new one. Historically, images of Asian males in film remain relatively limited to the roles of cook, waiter, busboy, delivery man, and/or dishwasher.[40] These low-wage, low-skilled male service workers with restricted screen time stand in stark contrast to the eventual outcomes of the white men who are triumphant, redeemed, and heroic in films like *Blade Runner* and *The Fifth Element*. The ineffective and connectedly gendered and feminized portrayals (see discussion below) of Asian cooks in SF films draw on negative stereotypes of Asian males that endure in U.S. society. In addition, the use of fragmented English by Asian chefs in both films allows for protagonists to symbolically retain ultimate power via white male American superiority within their future societies. "Otherness, when invoked in relation to cultural issues and media representations, is that it often tends to essentialize its object. Characteristics are thus attributed to certain groups which are apparently timeless and frequently demean."[41] Therefore, SF cinematic characterizations of Asian peoples and their cultural markers (the jobs they hold, the food they consume, the restaurants they own, and the languages they speak) are based in stereotypes that appear to be permanent and derisive/destructive.

Fear Comes to Fruition, the Other in Asian Restaurants Must Die

In several of the SF films screened for this project, the final result of othering Asian food in Asian restaurants is murdering an Asian chef or waiter working at the establishment. In the film *eXistenZ* (1999), Ted Pikul/Larry Ashen (played by white actor Jude Law) and Allegra Geller (played by white actress Jennifer Jason Leigh) begin their adventure in a virtual-reality game of the same name by being "magically" transported into a game emporium store through an *eXistenZ* game pod.[42] The dangers of Asian food and Asian restaurants are immediately presented by way of a poster in the emporium that emphatically warns "CHINESE RESTAURANT: WILL YOU MAKE IT OUT ALIVE?" When Pikul and Allegra eventually find their way to a "Chinese Restaurant" in the forest, they are served by a "Chinese Waiter" (portrayed by mainland Chinese born Oscar Hsu). The following exchange takes place while ordering food:

> Chinese Waiter: We have nice sea bass today. Shall I bring it for everyone?
>
> Pikul: We want the special. Did you hear me, Chinese Waiter? We want the special.
>
> Chinese Waiter: The special is for special occasions. I cannot give you the special.
>
> Pikul: But, this is a special occasion. It's her birthday.

Chinese Waiter: A birthday is a special occasion. I will therefore bring the special for everybody.

[All others sitting at the table leave.]

Pikul: I guess the special isn't very popular.

Allegra: I guess not.

. . . .

Chinese Waiter: Special order for the birthday girl. Hope you enjoy it very much.

[Allegra covers her mouth in disgust and looks away.]

Pikul: Look, it's our two-headed friend. It doesn't look too healthy. I think I lost my appetite.

Chinese Waiter: Oh, a shame, mutant reptiles and amphibians provide new and previously unimagined taste sensations. Shall I clear all this away?

Allegra: No, we're, um . . . happy.

Chinese Waiter: Very good, enjoy.[43]

The "two-headed friend" Pikul is referring to is a mutated amphibian that Allegra and Pikul run across in the "real world" outside of *eXistenZ*. In the above scene, audiences see the negative portrayal of Asian food in various incarnations. The food is made out of a mutant "frog, salamander, lizard thing." In fact, when Pikul begins eating the special, he states the food is "disgusting" but that he cannot force himself to stop eating it. "So-called dubious Asian foods" reflect the character of those who make it; Asians "are viewed as complicit in the ruination of their own culinary tradition" which leads to a "collective uneasy feeling about the perceived foreignness or alienness of the people who are in the business of selling it."[44] Pikul consumes yet another example of "dishonest" food in SF, as various parts of an organically fabricated gun are revealed hidden in its bowels. Another remnant of the "real world," this gun fires human teeth that Pikul extracts from his own mouth.

Pikul tells Allegra he has the "urge" and "needs" to kill Chinese Waiter, which she wholeheartedly encourages, even telling him to "enjoy it." Until this point, Pikul is referred to as a "marketing trainee" and a "PR nerd," portrayed as an ineffective, unprogressive, confused, scared character. Since white heterosexual men are generally threatened by other masculinities, "othered" men with lower perceived levels of sexuality are presented in SF storylines to "reinvigorate white manhood."[45] Chinese Waiter speaks with a slight lisp and higher tone of voice, wears a kerchief jauntily tied in an askew fashion around his neck, and when he walks he has a slight sway to his hips. As such, Chinese Waiter solidly represents the threat of an "effeminized, Orientalized other," similar to SF "homosexual menaces like Fu Manchu."[46] Pikul does express some doubt, telling Allegra the waiter is "too nice" (read not masculine enough) but eventually declares "I found this in my soup, and I'm very upset," killing Chinese Waiter with the gun filled with his own body's ammunition. The "constitutive inferiority and deficit" of Chinese Waiter is wholly punctuated by the fact that he is not given a name in the film apart from his singular service role, a reflection of the "prevailing one-dimensional portraits of Asians as cooks, waiters, and other fetishized objects of mainstream consumption."[47] The death of Chinese Waiter and his "otherness" in Chinese Restaurant symbolizes the final death of Pikul's less-than personality, replaced by a more certain and powerful heterosexual white masculinity.

The Asian eatery Wu's Diamond Garden Sea Food Restaurant and the owner/chef, Mr. Wu (played by Chinese and Japanese U.S.-born actor Keone Young), in *Men in Black 3* serve as a foreboding start to the action and a foreshadowing of multiple deaths in the film.[48] According to bell hooks, "Encounters with Otherness are clearly marked as more exciting, more intense, and more threatening. The lure is the combination of pleasure and danger."[49] In this early portion of the film, we certainly see all of these elements via an interesting take on the representation of Asian food, chefs, and restaurants in SF. Agents J (played by black actor Will Smith) and K (played by white actor Tommy Lee Jones) interrogate Wu after receiving a report that some humans are "suffering from intestinal worms of alien origin." J and K participate in the following exchange with Mr. Wu at his Diamond Garden Sea Food Restaurant:

Wu: Oh, K, J, so happy to see you. Uh, Mr. Wu get you your leggular table.

[K and J stare at Mr. Wu.]

Wu: You no hungly?

K: Show us the tanks Wu.

Wu: Oh, sure, sure, you look. Velly fresh.

K: Show us the tanks in the back.

Wu: Aah, so solly. No speaka English. You come back later, OK?

J: Save the chop-socky bullshit for the tourists, Wu.[50]

Wu, an alien posing as an Asian in New York, puts on an affected Asian accent for the agents, eventually breaking down into a New York borough accent once Agent J tells him to stop. This type of falsified, Asianized accent is termed "linguistic Orientalism" by Akihiko Hirose and Kay Kei-Ho Pih, whereby "this form of 'othering' further validates the claim of the authenticity of [the] dining experience."[51] Agents J and K are meant to fall victim to Wu's Asian act, or what Hirose and Pih further brand "self-Orientalism," since Mr. Wu is an alien posing as an Asian American.[52] The Asian/alien connection is clearly portrayed in *Men in Black 3*, perhaps more saliently than in any other SF film or production to date.

Later, Wu tells Agents J and K if they arrest him for selling "unlicensed, extraterrestrial foodstuffs," it is "a hate crime," to which K answers, forcibly stripping off Wu's apron and revealing his alien bottom half, "It would be if you were Chinese." In Wu's kitchen, white Agent K reveals both Wu's Asianness and alienness in one fell swoop, an exposure that was foreshadowed earlier by Agent J stating, "You don't have no balls, Wu." At the same time, Agent J seems like he has more respect for Wu as a fellow racial/ethnic minority, telling Agent K, "That was just mean, what you did to Wu back there. Snatched his skirt off, that's just disrespectful." There are a host of mixed messages throughout these few scenes that take place at Wu's Diamond Garden Sea Food Restaurant. On the one hand, Agent J seems to defend Wu, but on the other hand he derisively states, "Don't nobody want none of your nasty-ass noodles, Wu." Similarly, while Agent K degrades Wu by revealing his alien body parts and slapping him in the face multiple times with an alien fish, even at one point telling Wu he is a "piece of shit," he ultimately orders, with the intent to consume, a meal of shrimp and bok choy noodle soup complete with a moving eyeball. The storyline continues from there, but suffice it to say by the end of these scenes chef Wu is dead, several of the Asian restaurant workers are beaten unconscious, and the Asian restaurant is left in ruins. Prior to his death, Wu supplicates himself to the agents, falling back on linguistic and self-Orientalism speech patterns, stating "On behalf of my pathetic self and worthless children, you stay. Allow me most honorable benefit of serving you favorite noodles, K?" In effect, Wu represents a host of dyadic stereotypes of Asians in America. He is the embodiment of mixed messages: deceitful and honest, hardworking and opportunist, proud and meek, and, yes, Asian and alien.

Does Asian Equal Alien OR Does Alien Equal Asian?

Embarking on this project, I admittedly had much scholarship to read pertaining to SF history, Asian food and restaurants, orientalism, and general representations of Asians in popular culture. This nugget of an idea, ostensibly a simple question, "Why is there so much Asian food in science fiction?" turned into a much larger project than I initially anticipated. In some ways, I was at an advantage; reading the literature all at once forced me to connect the historical implications of racial domination and ethnic determinism found in early SF and other popular-culture products, and how this tradition continues to shape SF representations of Asianness, otherness, and alienness via food, chefs, and restaurants in recent cinematic reworkings of a seemingly everlasting trope legacy. Reading John Cheng's outstanding chapter "Human Martians and Asian Aliens: The Racial Nature of Wondrous Worlds," which addresses the onset of Asian presence and purpose in 1920s and 1930s SF, was a significant turning point in my research.[53] Cheng states,

> early twentieth-century racial views of Asians—or more appropriately, of "orientals" and "Asiatics"—gave its specific concerns, particularly the terrific potential of science and technology, their

> most powerful expression. Asians' status as inassimilable aliens within America anchored the various associations of science fiction's creatures, lending them a qualitative "alien" difference at a time when the term "alien" was not yet used in or related to science fiction.[54]

Later in his chapter, Cheng explains that other words were mentioned instead of "alien," given the rare use of the expression at the time. Instead, "terms such as 'foreign,' 'odd,' 'weird,' 'strange,' and 'beastly' were used in similar fashion and far more frequently in science fiction of the 1920's and 30's. In that era, 'alien' connoted difference; it did not denote creatures from outer space or other worlds."[55] Cheng's findings of the use (or nonuse, as it were) of the term *alien* and the genre's extremist and paranoiac demarcation of Asians to designate other beings from strange worlds, in combination with reading about California senator John Miller, who claimed in 1881 that the Chinese were "inhabitants of another planet," and the eventual SF insertion of "the large-brained, small-bodied man of the future" led me to question exactly where and when was the term, and image of, *alien* introduced?[56]

I thought of the small bodies, dark slanted eyes, and large brains/superior intelligence of the now-familiar "grey alien," found over and over and over again in nearly every film depicting these beings. Aliens are portrayed as abductors, they are invaders, they are tricksters, they have superior technology, they have special powers, they are all-knowing; for all of these reasons and more they are, perennially, to be feared. Many of the physical attributes of the grey alien mentioned here are stereotypically used to describe the bodies of Asians, and the other qualities listed above are echoes of SF's shameful yellow peril past. In none of my reading, including those by Cheng, numerous other race/SF theorists, or more modern orientalism analyses of SF, did anyone broach this subject. I could not confirm my suspicion through academic research, so I turned to the internet and I typed the question "Where does the grey alien come from?" I was met with the following:

> In 1933, the Swedish novelist Gustav Sandgren, using the pen name Gabriel Linde, published a science-fiction novel called Den okända faran (The Unknown Danger), in which he describes a

> race of extraterrestrials, "[. . .] the creatures did not resemble any race of humans. They were short, shorter than the average Japanese, and their heads were big and bald, with strong, square foreheads, and very small noses and mouths, and weak chins. What was most extraordinary about them were the eyes—large, dark, gleaming, with a sharp gaze. They wore clothes made of soft grey fabric, and their limbs seemed to be similar to those of humans."[57]

That Sandgren's novel was written during the same decades Cheng investigates as the pinnacle of injecting yellow peril messages into SF, joined with the fact that Sandgren used the Japanese as a reference point in his descriptions of the grey alien, confirms my suspicion that the initial (and everlasting) appearance of the grey alien in SF was built upon the otherized likeness of Asians already popularized/perpetuated/perpetrated within the genre. Cheng describes the purpose of the Asian presence in SF as follows: "the menace of Oriental Asians gave the conflict between science fiction's protagonists and the imagined creatures they encountered greater and more resonant significance. The association was clear: not only were Asians alien in America; they were also alien in outer space . . . alien in other space."[58] In addition, David Morley and Kevin Robins state that in SF, Japanese people (and by extension all Asians) are portrayed as "unfeeling aliens; they are the cyborgs and replicants," victims of stereotypes which "hold them to be sub-human, as if they have no feelings, no emotions, no humanity."[59] So, to answer the question *does Asian equal alien or does alien equal Asian*, my response is, according to the description of the grey alien found in *The Unknown Danger*, both.

Depictions of future Asian technology and culture (outside of Asian food, chefs, and restaurants) in SF have been, in fact, well-documented and critically discussed over the last two decades. This intersection, first dubbed "techno-orientalism" in 1995 by Morley and Robins, explores SF's longstanding tradition of representing both Asian peoples and their technologies as alien.[60] The people and technology connected to techno-orientalism are almost always viewed as foreign and dangerous in SF films, messages closely linked to modern reinterpretations of yellow peril. Consequently, I am faced with a further question: is the use of Asian food, chefs, and restaurants in

SF orientalism or techno-orientalism? My conclusion is that, overall, these representations reflect orientalism. While the city settings of *Blade Runner* and other SF stories have certainly been proven by many theorists to be techno-orientalist in scope, I find that in all films discussed here, Asian food, chefs, and restaurants are in no way presented as futuristic via science, economy, or technology. For example, while Mr. Kim's Thai restaurant has the capacity to float, the wooden barge slowly putters across the screen emitting smoke, sharply contrasting to futuristic cars zooming by at breakneck speeds in *The Fifth Element*. Kim does not use uber-modern technology on his ship—audiences see baskets of dried foods, lanterns, woks, and bowls with chopsticks—"simple" tools from a "simpler" time, a "simpler" people. Similarly, the Sushi Master in *Blade Runner*'s future world operates out of an everyday side-street noodle bar, serving his meals in the same "modest" bowls with chopsticks as found today and in the past. While eating at Chinese Restaurant in the woods, *eXistenZ*'s Pikul constructs a weapon of flesh and bone, not one made of technologically advanced futuristic metals. In these ways, as well as many more, the use of Asian food, chefs, and restaurants in SF relegates Asians to a "culture defined by what it lacks (modernity, rationality, universality); its 'Otherness' is defined in terms of the backwardness, the irrationality and the particularity of its values."[61]

Said states that orientalism "demonstrates a proclivity to divide, subdivide, and redivide its subject matter without ever changing its mind about the Orient as being always the same, unchanging, uniform, and radically peculiar object."[62] By representing Asian people, language, and culture in stereotypical and often veiled and menacing ways within SF, the "peculiar" object of Asian otherness is not only kept intact, but reinforced as a future certainty. At the same time, the superiority of white citizens (particularly white males and their affiliated patriarchy) continues well-forward into the future worlds of SF. Through the portrayal of Asian food, chefs, and restaurants in SF, "the production and reproduction of the exoticized racial signification of the 'Oriental other' are intimately linked to the authenticity of cultural otherness which, in turn, is connected to the authenticity of a culturally competent, cosmopolitan consumer experience."[63] I argue here that the "consumer experience" is not actually the people eating at the Asian restaurants Hirose and Pih studied; instead, the consumer is the audience at the movie theater and the experience is not just watching the film, but the assured continuation of white dominance in the "endless White future" of SF.[64]

Asian restaurants, and the food and chefs within, are a staple of American life; in fact, there are currently over 40,000 Chinese restaurants in the United States alone. Nevertheless, Asian food, chefs, and restaurants continue to represent strange, future, otherworldly outcomes with dreaded results in SF films, perhaps because "eating 'ethnic' food is a form of 'eating the Other' with problematic politics."[65] In our current "real world" of global culinary foodways exploration, non-Asian diners express "the desire not only to eat the metaphoric other, but also to explore the entire world and consume it."[66] The Asian restaurant is an "exotic place, an elsewhere" filled with strange, otherized food that "provides a valuable case of the growth and institutionalization of an 'alien' culture . . . .[and] 'alien foods.'"[67] The locations of Asian foods, chefs, and restaurants, in and out of film, are often suspect—physical, social, and interpersonal spaces where high attention is paid to perceived substandard, unhygienic levels of quality. However, the "disgust" some non-Asians express towards Asian restaurants "has little to do with food. Rather, it concerns an individual's sense of self within an imagined community against a perceived alien threat . . . the corrupting power of the Orient."[68]

Asian food, chefs, and restaurants exemplify the "different power dynamics [of] the ethnic and colonial relations being presented" in the SF films discussed in this chapter.[69] The "mythical" colonized/colonizer element of Asians in SF films is depicted through the reworked yellow-peril trope of the Asian chef as a "harbinger of doom" in such films as *The Fifth Element*, *Blade Runner*, and even *Men in Black 3*, as all bad things on earth begin with the action at Wu's Diamond Garden Sea Food Restaurant. One may even consider the bug-infested Asian noodles and rice as mythical signifiers of terrible things to come in *The Lost Boys* and *Titan A.E.* At the same time, films like *The Fifth Element* and *Blade Runner* illustrate future orientalized cities as places Caucasians continue to have utmost power within the globalized marketplace. We must also take into account a film like *Titan A.E.*, where white males are forced from their homes (and planets) of origin and put into lower class statuses, humiliated into the servitude of those alien races, briefly, in power. The heaping bowlfuls of Asian food in Asian restaurants served by Asian/alien cooks, often stereotyped by less-than-acceptable heteronormative levels of masculinity (remember the portrayal of Chinese Waiter in *eXistenZ* and the comment that Mr. Wu has "no balls" in *Men in Black 3*?), continue to embody otherness in techno-orientalized cityscapes. These recurrent images and messages may place some SF moviegoers into a type of perpetual serenity, literally consuming the "self-validating 'ethnic experience,' a mark of their tolerance and sophistication."[70] In this way, they are sure that even in a dystopian future some things remain true: they are the final colonizers of any given world or universe and are not, in fact, at the bottom of the racial/ethnic/human/species food chain after all.

NOTES

Introduction

1. Andrew P. Haley, *Turning the Tables: Restaurants and the Rise of the American Middle Class, 1880–1920* (Chapel Hill: University of North Carolina Press, 2011), 224.
2. "58% Eat at a Restaurant at Least Once a Week," *Rasmussman Reports, July 11, 2013,* http://www.rasmussenreports.com/public_content/lifestyle/general_lifestyle/july_2013/58_eat_at_a_restaurant_at_least_once_a_week; US Bureau of Labor Statistics, "Restaurant Industry Forecast Report Research," April 28, 2013, http://www.restaurant.org/Industry-Impact/Employing-America/America-work-here; National Restaurant Association, "2014 Restaurant Industry Forecast," n.d., http://www.restaurant.org/News-Research/Research/Forecast-2014.
3. Carson, L. Pierce, "Japanese Cuisine Has Increasing Appeal for American Palates," *Napa Valley Register*, November 30, 2010, http://napavalleyregister.com/lifestyles/food-and-cooking/japanese-cuisine-has-increasing-appeal-for-american-palates/article_922c990e-fc16-11df-8451-001cc4c002e0.html.
4. Jennifer 8. Lee, *The Fortune Cookie Chronicles: Adventures in the World of Chinese Food* (New York: Twelve Books, 2008).
5. David R. Chan, "Why Aren't There More Chinese Restaurant Chains?," *The Huffington Post*, May 6, 2013, http://www.huffingtonpost.com/Menuism/why-arent-there-more-chin_b_3188946.html.
6. Alice L. McLean, *Asian American Food Culture* (Santa Barbara: ABC-CLIO, 2015), xii.
7. For example, only chapters 1 and 5 of McLean's survey examine Asian restaurants in the United States, and only superficially.
8. One notable work that explores Chinese cuisine restaurants in Hawaii is David Y.H. Wu, "All You Can Eat Buffet: The Evolution of Chinese Cuisine in Hawaii," *Journal of Chinese Dietary Culture* 4, no. 1 (2008): 1–24. In this article, Wu discusses the influence of Japanese cuisine on Hawaiian Chinese restaurants (e.g., how sushi became an important and attractive item included in the "Chinese" buffet menu).
9. Robert Ji-Song Ku, Martin F. Manalansan, and Anita Mannur, eds. *Eating Asian America: A Food Studies Reader* (New York: New York University Press, 2013).
10. John Jung, *Sweet and Sour: Life in Chinese Family Restaurants* ([N.p.]: Yin and Yang Press, 2010).
11. Lee, *Fortune Cookie Chronicles.*
12. See, for example, J.A.G. Roberts, *China to Chinatown: Chinese Food in the*

West (London: Reaktion Books, 2002); Andrew Coe, *Chop Suey: A Cultural History of Chinese Food in the United States* (New York: Oxford University Press, 2009); Yong Chen, *Chop Suey, USA: The Story of Chinese Food in America* (New York: Columbia University Press, 2014); Haiming Liu, *From Canton Restaurant to Panda Express: A History of Chinese Food in the United States* (New Brunswick: Rutgers University Press, 2015); and Anne Mendelson, *Chow Chop Suey: Food and the Chinese American Journey* (New York: Columbia University Press, 2016).

13. In *Eating Chinese: Culture on the Menu in Small Town Canada* (Toronto: University of Toronto Press, 2010), Lily Cho provides an academic survey of local Chinese restaurants, however not in the United States but in Canada.
14. One work that addresses some of these points is Haiming Liu's *From Canton Restaurant to Panda Express,* which includes chapters on Kosher Chinese restaurants in the United States, American Chinese fast food, Chinese-cuisine chains in the United States and abroad (P.F. Chang's, for example), and the transnationality/globality of American-style Chinese cuisine.
15. While Robert Ji-Song Ku's *Dubious Gastronomy: The Cultural Politics of Eating Asian in the USA* (Honolulu: University of Hawaii Press, 2014) focuses on Chinese and Japanese cuisines in the United States, it emphasizes the politics behind specific dishes, such as the California Roll, for example, and only stresses restaurants through the framework of these specialties. Donna R. Gabaccia's *We Are What We Eat: Ethnic Food and the Making of Americans* (Cambridge: Harvard University Press, 2000) and David Beriss's and David Sutton's *The Restaurants Book: Ethnographies of Where We Eat* (Oxford: Berg, 2007) analyze ethnic food and the politics of restaurants, but treat Chinese and Japanese cuisine only superficially. David Y.H. Wu and Sidney C.H. Cheung, eds. *The Globalization of Chinese Food* (Honolulu: University of Hawaii Press, 2002) contributes to our understanding of how Chinese food became a transnational phenomenon. However, it does not focus on the United States and stops short of problematizing another Asian cuisines. On the other hand, Sucheng Chan and Madeline Yuan-yin Hsu, eds. *Chinese Americans and the Politics of Race and Culture* (Philadelphia: Temple University Press, 2008), Sherrie A. Inness, *Secret Ingredients: Race, Gender, and Class at the Dinner Table* (Basingstoke: Palgrave Macmillan, 2005), and Maria Ng and Philip Holden, eds. *Reading Chinese Transnationalism* (Hong Kong: Hong Kong University Press, 2006) all deal with Chinese cuisine in the United States, but do not fully address restaurant culture. Mimi Thi Nguyen and Thuy Linh Nguyen Tu's *Alien Encounters: Popular Culture in Asian America* (Durham: Duke University Press, 2007) includes a chapter entitled "The Chinese Restaurant Drive-Thru," but it is a survey of Chinese restaurants that resembles a blog entry. Other works that include only a chapter or two on Chinese restaurants are: Jack Goody, *Food and Love: A Cultural History of East and West* (London: Verso, 1999) and Barbara Gimla Shortridge and James R. Shortridge, eds. *The Taste of American Place: A Reader on Regional and Ethnic Foods* (Lanham: Rowman & Littlefield Publishers, 1999).
16. This category includes: Roy Choi, Tien Nguyen, and Natasha Phan, *L.A. Son: My Life, My City, My Food* (New York: Anthony Bourdain/Ecco, 2013); Marie

Rose Wong, *Sweet Cakes, Long Journey: The Chinatowns of Portland, Oregon* (Seattle: University of Washington Press, 2004); Alfred Yee, *Shopping at Giant Foods: Chinese American Supermarkets in Northern California* (Seattle: University of Washington Press, 2013); and (auto)biographical works on the Asian restaurant business, such as those by chef Eddie Huang (e.g., *Fresh off the Boat: A Memoir* [New York: Spiegel & Grau, 2013] and *Double Cup Love: On the Trail of Family, Food, and Broken Hearts in China* [New York: Spiegel & Grau, 2017]).

17. For example, David Meyers, Elise Meyers Walker, Jeff Chenault, and Doug Motz, *Kahiki Supper Club: A Polynesian Paradise in Columbus* (Stroud: History Press, 2014).
18. Chee-Beng Tan, ed. *Chinese Food and Foodways in Southeast Asia and Beyond* (Singapore: NUS Press, 2011), 4–9. Also see David Y.H. Wu's "Global Encounter of Diasporic Chinese Restaurant Food," pp. 75–103 in the same volume. Here, Wu defines chop suey as "Chinese cuisine overseas" and compares it to the foodways of Western cultural imperialism.
19. "P.F. Chang's International Locations," https://www.pfchangs.com/international.
20. "Panda Express Locations," https://en.wikipedia.org/wiki/Panda_Express.
21. Cooking Channel, *Restaurant Redemption*, http://www.cookingchanneltv.com/shows/restaurant-redemption.html.
22. Kevin Vollmers, "'Restaurant Redemption' Recap: Serving Up Some Good Drama!," The Community, *Entertainment Weekly*, October 28, 2014, http://community.ew.com/2014/10/28/restaurant-redemption-recap-chal-chilli/.
23. Virginia B. Wood, "What If Your Restaurant Doesn't Need Redemption?," *Austin Chronicle*, January 31, 2014, http://www.austinchronicle.com/food/2014-01-31/what-if-your-restaurant-doesnt-need-redemption; Melissa Chan, "Fresh Meadows Restaurant Owners Featured on Cooking Channel Show Say Eatery did not Need 'Redemption,'" *Queens Courier*, November 14, 2013, http://queenscourier.com/fresh-meadows-restaurant-owners-featured-on-cooking-channel-show-say-eatery-did-not-need-redemption.
24. Mimi Brodeur, "Fusion Fire Asian Restaurant's Menu Remains Unchanged after 'Restaurant Redemption,'" *The Patriot-News*, Dec. 11, 2014, http://www.pennlive.com/food/index.ssf/2014/12/fusion_fire.html.

CHAPTER 1

1. Ah Fong's, Beverly Hills, California, 1974 Menu. Los Angeles Public Library Menus Collection: http://dbase1.lapl.org/images/menus/fullsize/d/rb04084-04.jpg.
2. Ah Fong's, Beverly Hills, California, 1974 Menu. Los Angeles Public Library Menus Collection: http://dbase1.lapl.org/images/menus/fullsize/d/rb04084-02.jpg.
3. There are numerous important menu collections housed at Johnson and Wales University, Cornell University, Kansas State University, the New York Public Library, the Los Angeles Public Library, the City of San Francisco

Library, the University of Nevada, Las Vegas, and the University of Washington, to name only a few. These archives contain a wealth of resources on Asian cuisine in the United States, and deserve greater attention by foodways scholars. This essay will provide just a sampling of the menus in this area, and is by no means intended to be an exhaustive study of the subject.

4. Sau-ling Cynthia Wong, *Reading Asian American Literature: From Necessity to Extravagance* (Princeton: Princeton University Press, 1993), 55.
5. Ibid.
6. Ibid.
7. Anita Mannur, "'Peeking Ducks' and 'Food Pornographers': Commodifying Culinary Chinese Americanness," in *Culture, Identity, Commodity. Diasporic Chinese Literatures in English*, eds. Tseen Khoo and Kam Louie (Aberdeen: Hong Kong University Press, 2005), 20.
8. Ah Fong's, Beverly Hills, California, 1974 Menu. Los Angeles Public Library Menus Collection: http://dbase1.lapl.org/images/menus/fullsize/d/rb04084-05.jpg.
9. Mannur, "'Peeking Ducks,'" 24.
10. For a succinct overview of the Chinese experience in America, see Ronald Takaki, *Strangers from a Different Shore: A History of Asian Americans* (New York: Little, Brown and Company, 1998), especially chapters 3 and 6, which discuss nineteenth-century immigration and the establishment of Chinese ghettos (Chinatowns) and restaurants. For more on the Chinese culinary experience in the United States, see Jennifer Jensen Wallach, *How America Eats: A Social History of U.S. Food and Culture* (Lanham: Rowman and Littlefield, 2013), 170–178.
11. Vincent Cheng, "'A Four-Legged Duck?' Chinese Restaurant Culture in the U.S.," *China Media Research* 3, no. 2 (2007): 98.
12. Kristin Hoganson, "Food and Entertainment from Every Corner of the Globe: Bourgeois US Households as Points of Encounter, 1870–1920," *Amerikastudien/American Studies* 48, no. 1 (2003): 124.
13. Cheng, "'A Four-Legged Duck?,'" 99.
14. Ibid., 97.
15. Shun Lu and Gary Alan Fine, "The Presentation of Ethnic Authenticity: Chinese Food as a Social Accomplishment," *Sociological Quarterly* 36, no. 3 (1995): 541.
16. Cheng, "'A Four-Legged Duck?,'" 97.
17. Haiming Liu, "Chop Suey as Imagined Authentic Chinese Food: The Culinary Identity of Chinese Restaurants in the United States," *Journal of Transnational American Studies* 1, no. 1 (2009): 3.
18. Cheng, "'A Four-Legged Duck?,'" 101.
19. Ibid., 101–102.
20. Menu for the Oriental Grill, 714 K Street, Sacramento, California, 1916. University of California, Berkeley, Digital Archives: http://sunsite.berkeley.edu/cgi-bin/flipomatic/cic/chs1228.
21. Hoganson, "Food and Entertainment," 128.
22. Postcard of Cathay House, Boston, Mass., circa 1930–1945. Boston Public Library Photo Stream: http://www.flickr.com/photos/

boston_public_library/2381023464. Cathay House Menu (Front Cover), Los Angeles Public Library Menus Collection: http://dbase1.lapl.org/images/menus/fullsize/b/14244-FRONT.jpg.

23. Bob Lee's Lantern House, Boston, Mass., circa 1930–1945. Boston Public Library Photo Stream: http://www.flickr.com/photos/boston_public_library/2380187033/in/photostream.
24. Cheng, "'A Four-Legged Duck?,'" 99.
25. Some examples of "pagoda" restaurants were Los Angeles's Kim Ling Inn and Hong Kong Restaurant. These eateries became so iconic that exterior shots often doubled as menu covers. See Kim Ling Inn Menu, Jericl Cat's Photo Stream: http://www.flickr.com/photos/79761301@N00/2369300753/in/photostream; Hong Kong Restaurant Menu, Jericl Cat's Photo Stream: http://www.flickr.com/photos/79761301@N00/2369300139/in/photostream.
26. Edward W. Said, *Orientalism* (New York: Vintage Books, 1978). In short, Orientalism is the representation of Asia by "the West" in a stereotyped way that embodies a colonialist attitude.
27. G. Ace Yan and Carla Almeida Santos, "'China, Forever': Tourism Discourse and Self-Orientalism," *Annals of Tourism Research* 36 (2009): 297.
28. Akihiko Hirose and Kay Kei-Ho Pih, "'No Asians Working Here': Racialized Otherness and Authenticity in Gastronomical Orientalism," *Ethnic and Racial Studies* 34, no. 9 (2011): 1498.
29. Ibid.
30. Rey Chow, "'Have You Eaten?': Inspired by an Exhibit," *Amerasia* 31, no. 1 (2005): 20–21.
31. Karen Pyke and Tran Dang, "'FOB' and 'Whitewashed': Identity and Internalized Racism among Second Generation Asian Americans," *Qualitative Sociology* 26 (2003): 150–151.
32. Wong, *Reading Asian American Literature*, 57.
33. Sean Brayton and Brad Millington, "Renovating Ethnic Identity on *Restaurant Makeover*," *Social Identities: Journal for the Study of Race, Nation and Culture* 17, no. 2 (2011): 194.
34. Lu and Fine, "Presentation of Ethnic Authenticity," 539. For more on hyperreality, see Jean Baudrillard, *Simulacra and Simulation* (Ann Arbor: University of Michigan Press, 1994).
35. Chins Dinner Menu, 1944. New York Public Library, "What's on the Menu" Collection: http://menus.nypl.org/menu_pages/57394/explore.
36. Hoe Sai Gai Menu, 1949. New York Public Library, "What's on the Menu" Collection: http://menus.nypl.org/menu_pages/58478.
37. Forbidden City Menu, 1943. New York Public Library, "What's on the Menu" Collection: http://menus.nypl.org/menu_pages/48477/explore.
38. Joy Yong Co. Chinese and American Restaurant, Boston, 1945. Misconmike's Photo Stream: http://www.flickr.com/photos/mgwilkins/5561131336/.
39. Chop Sticks Chinese Restaurant and Cocktail Lounge Menu. University of Nevada, Las Vegas, Digital Collections, "Menus: The Art of Dining" Collection: http://digital.library.unlv.edu/objects/menus/4783.
40. Michael Luo, "As All-American as Egg Foo Yong," *New York Times*, September 22, 2004: http://www.nytimes.com/2004/09/22/dining/22CHIN.html.

41. Brayton and Millington, "Renovating Ethnic Identity," 186.
42. David Y.H. Wu, "Improvising Chinese Cuisine Overseas" in *The Globalization of Chinese Food*, eds. David Y.H. Wu and Sidney C.H. Cheung (Honolulu: University of Hawaii Press, 2002), 61.
43. Luo, "As All-American as Egg Foo Yong."
44. Wu, "Improvising Chinese Cuisine Overseas," 61. It is important to note that because of immigration laws, the 1940s was a time when American-born Chinese outnumbered the immigrant population. Thus many Chinese restauranteurs who played into such racial stereotypes were actually second, or even third, generation Americans, making the task especially unpleasant—a "necessary evil," which often earned the resentment of their community. While such individuals used incorrect grammar and pidgin English to reinforce stereotypes for survival, their pronunciation deployed a distinct Cantonese accent (which is very different than many other dialects in China), reflecting their cultural roots and ethnic identity.
45. "PY Chong Menu, c. 1940s," *Foodies in the Bible Belt*, blog, March 10, 2011: http://biblebeltfoodies.blogspot.com/2011/03/chinese-japanese-dirty-knees-look-at.html.
46. Don the Beachcomber Menu, Los Angeles Public Library Menus Collection: http://dbase1.lapl.org/images/menus/fullsize/f/rb04383-01.jpg.
47. Hoganson, "Food and Entertainment," 124.
48. Will Kymlicka, *Multicultural Odysseys: Navigating the New International Politics of Diversity* (Oxford: Oxford University Press, 2007), 130.
49. Luo, "As All-American as Egg Foo Yong."
50. Allan Lum's New Grand East Café, Los Angeles, Menu (Front Cover), Los Angeles Public Library Menus Collection: http://dbase1.lapl.org/images/menus/fullsize/j/rb03337-01.jpg.
51. J.A.G. Roberts, *China to Chinatown: Chinese Food in the West* (London: Reaktion Books, 2002), 152.
52. As quoted in Shehong Chen, "Reconstructing the Chinese American Experience in Lowell, Massachusetts, 1870s–1970s," *Institute for Asian American Studies Publications*, Paper 21 (2003): 17.
53. Calvin Lee, *Chinese Cooking for American Kitchens* (New York: G.P. Putnam's Sons, 1958), 29.
54. Toon Tien, Bronx, N.Y., 1948 Menu (Back Cover), New York Public Library, "What's on the Menu" Collection: http://menus.nypl.org/menu_pages/58143/explore.
55. Roberts, *China to Chinatown*, 152.
56. Andrew Coe, *Chop Suey: A Cultural History of Chinese Food in the United States* (New York: Oxford University Press, 2009), 219–220.
57. Forbidden Palace, Los Angeles, 1946 Menu (Front Cover), Los Angeles Public Library Menus Collection: http://dbase1.lapl.org/images/menus/fullsize/d/rb04238-01.jpg.
58. Golden Pagoda, Los Angeles, 1943 Menu (Front Cover), Los Angeles Public Library Menus Collection: http://dbase1.lapl.org/images/menus/fullsize/a/goldenpagoda-cov.jpg.
59. The Golden Pheasant, Chicago, 1946 Menu (Front Cover), Los Angeles Public

Library Menus Collection: http://dbase1.lapl.org/images/menus/fullsize/a/goldenpheasant-cov.jpg.

60. Hirose and Pih, "'No Asians Working Here,'" 1495.

61. Harley Spiller, "Late Night in the Lion's Den: Chinese Restaurant–Nightclubs in 1940s San Francisco," *Gastronomica: The Journal of Food and Culture* 4, no. 4 (2004): 94. I thank Harley for his valuable suggestions and insights.

62. Ibid., 98; Lion's Den, San Francisco, c. 1940s, U.S.S. Iwo Jima's Photo Stream: http://www.flickr.com/photos/41606952@N07/3888537374/.

63. Spiller, "Late Night in the Lion's Den," 98. For more on the literal and figurative consumption of ethnic culture in the United States, see Donna R. Gabaccia, *We Are What We Eat: Ethnic Food and the Making of Americans* (Cambridge: Harvard University Press, 2000).

64. Spiller, "Late Night in the Lion's Den," 98.

65. Ibid., 94.

66. Ibid., 100.

67. Ibid.

68. Madeline Y. Hsu, "From Chop Suey to Mandarin Cuisine: Fine Dining and the Refashioning of Chinese Ethnicity During the Cold War Era" in *Chinese Americans and the Politics of Race and Culture*, eds. Sucheng Chan and Madeline Yuan-yin Hsu (Philadelphia: Temple University Press, 2008), 174. Also see Takaki, *Strangers from a Different Shore*, chapters 10–12.

69. Sherrie A. Inness, *Secret Ingredients: Race, Gender, and Class at the Dinner Table* (New York: Palgrave Macmillan, 2005), 46.

70. Chen, "Reconstructing the Chinese American Experience," 17.

71. Lee, *Chinese Cooking for American Kitchens*, 30.

72. The Coral Reef, Sacramento, Calif., 1950s Menu (Back Page), Los Angeles Public Library Menus Collection: http://dbase1.lapl.org/images/menus/fullsize/j/rb03510-08.jpg.

73. Coe, *Chop Suey*, 210.

74. Lee, *Chinese Cooking for American Kitchens*, 29.

75. For more on how Cold War politics and Asian cuisine played out in the suburbs, see Mark Padoongpatt, "'Oriental Cookery': Devouring Asian and Pacific Cuisine during the Cold War," in *Eating Asian America: A Food Studies Reader*, eds. Robert Ji-Song Ku, Martin F. Manalansan, and Anita Mannur (New York: New York University Press, 2013), 186–207.

76. Coe, *Chop Suey*, 211.

77. Ibid., 215.

78. Edwin Tan's Chinese Gardens, San Bernardino, Calif., Menu Cover, Los Angeles Public Library Menus Collection: http://dbase1.lapl.org/images/menus/fullsize/a/15017-01.jpg.

79. Coe, *Chop Suey*, 216. For more on Hawaiian and Polynesian-themed cookbooks and their connection to popular restaurants such as Trader Vic's, as well as Cold War politics, see Amy Reddinger, "Pineapple Glaze and Backyard Luaus: Cold War Cookbooks and the Fiftieth State" in *Pressing the Fight: Print, Propaganda, and the Cold War*, ed. Catherine Turner (Amherst: University of Massachusetts Press, 2012), 193–208. Also see Padoongpatt, "'Oriental Cookery,'" 189–190.

80. The Don the Beachcomber restaurant expanded its menu to include Hawaiian and Polynesian dishes and also profited from this craze.
81. The China Trader, Burbank, Calif., Menu Image, Los Angeles Public Library Menus Collection: http://dbase1.lapl.org/images/menus/fullsize/d/rb00971-eyeback.jpg.
82. Mouling Restaurant, Hollywood, Menu (Front Cover), Los Angeles Public Library Menus Collection: http://dbase1.lapl.org/images/menus/fullsize/c/rb00961-01.jpg.
83. Mouling Restaurant, Hollywood, Interior Shots, Los Angeles Public Library Menus Collection: http://dbase1.lapl.org/images/menus/fullsize/c/rb00942-01.jpg.
84. For more on the rise of domestic Chinese cooking by non-Asian homemakers, see Katherine Parkin, *Food Is Love: Advertising and Gender Roles in Modern America* (Philadelphia: University of Pennsylvania Press, 2006), chapter 3. Also see Padoongpatt, "'Oriental Cookery,'" 200–202.
85. Hee Yong Guey Restaurant, Boston, Menu (Front Cover), Los Angeles Public Library Menus Collection: http://dbase1.lapl.org/images/menus/fullsize/g/rb00339-01.jpg.
86. Luo, "As All-American as Egg Foo Yong."
87. Cheng, "'A Four-Legged Duck?,'" 99.
88. Coe, *Chop Suey*, 210.
89. Luo, "As All-American as Egg Foo Yong."
90. Cheng, "'A Four-Legged Duck?,'" 99.
91. Haiming Liu and Lianlian Lin, "Food, Culinary Identity, and Transnational Culture: Chinese Restaurant Business in Southern California," *Journal of Asian American Studies* 12, no. 2 (2009): 138.
92. Coe, *Chop Suey*, 223.
93. Liu, "Chop Suey as Imagined Authentic Chinese Food," 17.
94. Coe, *Chop Suey*, 223.
95. Ibid., 221.
96. Ibid.
97. Harbin Inn, New York, 1970 Menu, New York Public Library, "What's on the Menu" Collection: http://menus.nypl.org/menu_pages/50234.
98. Jennifer 8. Lee, "Hunts for General Tso (Brief History of American Chinese Food)." *TED Talks*, July 2008: http://www.ted.com/talks/jennifer_8_lee_looks_for_general_tso.html.
99. Kuo Wah Café, San Francisco, 1960s Menu, New York Public Library, "What's on the Menu" Collection: http://menus.nypl.org/menu_pages/52082.
100. As quoted in Coe, *Chop Suey*, 224, 238–239. Kate Pickert, "A Brief History of Presidents Abroad," *Time*, March 31, 2009: http://www.time.com/time/nation/article/0,8599,1888528,00.html.
101. Coe, *Chop Suey*, 240.
102. La Société Bacchus et Epicurus, 1975 Menu (Front Cover), Los Angeles Public Library Menus Collection: http://dbase1.lapl.org/images/menus/fullsize/g/rb05321-01.jpg; La Société Bacchus et Epicurus, 1975 Menu (Courses), Los Angeles Public Library Menus Collection: http://dbase1.lapl.org/images/menus/fullsize/g/rb05321-03.jpg.

103. Gung Hay, Gardena, Calif., 1977 Menu (Front Cover), Los Angeles Public Library Menus Collection: http://dbase1.lapl.org/images/menus/fullsize/d/rb00017-cover.jpg; Gung Hay, Gardena, Calif., 1977 Menu (Page 4), Los Angeles Public Library Menus Collection: http://dbase1.lapl.org/images/menus/fullsize/d/rb00017-inside4.jpg.
104. Quoted in Hsu, "From Chop Suey to Mandarin Cuisine," 188.
105. Naomi Trostler and Liora Gvion, "Pleasures of the Table: Trends in Restaurant Menus: 1950–2000," *Nutrition Today* 42, no. 6 (2007): 257.
106. Amy Reddinger, "Eating 'Local': The Politics of Post-Statehood Hawaiian Cookbooks," *Nordic Journal of English Studies* 9, no. 3 (2010): 84.
107. Golden Dragon Café, Los Angeles, Menu (Front Cover), Los Angeles Public Library Menus Collection: http://dbase1.lapl.org/images/menus/fullsize/j/rb03582-01.jpg; Golden Dragon Café, Los Angeles, Menu (Introduction), Los Angeles Public Library Menus Collection: http://dbase1.lapl.org/images/menus/fullsize/j/rb03582-02.jpg.
108. Mandarin House, New York, 1965 Menu, New York Public Library, "What's on the Menu" Collection: http://menus.nypl.org/menu_pages/51890.
109. The Jade Palace, Chicago, 1960s Menu: http://tinyurl.com/dx6onjg.
110. Jade West, 1973 Menu (Front Cover). Los Angeles Public Library Menus Collection: http://dbase1.lapl.org/images/menus/fullsize/g/rb04689-01.jpg. Jade West, 1973 Menu (Back Cover). Los Angeles Public Library Menus Collection: http://dbase1.lapl.org/images/menus/fullsize/g/rb04689-04.jpg.
111. Don the Beachcomber, 1965 Menu. New York Public Library, "What's on the Menu" Collection: http://menus.nypl.org/menu_pages/47170.
112. Trostler and Gvion, "Pleasures of the Table," 258.
113. Ibid.
114. Chin's Village, Wellesley, Mass., Menu (Front Cover), Los Angeles Public Library Menus Collection: http://dbase1.lapl.org/images/menus/fullsize/c/rb01450-01.jpg.
115. Chin's Village, Wellesley, Mass., Menu (Inside Pages), Los Angeles Public Library Menus Collection: http://dbase1.lapl.org/images/menus/fullsize/c/rb01450-02.jpg; http://dbase1.lapl.org/images/menus/fullsize/c/rb01450-03.jpg.
116. Harbin Inn, New York, 1970 Menu, New York Public Library, "What's on the Menu" Collection: http://menus.nypl.org/menu_pages/50240/explore.
117. Lily Cho, "On Eating Chinese: Diasporic Agency and the Chinese Canadian Restaurant Menu," in *Reading Chinese Transnationalism*, eds. Maria Ng and Philip Holden (Hong Kong: Hong Kong University Press, 2006), 51.
118. Coe, *Chop Suey*, 251.
119. Trostler and Gvion, "Pleasures of the Table," 256.
120. Hsu, "From Chop Suey to Mandarin Cuisine," 174.
121. Samantha Barbas, "'I'll Take Chop Suey': Restaurants as Agents of Culinary and Cultural Change," *Journal of Popular Culture* 36, no. 4 (2003): 682.
122. Wong, *Reading Asian American Literature*, 61.
123. Ibid., 58.
124. Lu and Fine, "Presentation of Ethnic Authenticity," 547.

CHAPTER 2

1. Brandon Presser, "Next Stop, Quito: Our Top Cities for 2015," *The Daily Beast*, December 19, 2014: http://www.thedailybeast.com/articles/2014/12/19/next-stop-quito-our-top-cities-for-2015.html (last accessed February 24, 2017); "Quito," *Lonely Planet Online* (2016): https://www.lonelyplanet.com/best-in-travel/cities/2 (last accessed February 24, 2017).
2. Jennifer 8. Lee, *The Fortune Cookie Chronicles: Adventures in the World of Chinese Food* (New York: Twelve Books, 2008), 26.
3. Barbara Gimla Shortridge and James R. Shortridge, "Introduction," in *The Taste of American Place: A Reader on Regional and Ethnic Foods*, eds. Barbara Gimla Shortridge and James R. Shortridge (Lanham: Rowman & Littlefield, 1999), 1–20.
4. Soo Cheong (Shawn) Jang, Yinghua Liu, and Young Namkung, "Effects of Authentic Atmospherics in Ethnic Restaurants: Investigating Chinese Restaurants," *International Journal of Contemporary Hospitality Management* 23, no. 5 (2011): 663.
5. Evan Jones, *American Food: The Gastronomic Story* (New York: Vintage Books, 1981), 166–167; John Mariani, *America Eats Out* (New York: Lebhar-Friedman, 1999), 76–80; Rani Long, "10 Best Chinatowns Across the USA," *USA Today*, March 11, 2014: http://www.usatoday.com/story/travel/destinations/2014/03/08/chinatown-chinese-asian-food/6173601/ (last accessed February 24, 2017); Marie Rose Wong, *Sweet Cakes, Long Journey: The Chinatowns of Portland, Oregon* (Seattle: University of Washington Press, 2004), 265.
6. Mark Padoongpatt makes an intriguing argument that American women engaged with the "romance" and tragedy of U.S. global expansion via cookbooks and dinner menus. The twentieth-century "housewife" often "discovered" Asian cuisine through cookbooks, which made it safe for home preparation and white, suburban, middle-class consumption. The same "safe" mainstreaming of Chinese cuisine is what essentially drives Asian-inspired fast food chains today. Mark Padoongpatt, "Oriental Cookery," in *Eating Asian American: A Food Studies Reader*, eds. Robert Ji-Song Ku, Martin F. Manalansan IV, and Anita Mannur (New York: New York University Press, 2013), 186–207.
7. Andrew Coe, *Chop Suey: A Cultural History of Chinese Food in the United States* (New York: Oxford University Press, 2009), 246–247.
8. J.A.G. Roberts, *China to Chinatown: Chinese Food in the West* (London: Reaktion Books, 2002), 135–136, 144–145; Wong, *Sweet Cakes, Long Journey*, 263–265.
9. Quoted in Roberts, *China to Chinatown*, 151; Jiemin Bao, "Transnational Cuisine: Southeast Asian Chinese Food in Las Vegas," in *Chinese Food and Foodways in Southeast Asia and Beyond*, ed. Chee-Beng Tan (Singapore: NUS Press, 2001), 175–191.
10. Yong Chen, *Chop Suey, USA: The Story of Chinese Food in America* (New York: Columbia University Press, 2014, Kindle edition), locations 278, 301, and 321.
11. Ibid., location 754.

12. Ibid., locations 3766 and 3990.
13. Lee, *Fortune Cookie Chronicles*, 22–23, 57–58.
14. Haiming Liu, *From Canton Restaurant to Panda Express* (New Brunswick: Rutgers University Press, 2015), 71–73. The 1882 Act banned labor immigrants, and these provisions were extended in 1892 and 1902 to all U.S. territories.
15. Ibid., 75.
16. Jon D. Holtzman, "Food and Memory," *Annual Review of Anthropology* 35 (2006): 364–367; "Legendary Route 66: Harvey Hotels and Restaurants on Route 66," *Legends of America*: http://www.legendsofamerica.com/66-harveyhouse.html (last accessed February 24, 2017); "Harvey Houses: Civilizing the Old West," *Harvey Houses*: http://www.harveyhouses.net/ (last accessed February 24, 2017). Harvey House Restaurants first opened in 1876 at the Topeka Santa Fe Depot, along the Kansas Pacific Railroad line.
17. Jang, et al., "Effects of Authentic Atmospherics and Ethnic Restaurants," 664.
18. Maria Godoy, "Lo Mein Loophole: How US Immigration Law Fueled a Chinese Restaurant Boom," *The Salt*, NPR, February 22, 2016: http://www.npr.org/sections/thesalt/2016/02/22/467113401/lo-mein-loophole-how-u-s-immigration-law-fueled-a-chinese-restaurant-boom (last accessed March 25, 2017); John Jung, *Sweet and Sour: Life in Chinese Family Restaurants* (Cypress, Calif.: Yin and Yang Press, 2010), 9–22, 109–136.
19. Ian Cheney, dir., *In Search of General Tso*, Sundance Selects, 2014, DVD.
20. Barry M. Popkin, "Global Nutrition Dynamics: The World Is Shifting Rapidly Toward a Diet Linked with Noncommunicable Diseases," *American Journal of Clinical Nutrition* 84 (2006): 292–296.
21. Leonara Epstein, "15 Unforgivable Moments from The Late '90s/Early '00s Chinese Fashion Trend," *Buzzfeed*, March 14, 2011: https://www.buzzfeed.com/leonoraepstein/15-unforgivable-moments-from-the-late-90searly-00s-chinese-f?utm_term=.gkZ5YB7YOy#.cm7bv6mvRG (last accessed February 24, 2017).
22. For erroneous Chinese-inspired tattoos among North American youth, see: http://hanzismatter.blogspot.ca (last accessed February 24, 2017).

CHAPTER 3

1. Joshua Kurlantzick, *Charm Offensive: How China's Soft Power is Transforming the World* (New Haven: Yale University Press, 2007).
2. Dennis Hickey, "Imbalance in the Taiwan Strait," *Parameters* 43, no. 2 (2013): 43–53.
3. Chinese-American Restaurant Association, http://www.ca-ra.com/ (accessed April 21, 2017).
4. Eileen Yin-Fei Lo, *The Chinese Kitchen: Recipes, Techniques, Ingredients, History and Memories from America's Leading Authority on Chinese Cooking* (New York: Harper Collins, 1999).
5. Michael Browning, "Who Was General Tso and Why Are We Eating His Chicken?" *Washington Post*, April 17, 2002.

6. Kimberly Kohatsu, "Who Was General Tso and Why Are We Eating His Chicken?" *Huffington Post*, August 23, 2014.
7. Eric Hochman, "The Definitive General Tso's Chicken Page," http://www.echonyc.com/~erich/tso.htm (accessed April 21, 2017).
8. Shun Yao, "*Xin canting: pengyuan huiguan chaqi xindian xiangcai chushen shuogushi*" ("New Restaurant: Pengyuan Restaurant Opens in Xindian, the God of Hunan Cuisine Tells His Tale"), *China Times*, May 31, 2014, http://www.chinatimes.com/newspapers/20140531000219-260210 (accessed April 21, 2017).
9. Fuchshia Dunlop, "Hunan Resources," *New York Times*, February 4, 2007.
10. Ibid.
11. Shun Yao, "*Jingguo shengshenghuan Peng Chang-kuei fantai chuang Pengyuan*" ("Chiang Chin-kuo Kept Calling, Peng Chang-kuei Returned to Taiwan and Established Pengyuan Restaurant"), *China Times*, May 29, 2014, http://www.chinatimes.com/realtimenews/20140529004509-260405 (accessed April 21, 2017).
12. Lisa Marsh, "The Truth about Your Chinese Food: The Search for General Tso Premiers at the Tribeca Film Festival," *Epicurious*, http://www.epicurious.com/archive/blogs/editor/2014/04/the-truth-about-your-chinese-food-the-search-for-general-tso-premieres-at-the-tribeca-film-festival.html (accessed April 21, 2017).
13. James Flanigan, "Cooking Up a Powerhouse of Chinese Fast Food," *Los Angeles Times*, October 8, 2001.
14. Matt Krantz, "Panda Express Spreads Chinese Food across USA," *USA Today*, September 13, 2006.
15. "Cheng Zhengchang: Meiguo zhongcan dawang de gongfu xiongmao" ("Andrew Cherng: the 'Kungfu Panda' of the King of Chinese Food in America), http://news.sina.com.tw/article/20130921/10701595.html (accessed April 21, 2015).
16. "Xiongmao kuaican: meiguo de zhongshi maidanglao" ("Panda Express: America's Chinese McDonalds"), http://news.uschinapress.com/2017/0405/1101111.shtml (accessed April 21, 2017).
17. Bettijane Levine, "A Passion for Panda," *Pasadena Weekly*, July 1, 2011.
18. "Xiongmao kuaican: meiguo de zhongshi maidanglao" ("Panda Express: America's Chinese McDonalds"), http://news.uschinapress.com/2017/0405/1101111.shtml.
19. Timeline, "How it all Started," 2016: https://www.pandaexpress.com/ourfamilystory (last accessed April 29, 2017).

CHAPTER 4

Many thanks to Richard Sutch for his valuable support and counsel throughout this project and to the editors for their suggestions.

1. Menu available at: http://www.yellowpages.com/listings/1847849/menu; Mandy Potts, "Chili," *A Serving Life* (blog) (accessed April 5, 2014). See also: http://oshkoshchilicookoff.com (accessed April 5, 2014).

2. On Americans' embrace of ethnic food see Donna R. Gabaccia, *We Are What We Eat: Ethnic Food and the Making of Americans* (Cambridge: Harvard University Press, 1998), 226. Oshkosh population by race and ethnicity from the federal census of 2010. Statistics available online at: http://www.census.gov/2010census/popmap/ipmtext.php?fl=55. The term "ethnic food" is used regularly in two contradictory ways: as food "identified with an ethnic group other than one's own" and as "food that is cooked and served to express membership in one's own ethnic group." See Mark H. Zanger, "Ethnic Foods," in *The Oxford Companion to American Food and Drink*, ed. Andrew F. Smith (New York: Oxford University Press, 2007), 208.
3. Ladies of the Charity Circle, *The King's Daughters Cookbook: A Collection of Reliable Recipes from Experienced Housekeepers* (Oshkosh: W.M. Castle, Printer, 1891), 122. Online at the Library of Congress: https://archive.org/details/kingsdaughterscooofinn. See also Harva Hachten, *The Flavor of Wisconsin* (Madison: State Historical Society of Wisconsin, 1981). The Oshkosh cookbook is similar to those produced in other communities of the era. On reading community cookbooks see: Anne L. Bower, "Our Sisters' Recipes: Exploring 'Community' in a Community Cookbook," *Journal of Popular Culture* 31, no. 3 (1997): 137–151; Liora Gvion, "What's Cooking in America? Cookbooks Narrate Ethnicity: 1850–1990," *Food, Culture & Society* 2, no. 1 (2009): 53–76; Andrew P. Haley, "The Nation before Taste: The Challenges of American Culinary History," *The Public Historian* 34, no. 2 (2012): 53–78; Kennan Ferguson, "Intensifying Taste, Intensifying Identity: Collectivity through Community Cookbooks," *Signs* 37, no. 3 (2012): 695–717.
4. *Oshkosh (Wisc.) Daily Northwestern,* March 24, 1897; November 20, 1897; December 17, 1898.
5. *Oshkosh (Wisc.) Daily Northwestern,* December 24, 1902; October 21, 1902. Oshkosh Public Museum, Catalog no: P2001.48.30. Imperial Restaurant, circa 1903–1905.
6. Maxmillian Schele DeVore, *Americanisms* (New York: C. Scribner, 1872); John V. Bunn, *Bunn's Oshkosh Directory, 1903–04* (Oshkosh: Globe Printing, 1903).
7. Oshkosh Public Museum, Cat. No. P2001.48.5 19, 1908–1914.
8. "For a Café. Oshkosh Said to Be Lacking in One Where Theater Parties May Go," *Oshkosh (Wisc.) Daily Northwestern*, April 24, 1903.
9. "A Chinese Restaurant," *Oshkosh (Wisc.) Daily Northwestern*, December 11, 1902.
10. Allen Toy, "My Great-Grandfather," *Badger History* 10, no. 1 (1956): 2–3.
11. "He 'Does it Up Brown,'" *Oshkosh (Wisc.) Daily Northwestern*, December 6, 1905. For more photographs of the Toy Building, see David B. Holmes and Wenbin Yuan, *Chinese Milwaukee* (Charleston: Arcadia Publishing, 2008), 34–36.
12. "Chinese Restaurant," *Oshkosh (Wisc.) Daily Northwestern*, March 16, 1903; "Hong Kong Low Co. [ad]," *Oshkosh (Wisc.) Daily Northwestern*, April 4, 1903; "Charley Toy Entertains. Prepares a Chinese Feast for Some of His American Friends," *Oshkosh (Wisc.) Daily Northwestern*, May 4, 1903; "Hong Kong Low Co. [ad]" *Oshkosh (Wisc.) Daily Northwestern*, May 22, 1903; *Oshkosh (WI) Daily Northwestern*, October 8, 1903; "C. Toy to Milwaukee," *Oshkosh (Wisc.)*

Daily Northwestern, May 5, 1904; "He 'Does it Up Brown,'" *Oshkosh (Wisc.) Daily Northwestern*, December 6, 1905.

13. *Rhinelander (Wisc.) New North*, September 28, 1905.
14. Holmes and Yuan, *Chinese Milwaukee*, 31; "Calumet's Chinese Chop House," *(Milwaukee) Weekly Wisconsin*, October 23, 1897; *Rhinelander (Wisc.) New North*, September 28, 1905; "Moy Hee of China," *Saint Paul (Minn.) Globe*, July 20, 1901; Sherri Gebert Fuller, "Mirrored Identities: The Moys of St. Paul," *Minnesota History* 57 (Winter 2000/2001): 164; *Stevens Point (Wisc.) Journal*, February 25, 1905; "A Chinese Restaurant," *Oshkosh (Wisc.) Daily Northwestern*, December 11, 1902.
15. In 1900, the federal census enumerated 212 Chinese residents in Wisconsin; in 1910, 226.
16. Warren Belasco, *Food: The Key Concepts* (London: Bloomsbury, 2008), 1.
17. Ivan Light and Light and Charles Choy Wong identified this dilemma for Chinatown entrepreneurs of the era. See Ivan Light, "From Vice District to Tourist Attraction: The Moral Career of American Chinatowns, 1880–1940," *Pacific Historical Review* 43, no. 3 (1974): 367–394; Ivan Light and Charles Choy Wong, "Protest or Work: Dilemmas of the Tourist Industry in American Chinatowns," *American Journal of Sociology* 80, no. 6 (1975): 1342–1368; Ivan Light, "The Ethnic Vice Industry, 1880–1944," *American Sociological Review* 42, no. 3 (1977): 469. The representation of the Oriental as "both seductively childlike and threateningly sexual" is from Robert G. Lee, *Asian Americans in Popular Culture* (Philadelphia: Temple University Press, 1999), 10.
18. Kristin L. Hoganson, *Consumers' Imperium: The Global Production of American Domesticity, 1865–1920* (Chapel Hill: University of North Carolina Press, 2007); Jan Whitaker, *Tea at the Blue Lantern Inn: A Social History of the Tea Room Craze in America* (New York: St. Martin's Press, 2002); Andrew Coe, *Chop Suey: A Cultural History of Chinese Food in the United States* (New York: Oxford University Press, 2009), 148; Andrew P. Haley, *Turning the Tables: Restaurants and the Rise of the American Middle Class, 1880–1920* (Chapel Hill: University of North Carolina Press, 2011), 8–9; Paul Freedman, *Ten Restaurants That Changed America* (New York: Liveright Publishing, 2016); Anne Mendelson, *Chow Chop Suey: Food and the Chinese American Journey* (New York: Columbia University Press, 2016); Sinclair Lewis, *Main Street* (New York: New American Library, 1961 [1920]), 231. See Hoganson, 5–8, for a discussion of Kennicott's cosmopolitanism.
19. Chandler B. Beach and Chandler B. McMurry, eds., *The New Student's Reference Work for Teachers, Students and Families* (Chicago: F. E. Compton, 1914); Wisconsin Historical Society, "Oshkosh, Wisconsin—A Brief History": http://www.wisconsinhistory.org/Content.aspx?dsNav=N:4294963828-4294963805&dsRecordDetails =R:CS2390. Occupational distributions calculated using the 1900 IPUMS. See Steven Ruggles, Katie Genadek, Ronald Goeken, Josiah Grover, and Matthew Sobek, *Integrated Public Use Microdata Series*, version 6.0 [dataset] (Minneapolis: University of Minnesota, 2015): http://doi.org/10.18128/D010.V6.0.
20. *Bunn & Philippi's Oshkosh City Directory, 1889–90* (Oshkosh: E. W. Viall, 1889), 6–7.

21. "The Mikado!," *Oshkosh (Wisc.) Daily Northwestern*, December 24, 1885; "Costumed As Japs. All for the Mikado," *Oshkosh (Wisc.) Daily Northwestern*, October 11, 1889. Description of Daggett based on a photograph in the collection of the Oshkosh Public Museum. See: http://oshkosh.pastperfect-online.com/20004cgi/mweb.exe?request=record;id= BB46BAAE-57B7-4D44-ABFF-958913431006;type=102.
22. *Oshkosh (Wisc.) Daily Northwestern*, March 23, 1897.
23. "A Chinese Honeymoon," *Oshkosh (Wisc.) Daily Northwestern*, August 30, 1902; June 6, 1903; August 1, 1903. I was unable to find a review of the play in a Wisconsin newspaper. The plot summary comes from a small-city newspaper in Pennsylvania: "A Chinese Honeymoon," *Altoona (Pa.) Tribune*, Sept. 16, 1904. The critical commentary is an unsigned review that appeared in *The Theatre: Illustrated Monthly Review of Theatre and Theatrical Life* 2, no. 4 (1902) cited in James S. Moy, *Marginal Sights: Staging the Chinese in America* (Iowa City: University of Iowa Press, 1993), 10.
24. *Oshkosh (Wisc.) Daily Northwestern*, March 28, 1887.
25. "Ah Moy's Street Market," *Oshkosh (Wisc.) Daily Northwestern*, November 27, 1888.
26. "Food of All Nations Served at the Midwinter Fair," *Oshkosh (Wisc.) Daily Northwestern*, March 10, 1894.
27. "Chinese Dinner," *Oshkosh (Wisc.) Daily Northwestern*, November 15, 1902.
28. On the operation of Euro-American immigrant networks in Wisconsin in this era, see Simone A. Wegge, "Chain Migration and Information Networks: Evidence from Nineteenth-Century Hesse-Cassel," *Journal of Economic History* 58, no. 4 (1998): 957–986; Jon Gjerde, *From Peasants to Farmers: The Migration from Balestrand, Norway to the Upper Middle West* (New York: Cambridge University Press, 1985); Robert Clifford Ostergren, *A Community Transplanted: The Trans-Atlantic Experience of a Swedish Immigrant Settlement in the Upper Middle West, 1835–1915* (Madison: University of Wisconsin Press, 1988).
29. Holmes and Yuan, *Chinese Milwaukee*, 11. For information on Chinese by county, see Michael R. Haines and Inter-University Consortium for Political and Social Research, *Historical, Demographic, Economic, and Social Data: The United States, 1790–2002* (Ann Arbor: Inter-University Consortium for Political and Social Research, 2010): doi:10.3886/ICPSR02896.v3; Department of the Interior, Census Bureau, *Twelfth Census of the United States, Taken in the Year 1900* (Washington: United States Census Office, 1901).
30. "A Chinese Restaurant," *Oshkosh (Wisc.) Daily Northwestern*, February 3, 1891; "Celestials Made Glad," *Janesville (Wisc.) Daily Gazette*, February 9, 1891; "Chinese New Year. It Is Celebrated by the Mongolians of this City," *Oshkosh (Wisc.) Daily Northwestern*, February 9, 1891; "To Celebrate Sunday. Great Gathering of Chinamen to Take Place Here," *Oshkosh (Wisc.) Daily Northwestern*, January 21, 1898; "They Took in Appleton. Local Chinese Return from the Meeting of Chinese Masons. Went to the Paper City in a Bus and Returned as Far as Mensaba on the Inter Urban—Took a Four Piece Band with Them," *Oshkosh (Wisc.) Daily Northwestern*, October 10, 1898; "Chinese Freemasons in Oshkosh," *Oshkosh (Wisc.) Daily Northwestern*, February 9,

1899; "Oshkosh Becomes a Chinatown: Chinese Free Masons Gather Here from Country Round," *Oshkosh (Wisc.) Daily Northwestern*, November 5, 1900; "Celestials in Oshkosh. Thirty or More from Surrounding Cities Celebrate Chinese New Year," *Oshkosh (Wisc.) Daily Northwestern*, February 2, 1903; "Chinese Celebration. Celestials Have Jubilee over Horrible Death of Wrong Doer," *Oshkosh (Wisc.) Daily Northwestern*, July 27, 1903; "Celestial New Year," *Oshkosh (Wisc.) Daily Northwestern*, February 15, 1904.

31. "Sam Wah Kee is Master. Celestial Masons Adjourn Annual Session at Appleton," *Centralia (Wisc.) Enterprise and Tribune*, October 15, 1898; "Oshkosh Becomes a Chinatown. Chinese Free Masons Gather Here from Country Round," *Oshkosh (Wisc.) Daily Northwestern*, November 5, 1900; "Moy Hee, Mason of High Degree," *Minneapolis Journal*, April 11, 1902; "Chinese to Be Initiated. The Grand Master of the Lone We Tong Eng Ti to Conduct the Ceremony at 16 Pell Street To-night," *New York Times*, January 21, 1900; "Riding the Chinese Goat," *Alexandria (Va.) Gazette*, January 18, 1900.
32. On the power of Chinese-style social networks, see Mark Granovetter, "The Strength of Weak Ties," *American Journal of Sociology* 78, no. 6 (1973): 1360–1380. For a more recent formulation, see William R. Kerr and Martin Mandorff, "Social Networks, Ethnicity, and Entrepreneurship," *NBER Working Paper 21597* (Cambridge: National Bureau of Economic Research, 2015).
33. "Chinamen Chased. Angry Men After Them in Milwaukee," *Oshkosh (Wisc.) Daily Northwestern*, March 8, 1889.
34. Victor Jew, "'Chinese Demons': The Violent Articulation of Chinese Otherness and Interracial Sexuality in the US Midwest, 1885–1889," *Journal of Social History* 37, no. 2 (2003): 389–410; "Chinese Devils. Their Nefarious Practice in Milwaukee Exposed," *Oshkosh (Wisc.) Daily Northwestern*, March 7, 1889; "Chinamen Chased," *Oshkosh (Wisc.) Daily Northwestern*, March 8, 1889; "'String Them Up!'" *Oshkosh (Wisc.) Daily Northwestern*, March 9, 1889; "A Milwaukee Mob," *Oshkosh (Wisc.) Daily Northwestern*, March 11, 1889.
35. "Chinese Claims," *San Francisco Chronicle*, March 16, 1889; Holmes and Yuan, *Chinese Milwaukee*, 20; "Notes from Milwaukee," *Chicago Daily Tribune*, September 9, 1890.
36. Katherine Toy, personal communication, 2014.
37. "Death of Charlie Toy in China Recalls Early Life in Oshkosh," *Oshkosh (Wisc.) Daily Northwestern*, January 6, 1955; Toy, "My Great-Grandfather." The Chinese Exclusion case file of Moy Hee, a close relative, reported that the family owned large tracts of land in China and that Moy Hee's mother, Jun Shee, had bound feet, suggesting that Toy came from a prosperous family, despite his humble beginnings in the United States. See Fuller, "Mirrored Identities," 164.
38. "Death of Charlie Toy in China Recalls Early Life in Oshkosh," *Oshkosh (Wisc.) Daily Northwestern*, January 6, 1955; Toy, "My Great-Grandfather," 2–3; "Wah Kee, an Appleton Chinese Laundryman Has Been Back to China and

Returned," *Oshkosh (Wisc.) Daily Northwestern*, July 17, 1884; David Holmes, "Charlie Toy's Writing Translated by Gordon Toy," personal correspondence. In testimony to an Immigration Inspector in 1934, Toy said he first came to the United States in 1888 (after the Chinese Exclusion Act) and gave his birthdate as January 11, 1861. Chinese Exclusion Case file No. 2070/186 (Seattle), June 24, 1935.

39. Fuller, "Mirrored Identities," 164; *Bunn and Philippi's Oshkosh City Directory 1889–1890*; Toy, "My Great-Grandfather," 2–3.
40. The description of the interior of Toy's bazaar is based on the account of a New York Chinese merchant's store in the 1880s. See "John Chinaman in New York," *Elk County Advocate* (Ridgway, Pa.), March 18, 1880.
41. *Oshkosh (Wisc.) Daily Northwestern*, December 24, 1897.
42. "Fine Program," *Oshkosh (Wisc.) Daily Northwestern*, March 6, 1898.
43. "Chinaman on a Wheel," *Oshkosh (Wisc.) Daily Northwestern*, May 5, 1897.
44. "Chinamen Going Home," *Oshkosh (Wisc.) Daily Northwestern*, July 28, 1900.
45. Roger Daniels, *Guarding the Golden Door* (New York: Hill & Wang, 2005), 22.
46. Chinese Exclusion Case No. 7032/115, Moy Toy Nai alias Charley M. Toy (Seattle). Document dated October 5, 1894. Fuller reports that Moy Hee sought endorsements from some of the same prominent citizens. Fuller, "Mirrored Identities," 168.
47. Stanford M. Lyman, "The 'Chinese Question' and American Labor Historians," *New Politics* 7, no. 4 (2000): 113–148; Daniels, *Guarding the Golden Door*, 36.
48. Delber L. McKee, "'The Chinese Must Go!' Commissioner General Powderly and Chinese Immigration, 1897–1902," *Pennsylvania History* 44, no. 1 (1977): 37–51; "Seven Scooped In; Sam Wah Kee's Smuggling Party Interrupted," *Boston Globe*, January 14, 1901; Cynthia Y. Li, "The Other Great Wall: A Study of the Enforcement of the Chinese Exclusion Act," Honors College Thesis, Pforzheimer Honors College, Pace University, 2007.
49. "Starts for China," *Oshkosh (Wisc.) Daily Northwestern*, November 29, 1898.
50. *New York Times*, September 10, 1899.
51. This description of the Pacific Mail's detention center is based on J. F. Rose-Soley, "Chinese in Bond on the Mail Dock," *San Francisco Call*, November 6, 1898; cited in Robert Eric Barde, *Immigration at the Golden Gate: Passenger Ships, Exclusion, and Angel Island* (Westport: Praeger, 2008), 62–63.
52. "Charley Toy Arrives," *Oshkosh (Wisc.) Daily Northwestern*, September 11, 1899.
53. "Mrs. Toy and Family Here," *Oshkosh (Wisc.) Daily Northwestern*, October 19, 1905; "Death of Charlie Toy in China Recalls Early Life in Oshkosh," *Oshkosh (Wisc.) Daily Northwestern*, January 6, 1955.
54. "He 'Does it Up Brown'" *Oshkosh (Wisc.) Daily Northwestern*, December 6, 1905; "Governor Eats Chop Suey," *Oshkosh (Wisc.) Daily Northwestern*, September 14, 1908.
55. *Oshkosh (Wisc.) Daily Northwestern*, March 8, 1912; "New Palm Garden," *Oshkosh (Wisc.) Daily Northwestern*, June 28, 1912.
56. *Oshkosh (Wisc.) Daily Northwestern*, October 28, 1905. Golden Buck is Welsh Rarebit topped with a fried egg.

CHAPTER 5

1. For instance, a recent newspaper article reports that Hong Kong–style egg tart is more readily available than pizza in the Bath Beach community of Brooklyn, New York, due to the dramatic growth of Chinese population there: "布碌崙巴斯海灘華裔激增" [Rapid Growth of Chinese Population in Bath Beach, Brooklyn], *Singtao Daily* (East USA), April 11, 2014 (accessed January 31, 2016), http://ny.stgloballink.com/community/2014/0411/85695.shtml.
2. Chinese restaurant wait staff can be apologetic when a Chinese customer places an order for an item deemed "inauthentic." On several occasions, when Ting Man (coauthor) patronized a Chinese restaurant serving mainly a non-Chinese population, the wait staff had to steer him away from certain dishes such as spring roll, apologizing that the food was prepared specifically for "foreigners."
3. The following is an excellent study based on a rare archive of materials: Heather Lee, "A Life Cooking for Others: The Work and Migration Experiences of a Chinese Restaurant Worker in New York City, 1920–1946," in *Eating Asian America: A Food Studies Reader,* eds. Robert Ji-Song Ku, Martin F. Manalansan IV, and Anita Mannur (New York: New York University Press, 2013), 55–77.
4. The coauthors are grateful to Victoria Brown for suggesting this point about celebrity chefs. Any error here is of course ours.
5. David Y.H. Wu and Sidney C.H. Cheung, "Introduction. The Globalization of Chinese Food and Cuisine: Markers and Breakers of Cultural Barriers," in *The Globalization of Chinese Food*, eds. David Y. H. Wu and Sidney C.H. Cheung (Honolulu: University of Hawaii Press, 2002), 4.
6. Wendy Tan, *Chinese Dough Statuary: The Art and Work Presentations by Artist Kai Tai Chan* (New York: US-China Arts Exchange Center, 1998), 17–18.
7. "For Zurich Festival," *South China Morning Post*, January 6, 1969, 6; "親善訪問團飛瑞參加中國食品節" [Goodwill Mission Flies to Switzerland to Participate in the Chinese Food Festival], 香港工商日報, January 6, 1969, 6; 牛蔓, "「中國食品節」在海外" [Overseas "Chinese food festival"], Press Clipping, Kai Tai Chan Personal Archive.
8. R. Schwarz, "Aus Den Kochtopfen Chinesischer Kuchenmeister," *Hotel-und Gastgewerbe Rundschau*, March 1, 1969, 143.
9. The three chefs were 羅潤, 仇仕, and 林志榮.
10. Schwarz, "Aus Den Kochtopfen," 146.
11. The page boy was Ramsey Kok-king Lai.
12. They were 許劍萍, 岑少常, 姚玉珠 and 陶緒櫻.
13. Schwarz, "Aus Den Kochtopfen," 146; Nancy Hsu, "Page Boy Off on Three-Month Swiss Adventure," *South China Morning Post-Herald*, January 5, 1969, 1.
14. Schwarz, "Aus Den Kochtopfen"; Theo Denu, "Le Chef Chang Ching Nous Revele Le Secret Des 'Rouleaux Du Bonheur,'" *La Tribune De Geneve*, March 1, 1969, 7; "半島酒店徐太欣返港談及香港中國食品節在瑞士極受歡迎" [Tai Yan Tsui of Peninsula Hotel Returns to Hong Kong and Says the Hong Kong Chinese Food Festival Was Well Received in Switzerland], 華僑日報,

March 11, 1969, 7; "中國食品節瑞士感興趣" [The Swiss Are Interested in the Chinese Food Festival], 華僑日報, March 18, 1969, 5; 牛蔓.

15. Schwarz, "Aus Den Kochtopfen," 144.
16. 張志其,"洪顺樓兩員猛將:捏麪麵大師,點心主厨" ["Two Brave Warriors of Hung Shun Restaurant: A Dough Sculpture Master and a Dim Sum Chef], 地產工商快訊, April 12–18, 1991; "京華洒樓滿漢華筵序目" ["Blue Heaven Restaurant's Manchu-Han Imperial Feast Preface and Menu"], July 4, 1973, Kai Tai Chan Personal Archive.
17. 張志其.
18. Patricia Hughes, *Creative Doughcraft* (Lewes, U.K.: Guild of Master Craftsman Publications, 1999), 5; Margaret Blanche, *Inspirations in Dough* (Tunbridge Wells, U.K.: Search Press, 1998), 14.
19. Salt has long been a commonly recommended ingredient for dough or bread sculpture, but not sugar, the addition of which was Chan's original idea. For the use of salt in dough art, see Cheryl Owen, *Dough Folk Art* (New York: Sterling, 1995), 6; Joanna Jones, *Decorative Dough for Celebrations* (London: Merehurst, 1995), 6; Isolde Kiskalt, *Dough Crafts* (New York: Sterling, Lark, 1991), 8; Hughes, *Creative Doughcraft*, 4; Blanche, *Inspirations in Dough,* 10.
20. Peter Bart, *The Gross: The Hits, the Flops—The Summer That Ate Hollywood* (New York: St. Martin's Press, 1999), 219.
21. In Los Angeles, the *Mulan* première took place at the Hollywood Bowl.
22. Joseph M. Chan, "Disneyfying and Globalizing the Chinese Legend Mulan: A Study of Transculturation," in *In Search of Boundaries: Communication, Nation-States and Cultural Identities*, eds. Joseph M. Chan and Bryce T. McIntyre (Westport: Ablex, 2002), 236.
23. David Y. H. Wu and Sidney C.H. Cheung, eds., *The Globalization of Chinese Food* (Honolulu: University of Hawaii Press, 2002); J.A.G. Roberts, *China to Chinatown: Chinese Food in the West* (London: Reaktion Books, 2002).
24. Roberts, *China to Chinatown*, 9, 219.
25. Martin F. Manalansan IV, "Beyond Authenticity: Rerouting the Filipino Culinary Diaspora," in *Eating Asian America: A Food Studies Reader*, eds. Robert Ji-Song Ku, Martin F. Manalansan IV, and Anita Mannur (New York: New York University Press, 2013), 290–291.
26. Roberts, *China to Chinatown*, 11; Andrew Coe, *Chop Suey: A Cultural History of Chinese Food in the United States* (Oxford: Oxford University Press, 2009), 211; Yong Chen, *Chop Suey USA: The Story of Chinese Food in America* (New York: Columbia University Press, 2014), 23.
27. Quoted in Tan, *Chinese Dough Statuary*, 13.

CHAPTER 6

1. According to interviewees based in New York, Chinese Mainlanders who moved to New York in the 1950s, after the end of the Chinese Civil War, tended to be supporters of the Kuomintang (KMT, or Chinese Nationalist Party).
2. The Chinese TV series *A Native of Beijing in New York*, which came to the

small screen in 1994 and was filmed in the United States, is an excellent depiction of how the first wave of Chinese immigrants from Beijing struggled to adjust to life in NYC. This TV series garnered a considerable following in China and consequently played a prominent role in attracting attention to Chinese immigrants in the United States and particularly in NYC.

3. As for Chinese cuisine in the United States since the 1950s, David Y.H. Wu points out that, stateside, Chinese Mainlanders (some of whom were refugees), Taiwanese students, and Taiwanese immigrants strongly promoted a general type of Chinese cuisine regarded by David Wu as "Pan-China Cuisine." See David Y.H. Wu, "Global Encounter of Diasporic Chinese Restaurant Food," in *Chinese Food and Foodways in Southeast Asia and Beyond*, ed. Tan Chee-Beng (Singapore: National University of Singapore Press, 2011), 94–97.
4. From March 17 to March 22, 2015, I interviewed four representatives of the Flushing Taiwanese community regarding the evolution of Taiwanese cuisine, as well as the development of Taiwanese immigration there. The first interviewee was Mr. Chenghui Chuang (莊振輝), who is perhaps most representative of the local Taiwanese culinary industry insofar as Chuang's family in 1975 opened the First Delicious One, which was the first Taiwanese restaurant in Manhattan's Chinatown. The establishment thus served as a foundation for Taiwanese restaurants in Flushing. Later on, Mr. Chuang's brother and sister ran numerous businesses in the food industry: Fuguo Company (富國食品) sold fish balls and Ginchan Supermarket (錦昌超市) was a grocery store. In Flushing, Mr. Chuang ran many Taiwanese restaurants, including Huaxian Hotpot (華鄉石頭火鍋) in the 1980s, Fuhao Seafood Restaurant (富豪海鮮餐館) in the 1990s, Ice over Fire Banquet (冰火宴), which opened in 2008, and Taipei 101 (台北101), which opened in 2011. In addition to running these restaurants, Mr. Chuang has served as chair of the Flushing Culinary Association. I also interviewed Mr. Patrick Huang (Zai-tien Huang, 黃再添) and his wife Mrs. Suqing Yang (楊淑卿), both of whom have been residing in the greater NYC area since the 1970s. The fourth interviewee was Mr. Borcheng Hsu (許伯丞), who held many pivotal positions in associations representing the greater NYC area's Taiwanese community.
5. That is, cheap by contemporary standards.
6. According to my interview with Mingsen Lu on April 9, 2016, the Japanese were the first East Asian immigrants who settled down in Flushing (around the 1970s). The majority of them were businessmen and their dependents. Two principal reasons for these immigrants' selection of Flushing were convenient transportation (the terminal station served by the number 7 Train in Flushing) and the good quality of the surroundings at that time. During the 1970s, there was also a Japanese school in Queens. Later on, owing to problems with water quality and other issues, the Japanese moved to Fort Lee, New Jersey, and White Plains, New York.
7. From March 25 to April 7, 2016, I interviewed five representatives of the Flushing Taiwanese community regarding the evolution of Taiwanese cuisine, as well as the development of Taiwanese immigration there. The first interviewee was Sam Lin (Lin Qinfu, 林慶甫), who has run Coco Bubble Tea and

Iris Tea & Bakery in NYC. The second interviewee was Cheng San Lee (李正三), who started running Japanese and Chinese restaurants in 1974 (and continues to do so to the present); the locations of his restaurants have ranged from Manhattan and the Bronx to New Jersey. I also interviewed Mingsen Lu (呂明森, also known as Morris Lee) and James Huang (Shaolong Huang, 黃紹龍). Mr. Lu ran a well-known Japanese-style restaurant named Foliage in Flushing from 1983 to 1987. Mr. Huang has run Vivi Bubble Tea and Chi-Ken Taiwanese Popcorn Chicken Store in NYC. Interestingly, Mr. Huang is a second-generation Dachen Archipelago immigrant. The Dachen islands (大陳島) fell in 1955 to Chinese communist forces immediately after the KMT supporters there were evacuated to Taiwan, with the assistance of the United States Seventh Fleet. Dachen people settled down in different regions in Taiwan and some of them moved to New York, working as chefs in Chinese restaurants. James's father was a chef working in a restaurant specializing in Zhejiang cuisine (Zhejiang being the coastal Mainland Chinese province facing the Dachen Archipelago). The last interviewee was James C. Shau (Chongcheng Shau, 蕭忠正), who was one of the cofounders of the Empire Szechuan Group of New York, a chain of restaurants serving Chinese food in NYC.

8. Any culinary knowledge and activities that emerged from Taiwan should fall under the category of Taiwanese cuisine.
9. Almost all of my interviewees agreed that the research on overseas Taiwanese communities' Taiwanese cuisine should address both the cuisine's diversity and the immigrants' diversity. It is curious to note, however, that despite originally coming from Taiwan, the owners of restaurants selling Jiangsu–Zhejiang cuisine rarely add the word "Taiwan" to their signboards.
10. Mr. Mingsen Lu arrived in New York in 1971 and remains a resident of Flushing. He served as the first director of the Flushing Chinese Business Association, so he is quite familiar with the evolution of restaurants run by Taiwanese and Chinese Mainlanders. On a historical note, most Chinese restaurants in the United States during the late nineteenth century and the early twentieth century were run by Cantonese. Interview with Mr. Mingsen Lu, April 9, 2016.
11. In fact, before settling down in New York, Mr. Lu went to Tokyo to learn interior design and came to admire Japanese culture. Thus, Mr. Lu also goes by the name "Morisan," as well as his Anglicized name "Morris Lee" and his given Chinese name.
12. According to Yu-jen Chen's and Pin-tsang Tseng's research, this "high-end elite cuisine" emerged during the Japanese colonization of Taiwan (1895–1945), specifically in Taipei City, where Taiwanese elites benefited from the city's practical location for important gatherings and where some of Taiwan's cuisine originated. Basically, this "high-end elite cuisine" is a mixture of diverse components. For example, the majority of chefs in charge of preparing this cuisine came from Fuzhou in Fujian Province, but the ingredients and the preparation of this cuisine reflect a distinct combination of southern Fujian cuisine, Cantonese cuisine, and Japanese cuisine. See Yu-jen Chen (陳玉箴), "Nation, Class, and Cultural Presentation: 'Taiwanese Cuisine'

During the Japanese Colonial Era and Early Post-war Years in Taiwan" (**食物消費中的國家、階級與文化展演：日治與戰後初期的「臺灣菜」**), *Taiwan Historical Research* 15, no. 3 (2008): 139–186; Yu-jen Chen (**陳玉箴**), "Transformations of Consumption Space under Political Transition: 'Public Canteens' and 'Liquor Houses' in Post-war Taiwan: 1945–1962" (**政權轉移下的消費空間轉型：戰後初期的公共食堂與酒家**: 1945–1962), *Journal of History, NCCU* 39 (2013): 183–229; Pin-tsang Tseng (曾品滄), "From Ping Le You (平樂遊) to the Jiangshan Building (江山樓): The Transformations of Public Spaces in Taiwan's Drinking Parlors during the Mid-Japanese Colonial Period" (1912–1937), 從「平樂遊」到「江山樓」: 日治中期台灣酒樓公共空間意涵的轉型(1912–1937), in *Commercial Traditions in Taiwan: A Comparative Perspective*, ed. Yurou Lin (林玉茹) (Taipei: Academia Sinica, 2012), 519–549.

13. The Empire Szechuan Group of New York, which was cofounded by James C. Shau, Mrs. Yafeng Chang, and other partners, was the most successful chain of Chinese food stores run by Taiwanese immigrants in New York City from 1976 to the late 1990s.
14. Countries ruled by dictatorships typically have a blacklist (in Mandarin, the term is *heimingdan*, 黑名單) identifying citizens to be targeted, harassed, and exiled. In Taiwan during the KMT's non-democratic rule, the so-called National Security Bureau would cook up charges against citizens who advocated for democracy and protested the KMT for its monopolization of political power. Of course, blacklists have also been of service in Mainland China, where the ruling Chinese Communist Party polices opponents of the regime. Perhaps the most famous types of cases concern the students, professors, and others who led the Tiananmen Square Movement in mid-1989, and one of the most famous individual cases pertains to Dan Wang (王丹), whom the Chinese government has prohibited from re-entering China since 1998.
15. In overseas Taiwanese communities, the term *ku-shiang* has been closely associated with a song called "Homeland at Dusk" ("*Huanghun de Kushiang*," 黃昏的故鄉). This song has been sung countless times by both Taiwanese exiled to the United States and Taiwanese voluntarily residing abroad.
16. Interview with Chenghui Chuang on March 17, 2015.
17. Interview with Chenghui Chuang on March 17 and 19, 2015.
18. I conducted interviews with Mr. Chuang on March 17 and 19, 2015; with Mr. Hsu on March 18, 2015; with Mr. Patrick Huang on March 20, 2015; with Mr. James Huang on April 4, 2016; and with Mr. Mingsen Lu on April 9, 2016.
19. For research on Chinese food (including chop suey) in the United States, see the following works: Andrew Coe, *Chop Suey: A Cultural History of Chinese Food in the United States* (Oxford: Oxford University Press, 2009); Yong Chen, *Chop Suey, USA: The Story of Chinese Food in America* (New York: Columbia University Press, 2014).
20. Interviews with Mr. Chuang on March 17 and 19, 2015.
21. Interview with Mr. Lu on April 9, 2016.
22. Interviews with Mr. Chuang on March 17 and 19, 2015.
23. Ibid.
24. Ibid.

25. These snacks are typically small, casual servings of food that people consume between meals, not as a meal's first course.
26. Within the dietary contexts of Chinese cuisine, there is no accurate method for distinguishing appetizers from snacks. Within the context of the fan-cai principle, any foodstuff outside the category of meals (three meals a day) belongs to the category of snacks (小吃), which can be consumed anytime in any place on casual occasions. Within the context of the present research, even though some Taiwanese restaurants categorize snacks alongside appetizers, I apply the term "snack" rather than the term "appetizer" to my discussion of all of the foodstuffs outside the three standard meals of the day because the meaning of "snack" functions more accurately than the meaning of "appetizer." As for the fan-cai principle, it is a core component of Han Chinese people's dietary culture: "fan" (飯) refers to the staple foods of rice, noodles, and steamed buns; "cai" (菜) refers to the preparatory methods of steaming, deep-frying, light-frying, pickling, icing, and salting (and even refers to serving ingredients raw). The fan-cai principle simply calls for a combination of staple foods and variously prepared additional ingredients.
27. Many of these particular snacks originally derived from the Tainan area, an ancient city built up in the Qing era (1644–1911) by Taiwanese immigrants from Fujian Province and specifically from two prefectures, Zhangzhou Prefecture (漳州府) and Quanzhou Prefecture (泉州府). Of course these snacks differ from one another, but they have some aspects in common. First, these snacks function as between-meal snacks, meaning that they can be consumed at any time during the day, without restriction. Second, the snacks are readily available, as they are not considered haute cuisine, and thus constitute foodstuff for casual dining. Third, the most prevalent ingredients in these snacks include minced pork, glutinous rice, dried seafood (shelled shrimp and squid), and flour. Basically, cooks incorporate minced pork and dried seafood into either glutinous rice or flour to form the basis of such a snack. Fourth, these snacks exemplify an inheritance from Fujian Province's dietary customs: the shaping of snacks into balls that contain the staple ingredients of pork, seafood, and vegetables and that are often steamed, sometimes in a bouillon, rendering sweet and sour flavors.
28. In General, Taiwanese have long regarded pork legs as a dish possessing strong auspicious meaning because pigs' legs are associated with courage and, by extension, wealth. In Taiwan, dishes containing pork legs, whether braised or steamed, enjoy considerable popularity. Pork legs tend to be served with thin noodles because they symbolize longevity. Thus, pork legs with thin noodles have been closely associated with people's pursuit of both longevity and good fortune (or at least the avoidance of disaster). Pork legs with thin noodles are a staple at birthday parties and at celebrations marking the resolution of some troublesome business.
29. In Taiwan, adjacent to Wangluan (萬巒) is Ligang (里港), a place known for its preparation of trotter. Both are located in southern Taiwan's Pingdong County (屏東縣). Indeed, the entire county is prized for its pig-feeding techniques. The preparatory styles associated with Wangluan trotter have involved

braising, whereas Ligang trotter is generally steamed. The former dish is popular in Taiwan.

30. Chinese Mainlanders immigrated to Taiwan with the KMT military and political establishment, led by Chiang Kai-shek, in late 1949, on the heels of the KMT's military defeat by the Chinese Communist Party's military during China's long civil war (1927–1950). These exiled Chinese Mainlanders numbered approximately 600,000, many of whom were unmarried career soldiers. After completing the voyage to Taiwan, many of these soldiers resided in haphazardly constructed semi-permanent settlements (known as "military dependents" villages, 眷村) or were scattered across Taiwan in functioning military units.
31. According to current popular perception, which is not completely accurate, Taiwan is home to four basic ethnic groups: the earliest inhabitants of the island (aboriginal Taiwanese), Fujian Taiwanese, Hakka Taiwanese, and Chinese Mainlanders. More recently, Taiwan has received Southeast Asian immigrants and younger generations of Chinese Mainlander immigrants, many of whom are women intent on marrying Taiwanese bachelors.
32. "Breakfast Section," No. 1 East Restaurant menu.
33. Over time, these sorts of breakfasts have become fairly commonplace to restaurant-goers in Taiwan (restaurants there have been serving such morning repasts for at least two or three decades). Chinese-style breakfasts are a meal of choice chiefly among Chinese Mainlanders and would have been served at small diners located, for example, on a corner of a block of residential structures in military dependents' villages or close to schools.
34. "Snacks Section," No. 1 East Restaurant menu.
35. Yaodong Lu, "An Essay on Beef Noodles," (*Lunniuroumian*, 論牛肉麵) *China Times*, February 8, 1992; Yaodong Lu, "Another Essay on Beef Noodles," (*Hailunniuroumian*, 還論牛肉麵) *China Times*, February 15, 1992; Yaodong Lu, "One More Essay on Beef Noodles," (*Zailunniuroumian*, 再論牛肉麵) *China Times*, February 22, 1992.
36. Basically, Shanghai cuisine refers to the combination of dishes based in the lower Yangtze River delta. In terms of ingredients, it is widely known for its use of aquatic foodstuffs. In terms of cooking styles, it is known for steamed, lightly stir-fried, and stewed dishes. In traditional China, the lower Yangtze River region was a place where many literati resided, and hence, many regional dishes are closely associated with literati legends.
37. "Special Cold Dishes," No. 1 East Restaurant's menu.
38. For a history of Shanghai cuisine, see Mark Swislocki, *Culinary Nostalgia: Regional Food Culture and the Urban Experience in Shanghai* (Stanford: Stanford University Press, 2009). For a background on the dietary culture of the lower Yangtze River region in early modern China (the Ming-Qing eras), see Chunghao Pio Kuo, "The Making of Food and the Cultivation of Taste in the Lower Yangtze Region from the Wanli Reign to the Qianlong Reign," Master's Thesis, National Chi Nan University, 2003.
39. "Seafood," No. 1 East Restaurant's menu.

CHAPTER 7

1. Haiming Liu, “Chop Suey as Imagined Authentic Chinese Food: The Culinary Identity of Chinese Restaurants in the United States,” *Journal of Transnational American Studies* 1, no. 1 (2009): 1–24.
2. Raymond Douglas Chong, “The Yee Clan in Santa Barbara Chinatown: A Family Legacy in Gold Mountain,” *Gum Saan Journal* (2014): 54–63.
3. Joe Distefano, “The Secrets of Cantonese Cooking, America's First Chinese Cuisine,” *Serious Eats*, October 2014: http://www.seriouseats.com/2014/10/introduction-what-is-cantonese-chinese-cuisine.html.
4. Yong Chen, *Chop Suey, USA: The Story of Chinese Food in America* (New York: Columbia University Press, 2014); Andrew Coe, *Chop Suey: A Cultural History of Chinese Food in the United States* (New York: Oxford University Press, 2009); John Jung, *Sweet and Sour: Life in Chinese Family Restaurants* (Cyprus, Calif: Yin and Yang Press, 2010).
5. Jennifer 8. Lee, *The Fortune Cookie Chronicles: Adventures in the World of Chinese Food* (New York: Twelve Books, 2008).
6. Harley Spiller, “Dining, Drinking, Dancing: At the Lion's Den,” *Flavor & Fortune* 9, no. 3 (2002): 11, 12, 27, 28, and 29.
7. Mei-Mei Ling, *Chop Suey: A Collection of Simplified Chinese Recipes Adapted for the American Home* (Honolulu: South Sea Sales, 1953).
8. Jacqueline M. Newman, “La Choy: Going on Seventy Five,” *Flavor & Fortune* 11, no. 2 (2004): 5, 32, and 33.
9. Haiming Liu, *From Canton Restaurant to Panda Express* (New Brunswick: Rutgers University Press, 2015).
10. Raymond Douglas Chong, “Kubla Khan: A Chinatown Gateway,” *Flavor & Fortune* 19, no. 4 (2012): 15–17.
11. Ibid.
12. Raymond Douglas Chong and Tony Chong Osumi, “Far East Café and China-Meshi,” *Flavor & Fortune* 16, no. 1 (2009): 15, 16, and 17.
13. Raymond Douglas Chong, “The Far East Café: A Proud Legacy in Little Tokyo,” *Gum Saan Journal* (2013): 65–75.

CHAPTER 8

1. R. G. Carroll, “Chinese Laundries Gone: Restaurants are Many,” *Los Angeles Times*, May 27, 1924, 6.
2. “Made $20,000 a Year on Chinese Viands,” *New York Times*, October 13, 1916, 16.
3. Arthur Bonner, *Alas! What Brought Thee Hither?: The Chinese in New York, 1800–1950* (Madison, N.J.: Fairleigh Dickinson University Press, 1996), 97.
4. Grace Mayer, *Once upon a City: New York from 1890 to 1910* (New York: Macmillan, 1958), 417–418.
5. Renqiu Yu, “Chop Suey: From Chinese Food to Chinese American Food,” *Chinese America: History and Perspectives* 1, no. 1 (1987): 87–99.
6. “Chinatown ‘Slumming’ Parties Are Now the Fad,” *Washington Times*, March 29, 1903, 6.

7. "Chinese Restaurants: Those Uptown Becoming Increasingly Popular with 'Bohemian' Classes," *New York Tribune Illustrated Supplement,* February 3, 1901, B6.
8. "Growing Popularity of Chop Suey," *San Francisco Chronicle*, December 31, 1912, 6.
9. "Now for a Chop Suey Union. Federation of Labor Will Try to Organize the Chinese Restaurant Workers," *Chicago Daily Tribune,* July 6, 1903, 6; "Chop Suey Trust Octopus Has Tentacles in Chicago," *Chicago Daily Tribune*, July 15, 1903, 3.
10. "The 'Yellow Peril' hits Prescott hard. Chinese Restaurant Keepers in Northern City," *Tucson Daily Citizen,* December 27, 1906; "Investigates High Cost of Chop Suey," *Boston Daily Globe*, November 18, 1920, 17; "Union to Boycott Chinese Chop Suey," *Duluth News-Tribune,* June 25, 1905, 11.
11. "Chinese Mix Sin with Chop Suey. Investigators Find Laws of Morality and Health Ignored in Many Places. WHITE GIRLS EMPLOYEES. And Boys Escorting Mere Children Are Patrons in Oriental Restaurants," *Chicago Daily Tribune,* March 27, 1910, 3.
12. "Police Capture 178 in Chop Suey Raids," *New York Times*, April 15, 1918, 8.
13. "Yee Hee, a Chinese Held. Police Believe They Have Oriental Who Lured Girls," *Kansas City Star,* April 8, 1915, 3.
14. "Philadelphia Girls Held as White Slaves in Chinese Dens. Young Women Lured to New York Cause Two Arrests Here," *Philadelphia Inquirer,* June 16, 1921, 1, 5.
15. "Drugs Jail Chinese and White Woman. Waiters Battle Agents, Who Locate $1000 in Opium in Celestial's Restaurant," *Philadelphia Inquirer*, April 23, 1921, 3.
16. Karlyn Barker, "Chinese Restaurant Owners Complain to INS about Worker Restrictions," *Washington Post*, October 18, 1988, D3.
17. Frank Ching, "Drive Seeks End to Chinese Restaurant Raids," *New York Times,* March 12, 1971, 39.
18. Lena Williams, "Chinese Say Study Hurts Restaurants: Chinese Say Food Study Has Harmful Effect on Restaurants," *New York Times*, September 29, 1993, C1.
19. Joe Sing, "MSG and Chinese Restaurants," *Flavor and Fortune* 5, no. 4 (1998): 1–9.
20. Richard D. Lyons, "'Chinese Restaurant Syndrome' Puzzles Doctors," *New York Times,* May 19, 1968, 68.
21. "Thieves Beat Chinese. Restaurant Keeper in Omaha Robbed of $100," *Idaho Statesman*, July 12, 1907, 6.
22. "Jim Sing Victim of Assassin Says Klock. Chinese Restaurant Keeper at Domingo Murdered, Probably Robbed of Considerable Money and Body Cremated," *Albuquerque Journal*, May 27, 1910, 8.
23. "Queens Restaurant Owner Slain as He Thwarts Holdup by 2 Men," *New York Times,* April 13, 1980, 37.
24. Kevin J. Mullen, "The Golden Dragon Restaurant Massacre," *Shaping San Francisco's Digital Archive @ Found SF.* http://www.foundsf.org/index.php?title=The_Golden_Dragon_Restaurant_Massacre.

25. Mark E. Vogler, "Murder Charge Reinstated in Killing of Deliveryman," *Eagle-Tribune* (North Andover, Mass.), September 19, 2011.
26. Denny Lee, "Years of the Dragons," *New York Times*, May 11, 2003; Mark Jacobson, "The (Chinese) Gangs of New York," *Mr. Beller's Neighborhood*, March 8, 2003. https://mrbellersneighborhood.com/2003/03/the-chinese-gangs-of-new-york.
27. E-mail to John Jung from Ralph Young, September 29, 2009.
28. "Dr. Dowling Closes Restaurants as Menace to Public Health. One Chinaman Defies Authority and Goes to Jail—State Board Intends to Protect Public at All Hazards," *Times-Picayune* (New Orleans, La.), February 28, 1912, 7.
29. Gary Libby, "A Chinese-American Tragedy," The Chinese and American Friendship Association of Maine. https://cafammaine.org/2008/05/30/chinese-american-tragedy/.
30. Clara Veniard, "Rural Immigrant Entrepreneurs: Chinese Restaurants in Rural New Hampshire and Vermont," Undergraduate Honors Thesis, Department of Geography, Dartmouth College, 2001.
31. "Says Girls Work 70 Hours a Week. Chinese Restaurant Proprietor is Fined $10 and Costs," *Duluth News-Tribune* (Duluth, Minn.), December 16, 1915, 9.
32. Peter Kwong, *The New Chinatown* (New York: Hill and Wang, 1996), 141–147.
33. Steven Greenhouse, "Ollie's Restaurant Workers Sue, Complaining of Underpayment," *New York Times*, March 30, 2007, B3.
34. Amy Littlefield, "Former Employees Protest Outside Chinese Restaurant in Raynham," *Taunton Daily Gazette* (Taunton, Mass.), August 26, 2010.
35. Chinese Association Progressive, "CHECK, PLEASE! Health and working conditions in San Francisco Chinatown Restaurants," 2010. http://www.cpasf.org/content/check-please-1-out-2-workers-making-below-minimum-wage.
36. Renee Frojo, "Tsing Tao Restaurants in S.F. slapped with $300K Fine over Unpaid Wages," *San Francisco Business Times*, December 7, 2012.
37. Mark Rahner, "Labor Dept. Sues 3 Restaurants Over Wages, Overtime," *Seattle Times*, February 23, 2010.

CHAPTER 9

1. "Japanese Cuisine Goes Global," *New York Times*, December 9, 2013.
2. These feelings became more intense in the 1920s. See Izumi Hirobe, "American Attitudes toward the Japanese Immigration Question, 1924–1931," *Journal of American-East Asian Relations* 2, no. 3 (1993): 275–301.
3. Much has been written on the American-Japanese cultural encounter and its consequences: Yukiko Kimura, *Issei: Japanese Immigrants in Hawaii* (Honolulu: University of Hawaii Press, 1988); Jonathan J. Okamura, *Japanese American Contemporary Experience in Hawaii* (Honolulu: University of Hawaii Press, 2002); Jonathan J. Okamura, *The Japanese American Historical Experience in Hawaii* (Dubuque: Kendall Hunt, 2010); Gary J. Okihiro, *Cane Fires: The Anti-Japanese Movement in Hawaii, 1865–1945* (Philadelphia: Temple University Press, 1992).
4. "A Small-Sized Melting Pot," *Topeka State Journal*, June 1, 1911, 4.

5. "Hawaii and Japan," *Pacific Commercial Advertiser*, November 3, 1904, 4.
6. "Korea Gets in From the Orient," *Pacific Commercial Advertiser*, September 6, 1904, 7.
7. "Japanese Store Moved to Spokane," *Whitefish Pilot*, April 25, 1912, 1.
8. William McOmie, *The Opening of Japan, 1853–1855* (Leiden, Neth.: Global Oriental, 2006).
9. For an example, see Townsend Harris, *The Complete Journal of Townsend Harris: First American Consul and Minister to Japan* (Tokyo: Tuttle, 1930).
10. For a survey of the experiences of the first Prussian mission to Japan, see Frank Jacob, "Die Eulenburg-Expedition. Preußische Direktheit trifft japanische Zurückhaltung," in *Fremdbilder–Selbstbilder. Paradigmen japanisch-deutscher Wahrnehmung (1861–2011)*, ed. Stephan Köhn (Wiesbaden: Harrassowitz, 2014), 25–40.
11. For a survey on this topic, see Noboru Umetani, *O-yatoi gaikokujin: Gaisetsu* (Tokyo: Kajima Kenkyūjo Shuppankai, 1968).
12. "Traveling in Japan," *Grange Advance*, February 7, 1877, 7.
13. Some intellectuals, such as Fukuzawa Yukichi, argued in favor of integrating bread, milk, and meat into the daily diet of soldiers, due to their nutritional value. For this discussion, see Barak Kushner, *Slurp! A Social and Culinary History of Ramen* (Leiden, Neth.: Global Oriental, 2014), 110–111.
14. "The Japanese in Hawaii," *Pacific Commercial Advertiser*, October 29, 1885, 3.
15. "Notes on the Famous Japanese Curative Waters," *Hawaiian Star*, October 3, 1896, 1. A similar evaluation was made in "Korean Rebels Are Advancing," *San Francisco Call*, March 28, 1896, 2.
16. "Japanese Importers Rise," *Hawaiian Star*, February 26, 1900, 1.
17. *Hawaiian Star*, August 15, 1900, 4.
18. "New Japanese Steamers," *New York Tribune*, August 11, 1901, 7.
19. "Hawaii Good Customer for Mainland Markets," *Evening Bulletin*, July 16, 1908, 26.
20. *Maui News*, September 3, 1910, 5.
21. "European Wives of Japanese," *Yakima Herald*, October 24, 1901, 2.
22. Kushner, *Slurp!*, 125. *Washoku* translates as Japanese food, but with a nationalist agenda.
23. John Chapman, "British Naval Estimation of Japan and Russia, 1894–1905," *On the Periphery of the Russo-Japanese War*, Part I, Suntory Center Discussion Paper No. IS/04/475 (April 2004): 17–55.
24. On the battle of Tsushima see, Frank Jacob, *Tsushima 1905: Ostasiens Trafalgar* (Paderborn, Ger.: Schöningh, 2017).
25. For the global impact of the war, see Frank Jacob, *The Russo-Japanese War and Its Shaping of the 20th Century* (London: Routledge, 2017), forthcoming.
26. "Has a Fish Diet made the Japanese Brave and Strong," *Saint Paul Globe*, September 18, 1904, 31.
27. "Japs in Training," *Wichita Daily Eagle*, May 8, 1904, 18. The same article was published in part as "Japanese Officers and Their Pay," *Valentine Democrat*, August 4, 1904, 6.
28. "Japanese Food," *The Caucasian*, January 22, 1905, 6. Also printed in *Peninsula Enterprise*, February 4, 1905, 1.

29. For a detailed discussion of Japanese food during the Russo-Japanese War, see: H.D. Miller, "The Great Sushi Craze of 1905." Available online in two parts at http://eccentricculinary.com/the-great-sushi-craze-of-1905-part-1/ and http://eccentricculinary.com/the-great-sushi-craze-of-1905-part-2/ (last accessed February 12, 2017).
30. "Fisheries of Japan," *Nebraska Advertiser*, August 11, 1905, 4.
31. "The Japanese Amidst: Their Native Surroundings," *Baxter Springs News*, January 26, 1905, 2.
32. *The Commoner*, January 26, 1906, 3. The same article was published in the *Minneapolis Journal*: "Japan and the Japanese as Seen Through the Eyes of W. J. Bryan, Our 'Round the World' Correspondent," *Minneapolis Journal*, January 21, 1906, Part II, Editorial Section, 14.
33. "Japs Adopting Our Food," *Spokane Press*, December 10, 1908, 8. The article also stated: "For many years nine tenths of the food staples used by the Japanese population of the United States were imported from Japan, but the Japanese have recently been accustoming themselves to the use of American foods, as they have accustomed themselves to the American modes of living."
34. "Foreigners in Japan," *Point Pleasant Register*, July 20, 1910, 7.
35. "Japanese Food Boxes," *Devils Lake Weekly World*, July 4, 1913, 3. The article was printed in many other newspapers as well, including: *Pacific Commercial Advertiser*, December 15, 1908, 12; *Bridgeport Evening Farmer*, October 10, 1913, 13; *Bryan Daily Eagle and Pilot*, August 9, 1913, 3; *Bismarck Daily Tribune*, July 1, 1913, 2; *The Forest Republican*, December 24, 1913, 4; *Daily Capital Journal*, August 7, 1913, 8; "The Way the Japanese Live," *Hartford Herald*, November 18, 1908, 3.
36. "Japanese Food Boxes," *Devils Lake Weekly World*, July 4, 1913, 3.
37. "Tour of the World," *Edgefield Advertiser*, August 13, 1913, 4.
38. "Shortage of Japanese Food in San Francisco," *Honolulu Star-Bulletin*, December 16, 1915, 2.
39. *Seattle Star*, September 15, 1917, 9.
40. *Honolulu Star-Bulletin*, September 20, 1917, 3.
41. "Ishii, Back in US, Says Japan Does All It Can for Us," *New-York Tribune*, April 22, 1918, 4. Similar information is featured in "Viscount Ishii Has Arrived in US" *Evening Star*, April 22, 1918, 3.
42. "Quite Another Story," *Maui News*, December 7, 1917, 3.
43. Mary Alden Hopkins, "Cooking Familiar Dishes with a Foreign Accent," *New-York Tribune*, January 14, 1917, 8.
44. "Made-In-Japan Dinner: A Real Fairyland," *Daily Missourian*, May 18, 1917, 4.
45. "Use of Chopsticks in the Orient," *Free Trader-Journal*, September 19, 1918, 6.
46. "Officers Raid a Blind Pig," *Pacific Commercial Advertiser*, September 14, 1908, 7.
47. "Fennell Took Take to Jail," *Pacific Commercial Advertiser*, August 5, 1909, 1.
48. Ibid.
49. "Little Interviews," *Honolulu Star-Bulletin*, Friday, June 30, 1916, 4.
50. "Japanese Gets Badly Tangled in Law and Cannot Get Untwisted," *Semi-Weekly Maui News*, April 25, 1922, 1.
51. Ibid.

52. "Japanese Cafe is Wrecked," *Hawaiian Star*, June 5, 1907, 1. This was not the first Japanese restaurant that was destroyed by an angry crowd in the United States. During the Russo-Japanese War, a restaurant was destroyed for being too sympathetic towards Japanese victories in the war. See, "Tumbled Through Window," *Daily Capital Journal* (Salem, Oreg.), July 28, 1904, 5. However, the case in San Francisco caused a nationwide debate in U.S. newspapers and therefore deserves attention.
53. "Secretary Metcalf's Report," *Evening Statesman*, December 18, 1906, 3.
54. "Trouble with Japanese," *Daily Ardmoreite*, May 26, 1907, 1.
55. "Further Violence in San Francisco Would Arouse the Japanese," *Hawaiian Gazette*, May 28, 1907, 1.
56. "Hoodlums and International Peace," *Pacific Commercial Advertiser* (Honolulu), June 6, 1907, 4.
57. "The Question of Japanese Immigration," *Goodwin's Weekly: A Thinking Paper for Thinking People*, September 28, 1907, 2–3.

CHAPTER 10

1. H. Darr Belmer, *Tucson Citizen*, Monday, September 5, 1977.
2. Unless specifically stated in the notes, information from named people comes directly from interviews conducted by the author between 2013 and 2016. The author is extremely grateful to all who made themselves part of this study.
3. In 1960, forty-nine area residents spoke Japanese as their native tongue. Sixty-two residents were of Japanese descent. Tucson's growth between 1950 and 1960 was explosive. See Table 21 on pp. 4–31 and Table 80 on pp. 4–101 in U.S. Department of Commerce, Bureau of the Census, *Characteristics of the Population of Arizona: Number of Inhabitants, General Population Characteristic, General Social and Economic Characteristics, and Detailed Characteristics* (Washington, D.C.: US Government Printing Office, 1963).
4. Non-Nikkei finally embraced Japanese food when sushi became popular in the 1980s.
5. *Ethnopole* is a sociological term used to describe common meeting spots or enclaves for ethnic minorities that are located geographically within a larger urban area. See Michel S. Laguerre, *The Global Ethnopolis: Chinatown, Japantown and Manilatown in American Society* (New York: St. Martin's Press, 2000), 9–12.
6. "Orienting Your Diet," "Choose Tempura," "Japanese Tempura Easily Westernized," "Chicken Teri-Yaki is Fun to Eat," and "Japan's Food is Fun to Eat," *Stars and Stripes, Pacific,* May 23, 1958, 9–11.
7. Don Schellie, "It's Tempura Time," *Tucson Citizen*, February 5, 1962, 17.
8. Given that Kazuko was from Yokosuka, she was most likely a military bride, as there was (and is) a large U.S. naval presence in the city.
9. Schellie, "It's Tempura Time," 17.
10. "Advertisement: Wilmot Inn Bamboo Room," *Tucson Daily Citizen,* September 27, 1965, 43; "Advertisement: Wilmot Inn Bamboo Room," *Tucson Daily Citizen,* September 25, 1965, 43.

11. Sue and Homer Simpson, "Open Letter," *Tucson Daily Citizen*, May 7, 1964, 46.
12. For a detailed account of the history of Chinese food in the United States, see Andrew Coe, *Chop Suey: A Cultural History of Chinese Food in the United States* (Oxford: Oxford University Press, 2009).
13. "Advertisement: Tokyo Sukiyaki," *Tucson Daily Citizen*, October 10, 1964, 20.
14. "Advertisement: Tokyo Sukiyaki," *Tucson Daily Citizen*, December 30, 1964, 11.
15. "Advertisement: Tokyo Sukiyaki," *Tucson Daily Citizen*, April 17, 1965, 12.
16. Davis-Monthan Air Force Base in Tucson, one of the nation's largest, ensured that a fair number of the city's residents had lived in Japan.
17. When interviewed, the plate was the only item Sue kept from either Tokyo Sukiyaki or Sakura-ya.
18. Homer B. Tilton, "My Dream," *Math + Science Journal* 6, no. 15 (2009): 3.
19. Many of the Nikkei restaurateurs and their employees fondly remember seeing each other around midnight at Tucson International Airport when they all would go to pick up their weekly supplies from Los Angeles Fish Company, International Marine Products, and Hawaiian Fish Company. This continued well into the mid-1990s until Los Angeles-based distributors, such as the Japanese Food Company and Nishimoto Trading Company, set up regional shipping hubs in the Phoenix area and started direct truck deliveries to the restaurants.
20. Deborah Block, "Once Weekly Japanese Food is a Gourmet a la Jukebox," *Tucson Citizen*, May 4, 1977, 20.
21. Terry Greene Sterling, "Takuni Japanese Restaurant," *Arizona Highways*, https://www.arizonahighways.com/eat-sleep/dining/tanuki-japanese-restaurant (and interview).
22. Tom and Laurie Pew, "Dining Out: Tokyo Store," *Tucson Citizen*, September 4, 1982, 11.
23. Ibid., 9.
24. Sasha Issenberg, *The Sushi Economy: Globalization and the Making of a Modern Delicacy* (New York: Penguin, 2007), 96–98.
25. Barry Hellenbrand, "From the Folks who brought You Sony Comes a Fishy Ritual in the Raw," *Chicago Tribune*, March 24, 1980.
26. David Smollar, "Sushi Classes Giving Americans New Taste," *Los Angeles Times*, November 4, 1982.
27. Julie Szekely, "Sushi: Japanese Raw Fish Dish Challenging to Prepare," *Tucson Citizen*, May 2, 1984, 1B.
28. Ibid.
29. Nobu Nakajima, owner of the Yamato Restaurant (covered later in the chapter), also similarly reminisced about having to explain each piece of sushi in detail to customers willing to try it for the first time.
30. *Teppanyaki* steakhouses are native to Japan, but not traditionally Japanese. They began after the Second World War in Kobe, Japan. The first, Misono, was designed as a fusion Japanese-Western restaurant designed to showcase western-style foods.
31. John Jennings, "Japanese Kitchen," *Tucson Citizen*, September 16, 1982, 13.
32. The review from the *Tucson Citizen* critics was not particularly glowing, who wrote that "the name Maiko means something like 'apprentice geisha,'

and that struck us as an apt metaphor for the restaurant." Of the owners, the critics write that they appeared "inexperienced" and "untutored in the ways of market research and advertising," but eventually concluded that "the food and reasonable prices make Maiko well worth a visit." Tom Pew and Laurie Pew, "Food, Prices make Maiko Worth a Visit," *Tucson Citizen,* October 6, 1984, 6.

33. The first Tucson *matsuri,* Obon, began on August 8, 1981, with the first, small Obon festival being held by the recently established Japan-America Society of Tucson in the backyard of one of its members. Japan-American Society of Tucson, "Bulletin of the Japan-American Society of Tucson 1, No. 4," Tucson, Ariz., July 1981.
34. Japan-America Society of Tucson, "Newsletter 1. No. 1," Tucson, Ariz., September 1982.
35. For instance, one of the groups that regularly participated was the Tucson L5 Society, which promoted the colonization of outer space. The L5 society, for whatever reason, often attracted Caucasians with interests in Japanese culture.
36. Japan-America Society of Tucson, "Newsletter 1, No. 2," Tucson, Ariz., November 1982.
37. Japan-America Society of Tucson, "Newsletter 2, No. 2," Tucson, Ariz., October 1983.
38. Groups that entered booths included the University of Arizona Japan Club, Celestial Sleep Shop, University Express Travel, El Con Import Shop. Pleas for flea market items can be found in Japan-America Society of Tucson, "Newsletter 3, No. 3," Tucson, Ariz., November 1984.
39. Ibid. The Minyo Dancers and Kaneta's group began to perform together at the festival in 1984. Sometime after Azeka's death in 2001, the groups combined under Kaneta. She continues to teach Japanese dance in Tucson as of this study, practicing in her restaurant on Saturdays before opening for dinner.
40. This menu is from the 1985 celebration.
41. Various, including Minoru "Min" Yanagihashi, PhD (former president and treasurer of the Japan-America Society of Tucson) in discussion with author, May 2017; "Some History and Traditionis of Oshogatsu," "Newsletter 1, No. 3"; and "Invitation to a New Year's Celebration," between 1982 and 1986 from the Japan-America Society of Tucson.
42. Attendance figures are from Barbara Bowman Blair, "Press Release: 3rd Annual 'Aki Matsuri' (Japanese Fall Festival)," October 1984 and "Third Annual Fall Festival," informational write-up by the Japan-America Society of Tucson.
43. Japan-America Society of Tucson, "Newsletter 3, No. 2," Tucson, Ariz., October 1984; Japan-America Society of Tucson, "Newsletter 3, No. 3," Tucson, Ariz., November 1984.
44. Japan-America Society of Tucson, "Newsletter 4, No. 8," Tucson, Ariz., October 1985.
45. Japan-America Society of Tucson, "Newsletter 5, No. 3," Tucson, Ariz., October 1986.
46. At this point in the interview, Nakajimi became animated and shouted "*sugoi*! (amazing!)" while raising his arms.
47. Coley Ward, "Mr. on the Move: Building an An Empire," *Tucson.com,* June 10,

2010: http://tucson.com/entertainment/dining/mr-on-the-move/article_6239e3a6-1821-5b20-8984-d38a0f6211ac.html.

48. Kristen Cook, "Mr. An's Real 'No. 1 Son' to Open Downtown Tucson Eatery," *Arizona Daily Star*, August 4, 2016: http://tucson.com/business/tucson/mr-an-s-real-no-son-to-open-downtown-tucson/article_0c3b1ee6-d6e3-519d-9003-2ec7a9464d6c.html.
49. Ibid.; Adam Borowitz, "An the Move: After a Short-Lived Retirement, Mr. An Makes Plans to Expand His Restaurant Empire," *Tucson Weekly*, March 29, 2012: http://www.tucsonweekly.com/tucson/an-the-move/Content?oid=3268856.
50. Ward, "Mr. on the Move"; Cathalena E. Burch, "Tucson's Celebrity Restaurateur Sells Sakura," *Arizona Daily Star*, July 26, 2008: http://tucson.com/business/tucson-s-celebrity-restaurateur-sells-sakura/article_9a24d9a4-5fc9-5dd8-8e93-72c0436819ea.html.

CHAPTER 11

1. Mary Jane Weedman, "The Year of Asian Hipster Cuisine," *Grubstreet* (online), July 8, 2012: http://www.grubstreet.com/2012/07/asian_hipster_cuisine.html; Adam Platt, "Where to Eat 2013," *New York Magazine*, December 24, 2012; Nancy Matsumoto, "Stinky, Spicy, and Delicious: The Radical Reinvention of Asian American Food," *The Atlantic*, July 16, 2012; Linnea Covington, "The Rise of Asian Street Food," http://www.linneacovington.com/newyork-com.
2. Pierre Bourdieu, *Distinction: A Social Critique of the Judgment of Taste* (Cambridge: Harvard University Press, 1984).
3. Josée Johnston and Shyon Baumann, *Foodies: Democracy and Distinction in the Gourmet Foodscape* (New York: Routledge, 2015); Peter Naccarato and Kathleen LeBesco, *Culinary Capital* (New York: Berg, 2012).
4. Sarah Cappeliez and Josée Johnston, "From Meat and Potatoes to 'Real-Deal' Rotis: Exploring Everyday Culinary Cosmopolitanism," *Poetics* 41, no. 5 (2013): 433–455.
5. Johnston and Baumann, *Foodies*; Isabelle De Solier, *Food and the Self: Consumption, Production and Material Culture* (New York: Bloomsbury, 2013), 145–164.
6. Naccarato and LeBesco, *Culinary Capital*, 42.
7. Sang-hyoun Pahk, "Restaurant 2.0: Bringing Online Sociality to the Streets," in *Mission Street Food: Recipes and Ideas from an Improbable Restaurant*, eds. Anthony Myint and Karen Leibowitz (San Francisco: McSweeney's, 2011).
8. Ginette Wessel, Caroline Ziemkiewicz, and Eric Sauda, "Revaluating Urban Space through Tweets: An Analysis of Twitter-Based Mobile Food Vendors and Online Communications," *New Media & Society* 18, no. 8 (2016): 1636–1656.
9. Joyce Goldstein and Dore Brown, *Inside the California Food Revolution: Thirty Years That Changed Our Culinary Consciousness* (Berkeley: University of California Press, 2013).

10. Arianne Wing and Steve Banister, *Noodles through Escargots* (Hanford, Calif.: Civic Center Alliance, 2011).
11. Ibid.; Yong Chen, *Chop Suey, USA: The Story of Chinese Food in America* (New York: Columbia University Press, 2014).
12. Johnston and Baumann, *Foodies*, 204; Anita Mannur, *Culinary Fictions: Food in South Asian Diasporic Culture* (Philadelphia: Temple University Press, 2009).
13. Quoted in Goldstein and Brown, *Inside the California Food Revolution*, 31.
14. Rachel Wharton, "Don't Call It Fusion Cuisine," *Wall Street Journal*, February 28, 2014; Nobuyuki Matsuhisa, *Nobu: The Cookbook* (New York: Kodansha International, 2013), 10.
15. Carol Mighton Haddix, *Chicago Cooks: 25 Years of Food History with Menus, Recipes and Tips from Les Dames D'escoffier Chicago* (Chicago: Surrey Books, 2007), 51.
16. Mannur, *Culinary Fictions*, 188.
17. Ming Tsai, *Blue Ginger: East Meets West Cooking with Ming Tsai* (New York: Clarkson Potter Publishers, 1999).
18. Jean-Georges Vongerichten, *Asian Flavors of Jean-Georges* (New York: Broadway Books, 2007), 3.
19. Sara Dickerman, "Fusion Reaction: How America Fell in Love, and Then out of Love, and Then in Love All Over Again, with Asian-Influenced Cuisine," *Slate*, April 12, 2012: http://www.slate.com/articles/life/food/2012/04/asian_fusion_comeback_american_s_love_hate_relationship_with_asian_inspired_cooking_.html.
20. Felipe Fernandez-Armesto, *Near a Thousand Tables: A History of Food* (New York: Free Press, 2002).
21. Wharton, "Don't Call It Fusion Cuisine."
22. Ibid.
23. Kate Heyhoe, "Kate Heyhoe Interviews Susanna Foo," https://www.foodwine.com/food/egg/egg0297/foointer.html.
24. Anita Lo and Charlotte Druckman, *Cooking without Borders* (New York: Abrams, 2011).
25. Ibid.
26. Pete Wells, "Asian Fusion, the Latest Chapter," *New York Times*, January 3, 2012.
27. Weedman, "Year of Asian Hipster Cuisine."
28. Ibid.
29. Platt, "Where to Eat 2013."
30. Ibid.
31. Ibid.
32. Georgia Kral, "NYC's Hipster Asian Restaurant Trend Continues to Spread." *amNewYork*, February 6, 2014.
33. John Birdsall, "The Diss, Updated: Calling Asian Food 'Hipster,'" *Chowhound*, July 11, 2012: http://www.chowhound.com/food-news/120771/asian-hipster-food-disrespect-grub-street/#!.
34. Adam Platt, "The Chefs That Changed America: A Decade of David Chang and April Bloomfield," *Grub Street*, July 6, 2014: http://www.grubstreet.com/2014/07/adam-platt-on-david-chang-april-bloomfield-.html.

35. Alison Pearlman, *Smart Casual: The Transformation of Gourmet Restaurant Style in America*. (Chicago: University of Chicago Press, 2013), 2.
36. John Powers, "David Chang: The Anxiety of Influence," *Vogue*, September 5, 2012; Kevin Pang, "'Regular Dude' Chef Is Not Afraid to Mix It up—and Call It Simple American Food," *Chicago Tribune*, December 23, 2009.
37. David Chang and Peter Meehan, *Momofuku* (New York: Clarkson Potter Publishers, 2009), 8.
38. Pang, "'Regular Dude' Chef."
39. Powers, "David Chang."
40. Chang and Meehan, *Momofuku*, 29.
41. Chang and Meehan, *Momofuku*; Rachel Cooke, "David Chang: New York's King of the Pork Belly Bun," *The Guardian*, November 13, 2010.
42. Chang and Meehan, *Momofuku*, 31.
43. Minette Yao, "Bun Intended," *Cleaver Quarterly* 2, no. 3 (2014): 30–38.
44. Ibid., 31.
45. Powers, "David Chang."
46. Hillary Dixler, "Examining the Momofuku Pork Bun, a 10-Year NYC Favorite," *Eater*, September 24, 2014: http://www.eater.com/2014/9/24/6827659/momofuku-pork-buns-noodle-bar-david-chang-nyc.
47. Cooke, "David Chang."
48. Rob Patronite and Robin Raisfeld, "David Chang Opens His Spicy-Fried-Chicken-Sandwich Joint, Fuku, Today" *Grub Street*, June 10, 2015: http://www.grubstreet.com/2015/06/david-chang-fuku-fried-chicken-opens.html.
49. Lucky Peach, "Inside Momofuku Nishi," *Lucky Peach*, 2016: http://luckypeach.com/inside-momofuku-nishi/.
50. Ibid.
51. Pearlman, *Smart Casual*, 2–3; Powers, "David Chang."
52. Molly Young, "29 Minutes with Danny Bowien," *New York Magazine*, June 3, 2012.
53. Brett Martin, "Danny and the Electric Kung Pao Pastrami Test," *GQ Magazine*, November 12, 2012; Jeff Gordinier, "A Chef Regains His Focus: Danny Bowien Reopens Mission Chinese Food," *New York Times*, December 23, 2014.
54. Pete Wells, "Pastrami's Strange Dream," *New York Times*, July 25, 2012.
55. John Swansburg, "Empire of the Burning Tongue: How Mission Chinese Food Perfectly Encapsulates Our Post-Lovacore Moment," *New York Magazine*, December 3, 2012.
56. Lessley Anderson, "Chinese Takeout Artist," *Chowhound*, December 1, 2010: https://www.chowhound.com/food-news/67146/chinese-takeout-artist/.
57. Anthony Myint and Karen Leibowitz, *Mission Street Food: Recipes and Ideas from an Improbable Restaurant* (San Francisco: McSweeney's 2011).
58. "The Ten Best New Restaurants in America," *GQ Magazine*, February 15, 2012.
59. Danny Bowien and Chris Ying, *The Mission Chinese Food Cookbook* (New York: Anthony Bourdain Books, 2015).
60. Gordinier, "A Chef Regains His Focus"; Layla Khabiri, "Take a Look at the New, Old-School Menu at Mission Chinese Food," *Eater New York*, December 21, 2014: http://ny.eater.com/2014/12/21/7430123/

take-a-look-at-the-new-old-school-menu-at-mission-chinese-food; Tejal Rao, "Mission Chinese Food, Review: Hot, Hot, Melt-Your-Face-Hot," *Bloomberg Pursuits*, March 3, 2015.

61. Adam Platt, "Restaurant Review: At the New Mission Chinese Food, Danny Bowien Gets a Space to Match His Ambition," *The New Yorker*, May 3, 2015.
62. Ryan Sutton, "Meet Eater Young Gun Angela Dimayuga," *Eater,* Summer 2015: https://www.eater.com/a/young-guns-summer-2015/meet-eater-young-gun-angela-dimayuga.
63. Pete Wells, "Restaurant Review: Mission Chinese Food on the Lower East Side," *New York Times*, June 10, 2015.
64. Greg Morabito, "As a Christmas Surprise, Mission Chinese Food Launches Dim Sum Brunch," *Eater New York*, December 26, 2015: https://ny.eater.com/2015/12/26/10667038/mission-chinese-brunch-nyc.
65. Pete Wells, "Restaurant Review: Mission Chinese Food on the Lower East Side," *New York Times,* June 9, 2015: https://www.nytimes.com/2015/06/10/dining/restaurant-review-mission-chinese-food-on-the-lower-east-side.html.
66. Goldstein and Brown, *Inside the California Food Revolution*, 331.
67. Jessica Gelt, "Kogi Korean BBQ, a Taco Truck Brought to You by Twitter," *Los Angeles Times*, February 11, 2009; Andrew Romano, "Thanks to Twitter, America's First Viral Eatery," *Newsweek*, February 27, 2009.
68. Romano, "Thanks to Twitter."
69. Roy Choi, Tien Nguyen, and Natasha Phan, *L.A. Son: My Life, My City, My Food* (New York: HarperCollins Publishers, 2013); Gelt, "Kogi Korean BBQ."
70. Gelt, "Kogi Korean BBQ."
71. Oliver Wang, "To Live and Dine in Kogi L.A.," *Contexts* 8, no. 4 (2009): 69–71.
72. Choi, et al., *L.A. Son*, 296.
73. Ibid., 297.
74. Jeffrey M. Pilcher, *Planet Taco: A Global History of Mexican Food* (New York: Oxford University Press, 2012), 222; Wang, "To Live and Dine," 69–71; Lok Siu, "Twenty-First-Century Food Trucks: Mobility, Social Media, and Urban Hipness," in *Eating Asian America: A Food Studies Reader*, eds. Robert Ji-Song Ku, Martin F. Manalansan IV, and Anita Mannur (New York: New York University Press, 2013), 231–244.
75. Wang, "To Live and Dine," 69–71; Pilcher, *Planet Taco*, 222.
76. Jonathan Gold, "L.A. Restaurant Review: Chego the Sequel Opens with Familiar Pan-Asian Flavors," *Los Angeles Times*, July 5, 2013.
77. Chego, "About," http://eatchego.com.
78. Lesley Bargar Suter, "Roy Choi Turns a-Frame into a Hawaiian Paradise," *Los Angeles Magazine*, January 12, 2015.
79. Ibid.
80. A-Frame, "About," http://www.aframela.com.
81. Gold, "L.A. Restaurant Review."
82. Talde, "About," http://www.taldebrooklyn.com/about; Dale Talde and J.J. Goode, *Asian-American: Proudly Inauthentic Recipes from the Philippines to Brooklyn* (New York: L&S, 2015).

83. Talde, "About."
84. Talde and Goode, *Asian-American*, 19.
85. Johnston and Baumann, *Foodies*; Mannur, *Culinary Fictions*; Pilcher, *Planet Taco*, 222.
86. Laine Doss, "Talde at Thompson Miami Beach: 'You Build on Locals,'" *Miami New Times*, March 4 2015.
87. Condé Nast Traveler Editors, "19 Best Restaurants in Chicago," May 15, 2017: http://www.cntraveler.com/gallery/best-restaurants-in-chicago.
88. AvroKo, "Duck Duck Goat": http://www.avroko.com/blog/projects/duck-duck-goat.
89. Andy Ricker and J.J. Goode, *Pok Pok* (Berkeley: Ten Speed Press, 2013).
90. Chris Crowley, "How Chefs Embraced Global Techniques and Ingredients and Discovered a More Authentic Approach to 'Fusion Cuisine,'" *Grub Street*, April 18, 2017: http://www.grubstreet.com/2017/04/how-asian-american-chefs-are-creating-a-new-better-fusion.html.
91. Matsumoto, "Stinky, Spicy, and Delicious."
92. Marguerite Preston, "Leah Cohen on Pig & Khao's Dramatic First Year," *Eater New York*, October 11, 2013.
93. Christopher Koetke, "Embeya Chef Incorporates Training, Heritage, into His Cooking," *Chicago Tribune*, November 24, 2014.
94. Brad Weiss, "Configuring the Authentic Value of Real Food: Farm-to-Fork, Snout-to-Tail, and Local Food Movements," *American Ethnologist* 39, no. 3 (2012): 614–626.
95. Katy McLaughlin, "Recipe for an Outrageous Cookbook," *Wall Street Journal*, October 29, 2009.
96. "Baoburg, Modernist French Cuisine in Williamsburg, Launches a Weekday Brunch with New Items," *PRWeb*, May 6, 2014: http://www.prweb.com/releases/2014/05/prweb11814395.htm.
97. Ruth Brown, "Restaurant Guide 2012: Aviary, Restaurant of the Year," *Willamette Week*, October 23, 2012.
98. David Chang, "Foreword," in *Benu* by Corey Lee (New York: Phaedon Press, 2015), 16–17.
99. Lee, *Benu*, 23.
100. Paula Young Lee, "The Kimchi Revolution: How Korean-American Chefs Are Changing Food Culture," *Salon*, April 7, 2014: http://www.salon.com/2014/04/07/the_kimchi_revolution_how_korean_american_chefs_are_changing_food_culture.
101. Ibid.
102. Anthony Bourdain, "Foreword," in *The Mission Chinese Cookbook*, eds. Danny Bowien and Chris Ying (New York: HarperCollins, 2015), xi.
103. Amy Hanser and Zachary Hyde, "Foodies Remaking Cities," *Context* 13, no. 3 (2014): 44–49.
104. Adam Platt, "Where to Eat 2015," *New York Magazine*, December 12, 2014.
105. Sharon Zukin, *Naked City: The Death and Life of Authentic Urban Places* (New York: Oxford University Press, 2010); Sharon Zukin, "Consuming Authenticity: From the Outposts of Difference to Means of Exclusion," *Cultural Studies* 22, no. 5 (2006): 724–748.

CHAPTER 12

1. "The Best Burger in New York," *How I Met Your Mother*, Season 4, Episode 2, dir. Pamela Fryman, September 29, 2008.
2. Mita Banerjee, "Pork Chops and *alu gobi*: The (Un)Translatability of Culture in Mukherjee's *Jasmine*," in *Holding Their Own: Perspectives on the Multi-Ethnic Literatures of the United States*, eds. Dorothea Fischer-Hornung and Heike Raphael-Hernandez (Tübingen: Stauffenburg, 2000), 145. For culinary difference, see Linda Keller Brown and Kay Mussell, "Introduction," in *Ethnic and Regional Foodways in the United States: The Performance of Group Identity*, ed. Linda Keller Brown and Kay Mussell (Knoxville: University of Tennessee Press, 1984), 3–36.
3. In her study *The Chutneyfication of History*, Mita Banerjee uses the metaphor of the chutney, "an Indian relish made of fruit or vegetables, sugar, vinegar and spices" (9), to point to the uniqueness not only of each chutney, but to the idea that "the chutney, in the sense of a fictional version of history, is necessarily unique, even idiosyncratic" (9–10). Mita Banerjee, *The Chutneyfication of History: Salman Rushdie, Michael Ondaatje, Bharati Mukherjee and the Postcolonial Debate* (Heidelberg: Winter, 2002). For more information on contact zones, see Mary Louise Pratt, *Imperial Eyes: Travel Writing and Transculturation* (New York: Routledge, 2008).
4. Anita Mannur, "Culinary Nostalgia: Authenticity, Nationalism, and Diaspora," *MELUS* 32, no. 4 (2007): 11–31.
5. Michel Foucault, "Of Other Spaces," 1984, trans. Jay Miskowiec, *Diacritics* 16 (1986): 22–27.
6. Maria N. Ng, "Chop Suey Writing: Sui Sin Far, Wayson Choy, and Judy Fong Bates." *Essays on Canadian Writing* 65 (1998): 171–186. This essay was only available as an HTML file. Therefore, no page number can be attributed to the quote.
7. Edward Said considers "Orientalism as a discourse" that is "a Western style for dominating, restructuring, and having authority over the Orient." Edward Said, *Orientalism*, 1978 (New York: Vintage, 1994), 3.
8. Ruth Maxey, "'The East Is Where Things Begin': Writing the Ancestral Homeland in Amy Tan and Maxine Hong Kingston," *Orbis Litterarum* 60 (2005): 1–15.
9. Lisa Lau, "The Perpetuation and Development of Orientalism by Orientals," *Modern Asian Studies* 43 (2009): 571–590; 571.
10. "Stirring the Pot: The Future of Chinese Cuisine in the US," San Francisco, Youtube.com, Web June 18, 2012. https://www.youtube.com/watch?v=4VAXbl2CeoA.
11. Ralph Ellison, *Invisible Man* (1952; New York: Vintage, 1989), 266.
12. Saul-ling Cynthia Wong, *Reading Asian American Literature: From Necessity to Extravagance* (Princeton: Princeton University Press, 1993), 18; Claude Lévi-Strauss, "The Culinary Triangle," in *Food and Culture: A Reader*, eds. Carole Counihan and Penny van Esterik, 1997 (New York: Routledge, 2008), 36–43.
13. Roland Barthes, "Le bifteck et les frites," in *Mythologies*, (Paris: Éditions du Seuil, 1957), 72–74.

14. Ibid., 74.
15. Eileen Chia-Ching Fung, "Introduction to the Special Issue: Teaching Food and Foodways in Asian American Literature and Popular Culture," *Asian American Literature: Discourses and Pedagogies* 2 (2011): i–iii.
16. Wenying Xu, *Eating Identities: Reading Food in Asian American Literature* (Honolulu: University of Hawai'i Press, 2008), 12.
17. Wong, *Reading Asian American Literature*, 56.
18. Xu, *Eating Identities*, 8.
19. *Asian* is an umbrella term covering a large number of ethnic and national groups from Asia and will be specified in the selected texts to be discussed.
20. Stephanie Chan, "Review: Wenying Xu. *Eating Identities: Reading Food in Asian American Literature*. Honolulu: U of Hawai'i P, 2008," *Asian American Literature: Discourses and Pedagogies* 2 (2011): 77.
21. Mervyn Nicholson, "Eat–or Be Eaten: An Interdisciplinary Metaphor," *Mosaic* 24 nos.3–4 (1991): 191.
22. Donna Gabaccia, *We Are What We Eat: Ethnic Food and the Making of Americans* (Cambridge: Harvard University Press, 2000); Lily Cho, *Eating Chinese: Culture on the Menu in Small Town Canada* (Toronto: University of Toronto Press, 2010), 13.
23. Roland Barthes, "Toward a Psychosociology of Contemporary Food Consumption" (1961), in *Food and Culture: A Reader*, eds. Carole Counihan and Penny van Esterik, 1997 (New York: Routledge, 2008), 29.
24. Michelle Cliff, *No Telephone to Heaven*, 1987 (New York: Vintage, 1989), 75.
25. Tobias Döring, Markus Heide, and Susanne Mühleisen, "Writing/Eating Culture," in *Eating Culture: The Poetics and Politics of Food*, eds. Tobias Döring, Markus Heide, and Susanne Mühleisen (Heidelberg: Winter, 2003), 2.
26. Eric Hobsbawm and Terence Ranger, eds., *The Invention of Tradition*, 1983 (Cambridge: Cambridge University Press, 1984).
27. Susan Kalčik, "Ethnic Foodways in America: Symbol and the Performance of Identity," in *Ethnic and Regional Foodways in the United States: The Performance of Group Identity*, eds. Linda Keller Brown and Kay Mussell (Knoxville: University of Tennessee Press, 1984), 37.
28. This is not the case for my literary examples. A good example is Bharati Mukherjee's *Jasmine* (1990), in which the protagonist seems to be "an add-on, 'jazzing up' mainstream kitchens" (Banerjee, "Pork Chops," 148). Jasmine believes that "ethnicity can never be American" (Banerjee, "Pork Chops," 149).
29. Döring, Heide, and Mühleisen, "Writing/Eating Culture," 7.
30. Benedict Anderson, *Imagined Communities: Reflections on the Origin and Spread of Nationalism* (London: Verso, 1983). Benedict Anderson uses the phrase "imagined community" because "the members of even the smallest nation will never know most of their fellow-members, meet them, or even hear of them, yet in the minds of each lives the image of their communion" (6). In the case of Asian immigrants to North America, the term "community" and "imagined" are twofold: the community that is imagined in my literary examples is, on the one hand, that of the people with the same ethno-national background, living in a diaspora, and, on the other hand, that of the actual nation of the past to which the immigrants still feel connected.

These communities are imagined, first, because, as Anderson implies, none of the people will ever know all the members; second, it is only the assumption of national and ethnic identity that allows for such a creation; and, third, the idea of belonging to a nation in the past was already imagined at the moment of departure. Thus, none of these communities actually exists, but are imagined and seemingly stabilized and kept alive through the creation and perpetuation of rituals, predominantly in reference to foodways often accompanying celebrations.

31. Nicole Waller, "Past and Repast: Food as Historiography in Fae Myenne Ng's *Bone* and Frank Chin's *Donald Duk*," *Amerikastudien/American Studies* 40, no. 3 (1995): 485–486.
32. See Cuban sociologist Fernando Ortiz and his study *Cuban Counterpoint: Sugar and Tobacco*, trans. Harriet de Onís (New York: Alfred A. Knopf, Inc., 1947) and Carmen Birkle, *Migration—Miscegenation—Transculturation: Writing Multicultural America into the Twentieth Century* (Heidelberg: Winter, 2004).
33. Soja considers spatiality as socially constructed through the interaction between human beings and space. His Thirdspace is not the sum of two spaces (Firstspace and Secondspace) but the product of their interaction. Therefore, while still recognizable, the original spaces produce a new and, thus, Thirdspace. See Edward Soja, *Thirdspace: Journeys to Los Angeles and Other Real-and-Imagined Places* (Oxford: Blackwell, 1996).
34. "Thus we can hope to discover for each specific case how the cooking of a society is a language in which it unconsciously translates its structure–or else resigns itself, still unconsciously, to revealing its contradictions" (Lévi-Strauss, "The Culinary Triangle," 43).
35. Wong, *Reading Asian American Literature*, 57.
36. Cho, *Eating Chinese*, 132.
37. Gabaccia, *We Are What We Eat*, 103.
38. Wong, *Reading Asian American Literature*, 35.
39. See also his short story "Food for All His Dead" (1962), and on food pornography see his play *The Year of the Dragon* (1981; first produced 1974).
40. Frank Chin, *Donald Duk*, 1991 (Minneapolis: Coffee House Press, 1997).
41. Eileen Chia-Ching Fung, "'To Eat the Flesh of His Dead Mother': Hunger, Masculinity, and Nationalism in Frank Chin's *Donald Duk*," *Lit: Literature Interpretation Theory* 10, no. 3 (1999): 256.
42. Chin, *Donald Duk*, 64.
43. Fred Wah, *Diamond Grill*, 1996 (Edmonton, Alberta: NeWest Press, 2006), 179.
44. Ibid., 2.
45. Cynthia Sugars quoted in Joanne Saul, "'Auto-hyphen-ethno-hyphen-graphy': Fred Wah's Creative-Critical Writing," in *Asian Canadian Writing beyond Autoethnography*, eds. Eleanor Ty and Christl Verduyn (Waterloo, Ont.: Wilfrid Laurier University Press, 2008), 147.
46. Chin, *Donald Duk*, 63.
47. Ibid., 64.
48. Ibid.

49. Horace Kallen, *Culture and Democracy in the United States: Studies in the Group Psychology of the American Peoples* (New York: Boni and Liveright, 1924), 116, 124.
50. Chin, *Donald Duk*, 9.
51. Ibid., 1.
52. Ibid., 2.
53. Ibid., 42.
54. Fung, "'To Eat the Flesh of His Dead Mother,'" 262.
55. Chin, *Donald Duk*, 163.
56. Ibid., 1.
57. Ibid., 7.
58. Ibid., 172.
59. Wenying Xu, "Masculinity, Food, and Appetite in Frank Chin's *Donald Duk* and 'The Eat and Run Midnight People,'" *Cultural Critique* 66 (2007): 78.
60. Ibid., 83.
61. Ibid., 99.
62. M. Elaine Mar, *Paper Daughter: A Novel* (New York: Perennial, 2000), 50.
63. Ibid., 51.
64. Ibid., 161.
65. Ibid., 228.
66. Ibid., 52.
67. Ibid., 53.
68. Ibid., 172.
69. Ibid., 177.
70. Ibid., 178.
71. Ibid., 180.
72. Ibid., 225.
73. Ibid., 250.
74. Ibid., 250–251.
75. Roxanne N. Rashedi, "Disordered Eating, Agency, and Social Class: Elaine Mar's *Paper Daughter*," *Asian American Literature: Discourses and Pedagogies* 2 (2011): 38–44.
76. Kurt Dittmar, "Jüdische Ghettoliteratur: Die Lower East Side, 1890–1924," in *Amerikanische Ghettoliteratur: Zur Literatur ethnischer, marginaler und unterdrückter Gruppen*, ed. Berndt Ostendorf (Darmstadt: Wissenschaftliche Buchgesellschaft, 1983), 54.
77. Mar, *Paper Daughter*, viii–ix.
78. Amy Tan, *The Joy Luck Club* (New York: Ivy, 1989).
79. The daughters do not speak Chinese well; their mothers cannot express their tragedies in English but only in Chinese, and through rituals in which story-telling becomes an important task. In Kweilin, where they escaped from the Japanese, the Joy Luck Club became a means of survival.
80. Andrew Edgar, "Ritual," in *Key Concepts in Cultural Theory*, eds. Andrew Edgar and Peter Sedgwick (London: Routledge, 1999), 340–341.
81. Tan, *Joy Luck Club*, 21.
82. Robley Evans, "'Or Else This Were a Savage Spectacle': Eating and Troping Southern Culture," *Southern Quarterly* 30, nos. 2–3 (1992): 141.

83. Evans, "'Or Else This Were a Savage Spectacle,'" 141.
84. Ibid.; Barthes, "Toward a Psychosociology of Contemporary Food Consumption," 30.
85. Tan, *Joy Luck Club*, 195.
86. Ibid., 196.
87. William Boelhower quoted in Wong, *Reading Asian American Literature*, 70.
88. Tan, *Joy Luck Club*, 197.
89. Ibid., 95.
90. "[C]ultural self-empowerment" is achieved through Chinese traditions which, at the same time, could be considered "self-orientalizing tendencies" (Maxey, "'The East Is Where Things Begin,'" 1).
91. Evans, "'Or Else This Were a Savage Spectacle,'" 142.
92. Mary Douglas quoted in Wong, *Reading Asian American Literature*, 76.
93. Tan, *Joy Luck Club*, 40–41.
94. Ibid., 31.
95. Wong, *Reading Asian American Literature*, 31.
96. See also Fae Myenne Ng's "A Red Sweater," *American Voice* 4 (1986): 48–56; and Maxine Hong Kingston's *The Woman Warrior* (New York: Knopf, 1976).
97. Elizabeth Wong, *Kimchee and Chitlins* (1994), in *But Still, Like Air, I'll Rise: New Asian American Plays*, ed. Velina Hasu Houston (Philadelphia: Temple University Press, 1997), 395–450. "The controversial 1990 boycott of Korean American-owned stores in New York and the 1992 social upheaval most commonly known as the Los Angeles riots stand as two of the most prominent examples of interracial tensions between minorities, and specifically between African Americans and Asian Americans, in the United States." Ju Yon Kim, "The Difference a Smile Can Make: Interracial Conflict and Cross-Racial Performance in *Kimchee and Chitlins*," *Modern Drama* 53, no. 4 (2010): 533.
98. The term "chitlins" derives from "chitterlings," which are pork innards, hog bowels, or intestines.
99. Wong, *Kimchee and Chitlins*, 410.
100. Ibid., 444.
101. Ibid., 411.
102. Waller, "Past and Repast," 490.
103. Ibid., 491.
104. Salman Rushdie, "Imaginary Homelands" (1982) in *Imaginary Homelands: Essays and Criticism 1981–1991* (London: Granta, 1991), 9–21.
105. Barthes, "Toward a Psychosociology of Contemporary Food Consumption," 31.
106. Gabaccia, *We Are What We Eat*, 9.
107. Ellison, *Invisible Man*, 266.
108. Anita Mannur, *Culinary Fictions: Food in South Asian Diasporic Culture* (Philadelphia: Temple University Press, 2010), 20.
109. The Obama Sushi rolls were created by Ken Kawasumi at the Tokyo Sushi Academy. See R. Mansur, "Eat Obama," *Wonder How to Sushi*, Feb. 19, 2015, https://sushi.wonderhowto.com/news/eat-Obama-0117599/ (accessed Nov. 19, 2017).

CHAPTER 13

1. The expression appears in Herbert Asbury, *The Barbary Coast: An Informal History of the San Francisco Underworld* (New York: A.A. Knopf, 1933).
2. Tellingly, *Flower Drum Song*'s (1961) "Chop Suey"—an all-out musical homage to the dish—gives full credit to American inventiveness for the creation of the dish. Sung by Chinese American characters, the lyrics consist of an enumeration of American popular culture symbols.
3. Kwei Chen, "Chinese Definitions of Chinese Words," *American Speech* 2, no. 9 (1927): 416.
4. Ronald Takaki, *Strangers from a Different Shore: A History of Asian Americans* (Boston: Little, Brown, 1989); Haiming Liu, "Chop Suey as Imagined Authentic Chinese Food: The Culinary Identity of Chinese Restaurants in the United States," *Journal of Transnational American Studies* 1, no. 1 (2009): 1–24.
5. Harley Spiller, "Late Night in the Lion's Den: Chinese Restaurant-Nightclubs in 1940s San Francisco," *Gastronomica—The Journal of Food and Culture* 4 (2004): 94.
6. Esther Kim Lee, *A History of Asian American Theatre* (Cambridge: Cambridge University Press, 2006).
7. Andrew Coe, *Chop Suey: A Cultural History of Chinese Food in the United States* (Oxford: Oxford University Press, 2009).
8. Samantha Barbas, "'I'll Take Chop Suey': Restaurants as Agents of Culinary and Cultural Change," *Journal of Popular Culture* 36 (2003): 684.
9. Jinhee Choi, "National Cinema, the Very Idea," in *Philosophy of Film and Motion Pictures: An Anthology*, eds. Noël Carroll and Jinhee Choi (Malden, Mass.: Blackwell, 2006).
10. Anthony Wall, "Contradictory Pieces of Time and History," in *After Poststructuralism: Writing the Intellectual History of Theory*, eds. Tilottama Rajan and Michael J. O'Driscoll (Toronto: University of Toronto Press, 2002), 205.
11. Mikhail Bakhtin, *The Dialogic Imagination: Four Essays by M.M. Bakhtin*, eds. C. Emerson and M. Holquist, trans. M. Holquist (Austin: University of Texas Press, 1981), 84.
12. Ibid., 425–426.
13. Ibid., 253; Eduard Vlasov, "The World According to Bakhtin: On the Description of Space and Spatial Forms in Mikhail Bakhtin's Works," *Canadian Slavonic Papers/Revue Canadienne des Slavistes* 37, nos. 1–2 (1995): 378.
14. Michael Montgomery, *Carnivals and Commonplaces: Bakhtin's Chronotope, Cultural Studies, and Film* (New York: Peter Lang, 1993); Robert Stam, *Subversive Pleasures: Bakhtin, Cultural Criticism, and Film* (Baltimore: Johns Hopkins University Press, 1989); Joy Ladin, "Fleshing Out the Chronotope," in *Critical Essays on Mikhail Bakhtin*, ed. C. Emerson (New York: G.K. Hall, 1999), 212–236.
15. Ladin, "Fleshing Out," 218–219.
16. Ibid., 219.
17. Robert Warshow, *The Immediate Experience: Movies, Comics, Theatre and*

Other Aspects of Popular Culture (Cambridge: Harvard University Press, 2002).

18. David E. Ruth, *Inventing the Public Enemy: The Gangster in American Culture: 1918–1934* (Chicago: University of Chicago Press, 1996), 5.
19. See, for instance, Jonathan Munby, *Public Enemies, Public Heroes: Screening the Gangster from Little Caesar to Touch of Evil* (Chicago: University of Chicago Press, 1999).
20. Martha Nochimson, *Dying to Belong: Gangster Movies in Hollywood and Hong Kong* (Malden, Mass.: Blackwell, 2007), 6.
21. This interpretation is, therefore, diametrically opposed to Robert Warshow's, who claims the gangster to be "expressing that part of the American psyche which rejects the qualities and the demands of modern life, which rejects 'Americanism' itself" (Warshow, *Immediate Experience*, 100).
22. On the inclusivity of the chop suey joint, see Haiming Liu, *From Canton Restaurants to Panda Express: A History of Chinese Food in the United States* (New Brunswick: Rutgers University Press, 2015), 56.
23. Rebecca L. Epstein, "Appetite for Destruction: Gangster Food and Genre Convention in Quentin Tarantino's *Pulp Fiction*," in *Reel Food: Essays on Food and Film*, ed. Anne L. Bower (New York: Routledge, 2004), 197.
24. June's attitude towards boundaries is visually represented when, looking for a job, she literally steps into it, jumping behind the counter and starting to work without having been hired.
25. Lukas merely mimics what passes for Cantonese in the movie.
26. Ladin, "Fleshing Out," 230.
27. Asif Agha, "Recombinant Selves in Mass Mediated Spacetime," *Language and Communication* 27 (2007): 320–335.
28. When food is present, it generally serves to connote either class—poverty and hunger (*Beauty and the Boss* [1932]) or excessive opulence, ethnicity (spaghetti, beer), or both, as in the case of hot dogs, a symbol of middle-class American entertainment (*Central Park* [1932], *Change of Heart* [1934]).
29. Vince and Jules both have a strong aversive reaction when Vince mentions Europeans' habit of eating their fries with mayo rather than ketchup. Rebecca L. Epstein, "Appetite for Destruction."
30. Helene A. Shugart, "Sumptuous Texts: Consuming 'Otherness' in the Food Film Genre," *Critical Studies in Media Communication* 25, no. 1 (2008): 68–90; see also Diane Negra, "Ethnic Food Fetishism, Whiteness, and Nostalgia in Recent Film and Television" *Velvet Light Trap* 50 (2002): 62.
31. Paul Rozin, "The Selection of Food by Rats, Humans and Other Animals," in *Advances in the Study of Behavior*, vol. 6, eds. J. Rosenblatt, R.A. Hinde, C. Beer and E. Shaw (New York: Academic Press, 1976), 21–76; Claude Fischler, "Food Self and Identity," *Social Science Information* 27 (1988): 275–293.
32. Anne L. Bower, "Watching Food: The Production of Food, Film, and Values," in *Reel Food*, 1.
33. Laura U. Marks, *The Skin of the Film: Intercultural Cinema, Embodiment, and the Senses* (Durham: Duke University Press, 2000), back jacket.
34. Ibid., 153.

35. Jennifer Jensen Wallach, *How America Eats: A Social History of US Food and Culture* (Lanham: Rowman & Littlefield Publishers, 2013), 172–173.
36. Ibid., xi.

CHAPTER 14

1. Christopher W. Podeschi, "From Earth to Cosmos: Environmental Sociology and Images of the Future in Science Fiction Films," in *Cinematic Sociology: Social Life in Film*, eds. Jean-Anne Sutherland and Kathryn Feltey (Thousand Oaks, Calif.: Pine Forge Press, 2010), 237–252 (241).
2. Isiah Lavender III, *Race in American Science Fiction* (Bloomington: Indiana University Press, 2011), 8.
3. Ibid., 8.
4. Stephen Hong Sohn, "Introduction: Alien/Asian: Imagining the Racialized Future," *MELUS* 33, no. 4 (2008): 6.
5. Lavender III, *Race in American Science Fiction*, 14; Sharon DeGraw, *The Subject of Race in American Science Fiction* (New York: Routledge, 2007), 4–5; Betsy Huang, *Contesting Genres in Contemporary Asian American Fiction* (New York: Palgrave Macmillan, 2010), 9.
6. Jason Haslam, *Gender, Race, and American Science Fiction: Reflections on Fantastic Identities* (New York: Routledge, 2015), 74.
7. Edward W. Said, *Orientalism* (New York: Vintage, 1979), 7.
8. Lavender III, *Race in American Science Fiction*, 13. For lengthier discussions of the spread of yellow-peril messages in early SF, see the following publications: Christopher Frayling, *The Yellow Peril: Dr. Fu Manchu & The Rise of Chinaphobia* (New York: Thames & Hudson, 2014); DeGraw, *The Subject of Race in American Science Fiction;* Patrick B. Sharp, *Savage Perils: Racial Frontiers and Nuclear Apocalypse in American Culture* (Norman: University of Oklahoma Press, 2007); and Haslam, *Gender, Race, and American Science Fiction.*
9. Betsy Huang, "Premodern Orientalist Science Fictions," *MELUS* 33, no. 4 (2008): 24.
10. Jennifer Ann Ho, *Consumption and Identity in Asian American Coming-of-Age Novels* (New York: Routledge, 2005), 18; Robert Ji-Song Ku, Martin F. Manalansan IV, and Anita Mannur "An Alimentary Introduction" in *Eating Asian America: A Food Studies Reader*, eds. Robert Ji-Song Ku, Martin F. Manalansan IV, and Anita Mannur (New York: New York University Press, 2013), 5.
11. See Laurel Forster, "Futuristic Foodways: The Metaphorical Meaning of Food in Science Fiction Film," in *Reel Food: Essays on Food and Film*, ed. Anne L. Bower (New York: Routledge, 2004), 251–265; and Jean P. Retzinger, "Speculative Visions and Imaginary Meals: Food and the Environment in (Post-Apocalyptic) Science Fiction Films," *Cultural Studies* 22, nos. 3–4 (2008): 369–390.
12. Fran Wilde, Benjanun Sriduangkaew, Rochita Loenen-Ruiz, Ann Leckie, Aliette de Bodard, and Elizabeth Bear, "Food of the Future," *TOR.com:*

Science Fiction, Fantasy, the Universe, and Related Subjects, last modified January 30, 2014. Retrieved January 30, 2016. http://www.tor.com/2014/01/30/food-of-the-future-roundtable/.

13. Martha Jay, "Noodles: The Food of the Future?" *Accounting for Taste: Adventures in the Culture, History and Meanings of Food* (blog), last modified July 2, 2012. Retrieved January 30, 2016. http://accounting4taste.blogspot.com/2012/07/noodles-food-of-future.html.
14. *Soylent Green* (1973) is a SF film that depicts a nutritious wafer for consumption in a dystopian future. Reputedly made out of high-energy plankton from the ocean, it is later discovered that soylent green is made of human corpses. Significant to the arguments presented in this chapter, some have traced *Soylent Green*'s narrative to the short story *A Madman's Diary* (1918) written by Lu Xun, who is known as "the father of modern Chinese literature." See Robert Ji-Song Ku, *Dubious Gastronomy: The Cultural Politics of Eating Asian in the USA* (Honolulu: University of Hawai'i Press, 2014), 125.
15. Jason Sheehan, "Food in Science Fiction: In the Future We Will All Eat Lasers," NPR: WAMC Northeast Public Radio. Last modified July 13, 2013. Retrieved January 30, 2016. http://www.npr.org/2013/07/13/201181637/food-in-science-fiction-in-the-future-we-will-all-eat-lasers.
16. Retzinger, "Speculative Visions," 383.
17. Shun Lu and Gary Alan Fine, "The Presentation of Ethnic Authenticity: Chinese Food as a Social Accomplishment," *Sociological Quarterly* 36, no. 3 (1995): 539.
18. *The Lost Boys*, directed by Joel Schumacher (1987; Burbank, Calif: Warner Bros. Entertainment, 2015), DVD. While this film may not be viewed by some as SF, I argue these types of stories are located within one of SF's central themes—transformation; additionally, it is certainly part of the SF-adjacent fantasy genre.
19. Thank you very much to Warner Bros. Entertainment Inc. for the permission to reprint dialogue excerpts from *The Lost Boys*.
20. *Titan A.E.*, directed by Don Bluth, Gary Goldman, and Art Vitello (Los Angeles: 20th Century Fox, 2000), DVD.
21. Forster, "Futuristic Foodways," 264.
22. Yong Chen, *Chop Suey, USA: The Story of Chinese Food in America* (New York: Columbia University Press, 2014), 14; Wenying Xu, *Eating Identities: Reading Food and Asian American Literature* (Honolulu: University of Hawai'i Press, 2008), 8; Andrew Coe, *Chop Suey: A Cultural History of Chinese Food in the United States* (New York: Oxford University Press, 2009), 125; Ku, *Dubious Gastronomy*, 76–77.
23. *Men in Black* 3, directed by Barry Sonnenfeld (Culver City, Calif.: Columbia Pictures/Sony Pictures Home Entertainment, 2012), DVD.
24. *The Fifth Element*, directed by Luc Besson (1997; Culver City, Calif.: Columbia TriStar Home Entertainment, 2005), DVD.
25. *Blade Runner*, directed by Ridley Scott (1982; Burbank: Warner Bros, 1991), DVD (Director's Cut).
26. While the five films discussed in this chapter are used as examples of orientalism in SF, there are many more SF films that include Asian food, chefs, and

restaurants clearly depicted within or at least mentioned by central characters. These include *John Dies at the End* (2012), *Prometheus* (2012), *Cloud Atlas* (2012), *Push* (2009), *Sunshine* (2007), *Code 46* (2003), and *The Matrix* (1999), among others.

27. *Men in Black 3* is the exception to an all-white primary cast, where one of the two lead actors is played by an African American.
28. Scout, "Why Everyone Films at the Same Damn New York Chinese Restaurant," *Scouting NY*, last modified January 14, 2013. Retrieved January 30, 2016. http://www.scoutingny.com/why-everyone-films-at-the-same-new-york-chinese-restaurant/.
29. Said, *Orientalism*, 59.
30. For a few examples among many, see Forster, "Futuristic Foodways," 260; Retzinger, "Speculative Visions," 375; Timothy Yu, "Oriental Cities, Postmodern Futures: *Naked Lunch*, *Blade Runner*, and *Neuromancer*," *MELUS* 33, no. 4 (2008): 54–60; Jane Chi Hyun Park, *Yellow Future: Oriental Style in Hollywood Cinema* (Minneapolis: University of Minnesota Press, 2010), 51–81; and Adilifu Nama, *Black Space: Imagining Race in Science Fiction Film* (Austin: University of Texas Press, 2008), 58–60.
31. Yu, "Oriental Cities," 48.
32. See Park, *Yellow Future*, 64; and Nama, *Black Space*, 59, for full discussion of city living layout in *Blade Runner*.
33. Nama, *Black Space*, 58.
34. Asian chefs' quotes in this chapter are direct, in some cases adopted from closed-captioning when necessary, including missing words, mispronunciations, and replaced letters, each indicating English as a second language. This particular quote has been reproduced in numerous publications, indicating significant importance to the exchange.
35. Jennifer 8. Lee, *The Fortune Cookie Chronicles: Adventures in the World of Chinese Food* (New York: Twelve Books, 2008), 291.
36. Said, *Orientalism*, 26.
37. Chen, *Chop Suey, USA*, 85.
38. Robert Ferguson, *Representing 'Race': Ideology, Identity and the Media* (London: Arnold, 1998), 68.
39. Sharp, *Savage Perils*, 120; John Cheng, *Astounding Wonder: Imagining Science and Science Fiction in Interwar America* (Philadelphia: University of Pennsylvania Press, 2012), 174; David Morley and Kevin Robins, *Spaces of Identity: Global Media, Electronic Landscapes and Cultural Boundaries* (London: Routledge, 1995), 169.
40. Ho, *Consumption and Identity*, 15, 152; Ku, Manalansan IV, and Mannur, "An Alimentary Introduction," 5; Martin F. Manalansan IV, "Cooking up the Senses: A Critical Embodied Approach to the Study of Food and Asian American Television Audiences," in *Alien Encounters: Popular Culture in Asian America*, eds. Mimi Thi Nguyen and Thuy Linh Nguyen Tu (Durham: Duke University Press, 2007), 180.
41. Ferguson, *Representing 'Race,'* 69.
42. *eXistenZ*, directed by David Cronenberg (1999; Santa Monica: Miramax, 2016), DVD.

43. Thank you very much to writer and director David Cronenberg for permission to reprint dialogue excerpts from *eXistenZ*.
44. Ku, *Dubious Gastronomy*, 9, 56.
45. Haslam, *Gender, Race, and American Science Fiction*, 74.
46. Ibid., 88; Jeffrey Paul Chan, Frank Chin, Lawson Fusao Inada, and Shawn Wong, "Introduction" in *The Big Aiiieeeee! An Anthology of Chinese American and Japanese American Literature*, eds. Jeffrey Paul Chan, Frank Chin, Lawson Fusao Inada, and Shawn Wong (New York: Meridian, 1991), xiii.
47. Morley and Robins, *Spaces of Identity*, 137; Ho, *Consumption and Identity*, 3.
48. Naming the restaurant "Wu's Diamond Garden" reflects the practices of Chinese restaurant owners, whereby these types of designations "are strategies designed to reinforce the desire of diners for exotic experience" in Asian restaurants. Lu and Fine, "Ethnic Authenticity," 539.
49. bell hooks, "Eating the Other: Desire and Resistance" in *Eating Culture*, eds. Ron Scapp and Brian Seitz (Albany: State University of New York Press, 1998), 186.
50. *Men in Black 3* Content/Material License Agreement executed by Sony Pictures Post Production Services Inc. © 2012 Columbia Pictures Industries, Inc. and Hemisphere–Culver Picture Partners, I, LLC. All Rights Reserved. Courtesy of Columbia Pictures.
51. Akihiko Hirose and Kay Kei-Ho Pih, "'No Asians Working Here': Racialized Otherness and Authenticity in Gastronomical Orientalism," *Ethnic and Racial Studies* 34, no. 9 (2011): 1498.
52. Ibid., 1497–1499.
53. Cheng, *Astounding Wonder*, 147–178.
54. Ibid., 148.
55. Ibid., 174.
56. Huang, *Contesting Genres*, 95; John Rieder, *Colonialism and the Emergence of Science Fiction* (Middletown: Wesleyan University Press, 2008), 21.
57. Reproduced in multiple web pages and open-source books—original source unknown.
58. Cheng, *Astounding Wonder*, 163.
59. Morley and Robins, *Spaces of Identity*, 170, 172.
60. Ibid., see chapter 8, "Techno-Orientalism: Japan Panic," 147–173.
61. Ibid., 137.
62. Said, *Orientalism*, 98.
63. Hirose and Pih, "'No Asians Working Here,'" 1483.
64. De Witt Douglas Kilgore, "'The Best is Yet to Come'; or, Saving the Future: *Star Trek: Deep Space Nine* as Reform Astrofuturism" in *Black and Brown Planets: The Politics of Race in Science Fiction*, ed. Isiah Lavender III (Jackson: University Press of Mississippi, 2014), 31.
65. Rick Flowers and Elaine Swan, "Eating the Asian Other? Pedagogies of Food Multiculturalism in Australia," *PORTAL: Journal of Multidisciplinary International Studies* 9, no. 2 (2012): 2.
66. Laurier Turgeon and Madeleine Pastinelli, "'Eat the World': Postcolonial Encounters in Quebec City's Ethnic Restaurants," *Journal of American Folklore* 115, no. 456 (2002): 259.

67. Ibid., 259; Lu and Fine, "Ethnic Authenticity," 537–538.
68. Ku, *Dubious Gastronomy*, 147–148.
69. Flowers and Swan, "Eating the Asian Other," 28.
70. Lu and Fine, "Ethnic Authenticity," 547.

CONTRIBUTORS

BRUCE MAKOTO ARNOLD is an Assistant Professor within the Ohio State University Department of Educational Studies' program in the Philosophy and History of Education. He holds a PhD in American History from the Louisiana State University and Agricultural and Mechanical College where he wrote his dissertation on the lives of Japanese American children in Los Angeles before the Second World War. Additionally, he holds degrees in East Asian Studies, philosophy, and computer engineering. He specializes cultural history, Asian American history, masculinity, educational history and philosophy, and childhood studies.

ANNESSA ANN BABIC is a freelance writer and adjunct professor in New York, New York. She holds a PhD in American History from the State University of New York at Stony Brook and she specializes in women's studies, American social and cultural history, and transnational studies with an emphasis on the modern Middle East and U.S.-Turkish relations. She is the author and coeditor of several books, and has produced numerous book chapters, reference entries, book reviews, and journal articles. Her publications deal with nationalism, women's rights, women's liberation, transnational feminism, and travel literature. Most recently, she coedited an issue of *Food and Foodways* (with Tanfer Emin Tunç) and published on the manifestation, evolution, and incorporation of popular culture artifacts into our daily lives. She also has an active publishing career outside of academia, and is co-chair of the European Association of American Studies Women's Network Steering Committee.

CARMEN BIRKLE is Professor of North American Literary and Cultural Studies at Philipps University, Marburg. She has taught at the universities of Mainz and Vienna, and at Columbia University. Her research and teaching focus on ethnic and gender studies, literature and medicine, and popular culture. She is the author of *Women's Stories of the Looking Glass* (1996) and *Migration—Miscegenation—Transculturation*

(2004), editor of *Literature and Medicine: Women in the Medical Profession* (Parts I and II), and coeditor of *Communicating Disease* (2013). Her current research focuses on the intersection of literature, gender, and medicine in nineteenth-century America. Between 2014 and 2017, she was President of the German Association for American Studies.

MEGAN BOTT graduated from the University of Illinois at Springfield in 2014 with a Bachelor's Degree in Sociology and Anthropology and a minor in Women's and Gender Studies. Currently, she is a Program Manager for Project YES!, an AmeriCorps program that places members in schools and non-profits throughout Chicago.

SUSAN BOSLEGO CARTER is Professor Emerita of Economics from UC Riverside and the 2016–2017 Edward A. Dickson Emeritus Professor at UC Riverside. She received her PhD in Economics from Stanford University and has written widely on the economic history of women's work, labor history, education, and immigration. She is a general editor of *Historical Statistics of the United States, Millennial Edition* (2006) and past president of the Social Science History Association. Her book in progress explores the economic, social, political and cultural history of the Chinese restaurant in America.

INGRID E. CASTRO is Professor of Sociology and Director of Women, Gender, and Sexuality Studies at Massachusetts College of Liberal Arts. She received her PhD in Sociology, with Graduate Certificates in Gender Studies and Cinema Studies, from Northeastern University. Her qualitative research focuses on children, young adults, race, gender, and education, and applying a sociological lens to cinema studies. She is the lead editor of *Researching Children and Youth: Methodological Issues, Strategies, and Innovations* (Sociological Studies of Children and Youth, Volume 22), and her book chapters on film include *Children's Agency and Cinema's New Fairy Tale* and *Children, Innocence, and Agency in the Films of Steven Spielberg*, among others.

CLARENCE CHAN is the Director of the Physical Therapist Assistant Program at LaGuardia Community College, City University of New

York. A doctor of physical therapy with over twenty-five years of experience serving a diverse community in New York City, Dr. Chan integrates Eastern and Western medical concepts into his practice. Influenced by a family background where culinary art took center stage, Dr. Chan's unique clinical approach has been shaped by his early apprenticeship in a Chinese restaurant kitchen. Although he did not continue on the path of his family trade, Dr. Chan retains a keen interest in the development of Chinese food and culture, and the skills learned from his culinary career have helped him develop as a clinician and teacher. Dr. Chan incorporates those transferable skills into his classroom where he mentors the next generation of healthcare professionals, very much like his chef master mentored him.

RAYMOND DOUGLAS CHONG is a writer of stories, composer of poems, director of films, and lyricist. Raymond is a sixth generation American Born Chinese (ABC) from California, and holds a BS in Civil Engineering from the University of Southern California and an MS in Civil Engineering from San Jose State University. He is a Specially Appointed Professor at Shandong Jiaotong University in Jinan, China, and a Licensed Professional Engineer in Texas, a Professional Civil Engineer and a Professional Traffic Engineer in California, and a Professional Engineer in Saskatchewan. He has worked for various municipalities and consultancies in California, Texas, and Saskatchewan.

FRANK JACOB is an historian whose research interests cover modern Japanese history, transnational and global history, the history of secret societies, and the history of transatlantic socialism. He received his MA in History and Japanese Studies from the University of Würzburg (2010) before finishing his PhD in Japanese Studies at the University of Erlangen in 2012. He is the editor of numerous academic series and journals and has published several monographs, including *Secret Societies* (Kohlhammer, 2015) and *The Military Revolution in Early Modern Europe—A Revision* (coauthored with Gilmar Visoni-Alonzo, Palgrave 2016). His recent (co)edited volumes include *Prostitution—A Companion of Mankind* (Peter Lang, 2016), *War and Geography* (Schöningh, 2016) and *Russian and Soviet History in Film* (ALTIJA, 2016).

JOHN JUNG received his PhD in experimental psychology from Northwestern University (1962) and is Professor Emeritus at California State University, Long Beach. After entering retirement, he reflected on the lives of his immigrant parents and his siblings, the sole Chinese family in Macon, Georgia, where they operated a laundry from the 1920s to 1950s during the pre–civil rights era in his 2005 memoir, *Southern Fried Rice: Life in A Chinese Laundry in the Deep South.* Three additional books describe the lives of Chinese immigrants from the late 1800s through the middle of the twentieth century as they overcame harsh social prejudices and legal restrictions to succeed in running family businesses such as laundries (*Chinese Laundries: Tickets to Survival on Gold Mountain*, 2007), grocery stores (*Chopsticks in the Land of Cotton: Lives of Chinese Grocers in the Mississippi Delta,* 2008) and restaurants (*Sweet and Sour: Life in Chinese Family Restaurants*, 2010). A fifth book, *A Chinese American Odyssey: How a Retired Psychologist Makes a Hit as an Historian* (2014) describes Dr. Jung's decade of research, writing, and speaking about Chinese American history.

CHUNGHAO PIO KUO is currently a research fellow at the Center for General Education at Taipei Medical University. He is an historian of early modern China, specializing in food history, medical history, animal history, and environmental history. His dissertation explores the practice of pig-feeding and the consumption of pork in early modern China. His current projects include *Pigs, Pork, and Ham: From Farm to Table in Early Modern China* (University of Hawai'i Press, forthcoming) and *Animal Matters: Epidemic Diseases, Public Hygiene, and Food Safety in China, 1700–1900.*

ANDRÉE LAFONTAINE is Assistant Professor of American Studies at Aichi University, Nagoya, with a PhD in Film and Moving Image Studies from Concordia University, Montréal. Her work focuses on women's modernity in Depression-era Hollywood.

SHOON LIO is Assistant Professor of Sociology at the University of South Alabama. His research interests are in collective memory and the constitution of American national identity, food studies, social movements, and social theory. He is currently examining how the production and consumption of Asian American hipster cuisine constitutes culinary capital.

TONY TAI-TING LIU is an Associate Research Fellow at the Center for Contemporary China, National Chung Hsing University. He has a PhD and MA in International Politics from National Chung Hsing University and a BA in International Relations from the University of British Columbia. During his undergraduate studies in Canada, Tony worked as a translation editor and writer for *Perspectives Newspaper*, British Columbia's first English-Chinese student newspaper. He has also held visiting research positions at the Australian Catholic University (Institute for Social Justice) and University of Tübingen (European Research Center on Contemporary Taiwan, ERCCT). His research interests include Chinese foreign policy, China-Taiwan relations and East Asia international relations. Dr. Liu has contributed to a number of journals and volumes, such as *Journal of Current Chinese Affairs*, *The Ashgate Research Companion to Chinese Foreign Policy* and *The Routledge Handbook of Global Cultural Policy*.

HARLEY J. SPILLER, aka Inspector Collector, is a museum educator and Deputy Director of Franklin Furnace Archive, the international avant-garde arts organization. He has written for *The New York Times*, Abrams, Columbia University Press, Oxford University Press, and the University of California Press, and is the author of *Keep the Change: A Collector's Tales of Lucky Pennies, Counterfeit C-Notes, and Other Curious Currency* (Princeton Architectural Press, 2015).

TING MAN TSAO is a professor of English, teaching composition and literature at LaGuardia Community College, City University of New York. With a native fluency in Chinese, he majored in English at Shue Yan College. He holds an MA in Comparative Literature from the University of Washington and a PhD in English from Stony Brook University. Dr. Tsao has published articles in the fields of postcolonial studies, the medical humanities, creative nonfiction, pedagogy, higher education, and food studies. He is currently researching sexualization in animé fandoms. His book chapters have appeared in

Asian Crossings (Hong Kong University Press), *Pirates and Mutineers of the Nineteenth Century* (Ashgate), *Illness in the Academy* (Purdue University Press), *Papa, PhD* (Rutgers University Press), and *The American-Style University at Large* (Lexington). Dr. Tsao has also published in journals such as *Victorians Institute Journal, Teaching English in the Two-Year College, The History Teacher, Nursing Education Perspectives, Writing Macao*, and *Postcolonial Text.*

TANFER EMIN TUNÇ is an Associate Professor in the Department of American Culture and Literature at Hacettepe University, Ankara, Turkey. She received her PhD in American history from the State University of New York at Stony Brook, and her teaching and research interests include American social history, cultural studies, and women's studies. Her publications in Asian American studies range from articles and book chapters on the works of Ruthanne Lum McCunn, Paisley Rekdal, and Ping Chong; to co-edited collections such as *Positioning the New: Chinese American Literature and the Changing Image of the American Literary Canon* (Cambridge Scholars Publishing, 2010) and *The West in Asia and Asia in the West: Essays on Transnational Interactions* (McFarland Publishers, 2015); to the *Journal of Transnational American Studies*' special forum on Asian American studies (vol. 4, no. 1, 2012). Dr. Tunç has also examined the impact of war on American foodways, and her publications in this area include articles on food and the American Civil War (in the *European Journal of American Culture* and in *War & Society*), American World War I food propaganda (in *War and History*), food in 1950s atomic America (in *Cold War History*), as well as a co-edited special issue of *Food and Foodways* on World War II and the American Diet (vol. 25, no. 2, 2017). She is currently the vice president of the American Studies Association of Turkey and a board member of the European Association for American Studies.

INDEX

X

Y

Z